Financial Economics

Whilst many undergraduate finance textbooks are largely descriptive in nature the economic analysis in most graduate texts is too advanced for final year undergraduates. This book bridges the gap between these two extremes, offering a textbook that studies economic activity in financial markets, focusing on how consumers determine future consumption and on the role of financial securities. Areas covered in the book include:

- An examination of the role of finance in the economy using basic economic principles, eventually progressing to introductory graduate analysis.
- A microeconomic study of capital asset pricing when there is risk, inflation, taxes and asymmetric information.
- An emphasis on economic intuition using geometry to explain formal analysis.
- An extended treatment of corporate finance and the evaluation of public policy.

Written by an experienced teacher of financial economics and microeconomics at both graduate and postgraduate level, this book is essential reading for students seeking to study the links between economics and finance and those with a special interest in capital asset pricing, corporate finance, derivative securities, insurance, policy evaluation and discount rates.

Chris Jones is Senior Lecturer at the School of Economics at The Australian National University.

Financial Economics

Chris Jones

Routledge
Taylor & Francis Group
LONDON AND NEW YORK

First published 2008 by Routledge
2 Park Square, Milton Park, Abingdon, Oxon, OX14 4RN

Simultaneously published in USA and Canada
by Routledge
270 Madison Avenue, New York, NY 10016

Routledge is an imprint of the Taylor & Francis Group, an informa business

Typeset in Times New Roman by Keyword Group Ltd
Printed and bound in Great Britain by The Cromwell Press, Trowbridge, Wiltshire

British Library Cataloguing in Publication Data
A catalogue record for this book is available from the British Library

Library of Congress Cataloging-in-Publication Data
Jones, Chris, 1953-
Financial economics/Chris Jones.
p. cm.
Includes bibliographical references and index.
1. Finance. 2. Economics. I. Title.
HG173.J657 2008
332–dc22
2007032310

ISBN10: 0-415-37584-3 (hbk)
ISBN10: 0-415-37585-1 (pbk)
ISBN10: 0-203-93202-1 (ebk)

ISBN13: 978-0-415-37584-9 (hbk)
ISBN13: 978-0-415-37585-6 (pbk)
ISBN13: 978-0-203-93202-5 (ebk)

Contents

Figures

Boxes

Tables

1 Introduction

Individuals regularly make decisions to determine their consumption in future time periods, and most have income that varies over their lives. They initially consume from parental income before commencing work, whereupon their income normally increases until it peaks toward the end of their working life and then declines at retirement. An example of the income profile (I_t) for a consumer who lives until time T is shown by the solid line in Figure 1.1. When resources can be transferred between time periods the consumer can choose to smooth consumption expenditure (X_t) to make it look like the dashed line in the diagram.

Almost all consumption choices have intertemporal effects when individuals can transfer resources between time periods. Any good that provides (or funds) future consumption is referred to as a *capital asset*, and consumers trade these assets to determine the shape of the consumption profile. In Figure 1.1 the individual initially sells capital assets (borrows) to raise consumption above income, and later purchases capital assets (saves) to repay debt and save for retirement and the payment of bequests. These trades smooth consumption expenditure relative to income, where consumption profiles are determined by consumer preferences, resources endowments and investment opportunities.

There are physical and financial capital assets: physical assets such as houses and cars generate real consumption flows plus capital gains or losses, and financial assets have monetary payouts plus any capital gains or losses that can be converted into consumption goods. There are important links between them as many financial assets are used to fund investment in physical assets, where this gives them property right claims to their payouts. In frictionless competitive markets, asset values are a signal of the marginal benefits to sellers and marginal costs to buyers from trading future consumption. In effect, buyers and sellers are valuing the same payouts to capital assets when they make decisions to trade them, which is why so much effort is devoted to the derivation of capital asset pricing models in financial economics, particularly in the presence of uncertainty. Consumers will not pay a positive price for any asset unless it is expected to generate a net consumption flow for them in the future. In many cases these benefits might be reductions in consumption risk rather than increases in expected consumption. In fact, a large variety of financial securities trade in financial markets to facilitate trades in consumption risk.

While much of the material covered in this book examines trade in financial markets and the pricing of financial securities, there are important links between the real and financial variables in the economy. After all, financial markets function to facilitate the trades in real consumption, where financial securities reduce trading costs, particularly when consumption is transferred across time. Their prices provide important signals of the marginal valuations and costs of future consumption flows. To identify interactions between the real and

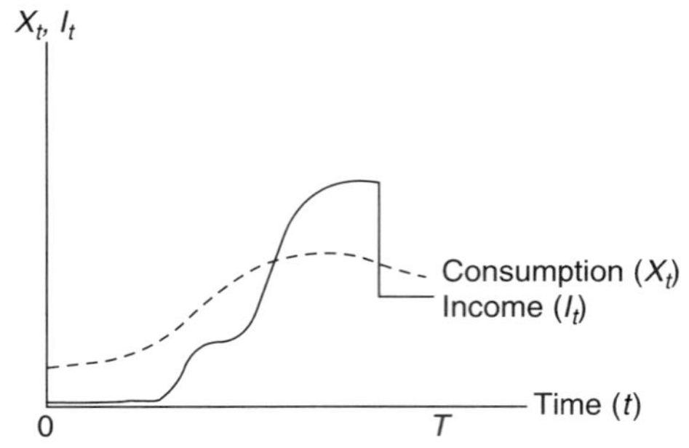

Figure 1.1 Income and consumption profiles.

financial variables in the economy, we examine the way capital asset prices change over time, and how they are affected by taxes, leverage, risk, new information and inflation. In particular, we look at how financial decisions affect real consumption opportunities.

A useful starting point for the analysis is the *classical finance model* with frictionless and competitive markets where traders have common information. In this setting the financial policy irrelevance theorems of Modigliani and Miller (1958, 1961) hold, where financial securities are a veil over the real economy. That is not to say these securities are irrelevant to the real economy, but rather, the types of financial securities used and the way they make payouts, whether as consumption, cash or capital gains, are irrelevant. This is an important proposition because it reminds us that the values of financial securities are ultimately determined by the net consumption flows they provide – in other words, by their fundamentals. While this model appears at odds with reality, it provides an important benchmark for gradually extending the analysis to a more realistic setting with trading costs, taxes and asymmetric information to explain the interactions we observe between the real and financial variables in the economy. Considerable progress has been made in deriving asset pricing models in recent years by linking prices back to consumption, which is the ultimate source of value because it determines the utility of consumers. Most of this work is undertaken in classical finance models, where departures from it attempt to make the pricing models perform better empirically.

This book aims to bridge the material covered in most undergraduate finance courses with material covered in a first-year graduate finance course. Thus, it can be used as a textbook for third-year undergraduate and honours courses in finance and financial economics. Another aim is to provide policy analysts with an accessible reference for evaluating policy changes with risky benefits and costs that extend into future time periods. The most challenging material is presented at the end of Chapter 4, where four popular consumption-based pricing models are derived, and in Chapter 8 on project evaluation and the social discount rate. I benefited enormously from reading many of the works listed in the References section, but two books were particularly helpful. The book by John Cochrane (2001) provides nice insights into the economics of asset pricing, and is well supported by the book by Yvan Lengwiler (2004) that carefully establishes the properties of the consumption-based pricing model where the analysis in Cochrane starts.

In this book I have expanded the material on corporate finance and included material on project evaluation. Corporate finance is an ideal application in financial economics because a large portion of aggregate investment is undertaken by corporate firms. It provides us with an opportunity to examine the role of taxes and the effects of firm financial policies on their market valuations. Welfare analysis is used in the evaluation of public sector projects, and to identify the efficiency and equity effects of resource allocations by trades in private markets. In distorted markets policy analysts use different rules than private traders for evaluating capital investment decisions. These differences are examined and we extend a compensated welfare analysis to identify the welfare effects of changes in consumption risk. For that reason the book may also be useful as a reference for courses in cost–benefit analysis, public economics and the economics of taxation. We now summarize the material covered in each of the following chapters.

1.1 Chapter summaries

Intertemporal decisions under uncertainty

Uncertainty obviously impacts on intertemporal consumption choices, where consumers, when valuing capital assets, apply discount factors to their future net consumption flows as compensation for the opportunity cost of time and risk. Rather than include both time and risk from the outset, we follow Hirshleifer (1965) in Chapter 2 by using certainty analysis to identify the opportunity cost of time. This conveniently extends standard atemporal economic analysis to multiple time periods without the complication of also including uncertainty. It is included later in Chapter 3 using a two-period Arrow–Debreu state-preference model, which is a natural extension of the certainty analysis in Chapter 2. By proceeding in this manner we establish a solid foundation for the more advanced material covered in later chapters. Some graduate finance books treat uncertainty analysis, and in some cases, state-preference theory, as assumed knowledge.

The certainty analysis commences in an *autarky economy* where individuals effectively live on islands. We do this to identify actions consumers can take in isolation from each other to transfer consumption to future time periods through private investment in capital assets. For example, they can store commodities, plant trees and other crops as well as build houses to provide direct consumption benefits in the future. While this is a simplistic description of the choices available to most consumers, it establishes useful properties that will carry over to a more realistic setting. In particular, it identifies potential gains from trade, where the nature of these gains is identified by gradually introducing trading opportunities to the autarky economy. We initially extend the analysis by allowing consumers to exchange goods within each time period (atemporal trade) where transactions costs are introduced to provide a role for (fiat) money and financial securities.

It is quite easy to overlook some of the important roles of money and financial securities in a more general setting with risk, taxes, externalities and asymmetric information. In a certainty setting without taxes and other distortions consumers use them to reduce the costs of moving goods around the *exchange economy*. Money and financial securities will coexist as a medium of exchange if they provide different cost reductions for different transactions. Since money is highly divisible and universally accepted as a medium of exchange, it reduces trading costs on relatively low-valued transactions. In contrast, financial securities are used for larger-valued transactions and trades with more complex property right transfers which are less easily verified at the time the exchanges occur.[1] If commodities are perfectly divisible, costless to transfer between locations, and traders have complete information about their quality and other important characteristics, the absence of trading costs will make money and financial securities redundant. Money is frequently not included in finance models due to the absence of trading costs on the grounds they are too small to play a significant role in the analysis. That also eliminates any transactions cost role for financial securities. When money is included in these circumstances it becomes a veil over the real economy so that nominal prices are determined by the supply of money.[2] Once trading costs are included, however, money and financial securities can have real effects on equilibrium outcomes.

When consumers can trade atemporally in frictionless competitive markets they equate their marginal utility from allocating income to each good consumed. This allows us to simplify the analysis considerably by defining consumer preferences over income on the basis that consumption bundles are being chosen optimally in the background to maximize utility. This continues to be the case in the presence of uncertainty when there is a single consumption good. However, with multiple goods, risk-averse consumers care not only about changes in their (expected) money income in future time periods but also about changes in relative commodity prices as both determine the changes in their real income.[3] This observation makes it easier to understand why in some pricing models the risk premiums are determined by changes in relative commodity prices.

The next extension to the autarky economy introduces *full trade* where consumers can trade within each period and across time (intertemporally) in a market economy. Initially we consider an exchange model where consumers swap goods in each time period and use forward commodity contracts to trade goods over time. The analysis is then extended to an *asset economy* by allowing consumers to trade financial securities. As noted by Arrow (1953), financial securities can significantly reduce the number of transactions. Instead of trading a separate forward contract for each good consumed in the future, consumers can trade money and financial securities with future payouts that can be converted into goods. Thus, money and financial securities can be used as a store of value to reduce the costs of trading intertemporally. But this introduces a wealth effect in the money market due to the non-payment of interest on currency. Whenever consumers hold currency as a store of value, they forgo interest payments on bonds; this acts as an implicit tax when the nominal interest rate exceeds the marginal social cost of supplying currency. Any anticipated expansion in the supply of fiat currency that raises the rate of price inflation and the nominal interest rate will increase the welfare loss from the non-payment of interest by further reducing the demand for currency. There are other important interactions between financial and real variables in the economy when we introduce risk and asymmetric information. By trading intertemporally in frictionless competitive markets, consumers equate their marginal rates of substitution between future and current consumption to the market rate of interest, and therefore use the same discount factors to value capital assets.

After extending the asset economy to allow investment by firms, we then examine the *Fisher separation theorem*. This gives price-taking firms the familiar objective of maximizing profit. Sometimes this objective is inappropriate. For example, shareholders are unlikely to be unanimous in supporting profit maximization when the investment choices of firms also affect the relative prices of the goods they consume. The Fisher separation theorem holds when these investment choices only have income effects on the budget constraints of shareholders. We then examine the effects of fully anticipated inflation in a classical finance model where the real economy is unaffected by changes in the rate of general price inflation. This establishes the Fisher effect where nominal interest rates change endogenously to keep the real interest rate constant, so that current asset prices are unaffected by changes in inflation. The real effects of inflation are obtained by relaxing assumptions in the classical finance model, including homogeneous expectations and flexible nominal prices.

Finally, the certainty analysis is completed by deriving asset prices for different types of securities such as perpetuities, annuities, share and bonds. In general terms, capital asset prices are determined by the size and timing of their net cash flows and the term structure of interest rates used to discount them. While this may seem a relatively straightforward exercise, it can become quite complicated in practice. There are many factors that can impact on the net cash flows and their discount factors, including, storage, investment opportunities, trading costs, inflation and taxes. After identifying the term structure of interest rates, we establish the fundamental equation of yield in a certainty setting. The term structure establishes the relationship between short- and long-term interest rates. This is important for pricing assets when their net cash flows are spread across a number of future time periods because the discount factors need to reflect the differences in their timing. Risk premiums are added to the short-term interest rates using an asset pricing model when the net cash flows are risky. These adjustments are derived later in Chapters 3 and 4. The equation of yield measures the economic return to capital invested in assets in each period of their lives. It identifies economic income as cash and consumption plus any capital gains or losses. Some asset prices rise over time, some fall and others stay constant. It depends on the size and timing of the cash flows they generate. Assets that delay paying net cash flows until later time periods must pay capital gains in subsequent years to compensate capital providers for the opportunity cost of time. In contrast, the prices of assets with larger immediate cash flows are much more likely to fall in some periods of their lives. In a frictionless competitive capital market every asset must pay the same economic rate of return as every other asset (in the same risk class). This is the *no arbitrage condition* which eliminates profit from security returns and makes them equal to the opportunity cost of time (and risk). It is an important relationship that appears time and again throughout the analysis in this book, and it provides extremely useful economic insights for predicting asset price changes and identifying the economic returns on assets.

The role of arbitrage can be demonstrated by computing the price of a financial asset with a net cash flow in the next period of X_1 dollars when the nominal rate of interest over the period is i_1. It has a present value of

$$PV_0 = \frac{X_1}{1+i_1}, \tag{1.1}$$

where the discount factor $1/(1 + i_1)$ converts future dollars into fewer current dollars to compensate the asset holder for the opportunity cost of delaying consumption expenditure. Whenever the current asset price (p_0) falls below PV_0 there is surplus with a net present value of

$$NPV_0 = \frac{X_1}{1+i_1} - p_0. \tag{1.2}$$

PV_0 is the most the buyer would pay for this asset because it is the amount that would need to be invested in other assets (in the same risk class) to generate the same net cash flow, with

$PV_0(1+i_1)=X_1$. In a frictionless competitive capital market arbitrage drives the market price of the asset (p_0) to its present value (PV_0). If the asset price results in $p_0(1+i_1)>X_1$ investors move into substitute assets which pay higher economic returns, while the reverse applies when $p_0(1+i_1)<X_1$. When the no arbitrage condition holds, the asset price is equated to the present value of its net cash flows, so that $NPV_0=0$. In these circumstances the discount rate (i_1) is the return every other asset (in the same risk class) pays over the same period of time.

Despite the simplicity of this example, it can be used to establish a number of very important properties that should apply to asset values. First, their net cash flows are payouts made to asset holders, and they are computed as gross revenue accruing to underlying real assets minus any non-capital costs of production. Second, the discount rate should in every way reflect the characteristics of the net cash flows being discounted. It should be the rate of return paid on all other assets in the same risk class over the same time period. If the payouts are made in six months' time the discount rate is the interest rate over that six-month period, while assets that make a continuous payout through time should be evaluated using a continuous discount factor. When the payouts are measured in nominal terms we use a nominal discount rate, and for those measured in real terms a real discount rate. In the presence of taxes we discount after-tax payouts using an after-tax discount rate. Finally, when the net cash flows are risky a premium is included in the discount rate to compensate asset holders for changes in their consumption risk. While these seem obvious points to make, they can nonetheless be easily overlooked in more complex present value calculations.

Uncertainty and risk

A key role of financial securities is to spread and diversify risk, and these issues are examined in Chapter 3. Many different types of securities trade in capital markets, including shares, bonds, options, futures, warrants and convertible notes. Traders use them to trade and diversify consumption risk and to obtain any profits through arbitrage. In a competitive capital market there is a perfect substitute for every traded security, so that no one can provide new risk trading opportunities by bringing a new security to the capital market. In other words, every new security can be replicated by creating a derivative security from existing traded assets. In this setting, traders have no market power because other traders can combine options, bonds and shares to create perfect substitutes for their securities. This activity is important for invoking the no arbitrage condition on security returns when there is uncertainty and plays an important role in making the capital market efficient in the sense that asset prices reflect all available information.

Chapter 3 extends the analysis in the previous chapter by including uncertainty using the *Arrow–Debreu state-preference model*. This establishes the classical finance model in an uncertainty setting where consumers have conditional perfect foresight, there are no trading costs and markets are competitive. It is equivalent to a certainty analysis where the characteristics of goods are expanded to make them state-contingent. The states of nature completely summarize all possible outcomes of the world in the future, and everyone in the economy agrees on the state space and can solve the equilibrium outcomes in the economy in every state. The only remaining uncertainty is over the state that will actually eventuate. Most of the economic intuitions for the equilibrium allocations in the certainty setting will carry over to this setting, except that consumers use stochastic discount factors to assess the values of capital assets.[4] If the capital market is complete, so that consumers can trade in every state of the world, they use the same *state-contingent discount factors* and have the same marginal valuations for risky capital assets.

Risk-averse consumers include a risk premium in their discount factors when valuing net cash flows on capital assets. This premium compensates them for risk imparted to their future consumption by the net cash flows. But while every consumer includes the same risk premium in their discount factors in the Arrow–Debreu model, they may not measure and price risk in the same way. One of the main objectives of finance research is to obtain an asset pricing model where consumers measure and price risk identically so that financial analysts can predict the market valuations of capital assets, and policy analysts can include a risk premium in the discount factors used to evaluate the net benefits on public sector projects. The first important step in this direction is to adopt von Neumann–Morgenstern expected utility functions to separate the probabilities consumers assign to states of nature from the utility they derive in each state. Since these preferences are time-separable with a state-independent utility function, they transform the Arrow–Debreu pricing model into the *consumption-based pricing model* where consumers face the same consumption risk and therefore measure and price risk identically.

Asset pricing models

Further assumptions are required, however, to make the consumption-based pricing model a simple linear function of a few (ideally one) factors that isolate market risk in the net cash flows to securities. We derive four popular pricing models as special cases of the consumption-based pricing model in Chapter 4. They include the *capital asset pricing model* (CAPM) derived by Sharpe (1964) and Lintner (1965), the *intertemporal capital asset pricing model* (ICAPM) by Merton (1973a), the *arbitrage pricing theory* (APT) by Ross (1976) and the *consumption-beta capital asset pricing model* (CCAPM) by Breeden and Litzenberger (1978) and Breeden (1979). All of them adopt assumptions that make the common stochastic discount factors of consumers linear in a set of factors that isolate aggregate consumption risk. And since these factors are variables reported in aggregate data, the models are relatively straightforward for analysts to use when estimating the current values of capital assets. In all of these models there is no risk premium for diversifiable risk in security returns because it can be costlessly eliminated by bundling risky securities in portfolios. Only the non-diversifiable (market) risk attracts a risk premium because it is risk that consumers must ultimately bear. Since this material is more difficult analytically, we follow standard practice by initially deriving the CAPM as the solution to the portfolio problem of consumers. In this two-period model consumers fund all their future consumption from payouts to securities where consumption risk is determined by the risk in their portfolios. Since they have common information they combine the same bundle of risky securities with a risk-free security, where market risk is determined by the risk in their common risky bundle (known as the market portfolio). Thus, they measure risk in the returns to securities by their covariance with the return on the risky market portfolio. This is a widely used model in practice because of its simplicity. There is a single measure of market risk in the economy that all consumers price in the same way, where the market portfolio is normally constructed as a value-weighted index of the traded risky securities on the stock exchange. The problem with this model lies in the simplifying assumptions, in particular, that of common information, no transactions costs and joint normally distributed returns.

When security returns are joint normally distributed the returns on security portfolios are completely described by their mean and variance. This is why the CAPM is based on a mean–variance analysis. The APT model is more general because it does not require security returns to be normally distributed. Instead, it is a linear factor analysis that isolates market risk empirically by identifying the common component in security returns. While the factors used are macroeconomic variables, they are not necessarily the source of the market risk in security returns. They are simply used to isolate it. We derive the APT model in a similar fashion to the derivation of the CAPM to demonstrate the role of arbitrage in eliminating diversifiable risk, and the role of mimicking portfolios to price the market risk isolated by the macro factors. The main weakness of this model is its failure to identify the set of common factors used by consumers.

In the last three sections we derive the CAPM and the APT, as well as the ICAPM and the CCAPM, as special cases of the consumption-based pricing model. Even though the analysis is slightly more complex, it provides much greater insight into the underlying economics in these pricing models. In particular, it links the risk in securities directly back to the risk in consumption expenditure. Since consumers derive utility from consumption and face the same consumption risk, they assess the risk in capital assets by measuring the covariance of their returns with changes in aggregate consumption. Additional factors are required when aggregate consumption risk also changes over time. Each model has its strengths and weaknesses, and by deriving them as special cases of the consumption-based pricing model, they can be compared more effectively.

Early empirical tests of these models focused on their ability to explain the risk premiums in expected security returns without considering how much risk was being transferred into real consumption expenditure. When testing the CCAPM, Mehra and Prescott (1985) looked beyond its ability to explain the risk in asset prices and examined whether the implied values of the (constant) coefficient of relative risk aversion and the (constant) rate of time preference were consistent with the risk in aggregate real consumption. Using US data, they discovered the equity premium and low risk-free real interest rate puzzles, where the premium puzzle finds the need to adopt a coefficient of relative risk aversion in the CCAPM that is approximately five times larger than its estimated value in experimental work, while the low risk-free rate puzzle finds the observed real interest rate much lower than the CCAPM would predict when the coefficient of relative risk aversion is set at its estimated value. Once it is set at the higher values required to explain the observed equity risk premium in security returns using the CCAPM, the predicted real interest rate is even higher. After summarizing these pricing puzzles we then look at subsequent attempts to explain them by modifying preferences and including market frictions.

Insurance with asymmetric information

As noted earlier, no risk premium is included in security returns for diversifiable risk in the consumption-based pricing models. This is referred to as the *mutuality principle*, and when it holds, we cannot assess the risk in security returns by looking solely at their variance. Instead, we need to measure that part of their variance that cannot be costlessly eliminated by bundling financial securities together or purchasing insurance. The diversification effect from bundling securities is examined in Chapters 3 and 4, while insurance is examined in Chapter 5. Insurance markets allow consumers to pool individual risks, which are diversifiable across the population. When insurance trades at actuarially fair prices (that is, at prices equal to the probability of their losses), consumers with von Neumann–Morgenstern preferences fully insure. They purchase less insurance and do not eliminate all the diversifiable risk from their consumption when there are marginal trading costs.

Governments and international aid agencies often justify stabilization policies on the grounds that private insurance markets are distorted by *moral hazard* and *adverse selection* problems. These are problems that arise when traders have *asymmetric information* – in particular, when insurers cannot costlessly observe the effort taken by consumers to reduce their probability of incurring losses, or distinguish between consumers with different risk. Dixit (1987, 1989) makes the important observation that stabilization policies can only be assessed properly when they are evaluated in the presence of the moral hazard and adverse selection problems. We provide a basis for doing this by formalizing equilibrium outcomes in the market for private insurance when traders have asymmetric information. Its effects are identified by comparing these outcomes to the equilibrium outcomes when traders have common information.

Derivative securities

There are frequently circumstances where individuals take actions now so they can delay making future consumption choices when uncertainty is partially resolved by the passing of time. Alternatively, they can eliminate some of the uncertainty in future consumption now by securing prices for future trades. *Options contracts* give holders the right but not the obligation to buy and sell commodities and financial assets at specified prices at (or before) specified times, while *forward contracts* are commitments to trade commodities and financial assets at specified prices and times. These derivative securities play the important role of facilitating trades in aggregate risk and allowing investors to diversify individual risk by completing the capital market. They also provide valuable information about the expectations of investors for future values of underlying assets. Strictly speaking, derivatives are financial securities whose values derive from other financial securities, but the term is used more widely to include options and forward contracts for commodities.[5] Micu and Upper (2006) report very large increases in the combined turnover in fixed income, equity index and currency contracts (including both options and futures) on international derivatives exchanges in recent years. Most of the financial contracts were for interest rates, government bonds, foreign exchange and stock indexes, while the main commodity contracts were for metals (particularly gold), agricultural goods and energy (particularly oil).

After summarizing the payouts to these contracts, we then look at how they are priced in Chapter 6. An economic model could be used to solve the stochastic discount factors in the consumption-based pricing model, but that involves solving the underlying asset prices. A preferable approach obtains a pricing model for derivatives that are functions of the current values of the underlying asset prices together with the restrictions specified by the contracts. Since the assets already trade we can use their current prices as inputs to the pricing model without trying to compute them. In effect, the approach works from the premise that markets price assets efficiently and all we need to do is work out how the derivatives relate to the assets themselves. This is the approach adopted by Black and Scholes (1973) whose option pricing model values share options using five variables – the current share price, its variance, the expiry date, exercise price and the risk-free interest rate. It is a popular and widely used model because this information is readily available, but it does rely on a number of important assumptions, including that they are European options with fixed exercise dates, the underlying shares pay no dividends and they have a constant variance. We do not derive the *Black–Scholes option pricing model* formally, preferring instead to provide an intuitive explanation for its separate components. Forward contracts are also valued using the current price of the underlying asset, the settlement date, margin requirements, price limits and storage costs when the asset is a storable commodity.

Corporate finance

In most economies a significant portion of aggregate investment is undertaken by corporate firms who can raise large amounts of risky capital by trading shares, bonds and other securities. In particular, they can issue limited liability shares that restrict the liability of shareholders to the value of their invested capital. In return, they are subject to statutory regulations that, among other things, specify information that must be reported to shareholders at specified times, and bankruptcy provisions to protect bondholders from undue risk. A significant fraction of the value of financial securities that trade in capital markets originate in the corporate sector. There are primary securities, such as debt and equity, as well as the numerous derivative securities written on them. In recent years a larger proportion of consumers hold these corporate securities, if not directly, then at least indirectly through their superannuation and pension funds. We examine the role of risk and taxes on corporate securities and on the market valuations of the firms who issue them in Chapter 7. In particular, we look at the effects of their capital structure and dividend policy choices. For expository purposes the classical finance model is an ideal starting point for the analysis because it establishes fundamental asset pricing relationships that can be extended to accommodate more realistic assumptions. In this setting, where consumers have common information in frictionless competitive capital markets, we obtain the *Modigliani–Miller financial policy irrelevance theorems*. They are generalized where possible by including risk and taxes before introducing leverage related costs and asymmetric information.

Most countries have a *classical corporate tax* that taxes the income corporate firms pay their shareholders but not interest payments on debt. This tax bias against equity encourages corporate firms to increase their leverage. Early studies looked for *leverage-related costs* to explain the presence of equity in a classical finance model, including bankruptcy costs, and lost corporate tax shields due to the asymmetric treatment of profits and losses, which both lead to optimal leverage policy choices. However, empirical studies could not find large enough leverage costs to offset the tax bias against equity, so Miller (1977) examined the combined effects of corporate and *personal taxes* and found that favourable tax treatment of capital gains could make equity preferable for investors in high tax brackets – that is, investors with marginal personal tax rates on cash distributions that exceed the corporate tax rate by more than their personal tax rates on capital gains. Most countries have progressive personal tax rates so that low-tax investors can have a tax preference for debt while high-tax investors have a tax preference for capital gains. Once both securities trade, Modigliani–Miller leverage will hold when consumers have common information. But this analysis by Miller produced the *dividend puzzle* where no fully taxable consumers have a tax preference for dividends over capital gains. Thus, shares pay no dividends in the *Miller equilibrium*. We examine a number of different explanations for this puzzle, including differential transactions costs, share repurchase constraints that restrict the payment of capital gains, and dividend signalling under asymmetric information. In the last section of this chapter we examine the *imputation tax system* used in Australia and New Zealand. This removes the double tax on dividends by crediting shareholders with corporate tax paid, where the corporate tax is used as withholding tax to discourage shareholders from realizing their income as capital gains in the future. Since capital gains are taxed at realization, rather than when they accrue inside firms, shareholders can reduce their effective tax rate on them by delaying realization. The corporate tax considerably reduces these benefits from retention by taxing income as it accrues inside firms.

Project evaluation and the social discount rate

Governments also undertake a large portion of the aggregate investment in most economies, where public sector agencies generally use different evaluation rules than those employed by private investors when markets are subject to distortions arising from taxes, externalities, non-competitive behaviour and the private underprovision of public goods. Private investors make investment choices to maximize their own welfare, while governments make investment choices to maximize social welfare. These objectives coincide in economies where resources are allocated in competitive markets without distortions (setting aside distributional concerns). However, when markets are subject to distortions private investors evaluate projects using distorted prices, while governments look beyond these distortions and evaluate projects by measuring their impact on social welfare. These differences are demonstrated in Chapter 8 by evaluating public projects that provide pure public goods in a tax-distorted economy with aggregate uncertainty. The analysis is undertaken in a two-period setting where consumers have common information and von Neumann–Morgenstern preferences.

Initially we obtain *optimality conditions for the provision of pure public goods* in the absence of taxes and other distortions to provide a benchmark for identifying the effects of *distorting taxes*. This extends the original Samuelson (1954) condition to an intertemporal setting with uncertainty where the current value of the summed marginal consumption benefits from the public good (MRS) is equated to the current value of the marginal resource cost (MRT). When these costs and benefits occur in the second period they are discounted using a stochastic discount factor, which, in the absence of taxes and other distortions, is the same as the discount factor used by private investors. However, in the presence of trade taxes (and other distortions) there are additional welfare effects when the projects impact on taxed activities. Any reduction in tax revenue is a welfare loss that increases the marginal cost of government spending, while the reverse applies when tax revenue rises. As a consequence of these welfare changes, projects in one period can have welfare effects that spill over into other time periods.

A conventional Harberger (1971) analysis is used to separate the welfare effects of each component of the projects, where this allows us to isolate the social benefits from extra public goods and the social costs of the tax changes made to fund their production costs.[6] By doing so we obtain measures of the *marginal social cost of public funds* for each tax; these are used as scaling coefficients on revenue transfers made by the government to balance its budget. For a distorting tax, each dollar of revenue raised will reduce private surplus by more than a dollar due to the excess burden of taxation, where the marginal social cost of public funds exceeds unity. When taxes are Ramsey optimal they have the same marginal social cost of public funds, where the welfare effects of the projects are independent of the tax used.

Compensated welfare measures are then used to isolate the changes in real income from each project, where a compensated gain is surplus real income generated at unchanged expected utility for every consumer. They are efficiency effects that ultimately determine the final changes in expected utility. We demonstrate this by generalizing the Hatta (1977) decomposition to allow variable producer prices and uncertainty. It solves actual changes in expected utility as compensated welfare changes multiplied by the shadow value of government revenue, where the shadow value of government revenue measures the aggregate change in expected utility from endowing a unit of real income on the economy. Since all the income effects are included in this scaling coefficient they play no role in project evaluation when consumers have the same distributional weights, and when they have different weights the distributional effects are conveniently isolated by the shadow value of government revenue.

Most public sector projects impact on consumption risk, where some projects are undertaken because they provide risk benefits, while for other projects the changes in risk are side effects. For example, governments in developing countries have frequently used commodity price stabilization schemes to reduce consumption risk, like the rice price stabilization scheme in Indonesia and the wool price stabilization scheme in Australia.[7] We measure risk benefits from projects by deducting the *expected compensating variation* (CV) from the *ex-ante CV*. The expected CV holds constant the utility of every consumer in every time period and every state of nature. Thus, it completely undoes the impact of each project on consumers, including changes in their consumption risk. In contrast, the ex-ante CV holds constant the expected utility of every consumer but without holding their utility constant in every state of nature. It is the amount of income we can take from consumers now without reversing the changes in their consumption risk from the project. When the expected CV is larger than the ex-ante CV consumers benefit from changes in consumption risk, while the reverse applies when the ex-ante CV is larger.

One of the most contentious issues in project evaluation involves the choice of *social discount rate* for public projects in economies with distorted markets. Harberger (1969) and Sandmo and Dréze (1971) find the social discount rate is a weighted average of the pre- and post-tax interest rates in the presence of a tax on capital income in a two-period certainty setting. By including additional time periods, Marglin (1963a, 1963b) finds it should be higher than the weighted average formula, while Bradford (1975) finds it should be approximately equal to the after-tax interest rate. Sjaastad and Wisecarver (1977) show how these claims can be reconciled by their different treatment of capital depreciation. When private saving rises to replace depreciation of public capital the discount rate becomes the weighted average formula in a multi-period setting. Others argue there are differences between private and social discount rates when project net cash flows are uncertain. Samuelson (1964), Vickery (1964) and Arrow and Lind (1970) argue the social discount rate should be lower because the government can raise funds at lower risk. Bailey and Jensen (1972) argue these claims are based on the public sector being able to overcome distortions in private markets for trading risk.

We derive the social discount rate by including a tax on capital income in the public good economy. This extends the analysis of Harberger and of Sandmo and Dréze where, in the absence of trade taxes, the weighted average formula holds in each state of nature. Once trade taxes are included, the social discount rate deviates from this formula when public investment impacts on trade tax revenue. The derivations of the discount rate by Marglin and Bradford are reconciled to the weighted average formula using the analysis in Sjaastad and Wisecarver.

1.2 Concluding remarks

Financial economics is a challenging subject because it draws together analysis from a number of fields in economics. Indeed, modern macroeconomic analysis uses general equilibrium models with money and financial securities in a multi-period setting with uncertainty. Time and risk are fundamental characteristics of the environment every consumer faces. In recent years activity in capital markets has expanded dramatically to provide consumers with opportunities to trade risk and choose their intertemporal consumption.

More and more people have become shareholders in private firms as they set aside funds for consumption in retirement. Professional traders in the capital market perform a variety of important services. Some gather information to find profitable investment opportunities, where this imposes constraints on firm managers and aligns their interests more closely to those of their investors. And by reducing trading costs they expand the aggregate consumption opportunities for the economy. Others specialize in trading insurance so that consumers can reduce individual risk from their consumption. While most finance courses focus on private activity, which is understandable given the desire students have to either work in private firms or as policy analysts with an understanding of how private markets function, there are nonetheless a number of important issues that are peculiar to the evaluation of public policy in economies with distorted markets.

This book attempts to identify fundamental principles that underpin activity in financial markets. Starting in a certainty setting the analysis is extended gradually so that readers can develop a framework for understanding how time and risk impact on the allocation of resources, both in the private and public sectors of the economy. By exposing the fundamental economic principles in financial markets, financial economics provides a clearer understanding of the material covered in the field of finance. For example, the capital asset pricing model makes much more sense, and can be used in a more informed way, when it is derived using standard demand–supply analysis. It helps us understand why consumers all hold the same risky bundles and why they price risk identically, as well as exposing the important role of the key assumptions made in the model.

2 Investment decisions under certainty

A lot of important insights are obtained from the standard consumer problem of an individual who maximizes utility by allocating a given amount of money income to a bundle of goods with benefits confined to the current period. In practice, however, most goods generate future consumption flows, and consumers regularly make choices to determine their future consumption by trading capital goods. Houses and cars are obvious examples of goods with future consumption flows, as are jars of honey or packets of biscuits. These goods are capital assets which, broadly defined, are goods that embody future consumption flows. They can be purchased from current income as a form of saving, or by borrowing against future income. Either way, they allow consumers to trade intertemporally.[1]

There are different ways of shifting consumption through time: some result from actions consumers take in isolation, such as storage and other private investment activities, while others arise from trading in the capital market. In Section 2.1 we follow the analysis in Hirshleifer (1965) by examining storage and other private investment opportunities in an *autarky economy* where consumers live in isolation on (imaginary) island economies. This conveniently separates capital investment undertaken directly by individuals themselves from investment made on their behalf by firms. Individuals can store goods, such as rice and apples, for future consumption, and they can also plant rice and apple trees to produce future consumption. Both are examples of private investment in capital assets. Additional opportunities arise when they can trade capital assets with each other in the *capital market*.[2]

The role of trade is examined in Section 2.2 by introducing it in stages. Atemporal trade is introduced to the autarky economy where consumers exchange goods in each time period but not over time. This first step conveniently allows us to summarize intertemporal consumption choices using dollar values of expenditure in each period. It is the basis for the standard Fisher (1930) analysis of intertemporal consumption choices over current and future expenditure. Since consumers equate the marginal utility from spending (real) income on each good in their bundle, the composition of the consumption bundle can be suppressed in the analysis. Fiat money (currency) is then included to identify its role as a medium of exchange, and we do this by initially ruling out currency as a store of value, where the demand for currency is determined by its ability to reduce trading costs in each time period. The final extension allows consumers to also trade across time periods in a *market economy*, where some save while others borrow due to differences in their preferences, income flows and/or the rate of interest (which equates aggregate borrowing and saving in a competitive capital market). These intertemporal transfers can be made without affecting aggregate consumption. It only requires consumers to have different marginal valuations for future relative to current consumption. And there is even greater scope to trade intertemporally when aggregate consumption can be transferred into the future through storage and other forms of investment.

Financial securities play a number of important roles in market economies, one of which is to reduce the costs of trading private property rights over resources. Most finance models ignore these costs because they are relatively small, but that diminishes their importance, particularly when there is uncertainty and asymmetric information between traders where property rights are more costly to trade. In a certainty setting with complete information, no transactions costs, and perfectly divisible capital goods, there is no role for financial securities. In reality, however, goods are not perfectly divisible and they are costly to move about, and financial securities, and in particular fiat money, can dramatically lower these costs by reducing the number of physical exchanges of goods and services. Without financial assets consumers would exchange goods numerous times before finally converting them into their preferred consumption bundle. Since these assets provide holders with claims to underlying real resources, they reduce the number of times goods are transferred between consumers. When financial securities trade in a market economy we refer to it as an *asset economy*.

Trading costs are introduced to the asset economy to illustrate what determines the optimal demand for financial securities in a certainty setting. These costs arise on atemporal and intertemporal trades, where different securities play different roles in reducing them. Fiat money is a liquid security used for relatively low-valued transactions, and is more widely accepted by traders. Its role as a store of value is undermined somewhat by the non-payment of interest on currency held for a period of time, so its primary role is as a medium of exchange. Consumers do carry currency between periods as a form of insurance when there is uncertainty, but most intertemporal trade is facilitated using financial securities. For example, firms issue bonds and shares to fund investment, particularly larger investments with economies of scale. These securities specify the terms and conditions that govern the resource transfers through time. In practice the most significant difference between bonds and shares, and the many other financial securities that trade, is the risk in their payouts. Indeed, a key role of financial securities is to facilitate trades over risky resource transfers, and we examine this in much greater detail in Chapters 3 and 4. In a certainty setting, however, financial securities summarize property right transfers between savers and borrowers, where savers forgo current consumption in return for future consumption, while the reverse applies for borrowers. In effect, the security is a contract that specifies the terms and conditions that govern these intertemporal resource transfers.

They also provide a mechanism for aligning (at least partially) the incentives of firm managers (as agents) to the interests of their investors (the principals). The task is greatly simplified when investors all have the same objective function for firms. Irving Fisher (1930) made the important observation that consumers make their investment and intertemporal consumption choices separately when they are price-takers. In particular, they choose investment to maximize wealth and then choose intertemporal consumption to maximize utility. This is referred to as the *Fisher separation theorem*, and it provides price-taking firms with the simple and unanimous objective by its investors to maximize profit. We demonstrate this theorem and consider how economic analysis is affected when it fails to hold. The firm's objective function is much more complicated when Fisher separation breaks down because investment choices depend on the intertemporal consumption preferences of its investors. Financial securities play an important role in aligning the interests of managers with those of their investors when there is uncertainty and asymmetric information.

For example, ordinary shareholders generally have voting rights over the decisions taken by firm managers, where a shareholder, or group of shareholders, can have a controlling interest in a firm when they hold or can influence more than 50 per cent of its shares. Also, specialist traders in the financial market gather information to identify profitable opportunities when share prices deviate from their fundamental determinants. On some occasions they purchase enough shares to change the way a firm operates by reorganizing or replacing its existing management, by merging it with another firm, or by liquidating its assets and closing it down entirely. That is why share prices provide important signals, not just about conditions that affect the underlying value of goods and services that firms produce, but also about the performance of their managers. Share prices fall when traders believe managers are performing poorly, and this acts as a discipline on them. Conversely, managers who perform well benefit their shareholders by driving up share prices. Indeed, share prices, and changes in them, provide important information to traders in capital markets.

Expected inflation in the general price level can affect capital asset values by changing their real economic returns. These real effects originate in a number of different ways so we start by initially demonstrating the Fisher effect in Section 2.3. It is where nominal asset returns move with fully anticipated inflation to preserve their real returns, and it arises in a classical finance model where all nominal variables adjust freely in frictionless competitive markets and traders have common information. This establishes an important benchmark for identifying the real effects of inflation when the key assumptions in the model are relaxed. In particular, we consider heterogeneous expectations and the wealth effects from the non-payment of interest on currency.

Arbitrage in competitive (frictionless) markets underpins all of the popular asset pricing models in finance. Indeed, it makes every security (in the same risk class) pay the same expected economic return in every time period, and makes any sequence of short rates of return consistent with the corresponding long rate of return over the same period. We demonstrate these propositions in Section 2.4 by pricing bonds and shares, and then use these prices to derive the Modigliani–Miller financial policy irrelevance theorems in the presence of taxes in a two-period certainty model. This analysis is extended later in Chapters 3 and 4 to accommodate uncertainty.

2.1 Intertemporal consumption in autarky

Fisher (1930) initially showed that price-taking agents use the net present value (NPV) rule to value capital assets when they can trade intertemporally in a competitive capital market. Before demonstrating this we start the analysis in an autarky economy to identify where the potential gains from trade come from in market economies. Storage and other private investment opportunities are also examined in this section.

2.1.1 Endowments without storage

Consider an autarky economy where each consumer ($h = 1, \ldots, H$) is endowed with N non-storable consumption goods $\bar{x}_t^h := \{\bar{x}_t^h(1), \ldots, \bar{x}_t^h(N)\}$ in each time period $t \in \{0, 1\}$. They consume bundles of these goods $x_t^h := \{x_t^h(1), \ldots, x_t^h(N)\}$ to maximize utility $u^h(x_0^h, x_1^h)$.[3] Since each consumer effectively lives on an island their optimization problem, in the absence of storage and private investment opportunities (and with superscript h omitted), can be summarized as

$$\max \left\{ u(x_0 x_1) \middle| \begin{matrix} x_0 - \bar{x}_0 \leq 0 \\ x_1 - \bar{x}_1 \leq 0 \end{matrix} \right\}.^4 \qquad (2.1)$$

With non-satiation the constraints in (2.1) binds and the equilibrium outcome is degenerate in the sense that everyone consumes their endowments.[5] Clearly, each consumer is like a shipwrecked Robinson Crusoe (but without Friday) living on a remote island where the consumption opportunities are as illustrated in Figure 2.1 for one of the commodities.

At the endowment point $\bar{x}$ the marginal rate of substitution between consumption of each good (n) tomorrow ($t=1$) and today ($t=0$) is the inverse of the slope of the indifference schedule, with:

$$MRS_{1,0}(n) = \frac{u_1'(n)}{u_0'(n)} = \frac{\lambda_1(n)}{\lambda_0(n)} \quad \forall n,^6$$

where $u_t'(n) = \partial u(n)/\partial x_t(n)$ for $t \in \{0, 1\}$, and $\lambda_0(n)$ and $\lambda_1(n)$ are the Lagrange multipliers for the endowments that constrain consumption of each good in each time period. In the absence of trade these multipliers are equal to the marginal utility from consuming a good in each period, where $\lambda_1(n)/\lambda_0(n) = 1/[1 + \rho(n)]$ is the personal discount factor the consumer uses to compute the current value of good n in the second period. Without trade the discount rate $\rho(n)$ can differ across goods and across consumers. For example, the personal discount rate for good b in the second period (measured in units of good n) is $\lambda_1(b)/\lambda_0(n) = 1/[1 + \rho(b, n)]$, where it is possible that $\rho(b, n) \neq \rho(n)$. These differences signal potential gains from trading goods within each period and across time, as consumers have different valuations for future consumption flows. And when they do, they have different valuations for capital assets in the autarky economy.

We can determine a consumer's *rate of time preference* for each good by measuring the personal discount rate for the constant consumption bundles along a 45 degree line through the origin in Figure 2.1. Any deviation in the discount factor from unity along this line is solely due to the timing of consumption, where a positive rate of time preference indicates the consumer's impatience for consuming the good, while the reverse applies when it is negative.[7]

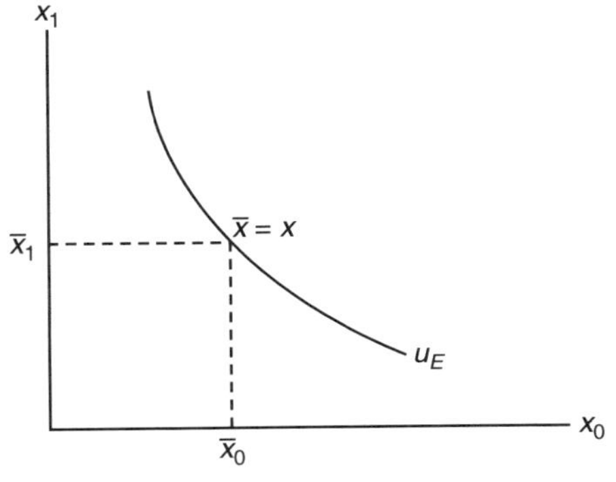

Figure 2.1 Interemporal consumption in autarky.

Thus, along the 45° line the discount rate is equal to the rate of time preference, but not otherwise (for strictly convex indifference curves).

2.1.2 Endowments with storage

Before introducing trade we look at private investment opportunities in the autarky economy of which storage is an obvious example. Suppose one or more of the goods can be stored so that consumers can transfer current endowments to the second period, the problem for each consumer becomes

$$\max\left\{u(x_0, x_1)\middle| \begin{matrix} x_0 - \bar{x}_0 \leq 0 \\ x_1 - \bar{x}_1 - (\bar{x}_0 - x_0) \leq 0 \end{matrix}\right\}, \tag{2.2}$$

with $\bar{x}_0(n) - x_0(n) > 0$ being the quantity of each good $n \in N$ stored. When consumers have standard preferences (to rule out corner solutions and non-satiation) the constraint on future consumption in (2.2) binds, but the constraint on current consumption may not. This is confirmed by using the first-order conditions to compute the discount factor, for each good (n), as

$$MRS_{1,0}(n) = \frac{\lambda_1(n)}{\lambda_0(n) + \lambda_1(n)} \equiv \frac{1}{1+\rho(n)}.$$

Notice how both constraint multipliers appear in the denominator when goods are storable. In effect, second-period consumption is constrained by the endowments in both periods, where consumers may choose to store every storable good, some of them, or none at all. The decision is determined by their marginal valuations for these goods at the endowment point, where two possibilities arise:

i Costless storage occurs, with $\bar{x}_0(n) - x_0(n) > 0$, if at the endowment point $MRS_{1,0}(n) > 1$. Since the constraint on current consumption in (2.2) is non-binding, we must have $\lambda_0(n) = 0$, so that $MRS_{1,0}(n) = 1$ at an interior solution, with $x_0(n) > 0$ and $x_1(n) > 0$. This equates the marginal utility from consuming the good in each period, as well as the marginal valuation of future consumption of all other goods measured in units of good n in the first period, where $MRS_{1,0}(k,n) = 1$ at all n, k.

ii No storage occurs, with $\bar{x}_0(n) - x_0(n) = 0$, if at the endowment point $MRS_{1,0}(n) \leq 1$. This is where consumers have a higher marginal valuation for the good (n) in the first period, and would therefore prefer to transfer some of the endowment from the second period (or consume their endowment when $MRS_{1,0}(n) = 1$).

The consumption opportunities for a storable good (n) are illustrated in Figure 2.2 by the frontier *DEF*. Storage allows the consumer to trade from the endowment point *E* along the segment *DE* of the frontier, which has slope −1 for costless storage. The good is stored when the slope of the indifference curve at the endowment point is flatter than line *DE* reflecting a higher marginal valuation for it in the second period.

Thus, storage allows consumers to exploit some of the potential gains from trade in the autarky economy when they have higher relative marginal valuations for consuming goods in the second period. But they cannot exploit potential gains from trade when they have

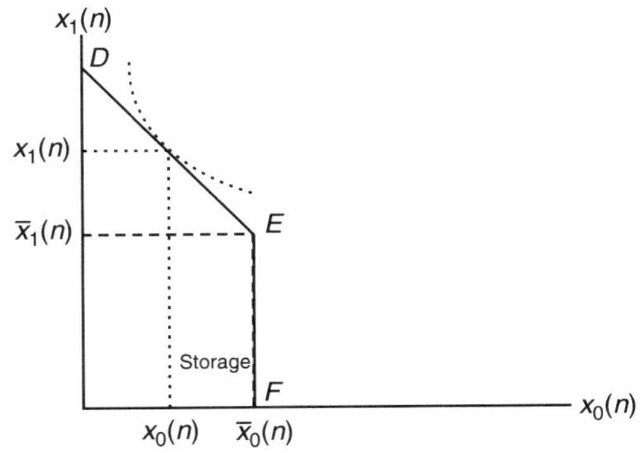

Figure 2.2 Costless storage in autarky.

higher relative marginal valuations for goods in the first period or when their marginal valuations for goods in each period differ from those of other consumers.

Box 2.1 Storage: a numerical example

Brad Johnson has 400 kg of rice which he can consume today (x_0) or store (z_0) and consume in 12 months time (x_1). He has no other income in each of the two periods and there are no storage costs. When he chooses consumption to maximize the utility function ln x_0 + 0.98 ln x_1 Brad will consume less rice next year than today, where his optimal consumption satisfies $x_1^* = 0.98\, x_0^*$. Using the budget constraint when it binds, with $x_0 = 400 - x_1$, he chooses $x_0^* \approx 202$ kg and $x_1^* \approx 198$ kg, where the difference is due to his marginal impatience for current consumption captured in the coefficient 0.98 in the utility function. When Brad consumes on the 45° line his marginal rate of substitution between consumption today and next year is $MRS_{0,1} = 0.98 = 1/(1 + \rho)$, where $\rho \approx 0.02$ is his marginal rate of time preference. Since he has a higher marginal valuation for current consumption his optimal consumption choice, which is illustrated in the diagram below at point A, lies to the right of the 45° line. Clearly, if Brad's marginal rate of time preference was zero he would consume on the 45° line.

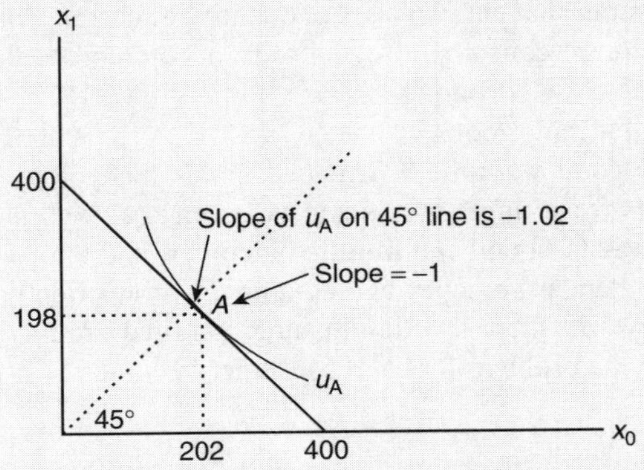

In reality, storage is costly due to wastage and the costs of providing storage facilities, and these costs contract segment *DE* of the consumption frontier in Figure 2.2. It they are constant marginal costs the segment *DE* of the consumption frontier gets flatter around point *E*, while fixed costs shift line *DE* to the left.

Box 2.2 Costly storage: a numerical example

When marginal storage costs are introduced into the optimization problem for Brad Johnson in Box 2.1 above, his budget constraint contracts around the endowment point and he consumes even less rice next year. Recall that with costless storage he consumes less rice in the second period due to his positive rate of time preference. The effects of storage costs are illustrated by introducing 2 per cent wastage, so that his optimal consumption choice now satisfies $x_1^* = 0.9604\, x_0^*$. Using the budget constraint in the presence of these costs when it binds, with $x_0 = 400 - x_1/0.98$, he consumes $x_0^* \approx 202$ kg and $x_1^* \approx 194$ kg. This outcome is illustrated in the diagram below at point B which is vertically below point A where he consumed previously when there were no storage costs. There is no change in current consumption here because the income effect offsets the substitution effect where the change in real income falls solely on consumption next period which falls by the storage costs of $202 \times 0.02 \approx 4$ kg.

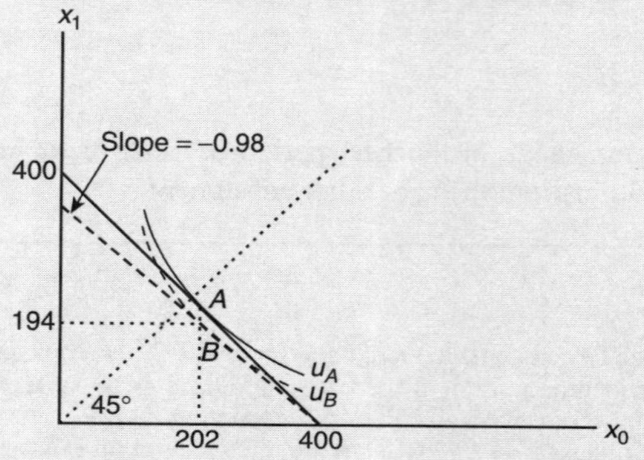

2.1.3 Other private investment opportunities

Consumers have other ways of converting current endowments into future consumption goods, and they differ from storage by providing the possibility of growth. In other words, they have private investment opportunities that convert a given quantity of current consumption goods into a larger quantity of future consumption goods. To accommodate them we define the second-period outputs for each consumer (h) as $y_1^h(z_0^h) := \{y_1^h(1), \ldots, y_1^h(N)\}$, which are produced by inputs of current goods, $z_0^h := \{z_0^h(1), \ldots, z_0^h(N)\}$, with $z_o^h(n) = \bar{x}_0^h(n) - x_0^h(n)$ being the input of each good n at time 0. This production technology is general enough to allow multiple outputs from single inputs and vice versa, as well as single outputs from single inputs. But as a way to bound equilibrium outcomes, and to make them unique for each consumer, we follow standard practice and assume the production possibility sets are strictly convex. In other words, there is a diminishing marginal productivity of investment and no fixed costs, where the problem for each consumer becomes

$$\max\left\{u(x_0, x_1)\left|\begin{matrix} x_0 + z_0 - \bar{x}_0 \le 0 \\ x_1 - \bar{x}_1 - y_1 \le 0 \end{matrix}\right.\right\}.^{8} \tag{2.3}$$

For optimally chosen consumption (with standard preferences) the personal discount factors for each good (n) are

$$MRS_{1,0}(n) = \frac{\lambda_1(n)}{\lambda_0(n) + \sum_j \lambda_i(j)\, MP(j,n)} \equiv \frac{1}{1+\rho(n)},$$

where $MP(j, n) = \partial y_1(j)/\partial z_0(n)$ is the marginal increase in the output of good j from investing another unit of good n.[9] This expression is similar to the discount rate with costless storage, where once again private investment opportunities raise the marginal utility of the current endowments when they are consumed in the second period. It is captured here by the term in the denominator that measures the marginal valuation of the goods used as inputs, $\Sigma_j \lambda_1(j)\, MP(j,n)/\lambda_1(n)$. Consumers will invest when, at the endowment point, they have a higher marginal valuation for future consumption, with $MRS_{1,0}(n) > \lambda_1(n)/\lambda_0(n)$.

The consumption opportunity set in the autarky economy with private investment is illustrated in Figure 2.3 when good n is the only input used to produce itself in the second period. You could think of it as corn planted now and harvested in the future. The non-linear segment DE of the consumption opportunity frontier maps the extra future consumption from private investment (with diminishing marginal productivity) onto the endowment point E.

Box 2.3 Private investment opportunities: a numerical example

Suppose we reconsider the consumption choices made by Brad Johnson in Box 2.1 by replacing storage with private investment where he can plant z_0 kg of rice today and harvest $y_1 = 30\sqrt{z_0}$ kg in 12 months' time. This technology has a positive marginal product of $dy_1/dz_0 = 15/\sqrt{z_0}$ kg, which diminishes with investment. Now his optimal consumption choices satisfy $0.98(x_0^*/x_1^*) = \sqrt{z_0}/15$, and are solved using the budget constraints on current and future consumption when they bind, with $x_0 = 400 - z_0$ and $x_1 = 30\sqrt{z_0}$, where $x_0^* \approx 269$ kg and $x_1^* \approx 344$ kg. This outcome is illustrated in the diagram below at point C where his indifference curve u_C has the same slope as his investment opportunity set when he invests $z_0^* \approx 131$ kg. Since there is a positive marginal product from initial investment, the extra real income raises Brad's utility above the levels achieved through storage earlier in Boxes 2.1 and 2.2, where we have $u_C > u_A > u_B$.

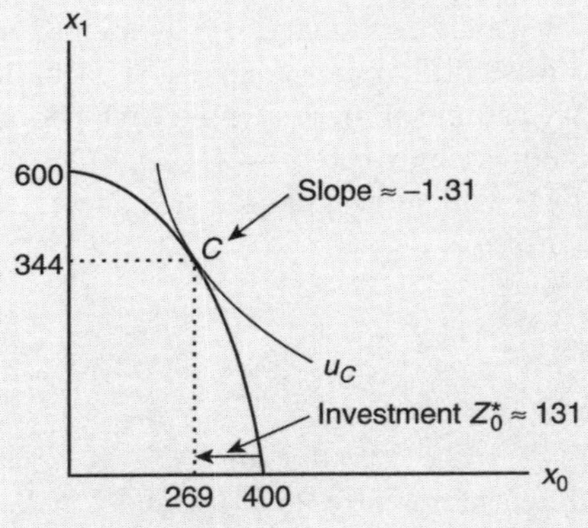

Even though there is no role for financial securities in the autarky economy the analysis has identified intertemporal consumption opportunities for individual consumers prior to trade and isolated the source of any potential gains from trade when consumers have different marginal valuations for goods in and between each time period.

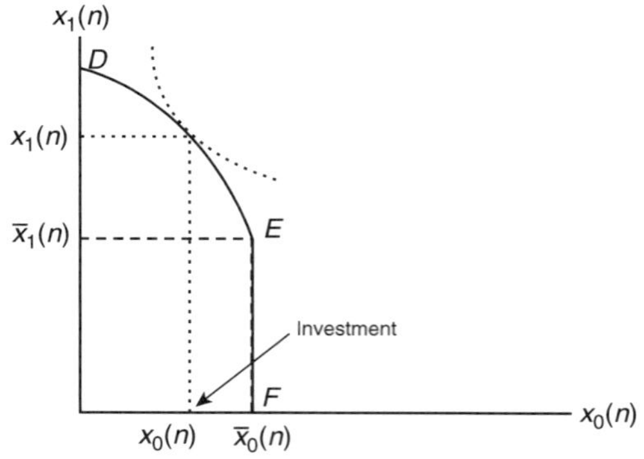

Figure 2.3 Private investment opportunities in autarky.

2.2 Intertemporal consumption in a market economy

We introduce trade into the autarky economy in this section by allowing consumers to exchange goods in a market economy. Initially they only trade their endowments within each time period, before eventually trading over time as well. This allows us to separate the roles of fiat currency (notes and coins) and financial securities as mediums of exchange and stores of value, where financial assets are used to reduce the costs of exchanging goods and to transfer expenditure between time periods.

2.2.1 Endowments with atemporal trade

Consumers who can barter and exchange goods in frictionless competitive markets have the same marginal valuations for each good in each time period for optimally chosen consumption. But without intertemporal trade they can have different marginal valuations for goods between time periods, in which case they will use different discount rates on future consumption flows when valuing capital assets. We assume all trades within each period are at competitively determined equilibrium commodity prices, where $p_t := \{1, \ldots, p_t(N)\}$ is the set of relative prices for the N goods at time $t \in \{0,1\}$ with good 1 chosen as numeraire. In this economy the consumer problem can be summarized as

$$\max\left\{u(x_0, x_1)\left|\begin{matrix} X_0 \le I_0 \\ X_1 \le I_1 \end{matrix}\right.\right\}, \tag{2.4}$$

where the market values of consumption and expenditure are $X_t \equiv p_t x_t$ and $I_t \equiv \bar{X}_t = p_t \bar{x}_t$, respectively. Any combination of the N goods can be purchased in each time period, subject to consumption expenditure being no greater than the market value of the endowments. And with atemporal trade these constraints apply to total expenditure and not the endowment of each good. Thus, there is a single constraint multiplier on the market value of income in each time period, rather than a separate multiplier for each good in each period, as was the case previously in the autarky economy.

> **Definition 2.1** The *endowment economy with atemporal trade* is described by $(u,\bar{x})$, where u is the set of consumer utility functions and $\bar{x}$ the set of current and future endowments for all H consumers. A competitive equilibrium in this economy is characterized by the relative commodity prices p_0^* and p_1^* such that:
>
> i $x_0^{h*}(n)$ and $x_1^{h*}(n)$, for all n, solve the consumer problem in (2.4) for all h;
>
> ii the goods markets clear in each period $t \in \{0, 1\}$, with $\Sigma\bar{x}_t^h(n) = \Sigma_h x_t^{h*}(n)$ for all h.

It is a unique equilibrium outcome when consumers have strictly convex indifference sets over bundles of consumption goods, but is unlikely to be Pareto efficient. All consumers have the same marginal rates of substitution between goods in the same time period when they can trade atemporally in frictionless competitive markets, with

$$MRS_0(n,k) = \frac{p_0(n)}{p_0(k)} \quad \forall n, k, h,$$

but they can have different marginal rates of substitution for goods in different time periods when they cannot trade intertemporally, with

$$MRS_{1,0}^h(n) = \frac{\lambda_1^h p_1(n)}{\lambda_0^h p_0(n)} \quad \forall n,$$

where $\lambda_1^h / \lambda_0^h$ are personalized discount factors on future income.[10] Once consumers exhaust the gains from atemporal trade we can reformulate the consumer problem over a single representative commodity (income), where the indirect utility function can be solved as

$$v(I) := \max\left\{u(x_0, x_1) \middle| \begin{matrix} X_0 \le I_0 \\ X_1 \le I_1 \end{matrix}\right\}^{11}, \tag{2.5}$$

with $I = \{I_0, I_1\}$. It is a maximum value function with income optimally allocated to bundles of goods in each period. In many applications we are not interested in the composition of these bundles, but rather in the value of consumption expenditure in each period, where the consumption opportunities are illustrated in Figure 2.4. This is the familiar analysis used by Fisher (1930) and Hirshleifer (1970). Clearly, consumption must be at the endowment when goods cannot be transferred between the two periods through storage, investment opportunities or trade. At this equilibrium allocation the personal discount rate on future income is the inverse of the slope of the indifference curve at the endowment point I, and it can differ across consumers with different endowments and preferences.

Before allowing consumers to trade intertemporally we consider the role of (fiat) money as a medium of exchange.

2.2.2 Endowments with atemporal trade and fiat money

Governments are monopoly suppliers of fiat money (notes and coins), which has two main roles – one is to reduce trading costs, while the other is to provide traders with a store of

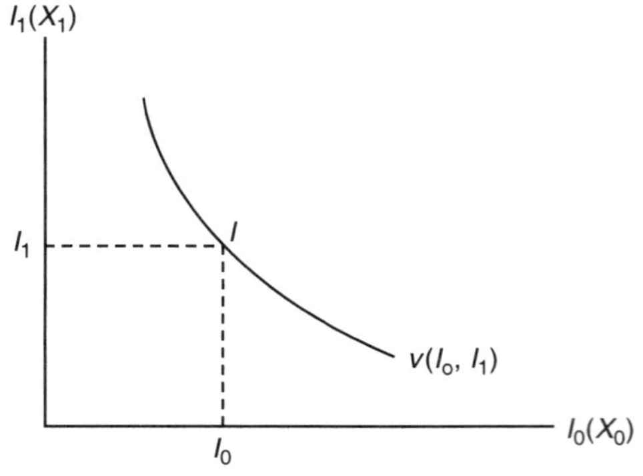

Figure 2.4 Consumption opportunities with income endowments and atemporal trade.

value (in nominal terms at least). By using currency, traders can significantly reduce the number of costly physical exchanges of goods and services in each time period, and we focus on this role by assuming currency cannot be used as a store of value. In other words, any currency the government supplies to the private economy by purchasing goods is redeemed in each period immediately after private trades are consummated. We avoid the need for any taxes by assuming currency is costless to supply.[12] Thus, there are no resource transfers through the government budget in this endowment economy with atemporal trade.

We define trading costs (measured in units of numeraire good 1) for each consumer as a constant proportion $\tau^h(n)$ of the market value of each good $n \in N$ traded. They are the same in each time period $t \in \{0, 1\}$ with $\tau^h(n) > 0$ for purchases when $x_t^h(n) > x_t^h(n)$, and $\tau^h(n) < 0$ for sales when $x_t^h(n) < \bar{x}_t^h(n)$. It is assumed here that they are strictly decreasing functions of the currency used in each period (m_t^h), where the problem for each consumer in the endowment economy with atemporal trade and fiat currency is

$$\max\left\{u(x_0, x_1)\middle|\begin{matrix} p_0 x_0 + \tau D_0 - p_0 \bar{x}_0 \le 0 \\ p_1 x_1 + \tau D_1 - p_1 \bar{x}_1 \le 0 \end{matrix}\right\}, \tag{2.6}$$

with $\tau := \{\tau(1), ..., \tau(N)\}$ being the trading costs for each good and $D_t := \{D_t(1), ..., D_t(N)\}$ the net demands for them, where $D_t(n) = p_t(n)[x_t(n) - \bar{x}_t(n)]$ for all n at each time $t \in \{0, 1\}$.

Definition 2.2 The *endowment economy with atemporal trade and (fiat) money* is described by $(u, \bar{x}, m)$, where m is the set of total currency supplied in each time period. A competitive equilibrium in this economy is characterized by the relative commodity prices p_0^* and p_1^* such that:

i $x_0^{h*}(n)$ and $x_1^{h*}(n)$, for all n, solve the consumer problem in (2.6) for all h;

ii the goods markets clear in each time period $t \in \{0, 1\}$, with $\Sigma_h \bar{x}_{t(n)}^h = \Sigma_h \bar{x}_t^{h*}(n)$, for all $n \neq 1$, and $\Sigma_h \bar{x}_t^h(1) = \Sigma_h x_t^{h*}(1) + \Sigma_h \tau^h D_t^h$.

As noted above, there is no government budget constraint in this economy as currency is costless to supply and no resources are transferred from consumers as seigniorage. That is the reason why currency does not appear directly in the budget constraints in (2.6), but indirectly through its impact on trading costs, where the final market-clearing condition in Definition 2.2 (ii) equates the sum of trading costs and consumption of good 1 to the aggregate endowment of good 1.

If trading costs are minimum necessary costs of trade they do not distort equilibrium outcomes, even though consumers cannot equate their marginal rates of substitution for goods in the same time period. For optimally chosen consumption in each period, we have

$$MRS_0(n,k) = \frac{p_0(n)[1+\tau(n)]}{p_0(k)[1+\tau(k)]} \quad \forall n,k,h,$$

where the trading costs do not cancel, even when they are the same for each good, as one may be purchased and the other sold. But if we deduct these costs from the marginal rates of substitution by shifting them to the left-hand side of the expression above, consumers will have the same net marginal rates of substitution for goods in the same time period. This is a signal of efficiency in the conventional Paretian sense when they are minimum necessary costs of trade. However, consumers can have different marginal rates of substitution for goods in different time periods, even without trading costs, when they cannot trade intertemporally. This was confirmed in the previous section where, in the presence of trading costs, we now have

$$MRS^h_{1,0}(n) = \frac{\lambda^h_1 p_1(n)[1+\tau(n)]}{\lambda^h_0 p_0(n)[1+\tau(n)]} \quad \forall n.$$

Optimally chosen currency demands in each time period satisfy

$$-\lambda_t \sum_n \frac{\partial \tau(n)}{\partial m_t} p_t(n)\big(x_t(n) - \bar{x}_t(n)\big) = 0 \quad \forall t \in \{0,1\} \quad \text{and} \quad \forall h.$$

Since there are no private costs to consumers from using currency in this setting they exhaust the benefits, with $\partial \tau(n)/\partial m_t = 0$ for all n. But any quantity of (almost) perfectly divisible currency will satisfy consumers in a certainty setting where nominal prices can be costlessly adjusted to preserve the market-clearing relative commodity prices. Thus, there is a *classical dichotomy* between the real and nominal variables in the economy, where the reduction in trading costs is independent of the quantity of currency supplied. When currency is held as a store of value there is an implicit tax on currency holders from the non-payment of interest which transfers real resources as seigniorage to the government budget, where fully anticipated changes in the supply of currency will have real effects through their impact on the nominal rate of interest. These wealth effects are examined later in Section 2.5.

2.2.3 Endowments with full trade

In this section consumers can trade within each period (atemporally) and across time (intertemporally), where initially goods are traded intertemporally by exchanging forward contracts that are promises to deliver specified quantities of goods. The analysis is extended to an asset economy by introducing a financial security so that consumers can transfer income between the two time periods. This allows us to compare equilibrium outcomes in the exchange and asset economies when *full trade* is possible to confirm the observation by Arrow (1953) that financial securities significantly reduce the number of choice variables for consumers in the first period. In particular, they choose the market value of their future consumption bundle without choosing its composition until the second period when their securities are liquidated.

Consider the exchange economy when consumers can trade intertemporally by exchanging forward contracts $f^h(n)$ for each good $n \in N$. The buyer receives a unit of good n in the second period for each contract purchased, with $f^h(n) > 0$ for the buyer and $f^h(n) < 0$ for the seller. These contracts trade in the first period at relative prices $p_f := \{p_f(1), \dots, p_f(N)\}$, where the consumer problem in the endowment economy with full trade and forward contracts is

$$\max\left\{u(x_0, x_1) \left| \begin{matrix} p_0 x_0 - p_0 \bar{x}_0 + p_f f \le 0 \\ p_1 x_1 - p_1(\bar{x}_1 + f) \le 0 \end{matrix} \right.\right\}^{13}, \tag{2.7}$$

with $f^h := \{f^h(1), \dots, f^h(N)\}$ being the forward contracts traded.

Definition 2.3 The *market economy with endowments and forward commodity contracts* is the triplet $(u, \bar{x}, f)$, where f is the set of forward contracts for H consumers. A competitive equilibrium in this economy is characterized by the relative commodity prices p_0^* and p_1^* and relative forward contract prices p^{f*} such that:

i $x_0^{h*}(n)$, $x_1^{h*}(n)$ and $f^{h*}(n)$, for all n, solve the consumer problem in (2.7) for all $h = 1, \dots, H$;

ii the goods market clear in each time period $t \in \{0, 1\}$, with $\Sigma_h \bar{x}_t^h(n) = \Sigma_h x_t^{h*}(n)$ for all n, and the market for forward contracts clears, with $\Sigma_h f^{h*}(n) = 0$ for all n.

Optimally chosen forward contracts (for an interior solution) satisfy the first-order conditions for each good n, with

$$-\lambda_0^h p^f(n) + \lambda_1^h p_1(n) = 0 \;\forall n, h.$$

In the absence of transactions costs and taxes consumers use the same discount factor $(\lambda_1^h/\lambda_0^h)$ to value income in the second period, where the prices of forward contracts satisfy:

$$P^f(n) = \frac{p_1(n)\lambda_1}{\lambda_0} \;\forall n.$$

Since they can now trade all goods intertemporally they have the same marginal rates of substitution for goods in different time periods, with

$$MRS_{1,0}(n, k) = \frac{p^f(n)}{p_0(k)} \;\forall n, k, h.$$

Thus, the equilibrium outcome is Pareto optimal. An implicit market rate of interest is embedded in these pricing relationships, and we confirm this by allowing consumers to trade a^h units of a risk-free security in the first period at market price p_a per unit, with $a^h > 0$ for buyers and $a^h < 0$ for sellers. The current value of the asset traded by each consumer is $V_0^h = p_a a^h$, and it has payouts in the future of $a^h R_1 \equiv V_0^h(1+i)$, where i is the risk-free interest rate, and $R_1 = p_a(1 + i)$ the gross payout on each unit of current income invested in the security. Now the problem for each consumer in the asset economy is summarized in (2.5) when income in each time period is defined as

$$\begin{aligned} I_0 &\equiv \bar{X}_0 - V_0, \\ I_1 &\equiv \bar{X}_1 - aR_1.^{14} \end{aligned} \tag{2.8}$$

In this setting consumers determine the market value of their consumption expenditure in each time period by trading the risk-free security.

Definition 2.4 An *asset economy* is a market economy with a financial security.

Definition 2.5 The *asset economy with endowments* is described by $(u, \bar{x}, a)$, where a is the set of asset holdings of all H consumers. A competitive equilibrium in this economy is characterized by relative commodity prices p_0^* and p_1^*, a security price p_a^*, and an interest rate i^* such that

i $x_0^{h*}(n)$ and $x_1^{h*}(n)$, for all n, and a^{h*} solve the consumer problem in (2.8) for all h;

ii the goods markets clear in each time period $t \in \{0, 1\}$, with $\Sigma_h \bar{x}_t^h(n) = \Sigma_h x_t^{h*}(n) \forall_n$, and the capital market clears, with $\Sigma_h a^{h*} = 0 \; \forall n$.

Without providing an explicit reason for using a financial security rather than forward contracts, the two economies in Definitions 2.3 and 2.5 above are identical. Indeed, they have identical real equilibrium outcomes where consumers choose the same consumption bundles in each period and have the same utilities. A proper description of the economy would require the introduction of trading costs that are reduced by trading forward contracts and the financial security. Realistically, both could trade when they have different marginal effects on these costs. Thus, the asset economy in Definition 2.5 implicitly assumes trading costs can be costlessly eliminated by using the financial security without forward contracts. It is certainly plausible that the financial security will reduce these costs more than forward contracts in most circumstances. When using forward contracts consumers trade a separate one for each good to determine the composition of their future consumption bundle. However, when using the financial security they choose the market value of their future consumption bundle, while its composition is determined in the second period using the security payout. This potentially reduces the number of choice variables in the first period from $2N$ with forward contracts to $N + 1$ with the financial security.

Later in Chapters 3 and 4 we extend the analysis to accommodate uncertainty where consumers choose portfolios of securities to spread risk. Despite the additional security trades, however, they still have fewer choice variables in the asset economy, where the optimal security trade by each consumer solves the first-order condition

$$-\lambda_0^h p_a + \lambda_1^h R_1 = 0 \; \forall h,$$

where the discount factor on future income becomes $\lambda_1/\lambda_0, = 1/(1 + i)$, which is the same for all consumers.[15] When the constraints in (2.8) bind we obtain the familiar net present value rule for pricing capital assets, where wealth is the discounted present value of income, with

$$W_0 = I_0 + \frac{I_1}{1+i} = \bar{X}_0 + \frac{\bar{X}_1}{1+i}.$$

This allows us to summarize the consumer problem in the endowment economy with frictionless competitive markets as

$$\max_{\{a\}} \left\{ v(I) \middle| W_0 = I_0 + \frac{I_1}{1+i} \right\}. \tag{2.9}$$

The asset choice distributes income across the two periods, and is ultimately determined by consumer preferences for the goods purchased in each period. The consumption opportunities are illustrated in Figure 2.5, where the slope of the budget constraint determines the rate at which income can be transferred between the two periods by trading the security.

Whenever consumers save a dollar of current income their future consumption expenditure rises by $1 + i$ dollars, while borrowing a dollar of future income raises their current consumption expenditure by $1/(1 + i)$ dollars. The budget constraint is linear as consumers are price-takers. When they are large in the capital market, and the interest rate rises with borrowing and falls with saving, the budget constraint is concave to the origin through the endowment point. Any bundle along (or inside) the budget constraint is feasible, where optimally chosen intertemporal consumption expenditure satisfies

$$MRS_{1,0}(I) = \frac{v_1}{v_0} = \frac{1}{1+i}.$$

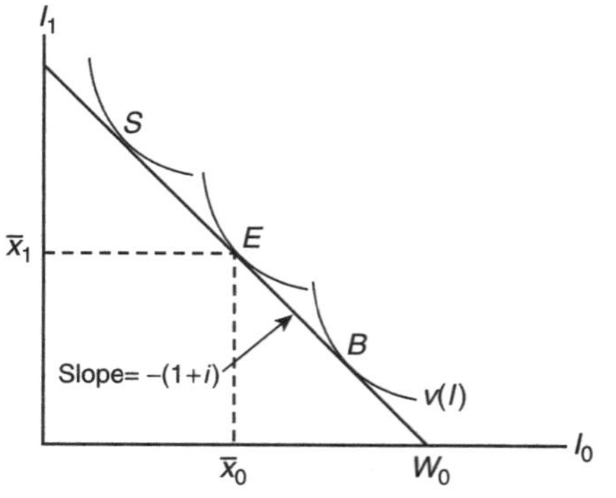

Figure 2.5 Consumption opportunities with income endowments, atemporal trade and a competitive capital market.

Three examples of the way consumers trade in the capital market are illustrated in Figure 2.5 with a saver at point *S*, a borrower at point *B*, and a non-trader who consumes the endowment at point *E*. The final equilibrium outcome for each consumer is determined by (i) the income endowments, (ii) the market rate of interest, and (iii) preferences. If the income endowments are skewed toward the first period, or interest rates are relatively high, consumers are more likely to save, and vice versa.

Box 2.4 Trade in a competitive capital market: a numerical example

Earlier in Box 2.1 we looked at the consumption choices made by Brad Johnson in a two-period setting. He has an endowment of 400 kg of rice today that could be transferred to the second period using storage and other private investment opportunities. Now we consider his intertemporal consumption choices when he can trade in a frictionless competitive capital market at a risk-free interest rate of 5 per cent over the year (but without storage and other private investment opportunities). By trading a risk-free security (a_0) he can transfer rice into the second period, where the constraints on his rice consumption in each period are $x_0 \leq 400 - a_0$ and $x_1 \leq 1.05\, a_0$, respectively. Based on his preferences in Box 2.1, his optimal consumption choices satisfy $0.98x_0^* = x_1^*/1.05$, and they are solved using the budget constraints when they bind, with $x_0^* \approx 202$ kg and $x_1^* \approx 208$ kg. Thus, his optimal demand for the risk-free security is $a_0^* \approx 192$ kg of rice. This outcome is illustrated in the diagram below at point *D* where his indifference curve u_D has a slope equal to -1.05, which is also the rate at which he can transfer rice between the two periods by trading the risk-free security. Notice how current consumption is the same as it was with costless storage in Box 2.1. Based on his preferences all the extra real income from interest received on saving is allocated to future consumption, where his utility (u_D) is higher than his utility in autarky (u_A) at point *A* in Box 2.1.

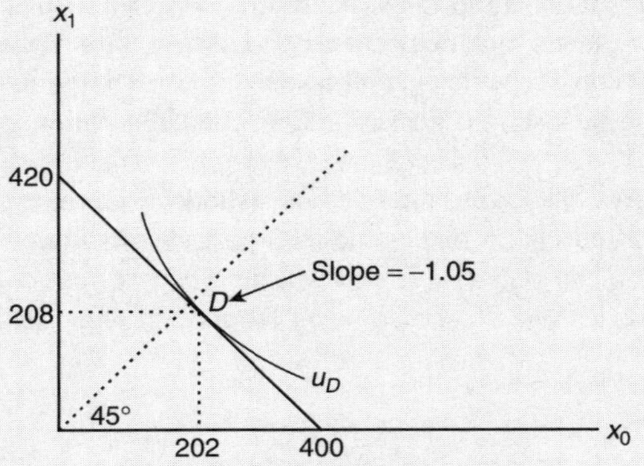

In a competitive capital market the interest rate equates aggregate saving and borrowing, with $\Sigma_h S^h = \Sigma_h B^h$, and since saving and borrowing decisions are determined by the distribution of income endowments over consumers in each time period and by their individual preferences, they also determine the interest rate in a closed economy. A stable equilibrium adjustment mechanism drives down the interest rate when $\Sigma_h S^h > \Sigma_h B^h$, while the reverse applies when $\Sigma_h S^h < \Sigma_h B^h$. It seems reasonable to expect higher interest rates will raise saving and reduce borrowing, which is what we normally observe in aggregate data, but it may not apply for every individual consumer due to the role of income effects.

To see this, consider the effects of raising the interest rate to i_1 for a consumer with standard convex preferences who initially saves at point *A* in Figure 2.6. The substitution effect

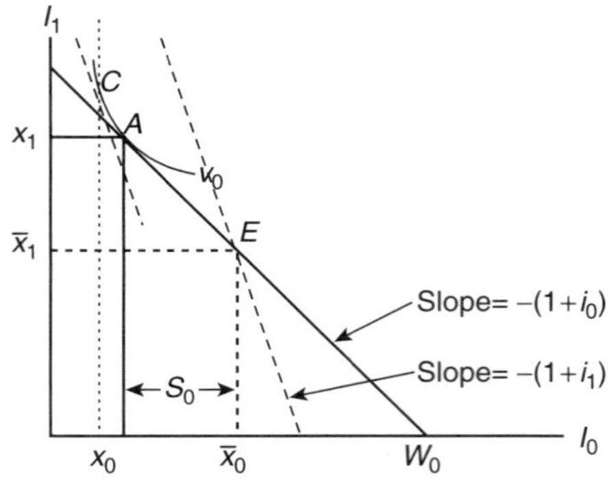

Figure 2.6 The relationship between saving and the interest rate.

unambiguously raises saving in the move from A to C. But the income effect works against the substitution effect when current consumption is a normal good because a higher interest rate generates additional real income at each level of saving. This moves the consumption bundle to the right of point C onto the new budget line through E. If the income effect is smaller than the substitution effect in absolute value terms then saving rises above its initial level at S_0, but if it is larger in absolute value terms saving falls below S_0. This seemingly anomalous case is more likely at higher initial saving S_0 because the income effect is larger. Clearly, saving always rises when current consumption expenditure is inferior, which seems unlikely. In this setting with income endowments the necessary condition for a higher interest rate to reduce saving is for current consumption expenditure to be normal, while the sufficient condition is that the income effect should be larger than the substitution effect in absolute value terms.

For a consumer who initially borrows, the higher interest rate will always reduce borrowing when current consumption expenditure is normal as the income and substitution effects work in the same direction. Borrowing can only rise in this setting when current consumption expenditure is inferior. These cases can be illustrated using Figure 2.7. After the interest

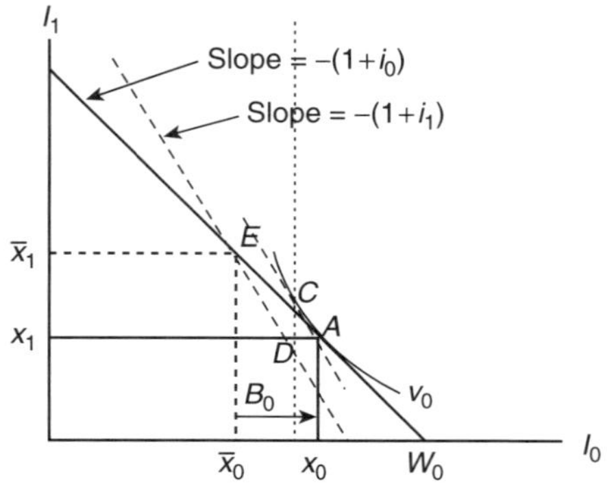

Figure 2.7 The relationship between borrowing and the interest rate.

rate rises to i_1 the consumer substitutes from *A* to *C* and borrowing declines. As real income falls the new consumption bundle must lie on the new budget constraint represented by the dotted line through the endowment point *E*. If it lies above the endowment point the consumer becomes a saver where borrowing unambiguously falls. But if current consumption expenditure is inferior the new bundle lies below point *D* on the new budget constraint. For borrowing to rise the income effect must be larger than substitution effect. But this case seems improbable as current consumption is unlikely to be inferior.

2.2.4 Asset economy with private investment opportunities

Most consumers can determine the size and timing of their income stream in future time periods through the labour–leisure choice and by investing in human capital. When older consumers leave the workforce, however, they have less scope to do this and the analysis with fixed income endowments in the previous section is perhaps more appropriate. In contrast, younger consumers make private investment choices that will determine the type of labour they can supply in future years; an obvious example is education that is undertaken to increase labour productivity. As a consequence, they are making choices not only about the type of work they want to do, but also about the amount of wage and salary income they want to earn in future years. There are occasions where consumers invest in education to achieve higher job satisfaction rather than higher wages, but we will abstract from that issue here.

Using the production technology defined earlier in the autarky economy, the market value of output in the second period for each consumer is $Y_1^h \equiv \Sigma_n p_1(n) y_1^h(n)$, which is produced by inputs in the first period with a market value of $Z_0^h \equiv \Sigma_n p_0(n) z_0^h(n)$. Once again, we assume the production opportunity set is strictly convex, where the problem for each consumer in the asset economy with private investment is summarized in (2.5) when income in each period is defined as

$$\begin{aligned} I_0 &\equiv \bar{X}_0 - V_0 - Z_0, \\ I_1 &\equiv \bar{X}_1 + aR_1 + Y_1. \end{aligned} \tag{2.10}$$

Definition 2.6 An *asset economy with private investment opportunities* is described by (u, $\bar{x}$, y (H), a), where $y(H)$ is the set of private production opportunities for the H consumers. A competitive equilibrium in this economy is characterized by relative commodity prices p_0^* and p_1^*, a security price p_a^* and an interest rate i^* such that

i $x_0^{h*}(n), x_1^{h*}(n)$ and $y_1^{h*}(n)$, for all n, and a^{h*} solve the consumer problem in (2.10) for all h;

ii the goods markets clear in each time period, with $\Sigma_h \bar{x}_0^h(n) = \Sigma_h x_0^{h*}(n) + \Sigma_h z_0^{h*}(n)$ for all n in the first period, $\Sigma_h x_1^h(n) + \Sigma_h y_1^{h*}(n) = \Sigma_h x_1^{h*}(n)$ for all n in the second period, and the capital market clears, with $\Sigma_h a^{h*} = 0$.

For optimally chosen investment we have $\lambda_0 = \lambda_1\, VMP$, where $VMP = 1 + i_Z$ is the value (at market prices) of the marginal product of capital investment; it is 1 plus the marginal rate of return on investment (i_Z). Since investors can equate their discount factors on second-period consumption by trading in the capital market, with $\lambda_1/\lambda_0 = 1/(1 + i)$, we can write the

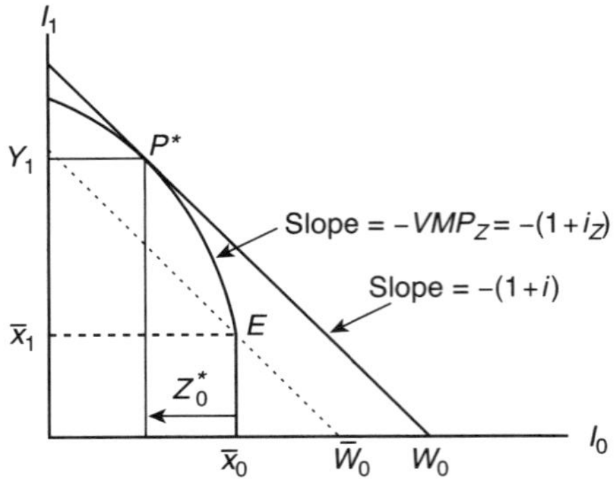

Figure 2.8 Consumption opportunities in the asset economy with private investment.

condition for optimally chosen investment as $VMP = 1 + i$. This tells us that consumers maximize wealth by equating the marginal return on investment to the market rate of interest, with $i_Z = i$. The consumption opportunities are illustrated in Figure 2.8.

Wealth in the absence of investment is equal to the discounted present value of the endowment at $\bar{W}_0$. Since the marginal return on investment exceeds the market interest rate at the endowment point E, with $i_Z > i$, the consumer can raise wealth to W_0 by investing Z_0^* (units of the numeraire good). At point P^* the marginal return from investment matches the market interest rate, which is the opportunity cost. Investing beyond point P^* would lower wealth because the capital market pays a higher rate of return. The optimal consumption bundle in the income space lies along the budget line through the production point P^*, where from the first-order conditions on the consumer problem in (2.10) we have

$$MRS_{1,0}(I) = \frac{\nu_1}{\nu_0} = \frac{1}{1+i} = \frac{1}{1+i_z}.$$

In this setting consumers separate their investment and consumption choices; they choose investment to maximize wealth which they then allocate to intertemporal consumption by trading in the capital market to maximize utility. Any other level of investment above or below Z_0^* in Figure 2.9 reduces wealth by moving the budget constraint down in a parallel fashion. In other words, investment choices have pure income effects on price-taking consumers so that maximizing wealth will also maximize their utility. Examples of non-optimal investment choices are illustrated in Figure 2.9 by the large black dots where the new budget constraint is the dotted line parallel to the budget line through P^* which maximizes wealth.

Investment only has income effects here because consumers are price-takers in the capital market. This is referred to as the *Fisher separation theorem* (Fisher 1730), and it has important implications for the objective functions of firms when they undertake investment on behalf of consumers.

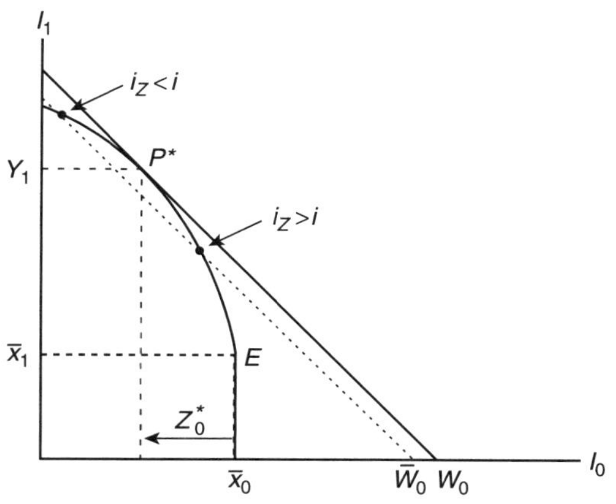

Figure 2.9 Optimal private investment with a competitive capital market.

Box 2.5 Private investment and trade: a numerical example

We now extend the analysis in Box 2.4 by allowing Brad Johnson to transfer rice to the second period by planting it on his farm using the technology in Box 2.3 and trading the risk-free security in a competitive capital market at a 5 per cent interest rate over the year. This means he has a single budget constraint, which in present value terms is

$$x_0 + \frac{x_1}{1.05} = 400 - z_0 + \frac{30\sqrt{z_0}}{1.05} = W_0.$$

Brad's wealth is maximized when private investment satisfies $15/\sqrt{z_0^*} = 1/1.05$, where $z_0^* \approx 248$ kg with $W_0^* \approx 602$. Based on his preferences in Box 2.1, his rice consumption in each period is chosen optimally when it satisfies $0.98x_0^* = x_1^*/1.05$. Using the budget constraint with maximized wealth, $W_0^* = x_0 - x_1/1.05 \approx 620$, we have $x_0^* \approx 304$ kg and $x_1^* \approx 313$ kg. These choices are illustrated in the diagram below, where wealth is maximised at point F on the investment frontier with consumption at point E which is on a higher indifference curve u_E than point D without private investment in Box 2.4.

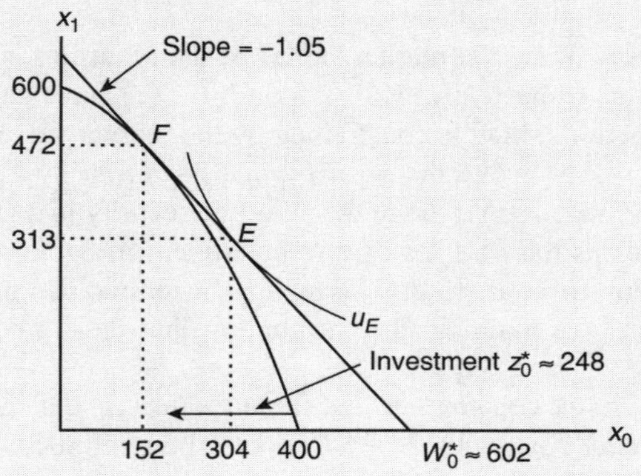

2.2.5 *Asset economy with investment by firms*

Finally, we extend the analysis to an economy where consumers have endowments of goods which they can trade within and between each time period in competitive markets. There are also J firms that perform the important task of moving resources to future time periods, where they do so at lower cost through specialization and large-scale production. To simplify the analysis we will assume goods are non-storable (although storage can easily be accommodated as a part of production) and there is no private investment by consumers. All investment is undertaken by firms who finance it by selling securities to consumers in the first period. In the second period they sell their output and use the proceeds to repurchase their securities from consumers. There is no government in the economy at this stage, so the only traders in the capital and goods markets are private agents. In many of the finance applications we examine in following chapters very little insight is gained by including production. For example, when deriving prices for assets with uncertain future returns we want to know how they are affected by risk-spreading opportunities provided in the capital market for risk-averse consumers. By including production we allow the supply of risky securities to change endogenously, but that adds little to the derivations of equilibrium asset pricing equations unless it provides new risk-spreading opportunities not already available to consumers using existing securities. Production is much more important in project evaluation where welfare changes depend on actual equilibrium outcomes. For that reason we include production in the asset economy, where the consumer problem is summarized in (2.8) when income in each period is defined as

$$\begin{aligned} I_0 &\equiv \bar{X}_0 - V_0 + \eta_0, \\ I_1 &\equiv \bar{X}_1 + aR_1, \end{aligned} \tag{2.11}$$

where $\eta_0 := \{\eta_0^1, \ldots, \eta_0^J\}$ is the set of profit shares in each firm j. Production by private firms is the only way resources can be transferred intertemporally in this economy without storage and private investment. In its absence, savers and borrowers would be confined to trading given resources with each other within each time period. Thus, in the asset economy with production consumers can transfer resources atemporally and intertemporally, where the problem for each firm $j = 1, \ldots, J$, is given by

$$\max\left\{\eta_0^j = V_0^j - Z_0^j \,\middle|\, a^j R_1 - Y_1^j(Z_0^j) \le 0\right\}, \tag{2.12}$$

with $V_0^j \equiv p_a a^j$ and $Z_0^j \equiv \Sigma_n p_0(n) z_0^j(n)$ being the market values of the securities supplied and inputs purchased in the first period, respectively, while $a^j R_1 = V_0^j(1 + i)$ is the payout to the risk-free security in the second period which is constrained by the market value of the output produced, $Y_1^j \equiv \Sigma_n p_1(n) y_1^j(n)$. We invoke the *no arbitrage condition* by allowing specialist firms (called financial intermediaries) to trade the risk-free security in a frictionless competitive capital market.[16] As was the case for private investment in Sections 2.1.3 and 2.2.4, the production structure for firms is general enough to accommodate multiple inputs and outputs for each firm, and we maintain the assumption that their production opportunity sets are strictly convex.

Optimally chosen investment in (2.12) equates the discounted value of the marginal product of investment to its opportunity cost, with $\lambda_1^j \, VMP^j = 1$.[17] The multiplier λ_1^j is a personal discount factor used by each firm j to evaluate the current value of future net cash flows, and this is confirmed by the first-order condition for optimally supplying the risk-free security, where $p_a = \lambda_1^j R_1 = \lambda_1^j p_a(1+i) = 0$. Thus, in the absence of taxes or transactions costs price-taking firms use the same discount factor on future cash flows, with $\lambda_1^j = 1/1(1+i)$. And since it is also the same discount rate used by consumers, the competitive equilibrium in this asset economy with production is Pareto optimal.

Definition 2.7 An *asset economy with production by firms is* described by $(u, \bar{x}, y(J), a)$, where $y(J)$ is the set of production outputs of the J firms. A competitive equilibrium in this economy is characterized by relative commodity prices p_0^* and p_1^*, a security price p_a^*, and an interest rate i^* such that:

i $x_0^{h*}(n)$ and $x_1^{h*}(n)$, for all n, and a^{h*} solve the consumer problem in (2.11) for all h;

ii $z_0^{j*}(n)$ and $y_1^{j*}(n)$, for all n, and a^{j*} solve the producer problem in (2.12) for all j;

iii the goods markets clear at each $t \in \{0, 1\}$, with $\Sigma_h \bar{x}_0^h(n) = \Sigma_h x_0^{h*}(n) + \Sigma_j z_0^{j*}(n)$ and $\Sigma_h \bar{x}_1^h(n) + \Sigma_j y_1^{j*}(n) = \Sigma_h x_1^{h*}(n)$ for all n and the capital market clears, with $\Sigma_h a^{h*} = \Sigma_j a^{j*}$

A formal derivation of the Fisher separation theorem is obtained by differentiating the consumer problem in (2.5) for a marginal increase in investment by firm j when income is defined in (2.11), with $aR_1 = V_0(1 + i)$, where the welfare change using the optimality condition for the risk-free security is

$$\frac{dv}{dZ_0^j} = \{-\lambda_0 + \lambda_1(1+i)\}\frac{dV_0}{dZ_0^j} = 0.$$ [18]

In frictionless competitive markets the investment and consumption choices of individual consumers and firms have no effect on commodity prices or the interest rate. And once investment is optimally chosen to maximize profit, it maximizes consumer wealth and utility. Formally stated the theorem is *'The investment decisions by individual consumers are independent of their intertemporal consumption preferences.'*

The crucial assumption is that of price-taking by firms and consumers, but the absence of transactions costs and taxes is also important. Trading costs drive wedges between borrowing and lending rates, and this can in some circumstances cause the theorem to fail. The important practical implication of this theorem is that all shareholders are unanimous in wanting firms to maximize profit. Indeed, once this objective is assigned to firms it invokes the conditions required for Fisher separation on the economic analysis. It is much easier for the capital market to create incentives for firm managers to act in the interests of their shareholders when their objective is to maximize profit. Mergers and takeovers are a threat to managers who do not maximize profit because their share prices are lower than they could be with better management.

Figure 2.10 is the familiar analysis in Hirshleifer (1970) that is used to illustrate the Fisher separation theorem in a two-period certainty model with production by firms. It is a natural extension of the standard two-period analysis in previous sections, where the representative firm j borrows capital from consumers by selling financial securities.[19] These funds are invested to maximize profit (η^j), which investors receive when the firm repurchases its securities in the second period. The representative investor h allocates the initial endowment of

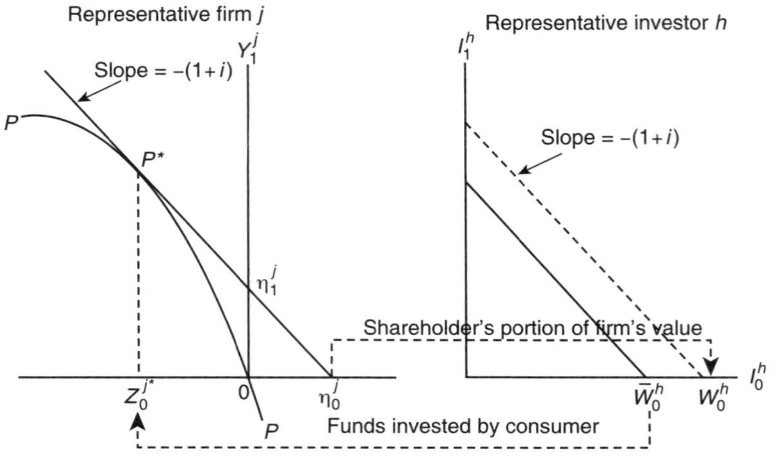

Figure 2.10 The Fisher separation theorem with firms.

income to current consumption and financial securities in a number of firms (to spread risk in an uncertainty setting). When the representative firm changes its investment decision it only has pure income effects on the investor's budget constraint, where the utility of every investor is maximized when it maximizes profit, and as a consequence, its market value.

Perhaps the easiest way to see how complicated things become when the Fisher separation theorem fails, is to consider a situation where investment decisions by individual firms affect the market rate of interest. In particular, suppose there is a positive relationship between them. Now the investment decision has both income and substitution effects on the budget constraints of investors, and it is no longer clear that profit maximization is the unanimous choice for firms. This conflict is illustrated in Figure 2.11, where additional

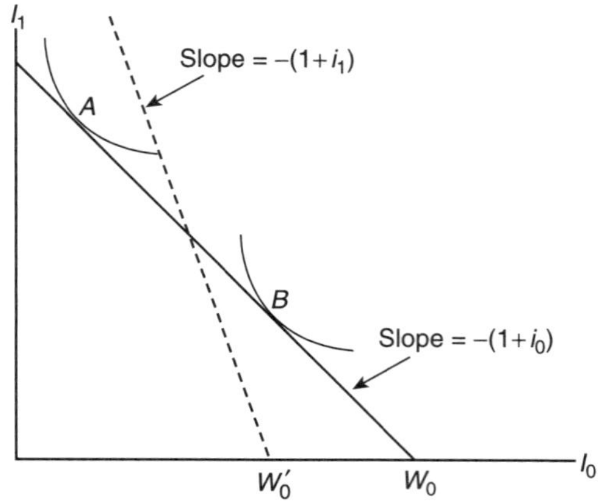

Figure 2.11 Investment when the Fisher separation theorem fails to hold.

investment changes both the slope and intercepts of the budget constraints of consumers by affecting the market rate of interest. Clearly, any consumer with consumption bundle B is made worse off by the investment decision, while the reverse applies to a consumer with bundle A. In circumstances like this the objective function of the firm cannot be solved independently of the preferences of its investors, where some type of voting mechanism is needed to trade off their competing gains and losses.

This conflict also applies more generally. Whenever a firm is able to affect the prices of its inputs and/or outputs it can have income and substitution effects on investors when they also consume the firm's output or supply its inputs. By way of example, consider a single-price monopolist whose investors consume its output. When it restricts output to make profit by driving up the product price, its investors are made better off by the higher profit but worse off by the higher product price. The relative costs and benefits depend on how much capital they invest in the firm relative to the value of the good consumed. Typically we assume investors in a single-price monopolist do not consume its product, or when they do they consume such a small amount that price changes have a negligible impact on their real income, where profit maximization is their unanimous objective function for the firm's managers.

A number of private and public institutions play an important role in supporting the Fisher separation theorem. Publicly listed companies are threatened by mergers and takeovers that help to align the interests of firm managers with those of their shareholders. Also, companies write contracts with managers that provide them with incentives to act in the interests of shareholders. For example, managers are frequently required to hold a portion of their wealth in the firm's shares or to hold call options written on them. They also include penalties for managers who do not perform. There are public regulations which specify the minimum information that firm managers must provide investors with, and competition policy is used to restrict the market power of firms. All these problems arise because investors do not have complete information about the actions taken on their behalf by firm managers. Traders in financial markets specialize in monitoring firms and will exploit any potential profits from replacing managers who under-perform. As specialists they perform this monitoring role at lower cost than investors would incur by monitoring firm managers themselves.

2.2.6 Asset economy with investment by firms and fiat money

There is no role for currency as a store of value in a certainty setting without trading costs when there is a risk-free security that pays interest. Due to the non-payment of interest on currency the opportunity cost of holding it over time is the forgone interest that could have been earned by holding the security instead. Currency was introduced to the endowment economy in Section 2.2.2 when it could be used as a medium of exchange to reduce costs of atemporal trade in each time period, but not as a store of value. In practice, currency has properties that make it a more effective medium of exchange, particularly for some trades, than a financial security, and we captured this previously by assuming they had different impacts on trading costs. While this explains why consumers use currency in each period, it does not explain why they use it as a store of value when no interest is paid. Any income transferred into the future would generate a larger consumption flow by using the risk-free security. On that basis, consumers would use currency in each period as a medium of exchange but not hold it over time unless there are other benefits from doing so. In the following analysis we overcome this problem by assuming it is too costly for consumers to choose different currency holdings in each period. Instead, they choose their currency holding in the first period and carry it over to the second period.

In the asset economy with fiat money and production the consumer problem is summarized in (2.5) when income in each period is defined as

$$\begin{aligned} I_0 &\equiv \bar{X}_0 - \tau_0 D_0 - V_0 - m_0 + \eta_0 + G_0, \\ I_1 &\equiv \bar{X}_1 - \tau_1 D_1 + aR_1 + m_0 + G_1.\text{[20]} \end{aligned} \tag{2.13}$$

The trading costs are defined here as a constant proportion of the market value of the net demands for goods, and are measured in units of good 1. They can differ across goods but are the same for sales and purchases, and are assumed to be decreasing functions of currency demand (m_0) in the first period. When consumers exchange goods for currency the government collects resources in the first period that it can spend, where G_t^h is the share of the value of government spending apportioned to each consumer h at each $t \in \{0, 1\}$. Total government spending in each period is $G_t = \sum_h p_t g_t^h$, with $g_t^h := \{g_t^h(1), \ldots, g_t^h(N)\}$ being the goods allocated to consumer h at each $t \in \{0, 1\}$. Thus, the market value of the net demands for goods in this setting in each period is $D_t = p_t(x_t - g_t - \bar{x}_t)$. We also allow the government to trade in the capital market, where $V_0^g = p_a a_0^g$ is the value of the risk-free security it holds, with $V_0^g > 0$ when it saves and $V_0^g < 0$ when it borrows. In the first period the constraint on government spending is $G_0^g + V_0^g = m_0^g$, while in the second period it is $G_1^g + m_0^g = V_0^g(1+i)$. Using the second-period constraint we can solve the value of the security traded by the government, as $V_0^g = (G_1 + m_0^g)/(1+i)$, where its budget constraint in present value terms becomes

$$G_0 + \frac{G_1}{1+i} = \frac{im_0^g}{1+i}. \tag{2.14}$$

In the second period the government collects seigniorage of im_0^g on the currency issued in the first period, and it is returned to consumers as government spending. In other words, the outputs the government produces are provided at no direct cost to consumers. They pay indirectly through the implicit tax on their currency holdings. We simplify the analysis by assuming firms do not use currency, where this leaves the problem for each firm j in (2.12) unchanged, and we make currency the numeraire good so that all prices are measured in money terms (which for convenience is referred to as dollars).

Definition 2.8 An *asset economy with fiat money and production by firms* is described by $(u, \bar{x}, y(J), a, m)$. *A* competitive equilibrium in this economy is characterized by relative commodity prices p_0, and p_1^*, a security price p_a^*, and an interest rate i^* such that:

i $x_0^{h*}(n)$ and $x_1^{h*}(n)$, for all n, and a^{h*} solve the consumer problem in (2.11) for all h;

ii $z_0^{j*}(n)$ and $y_1^{j*}(n)$, for all n, and a^{j*} solve the producer problem in (2.12) for all j;

iii the goods markets clear at each $t \in \{0, 1\}$, with $\sum_h \bar{x}_0^h(n) = \sum_h x_0^{h*}(n) + \sum_j z_0^{j*}(n)$ and $\sum_h \bar{x}_1^h(n) + \sum_j y_1^{j*}(n) = \sum_h x_1^{h*}(n)$ for all n, and the capital market clears with $\sum_h a^{h*} = \sum_j a^{j*}$.

A number of interesting issues arise when a financial security and currency can both be used by consumers to reduce trading costs. We assume the trading costs in both periods are reduced by using currency, while the risk-free security *only* reduces trading costs in the second period. The *optimality condition for the security trade* by each consumer is obtained from (2.13) as

$$-\lambda_0 + \lambda_1\left((1+i) - D_1\frac{\partial\tau_1}{\partial V_0}\right) = 0,$$

with $\partial\tau_0(n)/\partial V_0 = 0$ and $\partial\tau_1(n)/\partial V_0 < 0$, for all n, while the *optimal currency demand* solves

$$-\lambda_0\left(1 + D_0\frac{\partial\tau_0}{\partial m_0}\right) + \lambda_1\left(1 - D_1\frac{\partial\tau_1}{\partial m_0}\right) = 0,$$

with $\partial\tau_0(n)/\partial m_0 < 0$ and $\partial\tau_1(n)/\partial m_0 < 0$ for all n.[21] Notice that the condition for the optimal security trade above can be rearranged to provide a personal discount rate that will differ across consumers when they have different marginal changes in trading costs, with

$$\frac{\lambda_1}{\lambda_0} = \frac{1}{(1+i) - D_1(\partial\tau_1 / \partial V_0)}. \tag{2.15}$$

An obvious implication of this is that consumers will not value capital assets in the same way in these circumstances. The widely used equilibrium asset pricing models, which we examine in Chapter 4, assume there are no trading costs. But they have to be included to explain the demand for currency and the separate but related role for using financial securities rather than forward contracts. Indeed, financial securities are a less costly way to summarize the property right transfers when consumers trade intertemporally. A financial security that transfers income between the two periods is preferable to forward contracts because only one asset is exchanged (in a certainty setting), whereas a number of forward contracts are exchanged for goods and they must specify the quality, time and quantity of each good to be traded in the future. Thus, there are transactions costs benefits from using the risk-free asset which are likely to drive wedges between the discount rates consumer use to evaluate future consumption flows. As noted earlier in Section 2.2.2, however, the equilibrium allocation will still be Pareto efficient when the trading costs are minimum necessary costs of trade.

It is possible to confirm the proposition made earlier that, in the absence of trading costs, consumers will not hold currency as a store of value by solving the discount rate in (2.15) using the first-order condition for the security trade, with $\partial\tau_1/\partial V_0 = 0$, as $\lambda_1/\lambda_0 = 1/(1 + i)$, where the first-order condition for currency becomes $\lambda_1/\lambda_0 < 1$.[22] Since no interest is paid on currency, consumers can always increase their utility by allocating resources to the risk-free security rather than currency.

If we follow conventional analysis and assume trading costs are unaffected by the financial security the discount factor in (2.15) becomes $\lambda_1/\lambda_0 = 1/\ (1 + i)$, where the optimal currency demand solves

$$-D_0\frac{\partial\tau_0}{\partial m_0} - D_1\frac{\partial\tau_1}{\partial m_0}\frac{1}{1+i} = \frac{1}{1+i}.^{23} \tag{2.16}$$

This expression has a familiar interpretation because the left-hand side measures the present value of the marginal benefits from using currency as a medium of exchange, while the right-hand side is the present value of the opportunity cost, which is the forgone interest on the risk-free security. Once interest is paid on currency it becomes a perfect substitute for the security in a certainty setting. In much of the analysis in later chapters we assume there are no trading costs, which necessarily eliminates money from the asset economy. We do this to focus on the effects of taxes and firm financial policies on the capital market. The analysis in this section provides us with a way to think about how results in following sections may change when trading costs are included.

2.3 Asset prices and inflation

Asset prices change when inflation affects their expected real returns. Governments determine nominal price inflation in their economies by controlling the rate of growth in the nominal money supply. Money prices do not change over time if the money supply grows at the same rate as money demand.[24] However, it is not a trivial task for governments to match these growth rates, particularly when there is uncertainty about future outcomes. Money demand can be quite difficult to determine, especially in periods when there are large real shocks in economic activity. For example, the effects of large increases in the price of oil will depend on whether they are expected to be persistent or transitory, and are difficult to predict because people adjust to them over time. Moreover, governments have direct control over fiat money (notes and coins), but not broadly measured money, which includes cheque and other interest-bearing deposit accounts issued by both public and private financial intermediaries. Most governments control the broad money base by adjusting the quantity of currency on issue and by regulating the liquidity ratios of the assets held by financial institutions who create non-fiat money. They also intervene in bond markets to change interest rates when, in the absence of capital controls, domestic and foreign bonds are not perfect substitutes.

At the present time most developed countries have annual rates of general price inflation around 2–3 per cent. The rates of inflation are much higher in some developing countries, as they were in many developed countries during the 1970s and 1980s. There are costs and benefits of inflation. Some costs arise from the interaction between inflation and the tax system, while others arise from the income redistribution that takes place when inflation causes relative prices to change due to rigidities in nominal variables. For example, consumers with fixed money incomes lose from higher goods prices, while governments benefit from collecting revenue as seigniorage from the non-payment of interest on currency.

This section examines the way general price inflation affects current asset prices. To motivate the following analysis, consider a risk-free security that pays a nominal net cash flow in the second period of R_1 when the (expected) rate of inflation is π. In an economy with frictionless competitive markets its current price is

$$p_a = \frac{R_1}{1+i}, \tag{2.17}$$

where i is the nominal risk-free interest rate. Clearly, this asset price will not change with higher inflation when the nominal interest rate rises sufficiently to hold the real interest rate (r) constant.[25] In other words, if R_1 and $1 + i$ both rise at the expected rate of inflation there is no real change in the current value of the asset. If we assume, for the moment at least, that the net cash flows rise at the inflation rate, the change in the asset price will be determined by the way the nominal interest rate changes. This is confirmed by using the *identity* that defines the relationship between the nominal and real interest rates:

$$1+i \equiv (1+r)\,(1+\pi). \tag{2.18}$$

If the inflation rate is expected to rise we have the following possibilities:

i the nominal interest rate can rise with an unchanged real interest rate, where this leaves the asset price in (2.17) unchanged;
ii the nominal interest rate can stay constant and the real interest rate falls, where the asset price in (2.17) rises due to the lower opportunity cost of time;
iii the nominal and real interest rates can both change when the nominal rate rises by less than the inflation rate, where the lower real rate causes the asset price in (2.17) to rise, but by less than it would have with an unchanged nominal interest rate.

2.3.1 The Fisher effect

Ultimately the relationship between the nominal interest rate and the expected rate of inflation will depend on the way the economy adjusts to expected inflation. Consider a partial equilibrium analysis of the effects of higher expected inflation in the capital market, illustrated in Figure 2.12. In a two-period certainty setting there is single risk-free interest rate that is common to all financial securities in a frictionless competitive capital market. Aggregate saving (S) rises with the real interest rate because it is the opportunity cost of consuming now rather than later, while aggregate investment (Z) demand falls with the real interest rate because it is the

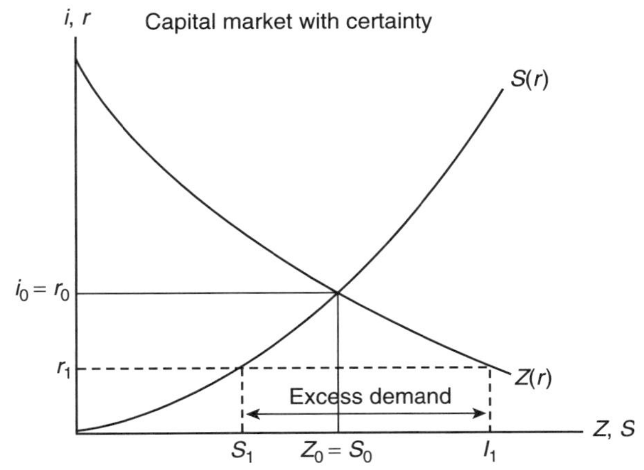

Figure 2.12 The Fisher effect.

cost of capital. In the absence of inflation, demand and supply are equated by the market-clearing nominal interest rate i_0, which is equal to the real interest rate r_0. Now suppose all borrowers (who sell financial securities) and savers (who purchase them) expect general price inflation over the next period at rate π_1. If, by way of illustration, traders in the capital market do not revise the nominal interest rate (so that i_0 stays constant), then from (2.18) the real interest rate declines to r_1. This creates an excess demand for capital as borrowing rises and saving falls, thereby exerting upward pressure on the nominal interest rate which continues to rise until the real interest rate returns to r_0 where investment demand is once again equal to saving. On that basis, the nominal interest rate rises to keep the real rate constant and preserve capital market equilibrium.

This important result is referred to as the *Fisher effect*, where, from (2.18), we have

$$\left.\frac{di}{d\pi}\right|_{dr=0} = 1 + r. \tag{2.19}$$

It holds in a classical finance model when the following conditions prevail:

i All nominal variables in the economy (including money wages, prices and the nominal interest rate) adjust freely in competitive markets.
ii Agents have homogeneous expectations about the rate of inflation.
iii There are no wealth effects in the money market
iv There are no taxes.

In this setting correctly anticipated changes in the nominal money supply will have no real effects as all nominal variables adjust to preserve the real economy. It holds in the asset economy with fiat money and production in Section 2.2.5 when the government pays interest on currency. Consider the consumer problem in (2.5) where the budget constraints in these circumstances are defined as

$$I_0 \equiv \bar{X}_0 - \tau_0 D_0 - V_0 - m_0 + \eta_0 + G_0,$$
$$I_1 \equiv \bar{X}_1 - \tau_1 D_1 + aR_1 + m_0(1+i) + G_1.$$

When trading costs are unaffected by the financial security, we know from (2.15) that the constraint multiplier on consumption in the second period becomes $\lambda_1 = \lambda_0/(1 + i)$, which allows us to rewrite the consumer problem as

$$\max\left\{ v(W_0) \middle| W_0 = \bar{X}_0 - \frac{\bar{X}_1}{1+i} - \tau_0 D_0 - \frac{\tau_1 D_1}{1+i} + \eta_0 + G_0 + \frac{G_1}{1+i} \right\}.^{26}$$

Whenever the government increases the supply of currency in the second period all nominal prices rise by the same proportion as the money supply, and nothing real happens because the Fisher effect in (2.19) holds.[27] Thus, the present value of the second-period endowments $\bar{X}_1/(1+i)$, trading costs $\tau_1 D_1/(1+i)$ and government spending $G_1/(1+i)$ are unaffected by the change in inflation. Neither is the profit share in each firm j:

$$\eta_0^j = \frac{p_1 y_1}{1+i} - p_0 z_0^j \quad \forall_j,$$

where p_1 and $1 + i$ both rise at the same rate. Since nothing real happens to the consumption opportunity sets of consumers, they choose the same bundle of goods in each period and get the same utility. It means anticipated changes in the money supply have no real effects in these circumstances. However, there is empirical evidence from some countries that nominal interest rates will rise with the rate of inflation over a long period of time. And this happens in economies where nominal interest payments are subject to distorting taxes so that the tax-adjusted Fisher effect needs to be even higher.[28] However, it is unlikely to hold in the short term or in economies where the conditions above do not apply. The most useful aspect of this analysis is that it provides a way of understanding what factors determine the real effects of expected inflation outside the classical finance model.

We now consider what happens when the first three conditions in the classical model outlined above are relaxed. The role of taxes will be examined in more detail in later chapters. If there are rigidities in more than one nominal variable in the economy then inflation can have real effects that will cause the Fisher effect to fail. In a Keynesian macroeconomic model with rigid money wages, monetary policy has real effects by altering the real wage and employment. Suppose a minimum wage leads to involuntary unemployment in the economy where an increase in the rate of growth in the money supply can raise aggregate output by pushing up the nominal prices of goods and services and reducing real wages.[29] Clearly, this stimulus in activity will be reversed when minimum wages are later adjusted to preserve them in real terms.[30] Any resulting changes in capital asset prices are determined by equilibrium adjustments to the relative prices of goods and services and the real interest rate, which can be estimated by using a computable general equilibrium model of the economy.

When agents form different expectations about the rate of inflation they expect different real interest rates, and this impacts on the capital market. By way of illustration, suppose borrowers expect a higher rate of inflation than do savers, with $\pi_B > \pi_S$. Since both face a common nominal interest rate when negotiating security trades, they must have different real interest rates which are solved using (2.18) as:

$$1+i = (1+r_B)(1+\pi_B) = (1+r_S)(1+\pi_S), \tag{2.20}$$

with $r_B < r_S$. This difference means borrowers are prepared to raise the nominal interest rate more than savers require to preserve their real return. The equilibrium nominal interest rate simultaneously raises the real return to savers and lowers the real cost of capital for investors, where the implicit interest rate subsidy is illustrated in Figure 2.13.

The lower real interest rate for borrowers causes capital asset prices to rise in the first period. Clearly, the reverse applies when savers expect a higher rate of inflation because they would want the nominal interest rate to rise more to preserve their real return than borrowers could afford to pay. This would act like an implicit tax on the capital market by driving down the equilibrium level of investment and saving.[31]

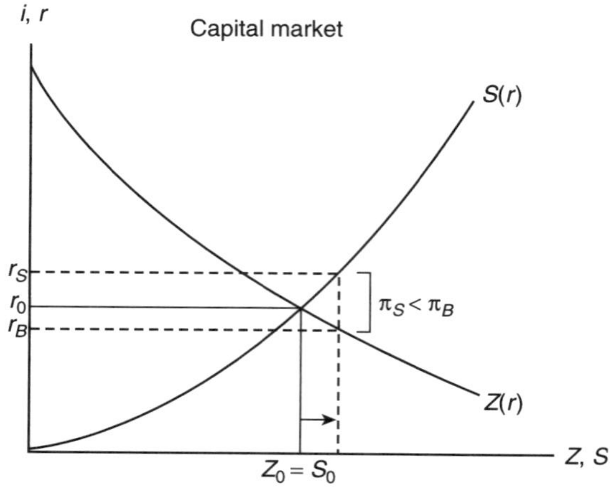

Figure 2.13 Different inflationary expectations.

2.3.2 Wealth effects in the money market

Changes in the rate of inflation have wealth effects when no interest is paid on currency. The private cost of holding currency is the nominal interest rate forgone on interest-bearing assets (with the same risk as currency). There are two components to this opportunity cost – one is the real interest return on bonds, while the other is the loss of purchasing power of currency due to inflation. If, as is normally the case, the social marginal cost of supplying currency is less than the nominal interest rate, then the non-payment of interest will impose a welfare loss on currency holders. In effect, they face a tax equal to the difference between the nominal interest rate and the marginal production cost which imposes a welfare loss on them. And this loss increases when higher expected inflation pushes up the nominal interest rate and reduces currency demand even further. Thus, changes in expected inflation have real effects on consumers that undermine the Fisher effect.

This welfare loss from the non-payment of interest on currency is illustrated in Figure 2.14, where the aggregate demand (m_d) for and supply (m_s) of real money balances are defined here as the nominal value of the notes and coins held by consumers divided by the consumer price index (CPI). For illustrative purposes we assume the marginal social cost of supplying currency (mc_s) is zero. In practice, however, it is positive but much smaller than the nominal interest rate. Initially the nominal interest rate i_0 equates money demand and supply, where the CPI is expected to rise at the same rate as the nominal money supply (broadly defined) in the next period of time.

Real money demand is determined by the marginal benefits consumers get from using currency, which for the most part is determined by the amount it reduces their trading costs as a medium of exchange and is therefore an increasing function of real income (y). Consumers maximize utility by equating their marginal benefits from using currency to the nominal interest rate, where the welfare loss is the cross-lined triangular region in Figure 2.14; it is a dollar measure of the forgone benefits due to the non-payment of interest. Currency holders are left with consumer

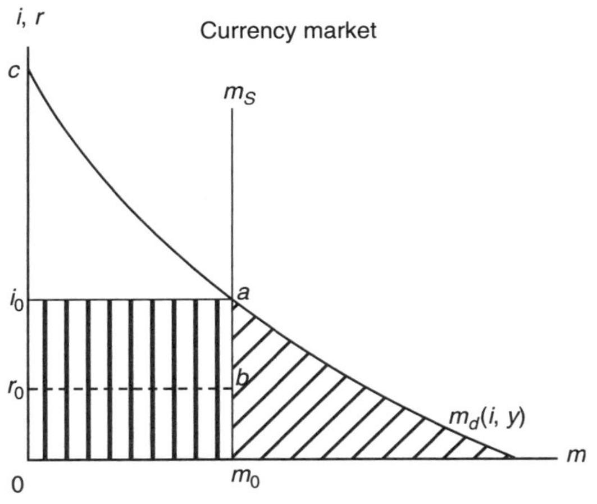

Figure 2.14 Welfare losses in the money market.

surplus of i_0ca, while the vertical-lined rectangle (i_0am_00) is revenue collected by the government as *seigniorage*; it is inflation tax revenue in i_0abr_0, plus revenue from not paying real interest on resources obtained with currency in r_0bm_00.

A simple example will illustrate how revenue is transferred to the government budget as seigniorage. Suppose the nominal interest rate is 15.5 per cent ($i_0 = 0.155$) when the expected inflation rate is 10 per cent ($\pi = 0.10$). From (2.18) we find the real interest rate is 5 per cent in the circumstances. Imagine the Central Bank prints a \$100 bill that the government uses (at time 0) to purchase corn from private traders at a money price of \$1 per kilo. It plants this corn at time 0 and uses the harvest at time 1 to redeem its liability to currency holders by selling them corn with a value of \$100 when the money price of corn is expected to be \$1.10 per kilo. The revenue transfers in the second period are summarized in Table 2.1.

Table 2.1 Revenue collected by the government as seigniorage

The government harvests gross revenue of \$115.50 when the price of corn per kg is \$1.10:	\$115.50 (105 kg)
Less corn sold by the government to redeem its \$100 bill at time 1:	\$100 (90.91 kg)
Seigniorage:	\$15.50 (14.09 kg)

We assume there is a (constant) 5 per cent real return from planting corn, so that 100 kg grows into 105 kg over the period. In the absence of inflation the government would have to sell 100 kg of corn to redeem its \$100 bill and would collect \$5 of seigniorage as the real return on investment (5 kg). But with 10 per cent price inflation it only has to sell 90.91 kg of corn at time 1 to redeem its \$100 bill, collecting \$15.50 of seigniorage with a real value of 14.1 kg. This includes \$10 inflation tax revenue as well as the \$5.50 real return on capital.

Box 2.6 Seigniorage in selected countries

Based on data reported by the International Monetary Fund (IMF) we obtain crude estimates of (gross) seigniorage as a proportion of GDP for the year ending December 2005 in the following countries. Notice how countries with relatively high nominal interest rates due to higher rates of inflation, such as Brazil, the Philippines and Zimbabwe, raise more seigniorage as a percentage of the GDP. In contrast, Japan raised (almost) no seigniorage in the calendar year 2005 because the nominal interest rate was zero. This is consistent with the Friedman rule that makes the optimal rate of inflation (ignoring distortions in other markets and the marginal cost of printing currency) negative and equal to the real interest. By driving the nominal interest rate to zero it eliminates the implicit tax on currency holders, and the government collects no revenue as seigniorage.

Country	*Currency/GDP (%)*[a]	*Interest rate (%)*[b]	*Seigniorage/GDP (%)*
Australia	4.76	5.5	0.26
Brazil	11.77	19.12	2.25
Canada	3.37	2.66	0.09
China – Mainland	34.46	3.33	1.15
China – Hong Kong	20.55	4.25	0.87
France	6.44	2.15	0.14
Germany	7.10	2.09	0.15
India	16.75	6.00	1.00
Indonesia	9.88	6.78	0.67
Japan	23.21	0.001	0.00
Malaysia	11.46	2.72	0.31
New Zealand	3.36	6.76	0.23
Philippines	10.64	7.314	0.78
Russian Federation	13.70	2.68	0.37
Singapore	12.04	2.28	0.27
Switzerland	10.93	0.63	0.07
Thailand	11.49	2.62	0.30
United Kingdom	3.49	4.70	0.16
United States	6.26	3.21	0.20
Zimbabwe	9.97	540.00	53.81

Source: International Financial Statistics On-line database, International Monetary Fund, for the year ending December 2005.

[a] Currency is measured using reserve money reported in data series (14) while GDP is measured using series (99b).

[b] The interest rate is the money market rate reported in series (60b) except in France and Zimbabwe, where we use a bank rate which is lower than the money market rate in other countries.

The welfare loss from higher expected inflation can be formally derived for the asset economy with currency and production in Section 2.2.5. We do this by aggregating consumer preferences using the individualistic social welfare function (W) of Bergson (1938) and Samuelson (1954), with

$$W = W(v),^{32} \tag{2.21}$$

where $v: = \{v^1, \dots, v^H\}$ is the set of indirect utility functions for consumers. By totally differentiating this welfare function, we have

$$dW = \sum_h \beta^h \left\{ dI_0^h + \frac{dI_1^h}{1+i} \right\},$$

with $\beta^h = (\partial W/\partial v^h)\lambda_0^h$ being the distributional weight for each consumer h, which measures the change in social welfare from marginally raising their wealth. In a conventional Harberger (1971) analysis consumers are assigned the same weights, with $\beta^h = \beta$ for all h, where a dollar measure of the change in social welfare is

$$\frac{dW}{\beta} = dI_0 + \frac{dI_1}{1+i},$$

with $dI_0 = \Sigma_h dI_0^h$ and $dI_1 = \Sigma_h dI_1^h$. The changes in aggregate income are obtained by summing consumer budget constraints in each time period, applying the first-order conditions for consumers and firms, and using the market-clearing conditions for the goods, currency and capital markets, where the dollar change in social welfare from marginally raising the rate of growth in the money supply becomes

$$\frac{dW}{dm_0^g}\frac{1}{\beta} = -D_0 \frac{\partial \tau_0}{\partial m_0}\frac{\partial m_0}{\partial m_0^g} - \frac{D_1}{1+i}\frac{d\tau_1}{\partial m_0}\frac{\partial m_0}{\partial m_0^g} = \frac{i}{1+i}\frac{\partial m_0}{\partial m_0^g} < 0,\text{[33]} \quad (2.22)$$

with $D_t = p_t(x_t - g_t - \bar{x}_t)$ being the market value of the net demand for goods at each time $t \in \{0, 1\}$. There is good intuition for this welfare change. A marginal increase in the money supply raises the nominal interest rate and reduces the private demand for currency. This exacerbates the welfare loss from the non-payment of interest on currency by the present value of the tax burden $i/(1 + i)$ multiplied by the change in the demand for currency $\partial m_0/\partial m_0^g$.[34]

We are now in a position to illustrate the welfare effect from changes in the expected rate of inflation. Suppose the government announces it will increase the rate of growth in the money supply (relative to money demand) over the next year. When the private sector believes the announcement, there are economic effects in both time periods:

i *At time 0.* Once traders expect a higher inflation rate the nominal interest rate rises to maintain equilibrium in the capital market. Currency holders respond to the higher nominal interest rate by reducing their demand for currency, where the excess supply of real money balances is eliminated by an immediate jump in the general price level. This exacerbates the welfare loss from the non-payment of interest on currency, which is spread across the real economy through resulting changes in private activity. This loss in wealth is illustrated as the cross-lined rectangle in Figure 2.15. It is larger for more interest-elastic money demand and a higher initial nominal interest rate. In any case, it will cause the Fisher effect to fail when the real interest changes.

ii *At time 1.* When the anticipated increase in the nominal money supply takes place it raises the general price level at the same rate. Thus, over the two periods, prices rise proportionately more than the nominal money supply due to the price jump in the first period.

Bailey (1962, pp. 49–53) formalized this wealth effect in a macroeconomic model of the economy. In its purest form, the classical model breaks down when no interest is paid on currency. A large literature looks at the feasibility of allowing private currencies to trade. Opponents raise concerns about the potential default problems that could cause bank runs and lead to financial crises, while those in favour argue there are incentives for private providers to coordinate them and to maintain the integrity of their currencies as a way to

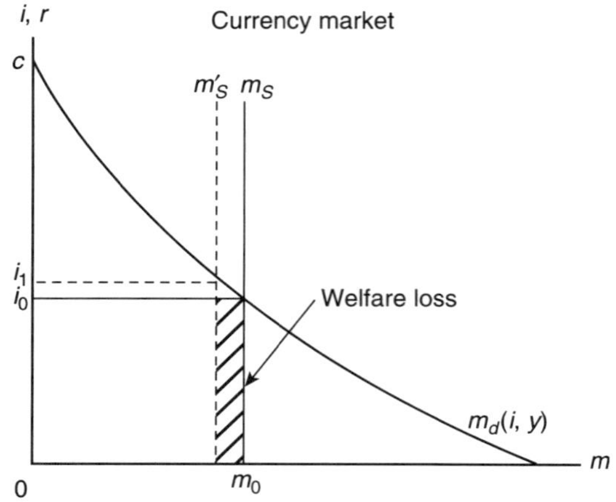

Figure 2.15 Welfare losses from higher expected inflation.

attract traders to use them. In a competitive environment there is pressure to pay interest on currency. And this can be done by dating notes and coins when they are issued and agreeing to pay holders interest at specified time periods during the year. Between these times traders negotiate discounts on trades made with currency as compensation for accrued interest. Indeed, this practice could be implemented by embedding computer chips in notes and (possibly) coins to record accrued interest and compute any discounts on trade between interest payments. Many supporters of private currency argue it removes the incentive for governments to use inflation as a hidden tax on consumers to finance their expenditure. But in recent times most governments have maintained low rates of inflation to minimize its adverse real effects on the economy, and this has mitigated, at least partially, the attraction of private currency.[35]

In summary, the way expected inflation affects capital asset prices depends on the real effects it has on the private economy. If the Fisher effect holds then changes in the expected rate of inflation will not affect current asset prices, and it does so in a classical macroeconomic model where financial variables are a veil over the real economy. Any anticipated changes in the money supply have no real effects in this setting. Even though it does not provide a realistic interpretation of what happens in practice, especially in the short term, it does establish the conditions for it to hold. Then, by relaxing them, we can determine how changes in expected inflation might impact in the real economy.

2.4 Valuing financial assets

Most financial securities have cash flows in a number of future time periods. To compute their values we need to know their size and timing, and then discount them for the opportunity cost (of time and risk). While the analysis in previous sections is undertaken in a certainty setting with two time periods, we will refer to expected future values here in preparation for the inclusion of uncertainty in the next chapter. The analysis is undertaken by extending the asset economy in Definition 2.7 to an infinite number of time periods and requiring the market-clearing conditions to hold in each of them.[36] The consumer problem in this infinite time horizon economy can be summarized as:

$$\max\left\{v(I)\middle|I_t = \bar{X}_t - V_t + \eta_t \forall_t\right\},^{37} \tag{2.23}$$

with $I = \{I_0, I_1, \ldots, I_8\}$. When consumers can trade in frictionless competitive markets they will use the same discount factors $\lambda_t/\lambda_0 = 1/(1+i_t)$ to evaluate future cash flows, where i_t is the interest rate on a long-term security that matures at time t. With standard preferences (to rule out non-satiation) we can write their budget constraints in (2.23) as

$$W_0 = I_0 + \frac{I_1}{(1+i_1)} + \frac{I_2}{(1+i_2)^2} + \cdots + \frac{I_\infty}{(1+i_\infty)^\infty},$$

where the current price of any security k becomes

$$P_{ak} = \sum_{t=0}^{\infty} \frac{\bar{R}_{kt}}{(1+i_t)^t}, \tag{2.24}$$

with $\bar{R}_{kt}$ being the (expected) payout to the security at time t. The long-term interest rates used in the discount factors are geometric means of the (expected) short-term interest rates in each period. The relationship between them is examined in the next section.[38]

2.4.1 Term structure of interest rates

Consider security k when it has a single expected payout of $\bar{R}_{k2}$ at the end of period 2, where its market value is

$$P_{ak} = \frac{\bar{R}_{k2}}{(1+i_1)(1+{}_1\bar{i}_2)},$$

with i_1 being the short-term interest rate for the first period, and ${}_1\bar{i}_2$ the (expected) short-term interest rate for the second period. The term structure of interest rates describes the relationship between these spot rates and the long-term interest rate over the two-year period (i_2). Ideally, it would be the term structure for another security with the same risk as the payouts on security k, but since it is unlikely that such a security will trade with enough different maturity dates to extract a full set of spot rates (especially when there are more than two time periods), we use the term structure of interest rates for government bonds and adjust the spot rates in each period for the risk in asset k.

If the *expectations hypothesis* holds, we can use the long-term interest rate (i_2) in place of the two spot rates, where the value of security k becomes:

$$P_{ak} = \frac{\bar{R}_{k2}}{(1+i_2)^2}.$$

There are two ways to carry a dollar forward over the two periods – one is to purchase a long-term security with a single payout at maturity, while the other is to purchase a short-term security in the first period and then to roll the payouts over into another short-term security in the second period. These alternatives generate the cash flows of $(1 + i_2)^2$ in the case of one long-term security and $(1+i_1)(1+{}_1\bar{i}_2)$ in the case of two short securities. When they are perfect substitutes (with the same risk), arbitrage in frictionless competitive markets equates their payouts:

$$(1+i_1)(1+{}_1\bar{i}_2)=(1+i_2)^2.$$

This is the expectations hypothesis where expected returns on combinations of short-term securities are the same as the returns on the long-term securities over the same time period. The long-term interest rate is the *geometric mean* of the short term interest rates,

$$i_2 = \sqrt{(1+i_1)(1+{}_1\bar{i}_2)} - 1,$$

and it differs from the *arithmetic mean* of the short rates,

$$i_2^A = \frac{i_1 + {}_1\bar{i}_2}{2},$$

due to the compounding effect of interest paid on interest in the second period.

Box 2.7 Differences in geometric and arithmetic means: numerical examples

The difference between the geometric mean and its arithmetic approximation for a two-period bond is illustrated by the following numerical examples. With consecutive short-term interest rates of 6 per cent and 5 per cent, respectively, the geometric mean is approximately 0.00118 percentage points lower than the arithmetic mean. It is 0.00122 percentage points lower for the lower consecutive short rates of 3 per cent and 2 per cent, respectively.

i_1	${}_1\bar{i}_2$	i_2	i_2^A
0.06	0.05	0.0549882	0.055
0.03	0.02	0.0249878	0.025

The *yield curve* reported in the financial press summarizes the term structure of interest rates for government bonds. Since long-term bond yields are approximately equal to the average of the expected spot rates in each period, the shape of the yield curve tells us how short-term rates are expected to change over time. This is illustrated by the three different yield curves in Figure 2.16. Spot rates are expected to decline along yield curve (a) and rise along yield

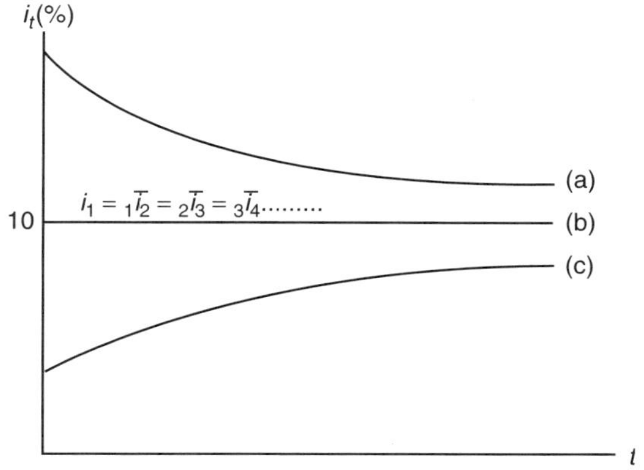

Figure 2.16 Yield curves for long-term government bonds.

curve (c), while they are constant for the flat term structure along yield curve (b). Exogenous shocks to the economy, such as changes in monetary policy and oil price shocks, shift the yield curve, which provides us with information about changes in the expectations of market traders.

Since long-term bond yields are known at the time the bonds trade, they contain forward spot rates that solve

$$(1+i_2)^2 = (1+i_1)(1+{}_1f_2),$$

with ${}_1f_2$ being the forward spot rate in the second year. Since we observe i_1 and i_2 we can compute ${}_1f_2$. Then, by taking the average annual yield for a three-year bond from the yield curve we can compute the forward spot rate in the third year, and so on until we obtain a complete set of forward rates. When the expectations hypothesis holds, these forward spot rates are equal to the expected spot rates in each period:

$$(1+i_1)(1+{}_1\bar{i}_2) = (1+i_2)^2 = (1+i_1)(1+{}_1f_2).$$

This justifies the use of long-term interest rates in the present value calculation in (2.24). When the net cash flows on security k contain more market risk than the net cash flows to government bonds, a risk premium is included in the discount factors using an asset pricing model similar to those considered later in Chapter 4. If the expectations hypothesis fails to hold the current price of any security k is computed using the expected spot rates:

$$p_{ak} = \sum_{t=1}^{T} \frac{\bar{R}_{kt}}{\prod_{s=1}^{t}(1+{}_{s-1}\bar{i}_s)}. \tag{2.25}$$

Empirical studies test the expectations hypothesis by regressing expected spot rates on the forward rates embedded in long-term bond yields:

$${}_1\bar{i}_2 = \alpha + \beta\ {}_1f_2.$$

Typically, past spot rates are used as measures of expected future spot rates on the assumption that investors' expectations are on average correct, where the hypothesis holds when $\alpha = 0$ and $\beta = 1$. Tease (1988) finds support for the expectations hypothesis using Australian data, while there is little support for it in overseas data. Some argue the failure of the hypothesis is evidence of a liquidity (risk) premium in long-term bond rates as they are costly to trade in periods prior to maturity. When it does fail to hold we can use empirical estimates of the expected short rates from these studies as the discount rates in the pricing equation in (2.25).

2.4.2 Fundamental equation of yield

In a frictionless competitive capital market capital assets must be expected to pay the same economic rate of return as all other assets in the same risk class in every period of their lives. This important relationship underpins the present value calculations used to compute asset prices. *Economic income* in any period of time measures the change in wealth. It is a measure of the potential consumption flow the initial capital will generate for the asset holder, and it can be a cash or direct consumption flow plus any capital gain. We derive the equation of yield by computing the expected price of capital assets in each future time period. Consider an asset which pays a stream of expected net cash flows at the end each year up to year T. Its current price (at $t = 0$) can be decomposed (with subscripts a and k omitted) as

$$p_0 = \frac{\bar{R}_1 + \bar{p}_1}{1 + i_1},$$

where $\bar{R}_1 + \bar{p}_1$ represents the expected market value of the potential consumption flow the security would fund in the second period. The current price sells at a discount on this payout to compensate the asset holder for time (and risk). In a similar fashion we can write the expected price of the asset at the end of each subsequent period as

$$\bar{p}_1 = \frac{\bar{R}_2 + \bar{p}_2}{\left(1 + {}_1\bar{i}_2\right)}, \bar{p}_2 = \frac{\bar{R}_3 + \bar{p}_3}{\left(1 + {}_2\bar{i}_3\right)}, \bar{p}_3 = \frac{\bar{R}_4 + \bar{p}_4}{\left(1 + {}_3\bar{i}_4\right)}, \bar{p}_{T-1} = \frac{\bar{R}_T + \bar{p}_T}{\left(1 + {}_{T-1}\bar{i}_T\right.}$$

In the absence of any further net cash flows beyond time T, the asset is expected to have no value at that time, with $p_T = 0$. By substituting these prices back down the chain we obtain the asset price in (2.25), and this becomes the pricing equation in (2.24) when the expectations hypothesis holds. Thus, between all adjacent time periods $\{t - 1, t\}$ we must have

$$\bar{p}_{t-1} = \frac{\bar{R}_t + \bar{p}_t}{(1 + {}_{t-1}\bar{i}_t)},$$

which can be rearranged as the *equation of yield*,

$$ {}_{t-1}\bar{i}_t = \frac{\bar{R}_t + \Delta\bar{p}_t}{\bar{p}_{t-1}}, \tag{2.26} $$

with $\Delta\bar{p}_t = \bar{p}_t - \bar{p}_{t-1}$ being the expected capital gain when the asset price rises. It is also referred to as the *holding period yield*, and is a very useful relationship for understanding how asset prices change over time, where some rise, others fall and others stay constant. In every time period the expected economic income $(\bar{R}_t + \Delta\bar{p}_t)$ per dollar of capital invested in the asset $(\bar{p}_{t-1})$ is equal to the expected rate of return on all other assets in the same risk class. Whenever ${}_{t-1}\bar{i}_t > (\bar{R}_t + \Delta\bar{p}_t)/\bar{p}_{t-1}$, investors sell security k and use the funds to purchase assets in the same risk class until $\bar{p}_{t-1}$ declines. Conversely, its price rises when investors expect ${}_{t-1}\bar{i}_t < (\bar{R}_t + \Delta\bar{p}_t)/\bar{p}_{t-1}$ because it pays a higher expected economic rate of return than other assets in the same risk class. In a frictionless competitive equilibrium we must have ${}_{t-1}\bar{i}_t = (\bar{R}_t + \Delta\bar{p}_t)/\bar{p}_{t-1}$, which is the *no arbitrage condition* where all profits are eliminated from asset prices.

To see how this relationship is useful in providing insight into the way asset prices change, consider four different payouts over the period from t–1 to t:

i $\bar{R}_t = 0$. In periods when there are no net cash/consumption flows the asset price must rise at the risk-adjusted rate of return for all assets in the same risk class, with ${}_{t-1}\bar{i}_t = \Delta\bar{p}_t/\bar{p}_{t-1}$. For example, shares that pay no dividends must be expected to pay capital gains at this rate to stop shareholders selling them. Also, the value of wine stored in an unused space must be expected to rise at the expected return on all other assets in the same risk class. The relationship determines when trees planted for commercial timber should be cut down or when to extract oil or other minerals from the ground. While the trees continue to grow at a rate that generates additional timber in the future with a market value greater than the opportunity cost of funds plus any opportunity cost from using the land they are growing on, they are left standing. Once the growth in the value of the extra timber falls below this hurdle the trees are cut down. The same rule determines the optimal time to extract oil and other minerals.[39] There is a private incentive to delay current consumption when doing so raises future consumption by more than the opportunity cost of time and risk for assets in the same risk class.

ii $\Delta\bar{p}_t = 0$. Assets must be expected to have net cash or direct consumption flows that yield an expected economic return sufficient to cover the opportunity cost of capital, with ${}_{t-1}\bar{i}_t = \bar{R}_t/\bar{p}_{t-1}$. The most obvious example is perhaps a bank deposit which pays market interest in each time period.

iii $\bar{R}_t < 0$. There are many investments that require cash outlays in the early years followed by expected revenues in future years. Mining companies search for oil and other minerals for a number of years before discovering anything, while information technology firms allocate resources to research and development for long periods of time to develop computing software and other products. Sometimes they have negative net cash flows in these periods, but their share prices must be expected to rise at a greater rate than the return on all other assets in the same risk class, with ${}_{t-1}\bar{i} < \Delta\bar{p}_t/\bar{p}_{t-1}$, to provide shareholders with the necessary economic return to hold their capital in these firms.

iv $\Delta\bar{p}_t < 0$. Cars and white goods are common examples of depreciating assets with prices that fall over time. They must have large enough cash flows to offset these capital losses and pay the same economic return as all other assets, with ${}_{t-1}\bar{i}_t < \bar{R}_t/\bar{p}_{t-1}$. This example provides an ideal opportunity to derive the *user cost of capital* for firms by rearranging the equation of yield in (2.26):

$$\bar{c}_t = {}_{t-1}\bar{i}_t - \bar{\Phi}_t = \frac{\bar{R}_t}{\bar{p}_{t-1}}, \tag{2.27}$$

where $\bar{\Phi}_t = \Delta\bar{p}_t/\bar{p}_{t-1}$ is the rate of change in the value of the asset over the period. It is the forgone expected return on all other assets in the same risk class (${}_{t-1}\bar{i}_t$) less the rate of capital gain ($\bar{\Phi}_t$). For depreciating assets $\bar{\Phi}_t, < 0$ measures the rate of economic depreciation that must be recovered from the net cash flows to preserve each dollar of wealth invested in the asset. Most governments examine the way their policies impact on the user cost of capital in each sector of the economy to determine how they affect private investment. Some implement policies, including, for example, tax reform and accelerated depreciation allowances, to reduce the user cost of capital and raise investment. Tax reform that reduces the excess burden of taxation can lower the used cost of capital in every sector, while accelerated depreciation allowances are targeted at specific activities and are therefore likely to cause efficiency losses.

Box 2.8 The equation of yield: a numerical example

Sunscreen Ltd is a publicly listed company whose current share price is \$15. It produces awnings, roller shutters and shade sails. If, in the absence of taxes and transactions costs, traders expect the economic earnings per share ($\overline{EPS}_k$) over the next year to be \$1.80, then by the equation of yield all other shares in the same risk class (k) must pay a rate of return of $\bar{i}_k = \overline{EPS}_k/\bar{p}_k = 0.12$. Moreover, when they expect the dividend yield to be 8 per cent at the end of the next year they must also expect the share price to rise by 4 per cent:

$$\Delta\bar{p}_k = \overline{EPS}_k - \overline{DIV}_k = 1.80 - \$1.20 = \$0.60,$$

with $\bar{p}_k = p_k + \Delta\bar{p}_k = \$15.60$. Financial analysts use measured earnings per share and information about the revenue and costs of Sunscreen over the period to estimate economic earnings per share. Those with better information than the market can make profits by trading the shares.

2.4.3 Convenient pricing models

Two pricing models are frequently used for making simple rule-of-thumb calculations. They are perpetuities which pay a fixed annual net cash flow in perpetuity, and annuities which pay a fixed annual net cash flow over a defined number of years. When shares are expected to pay a stable stream of dividends in the future we can approximate their value by using the pricing equation for the perpetuity. The present value of a security that pays a constant nominal net cash flow of $\bar{R}_p$ at the end of each year in *perpetuity* is

$$p_p = \frac{\bar{R}_p}{i}, \tag{2.28}$$

where i is the average annual yield on a perpetual government bond. If there are no government perpetuities we can use the average annual yield on a 50-year bond as a close approximation.

This pricing relationship is confirmed by noting that p_p is the amount that would have to be invested for ever at interest rate i to generate a net cash flow of $\bar{R}_p$ at the end of every year. Suppose the net cash flow is \$100 and the average annual yield on the long-term government bond is 5 per cent. Then the price of the perpetuity is \$2000. When the net cash flow is expected to grow at a constant rate g_p each year, the price of the perpetuity becomes

$$p_p = \frac{\bar{R}_p}{i - g_p}.$$

Annuities are more common because they provide a constant net cash flow over a specified number of years. They are popular securities for consumers wanting to fund a consumption flow over finite time periods. The current price of an annuity that pays net cash flows of $\bar{R}_p$ dollars at the end of each year for T years can be calculated as the combination of two perpetuities paying the same annual cash flow; one is purchased now and the other sold at the end of year T, so that, in present value terms, we have

$$p_{A0} = p_{P0} - \frac{p_{PT}}{(1+i)^T} = \frac{\bar{R}_P}{i}\left\{1 - \frac{1}{(1+i)^T}\right\}. \tag{2.29}$$

This calculation assumes the average annual yield to maturity on the perpetuity is the same as the average annual yield on the T-year government bond. For an annual cash flow of \$100 paid at the end of each year for 10 years, the price of the annuity is \$772.17 when the interest rate is 5 per cent.

2.4.4 Compound interest

Assets often have net cash flows over time intervals that do not coincide with the timing of the available interest rate data. We can use the compound interest formula to compute the discount rates in these circumstances. Compound interest is where interest is paid on interest. In other words, interest is paid and then reinvested in the asset. This raises the effective interest rate above the simple interest rate over the period, which can be demonstrated by computing the amount one dollar will grow into over a year when interest is paid m times:

$$\left(1 + \frac{i}{m}\right)^m = 1 + i_e,$$

where i is the simple interest rate and i_e the effective rate of interest. If the dollar is compounded m times each year for t years it will grow to

$$\left(1 + \frac{i}{m}\right)^{mt} = (1 + i_e)^t.$$

With continuous compounding a dollar will grow in 1 year into:

$$\lim_{m\to\infty}\left(1+\frac{i}{m}\right)^m = 2.718^i = e^i,$$

where 2.718 is the base of the natural logarithm. Thus, the effective rate of interest is 172 per cent for the simple interest rate of 100 per cent. With continuous compounding over t years it grows to:

$$\lim_{m\to\infty}\left(1+\frac{i}{m}\right)^{mt} = 2.718^{it} = e^{it}.$$

Box 2.9 Examples of compound interest

The benefits from compound interest can be illustrated for a simple interest rate of 5 per cent over 1 year for different values of m:

a for semi-annual interest ($m = 2$):

$$\left(1+\frac{0.05}{2}\right)^2 = 1.0506;$$

b for quarterly interest ($m = 4$):

$$\left(1+\frac{0.05}{4}\right)^4 = 1.0510;$$

c for continuous compounding ($m \to \infty$):

$$\lim_{m\to\infty}\left(1+\frac{0.05}{m}\right)^m = e^{0.05} = 1.0513.$$

There are a number of applications where compounding is important. Consider an asset with constant net cash flow paid continuously for T years, illustrated in Figure 2.17. A light bulb is an example when it provides a constant stream of light (L). Frequently the net cash flows are continuous over blocks of time and have uncertain lives, but we abstract from those complications here. This certain stream of net cash flows has a present value of:

$$p_L = \int_0^T \bar{R}_L e^{-it}\,dt.$$

The compound interest formula can be used to derive discount rates for cash flows that occur at times that do not coincide with the timing for reported interest rates. To illustrate this point, consider an asset k with net cash flows that occur eight times every 100 days from now. It has a present value of:

$$p_k = \sum_{t=1}^{8} \frac{R_{kt}}{(1+i_{100})^t},$$

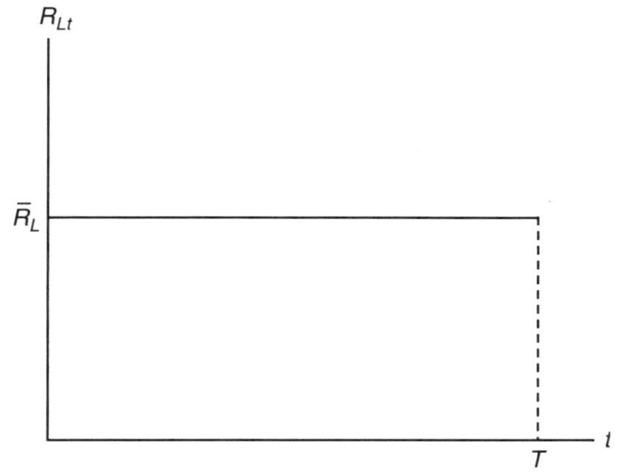

Figure 2.17 An asset with a continuous consumption stream.

where i_{100} is the 100-day interest rate embedded in the annual interest rate i, with:

$$(1+i_{100})365/100 = 1+i.$$

If the annual interest rate is 10 per cent the 100 day rate is 0.0265, which can be approximated as $i(100/365) = 0.0274$.[40]

2.4.5 Bond prices

A variety of different types of bonds are issued by private and public institutions. Government bonds are in general less risky than corporate bonds, as is evident from their lower returns, and they have different maturity dates ranging from 90 days to 20 (or more) years. There are three types of government bonds, which differ in their stream of future cash flows:

- i The *coupon* bond pays coupon interest on the face value of the bond in each period up to and including the date of maturity when it also repays the principal. The coupon interest rate can differ from the market interest rate over the life of the bond. It is a commitment made at the time the bond is sold.
- ii The *consol* is a coupon bond that pays coupon interest in perpetuity.
- iii The *discount* bond is a coupon bond with zero coupon interest. Thus, it pays a specified cash flow (for example, one dollar or one unit of real purchasing power) at maturity, but nothing in preceding time periods. (In effect, the current market price of a discount bond represents the capital that would need to be invested in a risk-free asset with interest payments reinvested until maturity.)

When there are differences in the coupon and market interest rates, the market and face values of the bonds diverge. Consider a government bond that pays 5 per cent coupon interest for 5 years on its face value of \$1000 that is redeemed at maturity. Its current market price is

$$p_B = \sum_{t=1}^{4} \frac{50}{\prod_{j=1}^{t}\left(1+i_j\right)} + \frac{1050}{\left(1+i_5\right)^5}.^{41}$$

When the coupon interest rate is less than the market rate the bond price sells at a discount on its face value, while the reverse applies when the market rate is lower than the coupon rate. This ensures the bond pays its holder a market rate of return, which is confirmed using the equation of yield, where, in each period of the bonds life, we have:

$$i_5 p_{Bt-1} = 50 + \Delta p_{Bt}.$$

In most countries public and corporate bonds trade prior to maturity on secondary boards at stock exchanges, where this provides information about the yield curve and the term structure of interest rates.

Corporate bonds can be long or short term and secured or unsecured, where secured bonds have a prior claim to the market values of specified assets when firms default on their interest payments. Even though bondholders have prior claims to the net cash flows they still face risk when shares have limited liability that restricts the losses of shareholders to the value of their invested capital. Once firms have losses that exceed the equity capital they must fall on the bondholders.[42]

2.4.6 Share prices

Since shares have residual claims to the net cash flows of firms they are typically more risky than debt, even when shares have limited liability. They also give shareholders valuable voting rights that can be used to influence the investment decisions of firms. The larger the proportion of shares any individual shareholder can influence, the more control they have over the firm. Share prices are ultimately determined by the value of their dividend payments, where

$$p_E = \sum_{r=1}^{\infty} \frac{DIV_t}{\left(1+i_{Et}\right)^t}, \tag{2.30}$$

with DIV_t being the dividend per share, and i_{Et} the expected economic return on all other assets in the same risk class, at each time t. To reduce the amount of notation in this and following sections we omit the variable identifying the firm.

Shareholders expect to receive income as cash dividends and/or capital gains in each period. Some shares pay variable dividends through time, while others pay a stable dividend stream. Either way they must be expected to pay the required economic return in each time period. Dividends are funded from the net cash flows of firms after paying interest to bondholders and maintaining the initial market value of the invested capital. This can be demonstrated by writing the equation of yield for a share as:

$$i_{Et} p_{Et-1} = DIV_t + \Delta p_{Et} = EPS_t, \tag{2.31}$$

where EPS_t is expected economic earnings per share at time t. Investors must expect each share to pay economic earnings over the period as a cash dividend and capital gain which is at least equal to the economic income paid on all other shares in the same risk class ($i_{Et}p_{t-1}$). This economic income is generated by the production activities of the firm issuing the share, with:

$$(1+i_{Et})p_{Et-1}S_{t-1} = X_t - (1+i_{Bt})B_{t-1} + V_t. \tag{2.32}$$

Here S_{t-1} is the number of shares issued by the firm at the beginning of the period. The market value of this equity at the beginning of the period, is $p_{Et-1}\ S_{t-1} = E_{t-1}$. X_t is the firm's net cash flow, which is equal to the gross revenue from selling output minus all the non-capital operating costs. It is the cash flow that can be distributed to capital providers in the firm. B_{t-1} is the market value of debt issued by the firm at the beginning of the period. We assume debt pays market interest at the end of the period (i_{Bt}) so that its face value is also its market value. Finally, $V_t = E_t + B_t$ is the expected market value of the firm at the end of the period. After rearranging (2.32) we can write the expected economic return on equity over the period as

$$i_{Et}E_{t-1} = X_t - i_{Bt}B_{t-1} + V_t - V_{t-1}.$$

Since shareholders have the residual claim on the firm's net cash flows their income is measured after repaying principal and interest to bondholders and recovering any fall in the market value of capital invested in equity. It is convenient to define the rate of economic depreciation as the rate of change in the market value of the firm:

$$\Phi_t = \frac{V_t - V_{t-1}}{V_{t-1}}. \tag{2.33}$$

This is negative when the firm's market value is expected to fall over the period and positive when it is expected to rise. This allows us to write the expected economic income paid to equity, as:

$$i_{Et}E_{t-1} = X_t - i_{Bt}B_{t-1} + \Phi_t V_{t-1} \tag{2.34}$$

When investors look at trading equity they compute its expected economic income, because that determines the change in their wealth. *Economic income* is what investors can consume over a period of time without reducing their initial wealth. In practice, however, economic income is quite difficult to measure because it includes capital gains or losses on assets held over the period. Many capital assets are purchased in prior periods, and unless there are active markets for identical assets the changes in their values must be estimated. Accounting rules and conventions are adopted to remove this subjectivity from reported income. Clearly, it would be possible for firms to manipulate reported income when capital gains or losses are subjectively determined. By reporting *measured income*, which is based on specified rules and conventions for computing depreciation in the values of capital assets, traders know how it is computed, and they can then make the necessary adjustments to convert it into economic income, which is the measure of income they care about because it isolates the true consumption gain.

2.4.7 *Price–earnings ratios*

Price–earnings (P/E) ratios for publicly listed shares are reported in the financial press in most countries. These ratios are used by traders and analysts in financial markets to assess the future profitability of shares, but they are based on measured rather than economic earnings. Thus, traders make adjustments to convert them into *ideal price–earnings ratios* that are obtained by rearranging (2.31):

$$\frac{p_{Et-1}}{EPS_t} = \frac{1}{i_{Et}}. \tag{2.35}$$

Box 2.10 Measured P/E ratios for shares traded on the Australian Securities Exchange

The P/E ratios listed below were compiled from data provided by the Australian Securities Exchange at the close of business on Friday 13 April 2007. They are average values for firms in 12 sectors of the economy with P/E ratios less than or equal to 150. Twenty-three firms had P/E ratios above this number and they were not included because in most cases they were large outliers that did not reflect the values reported for most firms. The standard deviations are included to indicate how the P/E ratios differ across firms in each sector; they differed most for firms in the health care sector and least for firms in the telecommunications sector.

Sector	*P/E Average*	*Standard deviation*	*No. of firms*
Consumer discretionary	24	19	107
Consumer staples	25	16	30
Energy	29	33	35
Financials, ex property	19	15	133
Property trusts	13	15	90
Health care	36	50	38
Industrials	19	12	130
Information technology	23	22	61
Materials	26	39	121
Telecommunication services	17	8	12
Utilities	56	34	8
Unclassified	73	33	2
All firms reporting PE (≤ 150):	23	26	767

Source: The data was obtained from the Australian Financial Review website at http://www.afr.com/home/sharetables/weekly/2007/4/13/CCsswk070413.csv, on 17 April 2007.

This tells us the number of years it takes for the share to repay its capital as economic income, and when the no arbitrage condition holds these ratios are the same for all shares in the same risk class. Any differences are due to differences in their market risk. Traders make investment decisions using the information contained in these ratios because they are based on economic income. In practice, however, the *measured P/E ratio* for each share is based on accounting (*A*) income:

$$\frac{p_{Et-1}}{EPS^A_{t-1}} = \frac{1}{i^A_{Et}}. \tag{2.36}$$

There are two reasons why this differs from the ideal ratio in (2.35):

i It uses the most recently reported earnings per share and is therefore backward-looking. In contrast, the ideal ratio is forward-looking because it uses expected future income. Indeed, the current share price is determined by future income, and not income in previous periods (unless it provides information about future income).
ii It uses measured income rather than economic income, for reasons discussed above.

By defining ideal P/E ratios it is possible to understand the information reported in the measured ratios. Occasionally they have very high values that suggest the shares will pay very low returns. For example, information technology (IT) stocks had measured P/E ratios as high as 60 during the IT boom at the end of the twentieth century. But this is explained by the low measured earnings in periods of research and development which do not include the expected capital gains included in economic income. Sometimes the reported P/E ratios are negative due to income losses. However, current share prices are determined by expected economic income, which cannot be negative. No investor pays a positive price for a share with expect economic losses. While losses are possible due to uncertainty, they must still expect profits. Financial analysts make these adjustments when using the reported ratios.

Box 2.11 Examples of large P/E ratios

Twenty-three firms with P/E ratios greater than 150 were not included in the data reported in Box 2.10. Four of them are summarized below, each of which has a very low measured earnings per share relative to the share price.

Firm	*P/E*	*Share price*	*EPS*
Victoria Pet	2100	0.21	0.0001
Mariner Bridge	6000	2.40	0.0004
Consolidated Minerals	8833.3	2.65	0.0003
Bakehouse Quarter	39100	3.91	0.0001

Source: The data was obtained from the Australian Financial Review website at http://www.afr.com/home/sharetables/weekly/2007/4/13/CCsswk070413.csv, on 17 April 2007.

The difference between measured and economic income can be illustrated by comparing economic earnings per share,

$$EPS_t = \frac{X_t - (1 + i_{Bt})B_{t-1} + \Phi_t V_t}{S_{t-1}},$$

with measured earnings per share,

$$EPS_t^A = \frac{X_t - (1 + i_{Bt})B_{t-1} + \Phi_t^A V_t}{S_{t-1}},$$

for the period from t–1 to t. Most of the difference arises from the way depreciation is computed, where Φ_t^A is *measured depreciation* and Φ_t *economic depreciation*. There are two main reasons for $\Phi_t^A \neq \Phi$.

First, measured depreciation is computed by applying decay factors to the written-down book values of the assets in the firm. There are basically two methods that can be used: straight line and diminishing value. But it is not uncommon for these asset prices to rise in some time periods. For example, firms with land and buildings in the central business districts of major cities frequently make capital gains on these assets even though they apply depreciation allowances to them when computing measured income. Moreover, there are circumstances where every physical asset depreciates in value while the overall market value of the firm appreciates. This occurs in periods when intangible assets such as goodwill are created, or when investments are made in activities that are expected to pay economic profits in the future. All these capital gains are included in economic depreciation (with $\Phi_t > 0$), while they are only included in measured income at the time the intangible assets actually trade. For example, when firms sell land and buildings they can report any capital gains at the time of sale, and not in the period when they actually occur. This makes measured income less than economic income in periods when the gains occur, but greater than economic income in periods when the assets are traded and the gains realized.

Second, since measured depreciation is based on initial prices paid for assets it is called *historic cost depreciation*, and it underestimates economic depreciation when there is general price inflation. The best way to illustrate this point is to consider the way economic depreciation in (2.34) is affected by anticipated inflation. Consider a situation where all nominal variables rise at the expected rate of inflation (π) to preserve the real economy. By using (2.18) we can write the expected nominal economic income on equity in (2.32) as:

$$\left(1+r_{Et}\right)\left(1+\pi\right)E_{t-1} = X_t - \left(1+r_{Bt}\right)\left(1+\pi\right)B_{t-1} + V_t,$$

where the net cash flows and value of the firm at time t rise by the expected rate of inflation. After rearranging this expression, the real *economic return to equity*, becomes:

$$r_{Et}E_{t-1} = \frac{X_t}{\left(1+\pi\right)} - r_{Bt}B_{t-1} + \frac{V_t - V_{t-1}\left(1+\pi\right)}{\left(1+\pi\right)}. \tag{2.37}$$

From this we can see that economic depreciation is the change in the market value of the firm that preserves the purchasing power of the initial capital invested at $t-1$. If we assume the measured and economic depreciation rates are equal in the absence of inflation, the *measured real return to equity*, which uses historic cost-based depreciation allowances, would be

$$r_{Et}^{A}E_{t-1} = \frac{X_t}{1+\pi} - r_{Bt}B_{t-1} + \frac{V_t - V_{t-1}}{1+\pi}. \tag{2.38}$$

Notice how this understates the firm's expenses and causes measured income to exceed economic income (all other things equal), with $r_{Et}^{A} > r_{Et}$, where expected inflation increases the effective tax rate on economic income when measured income is subject to tax.[43] Another way of summarizing this effect is to compare the economic depreciation rate,

$$\Phi_t = \frac{V_t - V_{t-1}(1+\pi)}{V_{t-1}(1+\pi)},$$

with the measured depreciation rate,

$$\Phi_t^A = \frac{V_t - V_{t-1}}{V_{t-1}}.$$

When V_t rises at the expected rate of inflation, nothing real happens to the economic depreciation rate, whereas the measured rate rises. The appropriate way to preserve measured depreciation allowances in these circumstances would be to scale up all the written-down book values of the firm's assets by $1 + \pi$ before applying the decay factors to them. This adjustment would at least preserve the purchasing power of the initial capital invested in the firm and stop the effective tax on economic income from rising when there is expected inflation.

2.4.8 Firm valuations and the cost of capital

Later in Chapter 7 we examine the impact of firm financial policy choices on their market values. We do this by defining the proportion of capital financed by debt at time $t-1$ as $b_{t-1} = B_{t-1}/V_{t-1}$, and the remaining proportion, financed by equity, as $(1-b_{t-1}) = E_{t-1}/V_{t-1}$, and this allows us to solve the market value of the firm at the beginning of the period using (2.34) as

$$V_{t-1} = \frac{X_t}{c_t}. \tag{2.39}$$

Here $c_t = (1-b_{t-1})\, i_{Et} + b_{t-1}\, i_{Bt} - \Phi_t$ is the user cost of capital in period t, that is, the cost of tying up each dollar of capital in the firm over the period from $t-1$ to t, where $(1-b_{t-1})\, i_{Et} + b_{t-1}\, i_{Bt}$ is the forgone return on all other assets in the same risk class, and Φ_t is the rate of capital depreciation. It is worth noting that while the user cost of capital is a weighted average of the costs of debt and equity, it is indeed the marginal cost of capital when the firm is a price-taker in all markets and changes in investment have no effect on the depreciation rate Φ_t. Thus, its investment choices cannot affect the market returns to debt and equity, or the market prices of capital assets. In the presence of uncertainty, however, changes in the debt–equity ratio (with investment held constant) can affect the returns to debt and equity by moving risk between them, but without affecting the overall value of the firm when there is common information. This is examined later in Chapter 7 by including uncertainty in the analysis. Once firms can affect the market risk or the underlying risk-free return there are additional terms in the user cost of capital.

Recall from Section 2.2 that the objective function of a competitive firm is to maximize profit, defined as

$$\eta_{t-1} = V_{t-1} - Z_{t-1}, \tag{2.40}$$

where the net cash flows are an increasing function of capital investment at the beginning of the period (Z_{t-1}), with $\partial X_{t-1}/\partial Z_{t-1} > 0$ and $\partial^2 X_{t-1}/\partial Z_{t-1}^2 < 0$. Leverage ($b_{t-1}$) is chosen to minimize the user cost of capital, with

$$\frac{\partial \eta_{t-1}}{\partial b_{t-1}}\bigg|_{dX_{t-1}=0} = \frac{V_{t-1}}{c_t}\left(i_{Et} - i_{Bt}\right) = 0, \tag{2.41}$$

while optimally chosen investment satisfies

$$\frac{\partial \eta_{t-1}}{\partial Z_{t-1}}\bigg|_{db_{t-1}=0} = \frac{\partial X_{t-1}}{\partial Z_{t-1}}\frac{1}{c_t} - \frac{\partial c_t}{\partial Z_{t-1}}V_{t-1} - 1 = 0. \tag{2.42}$$

When the no arbitrage condition holds in a certainty setting without taxes, debt and equity must pay the same rate of return, with $i_{Et} = i_{Bt}$, where the cost of capital is independent of leverage and (2.41) holds for all b_{t-1}. This is the Modigliani–Miller leverage irrelevance theorem in a certainty setting. The condition for optimally chosen investment in (2.42) equates the value of the marginal product of capital to its marginal user cost, with $\partial X_{t-1}/\partial Z_{t-1} = c_t$ when $\partial c_t/\partial Z_{t-1} = 0$. Once leverage affects the user cost of capital, investment cannot be choosen independently of the debt–equity choice, and Modigliani–Miller leverage irrelevance fails.

Box 2.12 The market valuation of a firm: a numerical example

Homemaker Ltd is a publicly listed company with expected net cash flows ($\bar{X}$) of \$168 million in 12 months' time and a current market value (V) of \$1200 million. In a frictionless competitive capital market where traders have common information the firm's expected used cost of capital ($\bar{c}$) is obtained using the equation of yield:

$$\bar{c} = \frac{\bar{X}}{V} = \frac{168}{1200} = 0.14.$$

In a certainty setting where debt and equity pay the same risk-free return (i), the change in the value of the firm over the year ($\bar{\Phi}$) is obtained from the user cost of capital, which is:

$$\bar{c} = i - \bar{\Phi} = 0.14.$$

If the risk-free rate is 5 per cent the market value of the firm declines by 9 per cent, ($\Phi = i - \bar{c} = 0.05 - 0.14 = -0.09$), so at the end of the year, we have

$$\bar{V} = V(1 - \bar{\Phi}) = 1200(1 - 0.09) = \$1092.$$

Later in Chapter 7 we introduce risk and taxes and find circumstances where the expected user cost of capital changes with leverage.

Problems

1 James allocates endowments of income between consumption today and consumption tomorrow by trading in a competitive capital market at interest rate i.

- i Illustrate his consumption opportunities in a diagram with dollars of consumption today on the x axis and dollars of consumption tomorrow on the y axis.
- ii Under what circumstances will James just consume his income endowments in each period?
- iii If James does not initially borrow or lend, will a rise in the market interest rate ever cause him to become a lender? Will he always be better off after the interest rate rises?
- iv Explain what conditions on preferences are required for James to lend less when the interest rate rises if he is initially a lender.
- v What happens to wealth measured in current dollars when the interest rate rises? What happens to wealth measured in future dollars when the interest rate rises?
- vi Explain what determines whether individuals enter the capital markets as borrowers or lenders. What role do financial securities play?
- vii Illustrate the change in James' consumption opportunities when transactions costs drive a wedge between the borrowing and lending rates of interest, with $i_B \neq i_L$.
- viii Identify the benefits to James, measured in current dollars, from introducing a capital market. Is it the same for all consumers?
- ix What determines the market rate of interest?

2 Bill is endowed with current income (M_0) and will receive a pension (P_1) in the second period which he allocates between consumption in the two periods in a competitive capital market at interest rate i. (Assume he has strictly convex indifference schedules over consumption expenditure in the two periods.)

- i Use a consumption space diagram to illustrate the way a tax on interest income affects Bill's budget constraint when it drives a wedge between borrowing and lending rates. Will this tax always cause him to trade less (i.e. reduce saving or borrowing) in the capital market when current consumption is a normal good?
- ii Examine the way Bill's budget constraint is affected by a lump-sum tax (T_0) in the current period which is returned to him in the second period (without interest). Will this cause him to save less when current and future consumption are normal goods?
- iii Use a diagram to illustrate the welfare change from replacing the pension with a non-tradable voucher of $V_1 = P_1$ dollars when Bill initially borrows. Would this raise the amount he borrows if current consumption is an inferior good? In your diagram identify the change in the interest rate that would alter his consumption in exactly the same way as the voucher–subsidy switch.
- iv Use a diagram to illustrate the welfare change from replacing the pension with a non-tradable voucher of $V_1 = P_1$ dollars when Bill initially saves. Does this cause his saving to fall when current consumption is a normal good? In your diagram identify the change in the interest rate that would alter his consumption in exactly the same way as the voucher–subsidy switch.

3 A farmer has 400 bushels of wheat, and he can convert wheat this year (x_1) into wheat next year (x_2) using the farming technology $x_2 = 50\sqrt{x_1}$. All prices are expected to remain constant between this year and next. Clearly, if the farmer plants his entire endowment he will earn a rate of return of 150 per cent on his investment.

i Illustrate the farmer's consumption opportunities in a commodity space $\{x_1, x_2\}$ diagram when he cannot access a capital market (i.e. he cannot borrow or lend). Write down his optimization problem when he derives utility from consuming wheat now and next year, and then derive the condition for optimally chosen investment. Illustrate this outcome in your diagram.

ii Suppose the farmer can borrow and lend at 25 per cent per annum. How much wheat should he plant? What are his consumption opportunities now? Why is his investment decision now independent of his tastes?

iii The farmer tells his neighbour that if the market interest rate were to rise to 50 per cent per annum he would plant only 278 bushels of wheat even though he could earn a 150 per cent return on his investment by planting the whole 400 bushels. Is the farmer investing too little wheat?

iv How much wheat should the farmer plant when he can borrow and lend at a zero market rate of interest?

v With the interest rate at which he can borrow and lend standing at 25 per cent, the farmer learns that he can borrow the equivalent of 300 bushels of wheat at a zero interest rate from a primary industry bank recently established by the government to stimulate farm investment. What is his optimal response to this scheme? What are his consumption opportunities?

4 Consider two projects with the following net cash flows:

Project	C_0	C_1	C_2
(a)	−5500	8000	
(b)	−5500		8500

The average annual yield on a two-period security is 10 per cent ($i_2 = 0.10$). In answering the following questions, assume this rate stays constant.

i Would you invest in either of the projects when the term structure of interest rates is flat?

ii Would you invest in either of the projects if the current spot rate is 5 per cent? What is the expected spot rate for the second year, $E({}_1i_2)$?

iii Would you invest in either of the projects if the expected spot rate for the second year is 5 per cent? What is the current spot rate, i_1?

iv Find the term structure of interest rates that would make you indifferent to the projects.

v Using the answers to parts (i), (ii) and (iii), isolate the important factors for the appraisal of projects with multi-period cash flows. What problems are encountered in practice when appraising projects?

vi What determines the term structure of interest rates, and how can they be calculated in practice?

vii How will project evaluation be biased if a flat discount rate is used to discount the net cash flows when the yield curve rises over the life of the project?

5 Consider the returns on the following three traded securities.

- S_{01} pays a 5 per cent return at $t = 1$ on dollars invested at $t = 0$;
- S_{12} pays a 12 per cent return at $t = 2$ on dollars invested at $t = 1$.
- S_{02} pays an average return of 9 per cent over the two periods paid at $t = 2$ on dollars invested at $t = 0$.

Construct a wealth-maximizing set of trades in these securities. Derive the maximization problem for an arbitrageur who starts with no initial wealth and sells one security to buy the other. Draw the budget constraint and the iso-profit lines in the security space and identify the profit from arbitrage. (Assume there are no taxes on security returns and the securities have equal risk over the two-year period.)

6 Derive and explain the fundamental equation of yield. (Carefully detail the assumptions you make.) Use it to explain how the price of a capital asset changes over periods of time when it generates no net cash flows. Why do people hold capital assets which generate no net cash flows, such as paintings, if their prices do not rise at the rate of interest?

7 A taxi cab company purchases its last car for \$22,000 at the beginning of the year and it is expected to have a market value of \$16,000 at the end of 12 months. Over the year the car is expected to generate \$35,960 in cab fees. If the company expects to pay \$17,000 in wages to a driver of the cab, \$6,000 in fuel costs and \$3,000 in other operating expenses (which do not include the cost of capital), what is the expected 12-month return on capital assets in the same risk class as this asset? (Assume all revenues are received, and operating costs paid, at the end of the period.) What is the risk premium if the riskless rate of return is 8 per cent?

8 Jordan owns a ride-on lawn mower that he expects will have a market value of \$3,800 at the end of the next 12 months when he receives a net cash flow of \$600 for mowing his neighbours' lawns. (Assume these are the only services the mower provides over the period.) Will the expected user cost of capital be 15 per cent if the mower has a current market value of \$4,000?

9 Consider the following cost–benefit analysis:

> How about considering the use of energy-efficient compact fluorescent lamps in place of the traditional incandescent (filament) globe?
>
> Let's compare the cost of operating a 60 watt incandescent globe with a life of 1,000 hours and costing \$1 against a compact fluorescent 11 watt lamp with a life of 8,000 hours and costing \$25. Due to its greater efficiency the 11 watt lamp provides light equivalent to the 60 watt globe.
>
> Using a domestic rate of 7.32 cents per kilowatt-hour for electricity and operating the lights for 10 hours per day, we find that after 8,000 hours of use (about 2 years and 3 months) the cost of using a globe was \$35.14 for power plus \$8 for the globes, a total of \$43.14. On the other hand, the lamp used \$6.44 worth of power and cost \$25 giving a total cost of \$31.44. This means a potential saving of \$11.70 - obviously, more lights and increased usage will mean a greater saving.
>
> On the same basis a 15 watt lamp compared with a 75 watt globe shows a possible saving of \$18.14!

These calculations make it hard to explain why people buy incandescent (filament) globes in preference to compact fluorescent lamps. Can you provide reasons why they do? Use a spreadsheet to compute the present values of the capital and recurrent costs of providing light from eight globes and one lamp. (Note that the electricity charge is 7.32 cents each hour when using a 1,000-watt appliance. Assume the electricity charges are paid every 62 days, and that the interest rate is 10 per cent per annum in each year.)

10 The price-earnings ratios for shares traded on the Australian Securities Exchange are reported on a regular basis to provide investors with information they can use to determine their security trades.

i Explain why these reported ratios differ across traded shares. What information do investors get from them? Should investors buy shares with high P/E ratios?

ii Examine the adjustments that investors would make to reported P/E ratios to convert them into ideal P/E ratios. Explain what the ideal ratios measure and why they differ across shares.

iii Consider reasons why the so-called *new technology stocks* have such high reported P/E ratios. Do stocks with more risk have higher or lower P/E ratios than stocks with less risk?

iv Explain why measured depreciation allowances differ from economic depreciation allowances. What are the factors that determine economic depreciation? How does expected inflation raise the effective tax on company income through measured depreciation allowances?

11 You have the following information. At $t = 0$ a firm issues $1,000 of debt with an interest cost of 20 per cent, and 1,000 shares with a market value of $1 (i.e., p_0 = $1). At $t = 1$ there are *expected* to be net cash flows (before interest, dividends and depreciation) of $600, an ex-dividend share price (p_1) of $1.20, and 5 per cent economic depreciation.

i Calculate and explain:

a the EPS, dividends per share and capital gains per share;

b the dividend yield;

c the earnings–price ratio; and,

d the P/E ratio.

ii How is the P/E ratio measured in practice, and why does it differ from the ideal P/E ratio?

12 The following financial data was reported for banks that trade on the Australian Securities Exchange. It was compiled at the close of business on Friday 13 April 2007, and was obtained from the *Australian Financial Review* website at *http://www.afr.com/home/sharetables/weekly/2007/4/13/CCsswk070413.csv*, on 17 April 2007.

Security description	*Share price ($) 13 April 2007*			*Net tangible assets ($)*	*Dividend yield (%)*	*Earnings per share(¢)*
	Day High	*Day Low*	*Last Sale*			
Adelaide Bank	15.71	15.26	15.45	6.01	3.95	84.92
ANZ Banking Group	30.40	30.11	30.33	8.53	4.12	200.00
Bank of Queensland	18.35	18.01	18.06	4.37	3.16	88.20
Bendigo Bank Ltd	17.08	16.99	17.01	5.06	3.17	81.20
C'wealth Bank of Aust.	51.99	51.57	51.80	10.23	4.58	320.70
Home Bld Soc.	15.40	15.30	15.32	4.72	2.87	54.00
Homeloans Ltd	0.98	0.97	0.97	—	5.15	5.09
Mackay Permanent	6.90	6.90	6.90	3.07	3.33	33.00
Mortgage Choice	3.21	3.17	3.20	0.40	4.06	16.10
National Aust. Bank	42.74	42.28	42.56	11.91	3.92	262.60
Rock Bld Perm	5.60	5.50	5.60	2.02	4.02	21.90
St George Bank	35.40	34.77	35.00	6.73	4.31	201.40
Westpac Banking	26.52	26.25	26.29	6.12	4.41	167.20
Wide Bay Aust. Ltd	12.40	12.35	12.35	3.37	4.57	60.52

Compute the measured P/E ratios for these banks and consider reasons why they might differ. Do they indicate the Home Building Society and the Rock Building Permanent are the most risky banks, while the ANZ Banking Group and Westpac Banking are the least risky banks? Calculate the dividends per share for each bank. Find examples of companies with negative P/E ratios and positive dividend yields and explain why it happens. Construct a similar table for a small group of companies in another sector of the economy. Can the ideal P/E ratio ever be negative?

13 Consider a sewing machine which generates a certain \$1,000 net cash flow at the end of each year for 5 years (with no residual value).

i Determine the price of this machine if the interest rate in each period is 10 per cent.

ii Calculate the rate of economic depreciation for this machine if it has no resale value at the end of its life.

iii Calculate the annual *rate* of depreciation allowed for tax purposes if the machine is depreciated on a straight-line basis over 5 years with zero residual value. Compare these allowances to economic depreciation in each year and consider whether they raise or lower the effective tax rate on the economic income generated by the sewing machine.

14 Historic cost based depreciation allowances can cause measured income to differ from economic income when: (a) allowed rates of depreciation (Φ_t^A) differ from economic rates of depreciation (Φ_t) and (b) there is expected inflation. This question demonstrates these differences for the nominal returns paid to shareholders in a corporate firm from period $t-1$ to t, where the *economic rate of return* is

$$i_{Et} = \frac{X_t - i_{Bt}B_{t-1} + \Phi_t V_{t-1}}{E_{t-1}},$$

and the *measured rate of return* is

$$i_{Et}^A = \frac{X_t - i_{Bt}B_{t-1} + \Phi_t^A V_{t-1}}{E_{t-1}}.$$

Let $E_{t-1} = B_{t-1} = \$500$.

i In the absence of inflation $V_t = \$950$, $X_t = \$80$, and $i_{Bt} = 0.03$. Calculate and compare economic and measured income in the absence of inflation when i $\Phi_t^A = -0.03$, and ii $\Phi_t^A = -0.05$.

ii Suppose inflation is expected to be 10 per cent over the period from $t-1$ to t, where $V_t = \$1{,}045$.

a Compute nominal economic income when the Fisher effect holds (in the absence of tax).

b Assume $\Phi_t^A = -0.05$. Compute nominal measured income when $i_{Bt} = 0.033$. Use historic cost based depreciation to calculate measured income.

c What happens to the effective tax rate on economic income if the tax is applied to nominal measured income?

15 There are a number of ways that changes in expected inflation can impact on capital asset prices. One is through wealth effects in the money market due to the non-payment on interest on currency (notes and coins) held by the private sector. Answer the following questions when the demand for real currency balances (in billions of dollars) is $m_d = 26 - 100i$, where i is the nominal rate of interest. (Assume m_d is unaffected by changes in real income.)

i What is the supply of real currency when the equilibrium nominal interest rate is 6 per cent? Calculate how much seigniorage there is when the rate of inflation in the general price level is expected to be 3 per cent. Explain how seigniorage transfers revenue to the Reserve Bank of Australia (RBA). Compute a dollar measure of the inefficiency when no interest is paid to currency holders and explain what this inefficiency measures. (Assume the RBA is a monopoly supplier that prints currency at a constant resource cost of 1 per cent of the quantity supplied.)

ii Now suppose currency holders expect an increase in the rate of inflation over the next year that raises the equilibrium nominal interest rate to 8 per cent. Compute the reduction in the demand for real currency balances and calculate a dollar measure (in millions) of the fall in the real wealth of currency holders. Carefully explain why this loss in wealth occurs and examine circumstances where it is larger for the same change in the nominal interest rate.

iii What would the real currency supply be if the RBA paid interest to currency holders? (Assume the RBA incurs no costs of paying interest, and interest is paid to eliminate inefficiency in the currency market.)

16 A gardening contractor buys a ride-on lawn mower which will generate a certain net cash flow of $5,000 at the end of each year for the next 2 years when it has a certain residual value of $1,000. (Assume all markets are competitive.)

i Compute economic depreciation on the mower in each of the two productive years of its life and compare it with measured straight-line depreciation when the risk-free interest rate is 5 per cent per annum. (Note that straight-line depreciation apportions the purchase price of the asset less its residual value equally over the 2 years of its life. Assume there is no expected inflation.)

ii Compute and compare the depreciation measures in part (i) when expected inflation increases all nominal variables by 2 per cent each year, including the net cash flows, the residual value of the mower and the nominal interest rate. Use this to explain why there are differences in measured and economic income. Identify circumstances where the Fisher effect holds and explain the forces that drive it. (Assume there is certainty.)

Explain why a change in the expected rate of inflation has real effects in the currency market when no interest is paid on notes and coins. Examine these real effects when there is a fall in the expected rate of inflation. How does the government raise revenue as seigniorage, and does this revenue fall when expected inflation declines?

3 Uncertainty and risk

Consumption goods in a certainty setting are characterized by their type (physical attributes), geographic location and location in time. For example, an apple in one location is different from an apple (with the same physical attributes) in another location, and it is also different from the same apple in different time periods. Indeed, consumers derive utility from the combination of characteristics that define them, which for an apple, include sweetness, size, colour, firmness and moisture content. In fact, it is possible to estimate the price of any good as the summed value of its characteristics using hedonic prices, which are consumer marginal valuations for each characteristic.[1] Uncertainty introduces randomness into future consumption through exogenous variability in the environment within which consumers live. Its effects may be confined to the variance it imparts to their consumption or a combination of that and its direct impact on their utility. Debreu (1959) captures uncertainty by expanding the characteristics used to define consumption goods by making them state-contingent, where all possible future states of the world are defined by unique combinations of a set of environmental variables. Consumers choose future consumption bundles that are contingent upon the realization of a final state of the world. In effect, they pre-commit to trades in specified states, where uncertainty is resolved when the true state eventuates.[2] This is the state-preference approach to uncertainty that extends a standard certainty analysis by expanding the commodity space to include goods that are state-contingent. When consumers with common beliefs about the outcomes in each state of nature can trade goods in competitive frictionless markets in each time period, over time and between states of the world, the familiar Pareto optimality conditions apply.

In the Debreu model consumers trade a full set of contingent commodity contracts which are commitments to exchange goods in specified states at agreed terms of trade. To make it a straightforward extension of the certainty model summarized in Definition 2.3, consumers have conditional perfect foresight and correctly anticipate equilibrium outcomes in each state of the world. In particular, every consumer correctly predicts their income and all the commodity prices. The only uncertainty is about which state becomes the actual (or true) state. In this setting the number of forward commodity contracts must increase to N times the number of possible states of the world so that consumers can trade all N commodities in every state.[3] Arrow (1953) extends the Debreu model by including risky financial securities so that consumers can transfer income (and consumption) between states by bundling securities into portfolios. In the *Arrow–Debreu economy* there are no transactions costs, the capital market is complete, and traders are price-takers with conditional perfect foresight. That makes it fully equivalent to the *asset economy* with certainty, summarized earlier in Definition 2.4. In a complete capital market consumers can trade every commodity in every state, where, in the absence of taxes and other market distortions, they equate their marginal valuations for goods.

Uncertainty provides an explanation for the large number of different types of securities that trade in capital markets. Consumers bundle them together in portfolios to choose patterns of consumption expenditure over uncertain states of nature. Indeed, in a complete capital market there are enough securities for them to trade in every state and spread risk according to their preferences. Financial securities play two important roles in spreading risk. The first is to eliminate *diversifiable (individual) risk* from consumption expenditure, while the second is to transfer *non-diversifiable (market) risk* across consumers. Whenever production activities in the economy are less than perfectly correlated, some of the variability in their net cash flows can be eliminated by bundling the securities used to finance them inside well-diversified portfolios. Consumers also face *idiosyncratic* (or *individual*) *risk* in their consumption expenditure that can be diversified across the population. For example, a given proportion of consumers will suffer a car accident and be harmed by adverse weather conditions. By purchasing insurance they create pools of funds for paying claims made by those incurring losses. Whenever individual risk trades at actuarially fair prices it is costlessly eliminated from consumption, where non-diversifiable risk is the only risk that will cause asset prices to sell at a discount in a frictionless competitive capital market. This is a fundamental property of all the popular asset pricing models we look at in Chapter 4.[4]

Financial securities facilitate the efficient transfer of market risk to consumers with lower relative risk aversion and/or better information. A large proportion of aggregate investment is financed by shares and bonds that consumers hold either directly in their own security portfolios or indirectly in mutual funds that are portfolios created by financial intermediaries. Indeed, a range of derivative securities are created to eliminate diversifiable risk from consumption and trade market risk at lower cost. For example, there are futures contracts for most major commodities that allow producers to reduce their exposure to price uncertainty on their outputs and inputs. Aluminium, crude oil, petroleum, wheat, wool, rice, sugar and coffee are all examples of commodities with futures contracts. Buyers give sellers a commitment to pay a set price for the delivery of a specified quantity and quality of a commodity at a specified point in time. Options contracts give holders the right, but not the obligation, to trade commodities and financial securities at specified prices on or before a specified time. They are used to replicate existing securities and to trade market risk.

A major objective of finance research is to derive an asset pricing model where every consumer measures and prices risk in the same way. It is used by private traders to value risky projects and by agencies in the public sector to evaluate the effects of government policies. Many traders in financial markets are specialists who collect information about the net cash flows on capital assets to identify securities with prices that do not fully reflect their fundamentals. By selling securities with high prices (relative to their fundamentals), and buying securities with low prices, they make profits through arbitrage. When these profits are eliminated the *no arbitrage condition* holds so that security prices reflect all available information about their fundamentals. Pricing models are also used in project evaluation by private firms and public agencies. Private firms seek profitable investment opportunities, while government agencies examine policy changes and public projects that will raise social welfare. But these two objectives rarely coincide in economies with distorted markets due to, for example, taxes, externalities and non-competitive behaviour.[5]

In this chapter we examine the role of uncertainty and risk on equilibrium outcomes in private market economies – in particular, how it affects capital asset prices. Knight (1921) distinguished between risk and uncertainty by identifying risk as circumstances where consumers assign numerical probabilities to random events, and uncertainty as circumstances where they do not (or cannot) assign such probabilities. The analysis commences in Section 3.1 by looking at consumer preferences under uncertainty and risk, starting with the generalized state preferences employed in the Arrow–Debreu economy. We then consider the expected utility approach that separates probabilities from utility at each random event. This was initially formalized by von Neumann and Morgenstern (1944) using common (objective) probabilities with state-independent consumption preferences. A large literature generalizes their approach by allowing different (subjective) probabilities and/or state-dependent consumption preferences. Despite the appeal of these extensions, however, the *von Neumann–Morgenstern expected utility* (NMEU) function is much more widely used in economic analysis because of its simplicity. Finally we consider *mean–variance analysis* as a special case of the expected utility approach. This is used in the four asset pricing models examined later in Chapter 4.

In Section 3.1 we derive an asset pricing equation in the two-period state-preference model of Arrow and Debreu where consumers have *conditional perfect foresight* based on common beliefs about the state-contingent commodity prices. This is a certainty-equivalent analysis that naturally extends the asset pricing model derived in the two-period certainty economy with production in Section 2.2.4. The *Arrow–Debreu pricing model* accounts for uncertainty in asset prices without explicitly isolating the probabilities consumers assign to random events. We modify this model in Section 3.2 by adopting (NMEU) functions to separate probabilities assigned to random events from the utility consumers derive from their expenditure in each event. This allows us to derive the *consumption-based pricing model (CBPM)* where in equilibrium consumers have the same consumption risk in a frictionless competitive capital market. Thus, we can summarize it using the set of common factors that explain the risk in aggregate consumption. The four popular asset pricing models examined in Chapter 4 differ by the way they isolate these common factors.

3.1 State-preference theory

Debreu made a very important contribution to standard general equilibrium analysis under uncertainty by expanding the definition of commodities to make them event-contingent. It is generally referred to as the state-preference approach to uncertainty.

3.1.1 The (finite) state space

Savage (1954) provides widely accepted definitions for the basic concepts of the theory of choice under uncertainty in the state-preference model, where a *state* is a complete description of all relevant aspects of the world, a *true state* is the one that actually eventuates when the uncertainty is resolved, while an *event* is a set of states. We assume the set of possible state $\mathcal{S}:=\{1,\dots,S\}$ and the number of time periods T are finite.[6] At each time $t=0,1,\dots,T$ there is a partition $\mathcal{E}_t$ of the state space $\mathcal{S}$, whose elements are events that can occur at that time.[7] Each event is a subset of the states in $\mathcal{S}$ and is outside the control of consumers. Consumers face most uncertainty in the first period where partition $\mathcal{E}_0$ has one event containing all the possible states of nature that can eventuate in the last time period T; this is the coarsest partition of $\mathcal{S}$. In contrast, when the uncertainty is resolved at time T there are S events in partition $\mathscr{E}_T$; this is the finest partition of $\mathscr{S}$. We can summarize the properties of the state space as follows:

i $\mathscr{S}$ is exhaustive – it contains all possible states of the world.
ii All $s \in \mathscr{S}$ are mutually exclusive – the occurrence of one state rules out the occurrence of any other state.
iii Every state $s \in \mathscr{S}$ is independent of the actions of consumers – both as individuals or as coalitions.
iv All consumers agree on s and classify every state in the same way.
v All consumers agree on the true state of the world in period T.

By conditions (i) and (ii) the state space identifies every possible description of the environment in the second period where each state is unique. Since consumers cannot influence the environment by property (iii), phenomena such as global warming are ruled out.[8] Properties (iii) and (iv) allow consumers to make binding agreements with each other: (iv) lets them make commitments that are conditional on specified contingencies, while (v) makes them enforceable.

An example of an event tree for three time periods is illustrated in Figure 3.1. There is a single event in the first period that contains all eight possible states, $\mathscr{E}_0: = \{e_0\}$, with $e_0: = \{\mathscr{S}\}$. In the second period the states are partitioned into three separate events, where $\mathscr{E}_1: = \{e_1, e_2, e_3\}$, with $e_1:= \{s_1, s_2, s_3\}$, $e_2:= \{s_4, s_5\}$ and $e_2:= \{s_6, s_7, s_8\}$. When one of these events is realized as an actual outcome in the second period ($t = 1$) some of the uncertainty is resolved as it contains the true state of the world in the final period ($t = 2$). In the true state all the uncertainty is resolved, and we have $\mathscr{E}_2:= \{e_4, e_5, e_6, e_7, e_8, e_9, e_{10}, e_{11}\}$, with $e_4:= \{s_1\}$,

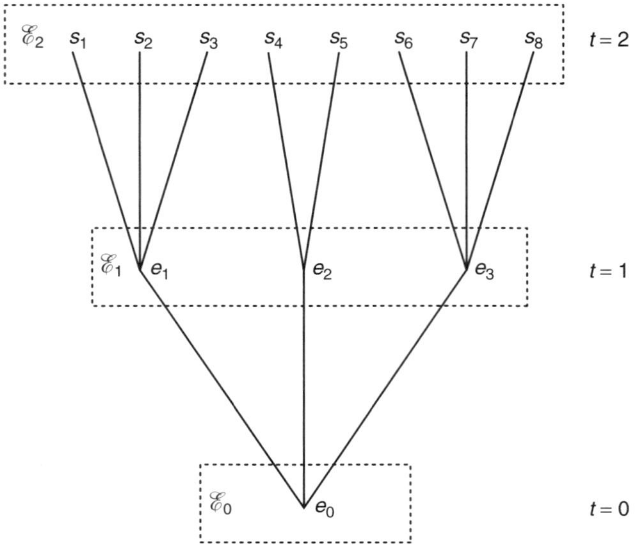

Figure 3.1 An event tree with three time periods.

$e_5 := \{s_2\}$, $e_6 := \{s_3\}$, $e_7 := \{s_4\}$, $e_8 := \{s_5\}$, $e_9 := \{s_6\}$, $e_{10} := \{s_7\}$, and $e_{11} := \{s_8\}$. Event-contingent goods are automatically located in time. Thus, in the presence of uncertainty they are defined by their physical attributes, their geographic location and by contingent events.

In a two-period analysis where uncertainty is completely resolved in the second period it makes more sense to define goods as state-contingent, rather than event-contingent, as the single event in $\mathscr{E}_0$ contains all the states, while there are as many events as states in $\mathscr{E}_1$. We adopt this terminology in the following analysis which is undertaken in a two-period setting. Consumer beliefs must clearly play an important role in determining equilibrium outcomes when there is uncertainty. With incomplete information they can have subjective probabilities that deviate from the *true* underlying objective probabilities. Further, consumers with different information can have different subjective probabilities.[9] It is clear from the event tree in Figure 3.1 that a considerable amount of information has to be processed to solve the event-contingent prices for each good, especially in the first period where all states are possible outcomes in the final period.

Each consumer must implicitly solve all the event-contingent commodity prices along each branch of the tree by computing the demands and supplies of every good in each state. In the following analysis we characterize equilibrium outcomes in the state-preference model when consumers have conditional perfect foresight.

Definition 3.1 (Conditional perfects foresight)

Consumers with conditional perfect foresight have common beliefs and correctly predict the commodity prices in each state of the world, with $p_s^h = p_s$ for all h.

If, in these circumstances, they can trade event-contingent claims for every commodity in every future time period the optimality conditions in a competitive equilibrium will have similar properties to those we are more familiar with in a certainty setting without taxes and trading costs. In particular, it will be a Pareto optimal allocation where consumers use the same event-contingent discount factors to value future consumption. In effect, they each make consumption choices for their entire life in the first period, and they do not expect to revise them in subsequent periods as the uncertainty is resolved.[10]

3.1.2 Debreu economy with contingent claims

The model of uncertainty in Chapter 7 of Debreu (1959) is for an economy where resources are privately owned and traded in competitive markets. There are no financial securities or money so consumers and producers instead exchange event-contingent claims to goods. These are *forward contracts* that specify the delivery of a unit of a commodity at a given location contingent on the occurrence of a specified event, with current prices determined by the event-contingent commodity prices. We initially restrict the analysis to two time periods and adapt the endowment economy in Section 2.2.3 by including production and expanding the commodity space to make goods state-contingent in the second period. In the first period each consumer ($h = 1, \dots, H$) now chooses a bundle of future consumption goods $x_s^h := \{x_s^h(1), \dots, x_s^h(N)\}$ that trade in competitive markets at expected future spot prices $p_s := \{p_s(1), \dots, p_s(N)\}$ in each state s. They do this to maximize a generalized utility function $u^h(x_0^h, x_1^h, \dots, x_s^h)$, where x_0^h is the current consumption bundle.[11] We assume consumers have conditional perfect foresight when they trade forward commodity contracts $f_s^h := \{f_s^h(1), \dots, f_s^h(N)\}$ at the state-contingent prices $p_{fs} := \{p_{fs}(1), \dots, p_{fs}(N)\}$, where $f_s(n) > 0$ is the amount of good n delivered to the consumer, and $f_s(n) < 0$ the amount sold, in state s.

Thus, the consumer problem in the Debreu economy with continent claims (omitting superscript h), can be summarized as

$$\max\left\{u(x_0, x_1, \dots, x_s)\left|\begin{array}{l} p_0x_0 - p_0\bar{x}_0 + \Sigma_s p_{fs} f_s - \eta_0 \le 0 \\ p_s x_s - p_s(\bar{x}_s + f_s) \le 0, \forall s \end{array}\right.\right\}, \tag{3.1}$$

where $\eta_0 := \{\eta_0^1, \dots, \eta_0^J\}$ are the profit shares in each of the J firms in the economy.[12]

In the previous chapter we saw how the consumer problem could be simplified when all goods are traded in frictionless markets in each time period. If consumers can also trade goods in every state, they will equalize their marginal utility of income in each time period and in each state. This allows us rewrite the problem in (3.1) as

$$\max\left\{v(I)\left|\begin{array}{l} X_0 - I_0 \le 0 \\ X_s - I_s \le 0, \forall s \end{array}\right.\right\},^{13} \tag{3.2}$$

where income $I := \{I_0, I_1, \dots, I_s\}$ is $I_0 \equiv \bar{X}_0 - F_0 + \eta_0$, with $F_0 = \Sigma_s p_{fs} f_s$, in the first period, and $I_s \equiv \bar{X}_s + F_s$ with $F_s = p_s f_s$, in each state in the second period. When forward contracts are traded optimally in frictionless competitive markets, they satisfy

$$p_{fs} = \varphi_s^h p_s \quad \forall s,^{14} \tag{3.3}$$

with $\varphi_s^h = \lambda_s^h / \lambda_0^h$ being the state-contingent discount factor used to value income in state s. It is the ratio of the constraint multipliers on the budget constraints in (3.2) which measure the marginal utility of future income in each state (with $\partial v^h / \partial I_s^h = \lambda_s^h$) relative to the marginal utility of current income (with $\partial v^h / \partial I_0^h = \lambda_0^h$).

Most asset pricing models in finance are derived in endowment economies where consumption risk is determined by endowment risk. Later in Chapter 8 we want to use the pricing models in project evaluation where production plays an important role in equilibrium outcomes. For that reason we include production, but simplify the analysis by ruling out private investment opportunities. Thus, all investment in the economy is undertaken by (j = 1, ... , J) firms who sell forward contracts $f_s^j := \{f_s^j(1), \dots, f_s^j(N)\}$ in the first period to fund expenditure on their inputs $z_0^j := \{z_0^j(1), \dots, z_0^j(N)\}$ which are used to produce the state-contingent $y_s^j := \{y_s^j(1), \dots, y_s^j(N)\}$. When they trade forward contracts, with $f_s^j(n) < 0$ for sales and $f_s^j(n) < 0$ for purchases of each good n in each state s, the problem for each firm in the two-period Debreu economy can be summarized (omitting superscript j) as

$$\max\left\{ \eta_0 = F_0 - Z_0 \,\middle|\, F_s - Y_1(Z_0) \le 0 \right\}, \tag{3.4}$$

where $F_0 = \Sigma_s p_{fs} f_s$ is revenue from selling futures contracts in the first period, $Z_0 = p_0 z_0$ expenditure on production inputs, $F_s = p_s f_s$ the market value of goods delivered on forward contracts in each state, and $Y_s = p_s y_s$ state-contingent sales revenue. While firms can produce multiple outputs using multiple inputs, we assume production sets are strictly convex. When forward contracts are traded optimally in frictionless competitive markets, they satisfy

$$p_{fs} = \varphi_s^j p_s \ \forall s. \quad (3.5)$$

where $\varphi_s^j = \lambda_s^j$ are the state-contingent discount factors used to value future income; they are the multiplier on the state-contingent payout constraints in (3.4).[15]

Both pricing models in (3.3) and (3.5) value forward contracts for each good by discounting their future spot prices, where all consumers and firms use the same discount factors in frictionless competitive markets, with $\varphi_s^h = \varphi_s^j = \varphi_s$ for all *h*, *j*. Thus, the equation for pricing forward contracts in the Debreu economy is:

$$p_{fs} = \varphi_s^j p_s \ \forall s. \quad (3.6)$$

Definition 3.2 The *Debreu economy with contingent claims* is described by (u, $\bar{x}$, $y(J)$), where u and $\bar{x}$ are, respectively, the vectors of utility functions and endowments for the H consumers, and $y(J)$ the vector of production technologies used by the J firms. In this economy where consumers have conditional perfect foresight a competitive equilibrium can be characterized by the vectors of relative commodity prices p_o and p_s^* for all s, and the vectors of forward contract prices p_{fs}^* for all s, such that:

i x_0^{h*}, f_s^{h*} and x_s^{h*} for all s, solves the consumer problem in (3.1) for all h;
ii z_0^{j*}, f_s^{j*} and y_s^{j*}, for all s, solves the producer problem in (3.4) for all j;
iii the goods markets clear at each $t \in \{0, 1\}$, with

$\Sigma_h \bar{x}_0^h(n) = \Sigma_h x_0^{h*}(n) + \Sigma_j z_0^{j*}(n)$ for all n and

$\Sigma_h \bar{x}_s^h(n) + \Sigma_j y_s^{j*} = \Sigma_h x_s^{h*}(n)$ for all n, s, and the forward market clears, with

$\Sigma_h f_s^{h*}(n) = \Sigma_j f_s^{j*}(n)$ for all n, s.

Since consumers with conditional perfect foresight agree on the future spot prices for the commodities they also use the same discount factors. But this unanimity breaks down when they have different information and form different expectations about the future spot prices.

3.1.3 Arrow–Debreu asset economy

Arrow (1953) extended the analysis of Debreu by introducing financial securities, but without formalizing their role by including trading costs. Since they are used to reduce the number of choice variables for consumers in the first period they are implicitly included to lower trading costs. This was noted earlier in the certainty analysis in Section 2.2.3, where instead of choosing the composition of their consumption bundles in the second period consumers chose the value of their consumption expenditure by trading a risk-free security. While there are more choice variables in the state-preference model where consumers determine expenditure in each state, the financial securities reduce the number of choice variables in the first period from at most $N(1 + S)$ in the Debreu economy to at most $N + S$ in the Arrow–Debreu economy.

The state-preference approach clarifies the role played by financial securities in spreading risk, where security demands are determined by preferences for patterns of consumption over the states of nature. As noted earlier, consumer preferences are determined by their beliefs about the likelihood of states, and the utility from consumption in them. These two components are separated later by using expected utility functions. Before doing so we derive an asset pricing equation in the Arrow–Debreu economy where consumers have the generalized state preferences in (3.1). This provides us with useful insights into the popular asset pricing models examined later in Chapter 4. In particular, it highlights the important role played by the restrictions they impose on consumer preferences and the distributions of the security returns.

In the asset economy ($k = 1, \ldots, K$) securities trade in a frictionless competitive capital market at prices $p_a := \{p_{a1}, \ldots, p_{ak}\}$. Consumers hold them in portfolios $a^h := \{a_1^h, \ldots, a_k^h\}$ with a current market value of $V_0^h = p_a a^h$, where $a_k^h > 0$ for units they purchase and $a_k^h < 0$ for units they sell.[16] These portfolios have state-contingent payouts, with $R_s^h = \sum_k a_k^h R_{ks}$, that determine the pattern of their future consumption expenditure which is illustrated in Figure 3.2 when consumers have no endowments in the second period. Thus, all their future consumption expenditure is funded from the security payouts.

When consumers have endowments in both periods we can write the budget constraints for the consumer problem in (3.2) as

$$\begin{aligned} I_0 &\equiv \bar{X}_0 - V_0 - \eta_0, \\ I_s &\equiv \bar{X}_s + R_s, \forall s, \end{aligned} \tag{3.7}$$

where $\eta_0 = V_0 - Z_0$ is profit in private firms which is paid to consumers as shareholders.[17] In the absence of trading constraints, optimally chosen security trades satisfy

$$\varphi^h R = p_a, \tag{3.8}$$

with φ^h being the $(1 \times S)$ row vector of state-contingent discount factors, R the $(S \times K)$ payout matrix and p_a the $(1 \times K)$ row vector of security prices.[18] The structure of the payout matrix R determines how much flexibility consumers have to choose their patterns of state-contingent consumption. In a complete capital market they can trade in every state of nature, which leads to the following definition.

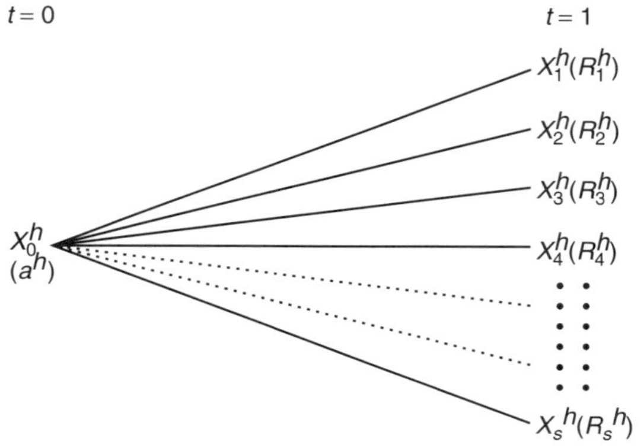

Figure 3.2 Commodity and financial flows in the Arrow–Debreu economy.

Definition 3.3 The *capital market is complete for consumers* when there are:

i as many linearly independent securities (K) as states of nature (S), with rank $[R] = S$; and
ii no constraints on consumer security trades.

Consider the following payout matrix for a full set of *conventional securities*, which have payouts in more than one state, in a three-state world:

$$R = \begin{matrix} & R_1 & R_2 & R_3 \\ s_1 & 1 & 0 & 1 \\ s_2 & 1 & 1 & 1 \\ s_3 & 0 & 1 & 1 \end{matrix}.$$

Securities 1 and 2 are risky, while security 3 is risk-free.[19] In a complete capital market consumers can create a full set of *primitive (Arrow) securities* with payouts in a single state of nature, where the payout matrix becomes

$$R^p = \begin{matrix} & R_1^p & R_2^p & R_3^p \\ s_1 & 1 & 0 & 0 \\ s_2 & 0 & 1 & 0 \\ s_3 & 0 & 0 & 1 \end{matrix}.$$

They are created by bundling conventional securities into portfolios, where R_1^p is obtained by purchasing a unit of conventional asset 3 and selling a unit of conventional asset 2, R_2^p by purchasing a unit each of conventional assets 1 and 2 and selling a unit of conventional asset 3, and R_3^p by purchasing a unit of conventional asset 3 and selling a unit of conventional asset 1.[20] Clearly, the two conditions in Definition 3.3 must hold for the capital market to be complete for consumers. They cannot trade in every state, even with a full set of linearly independent securities, when there are constraints on their security trades – in particular, short selling constraints that restrict borrowing.

In a complete capital market (where R is non-singular) price-taking consumers equate their discount factors in (3.8), with

$$\varphi = \varphi^h = p_k R^{-1}, \forall h,$$

where R^{-1} is the inverse of the payoff matrix. In an *incomplete capital market* they can have different state-contingent discount factors. Most formal analysis with incomplete markets provides no explicit reason for the absence of a full set of linearly independent securities. It is normally assumed, often implicitly, there are trading costs or consumers face borrowing constraints. It is important to model the incompleteness endogenously because it affects equilibrium outcomes, particularly with respect to their welfare effects. And we cannot automatically conclude there is market failure when transactions costs make the capital market incomplete. If they are minimum necessary costs of trade the equilibrium outcome is (Pareto) efficient when traders are price-takers. Any traders with a transactions cost advantage can supply securities with new patterns of returns across the states, and this gives them market power that can violate the competition assumption.

All investment in the Arrow–Debreu economy is undertaken by ($j = 1, \dots, J$) private firms who trade portfolios of financial securities $a^j := (a_1^j, \dots, a_k^j)$ in the first period with a market value of $V_0^j = p_a a^j$ to fund their input purchases (Z_0^j), with $a_k^j > 0$ units sold and $a_k^j < 0$ for units purchased. In the second period they make state-contingent payouts to securities (R_{ks}) from their net cash flows (Y_s^j), where the problem for each firm, is

$$\max\left\{\eta_0^j = V_0^j - Z_0^j \;\middle|\; V_s^j - Y_s^j(Z_0^j) \le 0, \forall s\right\}, \tag{3.9}$$

using $V_s^j = \Sigma_k a_k^j R_{ks}$ to denote the value of the security payouts in state s. In the absence of trading constraints their optimally chosen security trades satisfy

$$\varphi^j R = p_a, \tag{3.10}$$

with φ^j being the ($1 \times S$) row vector of state-contingent discount rates. In the following analysis firms (or their agents, financial intermediaries) trade securities to exploit any expected profits. This activity is especially important for the *no arbitrage condition* in models with taxes on security returns where consumers face borrowing constraints to restrict tax arbitrage.[21]

Definition 3.4 The *capital market is complete for firms* when there are:
i as many linearly independent securities (K) as states of nature (S), with rank $[R] = S$; and
ii no constraints on firm security trades.

In a complete capital market price-taking firms equate their state-contingent discount rates in (3.10):

$$\varphi = \varphi^j = p_a R^{-1}, \forall j.$$

When consumers and firms trade in frictionless competitive markets, we have the following definition:[22]

Definition 3.5 The *Arrow–Debreu asset economy* is described by $(u, \bar{x}, y(J), R)$,where R is the $S \times K$ payout matrix for a completed capital market (with rank $(R) = S$). In this economy, where consumers have conditional perfect foresight, a competitive equilibrium can be characterized by vectors of security prices p_a^*, commodity prices in the first period p_0^* and state-contingent commodity prices p_s^* such that:

i a^h x_0^{h*} and x_s^{h*}, for all s, solve the consumer problem in (3.2) with income defined in (3.7) for all h;

ii a^{j*}, z_0^{j*} and y_s^{j*}, for all s, solve the firm problem in (3.10) for all j;

iii the capital market clears, with $\Sigma_h a_k^{h*} = \Sigma_j a_k^{j*}$ for all k, and the goods market clear, with $\Sigma_h \bar{x}_0^h = \Sigma_h x_0^{h*} + \Sigma_j z_0^{j*}$ and $\Sigma_h \bar{x}_s^h + \Sigma_j y_s^{j*} = \Sigma_h x_s^{h*}$ for all s.

With more than two time periods the state-contingent variables are made event-contingent, where each event is a subset of the state space that identifies variables in a specified time period.

This is the same as the real equilibrium outcome in the Debreu economy in Definition 2.3 due to the absence of trading costs. They are different when trading costs are included and financial securities and forward contracts have different impacts on them. Indeed, there are circumstances where forward contracts and financial securities will both trade. To simplify the analysis we follow standard practice and rule out that possibility by excluding trading costs and forward contracts. When consumers and firms face the same payoff matrix R and vector of security prices they use the same discount factors in their pricing models in (3.8) and (3.10), respectively, with

$$\varphi = \varphi^h = \varphi^j = p_a R^{-1} \quad \forall h, j.$$

This leads to the *Arrow–Debreu pricing model* (ADPM),

$$\varphi R = P_a \ \forall\ h, j, \tag{3.11}$$

where the vector of discount factors (φ) are prices of the primitive (Arrow) securities.This is confirmed by using the payout matrix for a full set of primitive securities, where R^p is the identify matrix. For three states it is

$$R^p = I = \begin{matrix} & R_1^p & R_2^p & R_3^p \\ s_1 \\ s_2 \\ s_3 \end{matrix} \begin{bmatrix} 1 & 0 & 0 \\ 0 & 1 & 0 \\ 0 & 0 & 1 \end{bmatrix}.$$

Thus, by using (3.11), we have $\varphi = p_a^p$.

Box 3.1 Obtaining primitive (Arrow) prices from traded security prices

Three securities have the following market prices for the payouts in three possible states of nature:

Security	*Current Price ($)*	*Payouts ($)* *State 1*	*State 2*	*State 3*
ADL Share	12	0	15	30
Intec Share	21	60	0	20
Govt. Bond	19	20	20	20

Since the payouts to these securities are linearly independent (which means none of the securities can be replicated by combining the other two in a portfolio) we can solve the primitive (Arrow) prices using the following system of equations:

$$12 = \varphi_2\, 15 + \varphi_3\, 30$$

$$21 = \varphi_1\, 60 + \varphi_3\, 20$$

$$19 = \varphi_1\, 20 + \varphi_2\, 20 + \varphi_3\, 20$$

where $\varphi = \{0.3, 0.5, 0.15\}$. The risk-free interest rate can be obtained by pricing a risk-free bond that pays one dollar in every state, with $p_B = \Sigma_s\, \varphi_s = 0.95 = 1/(1 + i)$, where $i = 0.05$. The ADPM is not used in practice because the number of states is potentially large, and that makes them difficult to identify, particularly in a multi-period setting. The popular pricing models in finance proceed by adopting expected utility functions to decompose the state probabilities and discount factors embedded in the Arrow prices. We do this in following sections.

Arbitrage plays an important role in this model because it equates the prices of assets with the same state-contingent payouts. Thus, there are no arbitrage profits in a frictionless competitive capital market equilibrium, which leads to the following theorem.

Theorem 3.1 The *no arbitrage condition* holds in a competitive capital market described by (R, p_a) if and only if $\varphi R = p_a$ for $\varphi >> 0$.
Proof. Any arbitrage portofolio a^A (containing non-trivial elements and requiring no initial net wealth) with $Ra^A = 0$ must have a market value of:

$$p_a a^A = (\varphi R)\, a^A = \varphi(Ra^A) = 0. \qquad \square$$

It is important to understand what competition means in a state-preference model. Security trades by price-taking consumers and firms cannot change the risk-spreading opportunities available to the capital market. In other words, they cannot supply new securities as perfect substitutes can be created by bundling together existing traded securities. Formally, for any new security m, there exists a derivative security (d) such that $R_m = R_d = \sum_{k \neq m} a_k R_k$ where R_m is the column vector of state-contingent payoffs in R for security m, and R_d the vector of state-contingent payoffs from combining other traded assets $k \neq m$ in R.

It is straightforward to see how this condition holds in a frictionless complete capital market when consumers have common beliefs about the state-contingent commodity prices and state-contingent security returns. It is a much stronger requirement, however, when the capital market is incomplete. If trade is not possible in some states due to trading costs, no one will create new trading opportunities when traders face the same costs. Traders capable of creating new risk-spreading opportunities must have a cost advantage. For example, some firms may have production technologies that allow them to trade at lower cost in some states through their investment choices.[23] Before we can properly solve an equilibrium with an incomplete capital market it is important to specify the reasons why the incompleteness occurs in the first place. And this is particularly important for making any assessment about the welfare properties of the equilibrium outcome.

As a way to demonstrate the role of the no arbitrage condition, consider the arbitrage portfolio which combines security m with its perfect substitute (d), where the problem for the arbitrageur (A) is

$$\max\left\{\eta_0^A = \varphi a_m^A R_m + \varphi a_d^A R_d \;\middle|\; p_{am} a_m^A + p_{ad} a_d^A = 0\right\}. \tag{3.12}$$

Using the first-order conditions for this problem, we have $R_m/R_d = p_{am}/p_{ad}$. The role of arbitrage is illustrated in Figure 3.3 where the budget constraint passes through the origin because the portfolio is self-funding. The dashed iso-profit lines isolate combinations of security holdings with the same profit. There are profits from going long in security m and short in security d when the relative payouts on security m exceed its relative price, with $p_{am}/p_{ad} > R_m/R_d$. The portfolio C generates profit η^{AC}, but it is not an equilibrium unless constraints stop further trades. In fact, the demand for security m is unbounded whenever $p_{am}/p_{ad} > R_m/R_d$, while the reverse applies when $p_{am}/p_{ad} < R_m/R_d$. This arbitrage activity eliminates any profit by mapping the iso-profit lines onto the budget constraint, where in equilibrium $p_{am}/p_{ad} = R_m/R_d$.

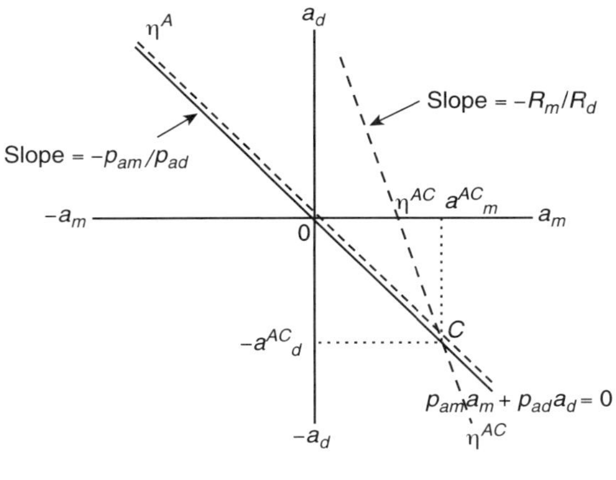

Figure 3.3 The no arbitrage condition.

3.2 Consumer preferences

The flow chart in Figure 3.4 provides a schematic summary of the relationship between the different preference mappings over uncertain consumption expenditure used in finance applications. In the following analysis we adopt the convention of placing a tilde (~) over random variables, where $\tilde{I}$ takes values from the set of state-contingent incomes, with $\tilde{I} = I_s$ for s ∈ $\mathcal{S}$. When objective probabilities (π_s) are assigned to states of nature the expectations operator is denoted $E(\cdot)$, while it is denoted $E^h(\cdot)$ for subjective probabilities (π_s^h), with $\Sigma_s \pi_s = 1$ and $\Sigma_s \pi_s^h = 1$ for all h, respectively. Similarly, state-independent preferences are denoted by utility function $U(\tilde{I})$, and state-dependent preferences by the function $U(\tilde{I}, s)$.[24]

In its most general form the Arrow–Debreu model employs *generalized state preferences*. These are preference mappings over the expanded commodity space where goods are characterised by type, location, time and event. But they do not separate probability distributions over states from the utility consumers derive in those states. In many applications it is useful to isolate the probability assessments made by consumers, where the most familiar approach uses the *von Neumann–Morgenstern expected utility* function (von Neumann and Morgenstern 1944). It weights the utility consumers derive in each state by its probability and then sums them over states, where the objectively determined probabilities are common to consumers and the utility functional is state-independent. All the popular pricing models examined in Chapter 4 adopt these preferences.

Savage (1954) extends the von Neumann–Morgenstern analysis by allowing consumers with different information to have different subjective probabilities. More recent work has moved away from the expected utility approach – for example, Machina (1982) relaxes the independence axiom – while others extend the expected utility approach – Mas-Colell *et al.* (1995) adopt state-dependent preferences with objective probabilities, while Karni (1985) adopts state-dependent preferences with subjective probabilities. Most of these extensions are subject to criticisms about the unrealistic nature of one or more of the axioms upon which they are based.[25] This is a reflection of how difficult it is to isolate subjectively assigned probabilities, particularly when the utility functions are state-dependent.

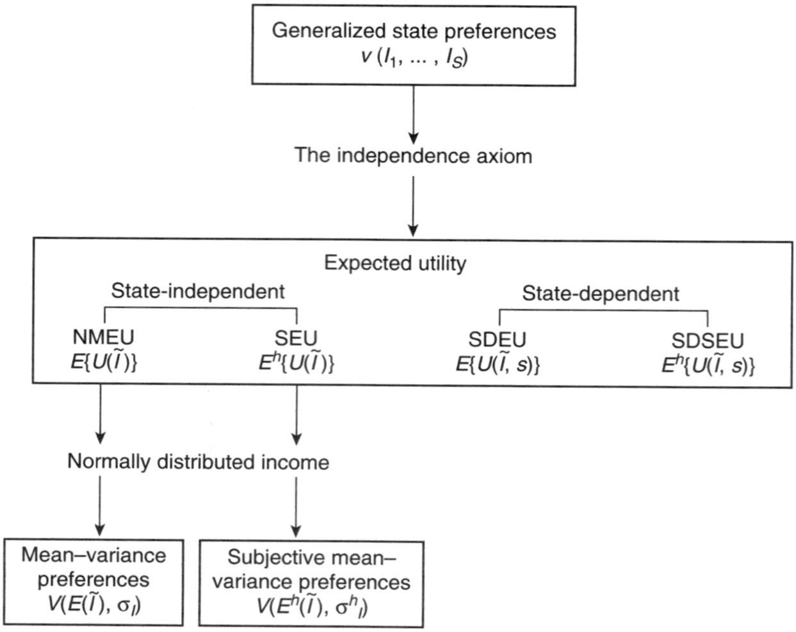

Figure 3.4 Consumer preferences with uncertainty and risk.

This separation is very useful because it identifies the important role of information when people form their probability beliefs, and different subjective probabilities result from consumers having different information. A lot of economic activity in financial markets involves gathering and trading information, where traders with different costs of obtaining information are likely to have different probability beliefs.

As noted earlier, the generalized state-preference function $v(\tilde{I})$ does not separate probabilities from utility over consumption expenditure in each state. It is based on the same minimal restrictions imposed on preferences in a certainty setting, where rankings over consumption bundles should be complete, transitive and continuous. Any risk assessment is embedded inside the generalized function itself. By adopting the *independence axiom*, which leaves preferences over any two random events unaffected by combining each of them with a common third event, we can measure consumer preference rankings using expected utility functions that separate the probabilities from utility over consumption expenditure. Also, when consumers assign objective probabilities to states and use state-independent utility functions to measure consumption benefits they have NMEU functions, denoted $E\{U(\tilde{I})\}$. Thus, any preferences they have for patterns of consumption expenditure over uncertain states are determined by the statistical properties of the probability density function.

While this utility function seems entirely appropriate for evaluating payoffs to lotteries which have objective probabilities that can be readily computed by consumers, like those associated with *roulette-wheel* type lotteries, it may not be suitable for evaluating consumption bundles that are contingent on random states of nature, like those associated with *horse-race* type lotteries.[26] Since states of nature are determined by combinations of a potentially large number of exogenously determined environmental variables, it seems more appropriate that consumers will assign subjective probabilities to them. In contrast, they can assign objective probabilities to random outcomes generated by roulette-wheel type lotteries because less information is needed and it is more accessible.

It seems reasonably clear from the way the NMEU function is derived that it focuses on individual risk from roulette-wheel type lotteries without recognizing (at least explicitly) the aggregate uncertainty from states of nature. For most individual risk there is good information about the probabilities of payouts, and when it is the only source of income uncertainty NMEU seems appropriate. But income is also subject to aggregate uncertainty about the states of nature, where consumers are much more likely to assign different probabilities to states, particularly when they have different information because it is costly to obtain.[27] Savage (1954) and Anscombe and Aumann (1963) recognize this by deriving the *subjective expected utility (SEU)* function $E^h\{U(\tilde{I})\}$. This assigns subjective probabilities to states of nature and uses a state-independent utility function to assess the benefits from consumption expenditure. Additional behavioural postulates are required for this function, which include the *sure-thing principle* that extends the independence axiom to state-contingent outcomes, and conditions to describe the way consumers form their probability beliefs.[28] This is a particularly useful extension because it isolates the role of costly information when consumers assign probabilities to states.

Subsequent work has argued that the SEU function should in fact be state-dependent because the same consumption bundle in one state may not generate the same benefits in another state. For example, consumers are unlikely to get the same benefits from a bundle of food in a state where they are healthy as they would get from the same bundle in a state where they are sick. Mas-Colell *et al.* (1995) respond to this problem by deriving a *state-dependent expected utility* function. They extend the NMEU function with objective probabilities by allowing state-dependent preferences, while Drèze (1987), Fishburn (1974), Grant and Karni (2004), Karni (1993) and Karni *et al.* (1983) derive *state-dependent subjective expected utility* functions. Unfortunately they all have drawbacks that result from their different behavioural postulates. For example, Drèze gives consumers the ability to determine states, while Fishburn has consumers making comparisons between mutually exclusive outcomes. It is a very difficult task to separate subjective probabilities from state-dependent preferences, a point that is perhaps best appreciated by noting that the expected utility function in these circumstances is $\sum_s \pi_s^h U(I_s, s)$. If consumers have the same probabilities we can identify the role of their state-dependent preferences by evaluating expected utility with constant consumption (which is where the consumption bundle is the same in every state). Alternatively, when they have state-independent preferences we can identify their subjective state probabilities by doing the same thing. But when they have subjective probabilities and state-dependent preferences it is not possible to separate them without placing additional restrictions on preferences.

A further extension to NMEU defines consumer preferences over the mean and variance in their consumption expenditure using the indirect utility function $V(\cdot)$. Many applications in economics adopt this approach to simplify the analysis. For example, all the asset pricing models examined in Chapter 4 use mean–variance analysis. Later in Section 3.3.3 we show there are two ways of justifying this approach – one assigns quadratic preferences to consumers, while the other requires consumption expenditure to be a normally distributed random variable. If consumers also assign objective probabilities to states of nature they have the mean–variance function $V(E(\tilde{I}), \sigma_1)$, where $E(\tilde{I})$ is expected consumption expenditure and σ_I its standard deviation, while they have the subjective mean–variance function $V(E^h(\tilde{I}),\sigma_I^h)$ when they assign subjective probabilities to states.

Box 3.2 Anecdotal evidence of state-dependent preferences

Aumann provides Savage with the example of a man whose sick wife has a 50 per cent chance of surviving an operation she must undergo. He is offered a choice between betting $100 dollars that she will survive the operation and betting the same amount on heads in the toss of a fair coin. It is argued that he will likely choose the bet on the operation if he loves his wife, because in the event that she dies he could win $100 on the coin toss when it is worth very much less to him. Aumann argues this is an example of a situation where the value is state-dependent. Savage responds by arguing it can be accommodated in a model with SEU when preferences are state-independent by making the full set of consequences from the lotteries available in every state. But that would require making comparisons between incompatible outcomes where, in the example provided by Aumann, one outcome has the man winning $100 dollars and his wife dies in a state where she survives the operation. These exchanges between Aumann and Savage are published in Drèze (1987).

3.2.1 Von Neumann–Morgenstern expected utility

Most empirical applications in finance adopt NMEU functions because they simplify uncertainty analysis considerably. Consumers with state-independent preferences choose patterns of consumption across states based on their risk aversion, relative commodity prices and the state probabilities. And by trading in a frictionless competitive capital market with common probabilities they have the same growth rates in marginal utility over time. That means consumers will face the same consumption risk, which is why the popular consumption-based pricing models we examine in Chapter 4 are functions of factors that determine aggregate consumption risk. But NMEU has obvious limitations – in particular, state-independent preferences may not be appropriate in such applications as the economics of health care insurance.[29] Once we relax state-independence and/or common objective probabilities consumers can face different consumption risk where the asset pricing equations are functions of a much larger number of factors. The behavioural postulates for the NMEU preferences are summarized as follows:

i The *standard preference relation* ($\succcurlyeq$) applies to rankings of consumption bundles (in the $(1 + S)$-dimensional commodity space), where $\succcurlyeq$ is complete, transitive and continuous.
ii The *independence axiom* holds – so that common alternatives within each state are irrelevant when ranking money payoffs to lotteries. For example, the preference ranking over two lotteries L and L' will not be changed by combining them both with a third lottery L''. Thus, if $L \succcurlyeq L'$ then $[(1 - \pi'')L + \pi''L''] \succcurlyeq [(1 - \pi'')L' + \pi''L'']$ when the independence axiom holds.
iii The preference relation $\succcurlyeq$ is *state-independent.*
iv Consumers assign *objective probabilities* to lotteries and states.

There is evidence from behavioural experiments that the independence axiom is violated in practice. The most widely cited example is referred to as the *Allais paradox* (Allais 1953) which finds people ranking the lotteries summarized in Table 3.1 in a manner that is inconsistent with the independence axiom. Most people choose A over B and C over D, but when the independence axiom holds D is preferred to C (whenever A is preferred to B).

Table 3.1 Lottery choices: the Allais paradox

	Probability of \$5m	*Probability of \$1m*	*Probability of \$0*
A	0	1.0	0
B	0.1	0.89	0.01
C	0.1	0	0.9
D	0	0.11	0.89

Empirical tests of the consumption-based pricing models suggest the state-independence assumption may also be violated in practice. Experimental studies find evidence of consumers placing more weight on bad outcomes than they do on good outcomes. Benartzi and Thaler (1995) and Barberis *et al.* (2001) model this as loss aversion for consumers with state-independent preferences, but it may in fact be evidence that they have state-dependent preferences. Indeed, even anecdotal evidence suggests that a significant proportion of consumption benefits do depend on states of nature, particularly with respect to personal health, but also the prevailing weather conditions.

There is also evidence that consumers assign different subjective probabilities to states of nature due to differences in their information sets. Traders in financial markets gather information about the fundamental determinants of the future payouts to securities. By specialising in particular types of securities they get information at lower cost and make profits – at least until the information is reflected in security prices. When the efficient markets hypothesis holds in its strongest form, security prices reflect all past and current information as well as security prices in past periods. But there is evidence that profits can be made from systematic trading rules. For example, there is a *weekend effect* where security prices fall over weekends when markets are closed, a *January effect* in the US where security prices are systematically higher at the beginning of the month, a *small-firm effect* where firms with relatively low market values paid higher rates of return on average than the entire stock market index over the period between 1960 and 1985, and a *closed end fund effect* where the value of mutual funds that bundle together a fixed number of shares trade at lower valuations than the sum of the market valuations of their shares.

Despite these concerns about the NMEU approach to measuring consumer preferences in the presence of uncertainty and risk, it is widely used in economic analysis. With multiple time periods most analysts make the expected utility function time-separable with a constant subjective discount factor (δ), where, for an infinitely lived agent, we have:

$$EU_t = E_t \sum_{j=0}^{\infty} \delta^j \left\{ U(\tilde{I}_{t+j}) \right\},^{30} \tag{3.13}$$

with $0 < \delta \leq 1$ being a measure of impatience for future consumption expenditure which is determined by the rate of time preference (ρ), with $\delta = 1/(1 + \rho)$.

As noted earlier, consumers who can trade in every state of nature will, in the absence of trading costs or other market frictions, have the same expected growth rate in their marginal utilities and, as a consequence, face the same consumption risk. For that reason they measure risk in securities by their contribution to aggregate consumption risk. This is demonstrated in Section 3.3 below by using NMEU to derive the *consumption-based pricing model (CBPM)* from the ADPM in (3.11).

3.2.2 Measuring risk aversion

Risk aversion plays a key role in determining the equilibrium risk premium in security returns, and there is evidence that it changes with wealth; consumers with relatively more wealth are likely to be marginally less risk-averse. In project evaluation analysts include a risk premium in discount factors on risky net cash flows, and the task is less complex when consumers measure and price risk in the same way. In effect, risk aversion measures the degree of concavity in the utility function over uncertain consumption expenditure. An example is shown in Figure 3.5 where income can vary between I_1 and I_2 with probabilities π_1 and π_2, respectively. To simplify the analysis we assume there is one future time period. With state-independent preferences we can map utility from consumption in each state using the function $U(\tilde{I})$, where the loss in utility from facing the variance in income is $U(\bar{I}) - EU(\tilde{I})$ for $\bar{I} = E(\tilde{I})$. In monetary terms the consumer is prepared to forgo income $RP(\bar{I}) = \bar{I} - \hat{I}$ to receive $\hat{I}$ with certainty. Clearly, this difference rises with the degree of concavity of the utility function.

Arrow (1971) and Pratt (1964) define a number of widely used measures of risk aversion. The first of them is:

Definition 3.6 The *coefficient of absolute risk aversion* (ARA) measures the curvature of the utility function as

$$ARA := -\frac{U''(I)}{U'(I)} \tag{3.14}$$

For a strictly concave utility function, such as the one illustrated in Figure 3.5, a negative second derivative makes ARA positive. One way of isolating this measure of risk aversion is to take a second-order Taylor series expansion around $\bar{I}$ for the relationship that defines the risk premium (*RP*) in Figure 3.5, where $EU(\tilde{I}) = U[\bar{I} - RP(\bar{I})]$, as

$$RP(\bar{I}) = -\frac{1}{2}\sigma_I^2 \frac{U''(\bar{I})}{U'(\bar{I})} = \frac{1}{2}\sigma_I^2 ARA.$$ [31]

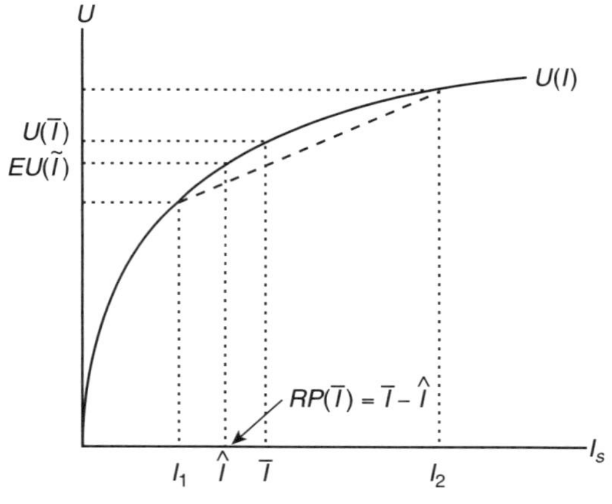

Figure 3.5 Consumption with expected utility and objective probabilities.

The utility function exhibits *constant absolute risk aversion* when ARA is independent of the level of income, it exhibits *decreasing absolute risk aversion* (DARA) when ARA declines with income, and *increasing absolute risk aversion* (IARA) when ARA rises with income. DARA has some intuitive appeal because consumers with relatively high incomes (and wealth) are less averse to risk at the margin. When ARA declines as income rises the utility function becomes less concave because U'' falls more than does U'.

Perhaps the most widely used measure of risk aversion is the following:

Definition 3.7 The *cofficient of relative risk aversion* (RRA) is a normalization of ARA that accounts for the initial value of consumption:

$$RRA: = -\frac{U''(I)}{U'(I)}I. \tag{3.15}$$

It is obtained as the coefficient on the variance in the proportional, rather than absolute, change in consumption expenditure.[32] Anecdotal evidence suggests consumers with higher income (and wealth) have a lower ARA. But this may well be consistent with all consumers having the same RRA. Indeed, there are empirical studies that find support for preferences with a *constant coefficient of relative risk aversion* (CRRA). Alternatively they could have *decreasing relative risk aversion* (DRRA) or *increasing relative risk aversion* (IRRA), as none are ruled out by the conventional restrictions imposed on preferences in consumer theory. It is ultimately an empirical question what values ARA and RRA take for consumers, and whether they rise or fall with wealth.

There is more empirical support for DARA than there is for DRRA. Barsky *et al.* (1997) used survey data to find that RRA rises and then falls with wealth, while Guiso and Paiella (2001) used survey data to find that DARA and IRRA. Experimental studies by Gordon *et al.* (1972), Binswanger (1981) and Quizon *et al.* (1984) found support for IRRA because the fraction of wealth consumers invest in risky securities declines with their wealth, contrary to US household data where the fraction of wealth consumers invest in risky securities increases as their wealth increases. Peress (2004) includes costly information to explain these conflicting observations, where increasing returns to information acquisition are large enough to overturn the tendency for consumer portfolio shares to decrease with wealth. Estimates of the value of the coefficient of RRA range from near 0 to 2. For example, Friend and Blume (1975) obtain an estimate from US household data around 2, and Fullenkamp *et al.* (2003) use data from a television game show with large amounts of money at stake and find a value in the range from 0.6 to 1.5.

3.2.3 Mean–variance preferences

Most consumption-based pricing models are derived using mean–variance analysis where preferences for future consumption can be completely described by the first two moments of the probability distribution over state-contingent outcomes. This occurs when consumption expenditure is normally distributed, or when consumers have mean–variance preferences.[33] Either way, the utility functions must be state-independent for consumers to care only about the statistical distribution of their future consumption. Any preference they have for consuming in one state over another is determined solely by their probabilities, where the one with higher probability is preferred. A mean–variance analysis adopts one of the two state-independent utility functions in Figure 3.4, where expected income with objective probabilities is defined as $E(\tilde{I})=\Sigma_s \pi_s I_s$, and with subjective probabilities as $E^h(\tilde{I})=\Sigma_s \pi_s^h I_s$, while the variance in income is defined as $\sigma_I = E[\tilde{I}-E(\tilde{I})]^2$ and $\sigma_I^h = E^h[\tilde{I}-E^h(\tilde{I})]^2$, respectively.

3.2.4 Martingale prices

Traders in financial markets form expectations about the economic returns to securities that can be paid as a combination of capital gains and cash distributions. By exploiting any profits they invoke the no arbitrage condition on security returns. This activity highlights the important role of information, where traders compute the statistical properties of the net revenues generated by underlying real assets from which security returns are paid. The income paid to shareholders ultimately comes from production activities by the firms who issue shares, and investors gather information about these activities as well as any other conditions that will affect the economic income they generate. Traders who can acquire and process information more efficiently can make profits by finding assets with the same risk paying different expected returns. This arbitrage activity, if unrestricted, will feed private information into current security prices until assets with the same risk pay the same expected returns in a competitive equilibrium. Unless traders have more information than does the market (which is the public information reflected in current security prices) they cannot expect to make profits from trading securities. In particular, no trading rule can outperform a buy and hold strategy when the no arbitrage condition holds.

Loosely speaking, this is referred to as the *efficient markets hypothesis*. Fama (1970) argued the capital market is efficient when the information of traders is included in security prices, and identified three different versions of efficiency based on three different information sets: a weak form of efficiency when information is based on past prices; a semi-strong form of efficiency when the information is past prices plus publicly available information; and a strong form of efficiency when the information also includes insider information. There is considerable interest in finding an economic model of asset pricing that is consistent with the efficient markets hypothesis.[34] Samuelson (1965) did this using a *martingale model*, where random variable x_t is a martingale with respect to an information set ω_t if it has $E(x_{t+1}|\omega_t) = x_t$, with $E(\cdot)$ being the expectations operator. By a process of iteration the expected future values of the variable are the same as its current value. Samuelson argued security prices will be a discounted martingale if consumers are risk-neutral. Basically, the prices of securities paying only capital gains must rise at the risk-free interest rate when the no arbitrage condition holds for risk-neural consumers. And that makes discounted future prices equal to current prices.[35]

The martingale model can be demonstrated by writing the state-contingent discounts factors in (3.11) as $\varphi_s = 1/(1 + i_s)$ for all s. When consumers are risk-neutral these discount factors become $\varphi_s = \pi_s/(1 + i)$ for all s, where $1/(1 + i)$ is the price of a risk-free bond, with $\Sigma_s\varphi_s = 1/(1 + i)$. Moreover, when payouts in R are security prices (without dividend payments), with $R_{ks} = p_{aks}$ for all k, s, the ADPM in (3.11) can be decomposed as:

$$\frac{E(\tilde{p}_{ak})}{1+i} = \sum_s \frac{\pi_s p_{aks}}{1+i} = p_{ak} \forall k.$$

Prices deviate from this discounted martingale model when consumers are risk-averse as their discount factors are a combination of risk preferences and probability assessments about the states. Ross (1977a) showed that we can always derive a normalized expectations operator that makes security prices discounted martingales. This is achieved by normalizing the vector of state-contingent discount rates, which are prices of primitive (Arrow) securities, as $\pi_s^* = \varphi_s/\Sigma_s\varphi_s$ for all s, where $\Sigma_s\varphi_s = 1/(1+i)$ is the price of the risk-free bond that pays one unit of the numeraire good in every state. These normalized prices have the same property as probabilities, with $\Sigma_s\pi_s^* = 1$ but they are not strictly probabilities, unless consumers are risk-neutral. For risk-averse consumers the normalized Arrow prices are combinations of subjective probability assessments about the likelihood of states and their preferences for transferring income between states and the current period. By using these normalized prices as the expectations operator we can rewrite the ADPM in (3.11) as:

$$\frac{\pi^* R}{1+i} = p_a,$$

with $\pi^* := (\pi_1^*, \ldots, \pi_S^*)$. Clearly, when the payouts in R are security prices, we have $E^*(R_k)/(1+i) = \pi^* R_k/(1+i) = p_{ak}$ for all k, using the normalized expectations operator $E^*(\cdot)$ with normalized Arrow prices as probabilities. Thus, security prices are discounted martingales based on the normalized expectations operator. These normalized Arrow prices are frequently referred to as risk-neutral probabilities because they play the same role as probabilities when security payoffs are discounted using the risk-free return. Indeed, when consumers are risk-neutral the normalized Arrow prices are probabilities, with $\pi_s^* \neq \pi_s$ for all s, but when they are risk-averse the normalized prices contain a risk premium, and $\pi_s^* \neq \pi_s$ for all s.

Box 3.3 Obtaining martingale prices from traded security prices

As a way to illustrate how the (discounted) martingale pricing model is used to value capital assets, we derive a normalized expectations operator by dividing the primitive (Arrow) prices in Box 3.1 by their sum ($\Sigma_s\phi_s = 1/(1+i) = 0.95$), where

$$\pi^* \approx \{0.32, 0.52, 0.16\}.$$

These normalized prices are used to value the payouts on capital assets when they are discounted by the risk-free interest rate. For the three traded securities in Box 3.1, we have

$$p_{\text{ADL share}} = \frac{0.52 \times 15}{1+i} + \frac{0.16 \times 30}{1+i} \approx 12;$$

$$p_{\text{Intec share}} = \frac{0.32 \times 60}{1+i} + \frac{0.16 \times 20}{1+i} \approx 21;$$

$$p_{\text{Govt. Bond}} = \frac{0.32 \times 20}{1+i} + \frac{0.52 \times 20}{1+i} + \frac{0.16 \times 20}{1+i} \approx 19.$$

This example makes it clear how normalized Arrow prices are state probabilities for risk-neutral consumers. We can see the role of risk aversion in the Arrow prices by comparing the normalized expectations operator in the martingale model to the state probabilities (π), where:

$$\pi \approx \{0.35, 0.55, 0.10\}$$

Risk aversion places extra weight on payouts in the third state and less weight on payouts in the first two states.

Notice how the normalized expectations operator shifts the risk premium from the discount rates (φ) in (3.11) to the expectations operator π^*.

3.3 Asset pricing in a two-period setting

In this section we derive the consumption-based pricing model (CBPM) in a two-period setting by assigning NMEU functions to consumers in the Arrow–Debreu asset economy. As noted above, there are four popular pricing models in finance that are special cases of the CBPM where consumers have the same consumption risk. Thus, they measure and price the risk in capital assets in the same way.[36] As preparation for the analysis in Chapter 4, we examine the properties of the CBPM. In particular, we look at why consumers have the same consumption risk, and why diversifiable risk attracts no risk premium. We extend the CBPM by adopting power utility functions and mean–variance analysis. Both simplify the analysis considerably: power utility makes consumption expenditure in each time period a constant proportion of wealth, and mean–variance analysis restricts the information needed to summarize the statistical properties of consumption expenditure.

3.3.1 Asset prices with expected utility

In a two-period setting most analysts make the NMEU function time-separable, with

$$EU = U(I_0) + \delta E\{U(\tilde{I})\}, \tag{3.16}$$

where $0 < \delta \leq 1$, and $E\{U(\tilde{I})\} = \Sigma_s \pi_s U(I_s)$. By using these preferences we can rewrite the ADPM in (3.11) as *the consumption-based pricing model* (CBPM),

$$E(\tilde{m}\,\tilde{R}) = p_a, \tag{3.17}$$

where $E(\cdot) = \Sigma_s \pi_s(\cdot)$ is the common expectations operator, $\tilde{m} = \delta U'(\tilde{I}) / U'(I_0)$ the stochastic discount factor, which is also referred to as the *pricing kernal* or *state price density*, and

> **Box 3.4 Using the CBPM to isolate the discount factors in Arrow prices**
>
> We can decompose the primitive (Arrow) prices obtained in Box 3.1 earlier by using the CBPM. When consumers with common expectations use the state probabilities π: = {0.35, 0.55, 0.10} their stochastic discount factors are obtained by dividing the Arrow prices by their respective probabilities, with $m_s = \varphi_s/\pi_s$, where:
>
> $$m \approx \{0.86, 0.91, 1.50\}.$$
>
> By using these discount factors and the state probabilities we can decompose the three security prices in Box 3.1 as follows:
>
> $$p_{\text{ADL Share}} = (0.55 \times 0.91 \times 15) + (0.10 \times 1.50 \times 30) \approx 12,$$
>
> $$p_{\text{Intec Share}} = (0.35 \times 0.86 \times 60) + (0.10 \times 1.50 \times 20) \approx 21,$$
>
> $$p_{\text{Govt. Bond}} = (0.35 \times 0.86 \times 20) + (0.55 \times 0.91 \times 20) + (0.10 \times 1.50 \times 20) \approx 19.$$

$\tilde{R} = (\tilde{R}_1, \ldots, \tilde{R}_K)$ the vector of random payouts to the $k = 1, \ldots, K$ securities. By using NMEU we can separate risk assesments from the marginal utility derived from consumption expenditure in the stochastic discount factor in (3.11) as $\tilde{\varphi} = \tilde{\pi}\tilde{m}$.

Since consumers use the same expectations operator $E(\cdot)$, and face a common payoff matrix R and common vector of security prices p_a, they have the same stochastic discount factor in the CBPM.[37]

Box 3.5 Using the CBPM in (3.18) to compute expected security returns

The decomposition in (3.18) can be confirmed by using the state probabilities $\pi := \{0.35, 0.55, 0.10\}$ and stochastic discount factors $m \approx \{0.86, 0.91, 1.50\}$, derived in Box 3.4, to compute the current prices of the three securities in Box 3.1. Since the price of a risk-free bond that pays one dollar in each state is $E(\tilde{m}) = 0.95$, the risk-free interest rate is i = 0.0526316. The expected payouts and rates of return for each security, together with their covariance terms, are summarized below.

Security	$E(\tilde{R}_k)$	$\text{Cov}(\tilde{m}, \tilde{R}_k)$	$E(\tilde{i}_k)$	$\text{Cov}(-\tilde{m}, \tilde{i}_k)$
ADL Share	11.25	1.3125	–0.0625	–0.109375
Intec Share	23	–0.85	0.0952381	0.040476
Govt. Bond	20	0	0.0526316	0

Using the pricing equation in (3.18), with $p_k = E(\tilde{m})E(\tilde{R}_k) + \text{Cov}(\tilde{m}, \tilde{R}_k)$, we have:

$$p_{\text{ADL Share}} = (0.95 \times 11.25) + 1.3125 = 12,$$

$$p_{\text{Intec Share}} = (0.95 \times 23) - 0.85 = 21,$$

$$p_{\text{Govt. Bond}} = (0.95 \times 20) + 0 = 19.$$

It is possible to obtain a so-called beta model from (3.17) by writing the price of any risky security k as

$$E(\tilde{m}, \tilde{R}_k) = E(\tilde{m})E(\tilde{R}_k) + \text{Cov}(\tilde{m}, \tilde{R}_k) = p_{ak}.^{38} \tag{3.18}$$

After defining random security returns as $\tilde{R}_k = (1 + \tilde{i}_k)p_{ak}$, and solving the price of the risk-free bond that pays one dollar in every state as $E(\tilde{m}) = 1/R_F = 1/(1+i)$, we have

$$\bar{i}_k - i = \beta_{mk}\lambda_m,^{39} \tag{3.19}$$

where $\beta_{m,k} = \text{Cov}(-\tilde{m}, \tilde{i}_k)/\text{Var}(\tilde{m})$ is the beta coefficient that measures the quantity of market risk in security k, and $\lambda_m = \text{Var}(\tilde{m})/E(\tilde{m})$ the price of market risk which is independent of k.

Box 3.6 Using the CBPM in (3.19) to compute expected security returns

To use the beta version of the CBPM in (3.19) we need to calculate the random rates of return for each of the three securities (k) in Box 3.1 using $\tilde{i}_k = \tilde{R}_k / p_k - 1$. They are summarized below with their expected values and covariance with the stochastic discount factor.

	Security returns				
Security	*State 1*	*State 2*	*State 3*	$E(\tilde{i}_k)$	$\text{Cov}(-\tilde{m},\tilde{i}_k)$
ADL Share	−1	0.25	1.5	−0.0625	−0.109375
Intec Share	1.8571429	−1	−0.047619	0.0952381	0.040476
Govt. Bond	0.0526316	0.0526316	0.0526316	0.0526316	0

We obtained these expected returns for each security as the probability-weighted sum of their returns in each state, using $\pi: = \{0.35, 0.55, 0.10\}$. They can also be obtained by using the beta model in (3.19), with $E(\tilde{i}_k) = i + \beta_{m,k}\lambda_m$, where $\beta_{mk} = \text{Cov}(\tilde{m},\tilde{i}_k)/\text{Var}(\tilde{m})$ and $\lambda_m = \text{Var}(\tilde{m})/E(\tilde{m})$. For the stochastic factors computed in Box 3.5, with $m \approx \{0.86, 0.91, 1.50\}$, we have $E(\tilde{m}) = 0.95$ and $\text{Var}(\tilde{m}) = 0.0341883$, where:

$$E(\tilde{i}_{\text{ADL Share}}) = 0.0526316 - (3.1991928 \times 0.0359877) \approx -0.0625,$$

$$E(\tilde{i}_{\text{Intec Share}}) = 0.0526316 + (1.183919 \times 0.0359877) \approx 0.0952381,$$

$$\tilde{i}_{\text{Govt. Bond}} = 0.0526316 + (0 \times 0.0359877) = 0.0526316.$$

In practice the stochastic discount factors in (3.17) are (potentially complex) non-linear functions of a large number of exogenously determined variables in the economy. Thus, the two versions of the CBPM in (3.18) and (3.19) are difficult to obtain from observable data. The popular pricing models examined later in Chapter 4 rely on additional assumptions to make the stochastic discount factor linear in a small number of state variables reported in aggregate data. While that makes them easier to use, they are less robust empirically.

The CBPM in (3.17) provides a number of very useful insights into the way expected security returns are affected by risk. First, in equilibrium the (risk-free) interest rate (i) is determined by the rate of time preference (ρ), consumer risk aversion and the growth in aggregate consumption expenditure. To see why that is the case, use $\delta = 1/(1 + \rho)$ to write $E(\tilde{m}) = 1/1+i)$, as:

$$1 + i = (1+\rho)\frac{U'(I_0)}{EU'(\tilde{I})}.$$

Risk-neutral consumers (with constant $U'(I)$) have a rate of time preference equal to the interest rate (with $\rho < i$). Expected consumption growth and risk aversion both cause the rate of time preference to fall below the interest rate. We have $\rho < i$ with (a) consumption growth and no uncertainty, where $U'(I_0) > U'(I_1)$ and (b) no expected consumption growth and uncertainty (with $E(\tilde{I}) = I_0$ and $\sigma_{\tilde{I}}^2 > 0$), where risk aversion drives down expected utility (with $EU'(\tilde{I}) < U'(I_0)$).

Second, no premium is paid for diversifiable (idiosyncratic) risk when it can be costlessly eliminated in a frictionless competitive capital market. This is referred to as the *mutuality principle*, where consumers use financial securities to pool this risk and eliminate it from their consumption. When the return on a risky security j (with $\sigma_j^2 > 0$) has zero covariance with aggregate consumption ($\text{Cov}(\tilde{m}, \tilde{i}_j) = 0$), then from (3.19) its expected return must be equal to the risk-free return, with $\bar{i}_j = i$. Only market risk is priced by the CBPM when diversifiable risk can be costlessly eliminated from consumption.[40]

Third, in a complete capital market the competitive equilibrium outcome in the Arrow–Debreu asset economy is Pareto optimal where consumers have the same stochastic discount factor ($\tilde{m}$) in (3.17). Thus, they have the same discounted growth in their marginal utility from consumption, and with diminishing marginal utility, changes in marginal utility are negatively correlated with changes in consumption so that consumers face the same consumption risk. Thus, security returns that covary positively with aggregate consumption pay a risk premium because they contribute to consumption risk. In general, however, the functional relationship between the risk premium on security returns and their covariance with aggregate consumption is non-linear due to the concavity of the utility function. Thus, we cannot replace the beta coefficient in (3.19) with a consumption-beta coefficient without placing further restrictions on preferences and/or the stochastic properties of aggregate consumption and security returns.

One of the most common ways of obtaining a closed-form solution for the stochastic discount factor in (3.17) is to adopt a *power utility function*, which normally takes the form

$$U(\tilde{I}_{t+1}) = \begin{cases} \dfrac{\tilde{I}_{t+1}^{1-\gamma}}{1-\gamma}, & \text{for } \gamma \neq 1, \\ \ln(\tilde{I}_{t+1}), & \text{for } \gamma = 1, \end{cases} \tag{3.20}$$

where γ is the CRRA.[41] Since it has a constant CRRA there is a one-to-one mapping between changes in marginal utility and changes in aggregate consumption. This is confirmed by using these functions to solve the stochastic discount factor in (3.17) as:[42]

$$\tilde{m}_{t+1} = \begin{cases} \delta(\tilde{I}_{t+1}/I_t)^{-\gamma}, & \text{for } \gamma \neq 1, \\ \delta(\tilde{I}_{t+1}/I_t)^{-1}, & \text{for } \gamma = 1. \end{cases} \tag{3.21}$$

By using them to measure the wealth of an infinitely lived representative consumer, we have

$$W_t = \begin{cases} E_t \sum_{t=1}^{\infty} \delta^t (\tilde{I}_{t+1}/I_t)^{-\gamma} \tilde{I}_{t+1} = E_t \sum_{t=1}^{\infty} \delta^t (1+\tilde{g}_{t+1})^{-\gamma} \tilde{I}_{t+1}, & \text{for } \gamma \neq 1, \\ E_t \sum_{t=1}^{\infty} \delta^t (\tilde{I}_{t+1}/I_t)^{-1} \tilde{I}_{t+1} = \dfrac{\delta}{1-\delta} I_t & \text{for } \gamma = 1, \end{cases} \tag{3.22}$$

where $\tilde{g}_{t+1} = (\tilde{I}_{t+1} - I_t)/I_t$ is the growth rate in consumption in period t. With log utility ($\gamma = 1$) consumption is a constant proportion of wealth in each period, where the stochastic discount factor over period t to $t + 1$ is equal to $\tilde{m}_{t-1} = 1/(1+\tilde{i}_{W,t+1})$ with $\tilde{i}_{W,t+1}$ being the return on wealth.[43] There is a linear relationship between the expected return on securities and their covariance with aggregate consumption for both versions of the power utility function in (3.20) when security returns are jointly log-normally distributed with aggregate consumption.[44]

Box 3.7 Consumption with log utility: a numerical example

An infinitely lived consumer with current wealth of \$1.5 million and a rate of time preference that makes $\delta = 0.95$ will consume approximately \$78,947 when they have the log utility function in (3.20) with $\gamma = 1$. This is confirmed by using the solution to wealth in (3.22), where

$$I_t = [(1-\delta)/\delta]W_t = 0.052631578 \times \$1,500,000 \approx \$78,947.$$

Another important feature of power utility functions is the inverse relationship between the elasticity of intertemporal consumption expenditure (Ω) and CRRA. Both are measures of the curvature of the utility function over consumption expenditure, where the first relates to differences over time and the second to differences over uncertain outcomes in each period. This inverse relationship is confirmed by using (3.20), with $\gamma \neq 1$, to write the marginal rate of substitution between consumption over time as

$$\frac{U_1'}{U_0'} = \delta\left(\frac{I_1}{I_0}\right)^{-\gamma}.$$

After taking the log of this expression we obtain the elasticity of intertemporal consumption expenditure:

$$\Omega = -\frac{d\,\text{In}(I_{t+1}/I_t)}{d\,\text{In}(U_{t+1}'/U_t')} = \frac{1}{\gamma}. \tag{3.23}$$

This tells us how sensitive intertemporal consumption is to changes in its relative cost, where changes in the marginal rate of substitution are driven by changes in the relative price of consumption over time. Thus, when consumers with power utility have a high CRRA they dislike changes in consumption within each period and also across time periods, while the reverse applies when they have a low CRRA. In other words, highly risk-averse consumers regard consumption as highly complementary across uncertain outcomes and also across time periods. They prefer smooth consumption flows over their lives.[45]

3.3.2 The mutuality principle

To demonstrate the way consumers can costlessly eliminate diversifiable risk from their consumption in a complete capital market, we consider a two-period endowment economy with two states of nature.[46] In the good state (G) individuals consume their income endowments (which they can transfer between periods by trading securities), while they incur a common income loss L in the bad state (B). The bad state occurs with exogenous given probability π_B and the good state with probability $\pi_G = 1 - \pi_B$, for all consumers. To simplify the analysis we allow consumers to trade a full set of primitive (Arrow) securities in the first period, one for each state, with respective prices p_{aB}^P and p_{aG}^P. They use them to transfer their consumption expenditure over time and between states to maximize NMEU functions, where the consumer problem can be summarized as:

$$\max\left\{U(I_0) + \pi_B\delta U(I_B) + \pi_G\delta U(I_G) \;\middle|\; \begin{aligned} I_0 &= \bar{X}_0 - p_{aB}^P a_B - p_{aG}^P a_G \\ I_B &= \bar{X}_1 - L + a_B \\ I_G &= \bar{X}_1 + a_G \end{aligned}\right\} \tag{3.24}$$

To simplify the analysis we remove any aggregate uncertainty by fixing the income endowment ($\bar{X}_1$) in the second period and invoking the law of large numbers to make the aggregate loss in income certain at $\pi_B HL$, where $\pi_B H$ is the proportion of the population (H) who incur loss L.[47] The only uncertainty consumers face here is whether or not they fall into that group. Using the first-order conditions for the optimally chosen security trades, they transfer income between the two states until

$$MRS_{B,G}(I) \equiv \frac{\pi_B \delta U'(I_B)}{\pi_G \delta U'(I_G)} = \frac{p^P_{aB}}{p^P_{aG}} \equiv MRT_{B,G}(I), \tag{3.25}$$

where $MRT_{B,G}(I)$ is the marginal cost of transferring income from the good to the bad state. In a frictionless competitive capital market the security prices solve as $p^P_{aB} = \pi_B/(1+i)$ and $p^P_{aG} = \pi_G/(1+i)$.[48] After substituting them into (3.25) we have $U'(I_B) = U'(I_G)$, where risk-averse consumers eliminate risk from their consumption expenditure, with $I_B = I_G$. This equilibrium outcome is located on the 45° line in Figure 3.6. In the absence of a capital market, consumers would locate at their income endowment point E.

Notice from (3.25) that the indifference curves must have a slope equal to the relative probabilities of the two states (π_B/π_G) along the 45° line. At the endowment point risk-averse consumers have a marginal valuation for bad state consumption that exceeds its relative cost (with $MRS_{B,G}(I) > \pi_B/\pi_G$). The gains from transferring income from the good to the bad state are maximized by trading to $\hat{I}$ on the 45° line where consumption risk is eliminated. Thus, in a frictionless complete capital market there is no risk premium in security returns for diversifiable risk because it can be costlessly eliminated. This is confirmed by using the equilibrium security prices $p^P_{aB} \equiv \pi_B/(1+i)$ and $p^P_{aG} = \pi_G/(1+i)$ to compute consumer wealth at an interior solution when the three budget constraints in (3.24) bind, where:

$$\begin{aligned} W_0 &= \bar{X}_0 - \frac{\pi_B a_B + \pi_G a_G}{1+i} + \frac{\pi_B(\bar{X}_1 - L + a_B)}{1+i} + \frac{\pi_G(\bar{X}_1 + a_G)}{1+i} \\ &= \bar{X}_0 + \frac{\bar{X}_1 - \pi_B L}{1+i}. \end{aligned} \tag{3.26}$$

It is the same as wealth when the primitive securities are replaced by a risk-free bond that stops consumers transferring income between the states to smooth consumption. In other words, wealth is independent of the amount of income transferred between the good and bad states when security prices are based on their relative probabilities. Thus, we have:

> **Definition 3.8 (The mutuality principle)**
> In a frictionless competitive capital market with common information, diversifiable risk is costlessly eliminated from consumption and attracts no risk premium in expected security returns. Only non-diversifiable (market) risk attracts a risk premium in these circumstances.

The mutuality principle can fail to hold when there are transactions costs, asymmetric information and state-dependent preferences. Each will now be examined in turn. In the presence of a constant marginal cost (τ) of trading primitive securities (with $\tau > 0$ when $a_s > 0$, and $\tau < 0$ when $a_s < 0$, for $s \in \{B, G\}$) we have

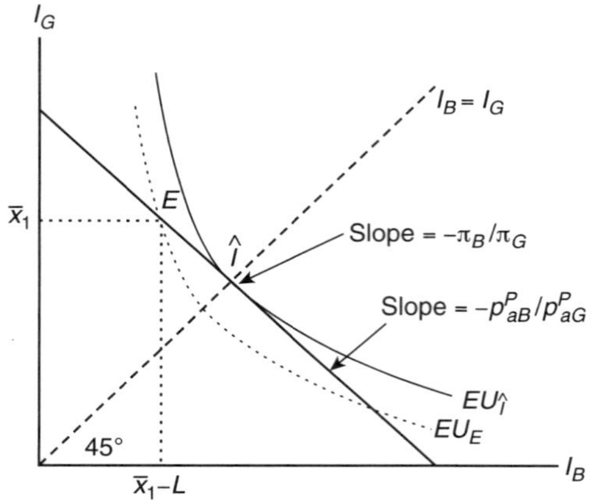

Figure 3.6 The mutuality principle.

$$\frac{\pi_B + \tau}{\pi_G - \tau} > \frac{\pi_B}{\pi_G}.$$

Thus, risk-averse consumers no longer eliminate all the diversifiable risk from their consumption expenditure. The effects of trading costs are illustrated in Figure 3.7, where they contract the consumption opportunity set around the endowment point E. Consumers choose an equilibrium allocation such as $\hat{I}$ which lies off the 45° line.

Asymmetric information can also cause the mutuality principle to fail. When traders have different information and form different beliefs, the primitive security prices can deviate from the discounted state probability assessments made by consumers, thereby resulting in equilibrium allocations off the 45° line. Other problems can arise from asymmetric information

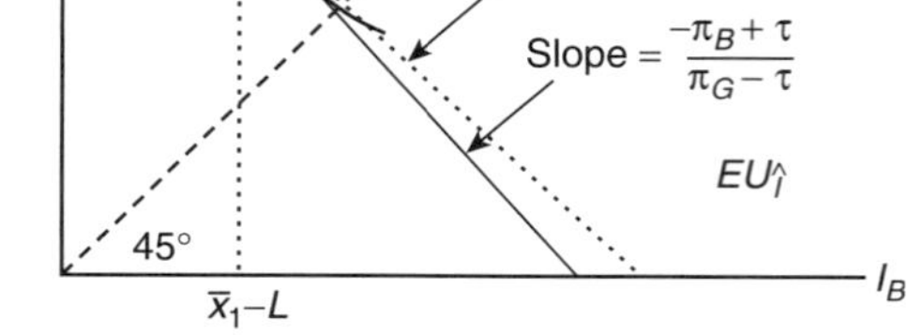

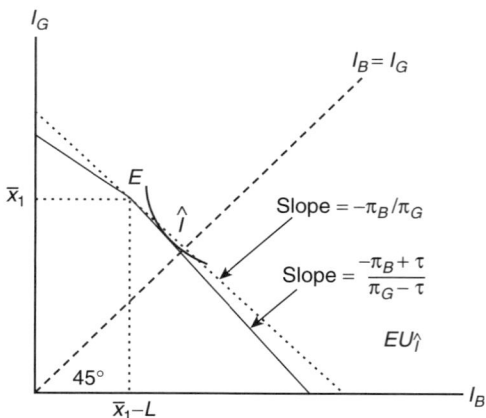

Figure 3.7 Trading costs.

when consumers can affect their probabilities of incurring losses by expending effort, or when they have different loss probabilities. These issues are examined later in Chapter 5.

Consumers with *state-dependent preferences* will not in general eliminate diversifiable risk from their consumption expenditure, even when they can do so costlessly. Indeed, we observe situations where consumers get different utility from the same real consumption bundle in different states of nature. An obvious example is where states of nature determine a consumer's health which changes the way utility maps from real consumption. If, for example, they get more utility from every consumption bundle in the good state they will not choose to equate their consumption in each state when faced with primitive security prices $p_{aB}^P = \pi_B/(1+i)$ and $p_{aG}^P = \pi_G/(1+i)$. This can be formalized by assigning to each consumer the state-dependent expected utility function,

$$EU = U_0(I_0) + \delta\pi_B U(I_B, B) + \delta\pi_G U(I_G, G), \tag{3.27}$$

where the optimally chosen allocation of consumption across the two states must now satisfy

$$\frac{\pi_B \delta U'(I_B, B)}{\pi_G \delta U'(I_G, G)} = \frac{\pi_B}{\pi_G}. \tag{3.28}$$

It is now possible that $U'(I_B,B) \neq U'(I_G,G)$ when $I_B = I_G$. An example is illustrated in Figure 3.8, where the optimal allocation of consumption occurs at $\hat{I}$, with $I_B < I_G$, because the consumer has a higher net marginal valuation for consumption in the good state on the 45° line. Even though consumers can costlessly eliminate risk from their consumption, they choose not to do so because they get more utility at the margin from consumption in the good state over the bad state. If transactions costs raise the relative cost of good state consumption the consumer bears even more risk.

This example also conveniently demonstrates why it is difficult in practice to separate risk from preferences over consumption when consumers have subjective probabilities and state-dependent utility. Whenever primitive security prices deviate from their state probabilities, with $\pi_B/\pi_G \neq p_{aB}^P/p_{aG}^P$, the relationship between the slopes of the indifference schedule and

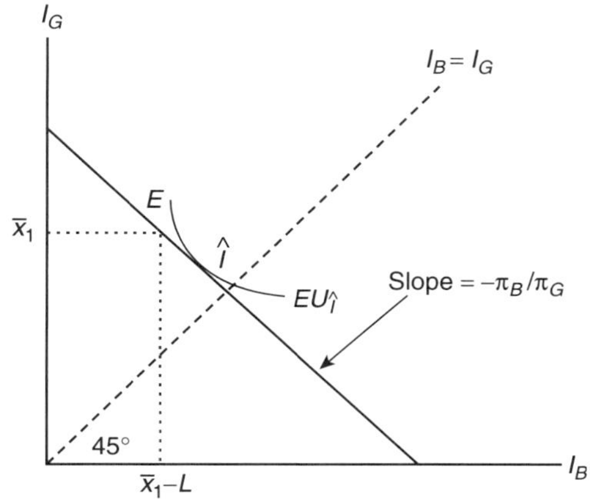

Figure 3.8 State-dependent preferences.

budget constraint are combinations of probability assessments and consumption benefits. By using the state-dependent subjective expected utility function,

$$EU = U_0(I_0) + \delta \sum_s \pi_s^h U(I_s, s), \tag{3.29}$$

to decompose the ADPM in (3.17), we have

$$E_0^h(\tilde{m}^h \tilde{R}) = p_a, \tag{3.30}$$

where $E_0^h(\cdot) = E_s \pi_s^h(\cdot)$ is the subjective expectations operator that is based on information available at time 0. Since consumers face the same random payouts ($\tilde{R}$) and security prices (p_a), they face the same Arrow security prices. But they do not decompose them in the same way when they use different state probabilities, with $\varphi_s = \pi_s^h m_s^h$ for all h. It is possible to identify their subjective probabilities when they have state-independent preferences. And we do so by computing the slopes of their indifference schedules on the 45° line with constant

Box 3.8 The mutuality principle: a numerical example

Janet consumes a single good corn (x) in each of two periods to maximize expected utility, $\ln x_0 + \pi_B 0.95 \ln x_B + \pi_G 0.95 \ln x_G$, where x_0 is current consumption and x_B and x_G bad and good state consumption, respectively, in the second period with probabilities $\pi_B = 0.4$ and $\pi_G = 0.6$. She has 2140 kg of rice in the first period which is allocated to current consumption and two primitive securities, a_B and a_G. Each security pays a kilo of corn in the bad and good states, respectively, and trade at current prices p_B and p_G (measured in units of corn), where Janet's budget constraint is

$$x_0 + p_B a_B + p_G a_G \leq 2140.$$

Thus, she consumes $x_G = a_G$ in the good state, and $x_B = a_B - 500$ in the bad state where there is a loss of 500 kg of corn due to theft. Since 40 per cent of the population always incurs this loss it is diversifiable risk (by the law of large numbers) and there is no aggregate risk in the economy. In a frictionless competitive capital market, with $1/(1 + i) = 0.95$, the primitive security prices are equal to $p_B = \pi_b/(1 + i) = 0.38$ and $p_G = \pi_G/(1 + i) = 0.57$.

When Janet makes her utility-maximizing consumption choices, they satisfy

$$\frac{\pi_B 0.95 x_0}{x_B} = \frac{\lambda_B}{\lambda_0} \text{ and } \frac{\pi_G 0.95 x_0}{x_G} = \frac{\lambda_G}{\lambda_0},$$

where λ_0, λ_B and λ_G are the Lagrange multipliers for her three constraints. Since optimally chosen security demands satisfy $p_B = \lambda_B/\lambda_0 = \pi_B/(1 + i)$ and $p_G = \lambda_G/\lambda_0 = \pi_G/(1 + i)$, Janet consumes $x_0^* = x_B^* + x_G^* = 1{,}000$ kg, with $x_B^* = a_B^* - 500 = 1{,}000$ kg and $x_G^* = a_G^* = 1{,}000$ kg. Thus, the mutuality principle holds here because all the diversifiable risk has been eliminated from her second-period consumption.

consumption across the states. Since $U'(I_B, B) = U'(I_G, G)$ in (3.28) when $I_B \neq I_G$, the slopes of the indifference schedules are equal to the ratios of the state probabilities. Alternatively, we could do the same thing to identify the state-dependent preferences of consumers when they have objective probabilities. But with subjective probabilities and state-dependent preferences we cannot identify their risk assessments without imposing additional restrictions on their preferences or the probability distributions.

3.3.3 Asset prices with mean–variance preferences

We saw in Section 3.3.1 how consumers use the same stochastic discount factors in the CBPM in (3.17). Without making further assumptions, however, the task of estimating the stochastic discount factors in (3.17) is potentially complex. In each time period the variance in aggregate consumption expenditure depends on the variance in income as well as the variance in relative commodity prices in all future time periods. Thus, even with time-separable expected utility, consumption in each period is a function of wealth, which is the discounted present value of all future consumption flows. And relative commodity prices matter because they determine the real consumption opportunities in each future time period. In a general equilibrium setting, aggregate consumption is likely to be a non-linear function that is potentially cumbersome to use in computational work. But even if we manage to solve it as a function of one or a small number of aggregate variables, we also need to measure the stochastic properties of the randomness they impart to aggregate consumption. Popular pricing models in finance adopt mean–variance analysis, where these two moments completely summarize the impact of risk in aggregate consumption on the utility of consumers. There are two ways to invoke a mean–variance analysis on the CBPM in (3.17).

i Consumers with *quadratic preferences* care only about the mean and variance in their (real) consumption expenditure.[49] An example is the utility function $U(\tilde{I}) = a\tilde{I} - \frac{1}{2}b\tilde{I}^2$ which makes the stochastic discount factor

$$\tilde{m} = \delta\left(\frac{a - b\tilde{I}}{a - bI_0}\right),$$

where the pricing equation for any security k in (3.19), using $\tilde{R}_k(1+\tilde{i}_k)p_{ak}$ and $E(\tilde{m}) = 1/(1+i)$, becomes

$$\bar{i}_k - i = \psi \operatorname{Cov}(\tilde{I}, \tilde{i}_k), \tag{3.31}$$

with $\psi = -(1 + i)\,[\delta b/(a - bI_0)]$ being a constant coefficient. By creating a derivative security with unit sensitivity to the risk in aggregate consumption expenditure (with $\operatorname{Cov}(\tilde{I}, \tilde{i}_I) = \sigma_I^2$ we can write the asset pricing model in (3.19) as

$$\bar{i}_k - i = \beta_{Ik}\lambda_I,^{50} \tag{3.32}$$

where $\beta_{Ik} = \operatorname{Cov}(\tilde{i}_I, \tilde{i}_k)/\sigma_I^2$ is the consumption-beta coefficient for security k, and $\lambda_I = (\bar{i}_I - i)/\sigma_I^2$ the premium for consumption risk. The derivative security is a *mimicking portfolio* constructed to replicate the risk in aggregate consumption (with $\beta_{II} = 1$) where the pricing equation in (3.32) differs from (3.19) by measuring risk in security returns by their covariance with aggregate consumption rather than the discounted change in marginal utility. In effect, quadratic preferences make changes in aggregate consumption a proxy for changes in marginal utility. And the model also holds unconditionally in a multi-period setting (which means it is independent of the time period) when the risk-free return is constant and security returns are identical and independently and identically distributed to rule out shifts in the investment opportunity set over time.

ii Wherever possible we try to minimize the restrictions imposed on consumer preferences. Thus, a preferable approach to adopting quadratic preferences is to assume aggregate consumption is *normally distributed* where its probability distribution is fully described by the mean and variance, with:[51]

$$E(e^{\tilde{I}}) = e^{E(\tilde{I}) + \frac{1}{2}\sigma_{\tilde{I}}^2}.^{52}$$

The *normal distribution* is a symmetric bell-shaped function with almost all the probability mass within three standard deviations of the mean. An example is shown in Figure 3.9 for the return on an asset with a mean of 10 per cent and standard deviation of 12 per cent. It can be a derivative security created by bundling traded securities together in a portfolio. There is a 68.26 per cent probability that the asset return will lie within one standard deviation of the mean (–2 and 22 percentage points), a 95.44 per cent probability it will lie within two standard deviations of the mean (−14 and 34 percentage points), and a 99.74 per cent probability it will lie within three standard deviations of the mean (–26 and 46 percentage points). (These probabilities are represented by the areas below the distribution function over the respective deviations from the mean in Figure 3.9.)

When all future consumption is funded from payouts to a portfolio (*P*) of securities we can map utility indirectly over the mean and standard deviation in its expected return, as $V(\bar{i}_P, \sigma_P)$. For risk-averse consumers the function increases with the mean and falls with the standard deviation. In other words, higher expected consumption makes consumers better off, while a larger variance makes them worse off. An indifference curve for a risk-averse consumer is illustrated in Figure 3.10 as $V_{RA}(\bar{i}_P, \sigma_P)$. Since utility declines with additional risk it has a positive slope, which becomes steeper with increasing disutility. The slope of the line tangent to the indifference curve at any point in the consumption space (like point *A* in Figure 3.10) tells us the consumer's marginal valuation for risk; it is their price of risk (σ_P).

To understand how risk aversion impacts on the asset pricing models examined later in Chapter 4, we frequently consider what happens when consumers are risk-neutral. The indifference curve for a risk-neutral consumer is illustrated in Figure 3.10 as the

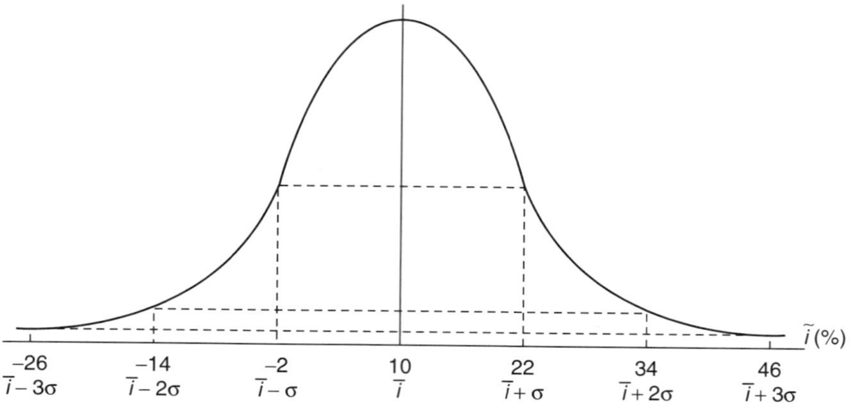

Figure 3.9 Normally distributed asset return.

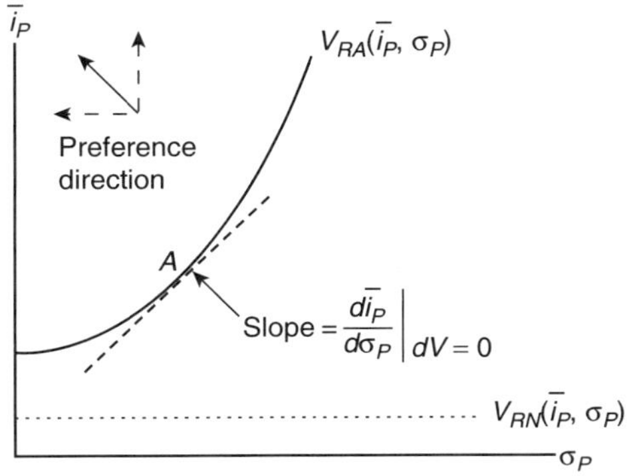

Figure 3.10 Mean–variance preferences.

dotted line labelled $V_{RN}(\bar{i}_P, \sigma_P)$. It is horizontal because utility is unaffected by changes in risk, where no risk premium is required to get consumers to bear consumption risk. In these circumstances the returns on all the risky assets are equal to the risk-free interest rate.

In a two-period setting consumption risk originates from aggregate uncertainty in second-period endowments and production. As owners of the endowments and shareholders in firms, consumers ultimately bear this non-diversifiable risk. When they have quadratic preferences, or second-period consumption is normally distributed, we can write their NMEU function in a two-period setting as

$$EU = U_0(I_0) + V(\bar{I}, \sigma_I).$$

The asset pricing models examined in Chapter 4 use mean–variance analysis. It conveniently makes the stochastic discount factor in the CBPM in (3.17) linear in the factors (state variables) that isolate the market risk in aggregate consumption.[53]

3.4 Term structure of interest rates

Capital assets with net cash flows over multiple future time periods are valued by discounting them for the opportunity cost of time and risk. Long-term stochastic discount factors are used for net cash flows in each time period, and they are the product of a full set of short-term stochastic discount factors, one for each consecutive time period up to the date of the cash flows. For example, the present value (at time t) of random cash flows in some future period $T > t$ is computed using the long-term stochastic discount factor

$$\tilde{m}_T = \delta^{T-t} \frac{U'(\tilde{I}_T)}{U'(I_t)}. \tag{3.33}$$

This can be decomposed as

$$\tilde{m}_T = {}_t\tilde{m}_{t+1} \cdot {}_{t+1}\tilde{m}_{t+2} \cdot \ldots \cdot {}_{T-1}\tilde{m}_T, \tag{3.34}$$

where ${}_{t-1}\tilde{m}_t = \delta U'(\tilde{I}_t)/U'(\tilde{I}_{t-1})$ is the short term discount factor over each period $t-1$ to t.[54]

Using this decomposition we can write the current (at time t) market price of security k with payouts over T periods as

$$P_{akt} = E_t\left(\sum_{j=0}^{T}\prod_{w=t}^{t+j} {}_{w-1}\tilde{m}_w \tilde{R}_{k,t+j}\right) = E_t\left(\sum_{j=0}^{T} \tilde{m}_{t+j}\tilde{R}_{k,t+j}\right).$$

Since long-term discount factors are based on long-term interest rates, and short-term discount factors on expected short-term interest rates, the expected short- and long-term interest rates are related to each other by arbitrage. The term structure of interest can be identified by comparing the long-term stochastic discount factors for government bonds with different dates to maturity. As government bonds are not (in general) subject to default risk their returns are (approximately) risk-free. That means they make the same payouts at every event in each time period, even though the risk-free interest rate can change over time.[55] If there is a full set of long-term government bonds with maturity dates in each future time period we can obtain a full set of forward spot rates. And they are equal to the expected spot rates when the (pure) expectations hypothesis holds.

Consider a discount bond that pays a unit of real purchasing power in the second year of its life (with $R_{B2} = 1$).[56] Using the CBPM in (3.17) in a multi-period setting, its current price (at $t = 0$) is equal to the expected value of the (long-term) stochastic discount factor, which we can decompose, using (3.34), as

$$E_0(\tilde{m}_2) = E_0({}_0\tilde{m}_1 \cdot {}_1\tilde{m}_2) = E_0({}_0\tilde{m}_1)E_0({}_1\tilde{m}_2) + \text{Cov}_0({}_0\tilde{m}_1, {}_1\tilde{m}_2) \tag{3.35}$$

where $E_0({}_0\tilde{m}_1)E_0({}_1\tilde{m}_2)$ is the current value of holding two short-term discount bonds expected to pay a unit of real purchasing power in the second period. Since the interest rate in the first period is known (at $t = 0$), we have $E_0({}_0\tilde{m}_1) = 1/(1+i_1)$, where i_1 is the interest rate in the first period. We also know the average annual yield to maturity (i_2) on the long-term bond as it also trades in the first period, where $E_0({}_1\tilde{m}_2) = 1/(1+i_2)^2$. However, the interest rate on the second-period short-term bond is uncertain (at $t = 0$) as it trades at the end of the first period (at $t = 1$). A forward spot rate (${}_1f_2$) is embedded in the price of the long-term bond, with:

$$E_0(\tilde{m}_2) = \frac{1}{(1+i_1)(1+{}_1f_2)}. \tag{3.36}$$

When two short-term bonds are perfect substitutes for the long-term bond, the forward rate is equal to the expected spot rate. The relationship between these spot rates can be obtained by writing the current value of the short-term stochastic discount factor in the second period as $E_0({}_1\tilde{m}_2) = 1/[1 + E_0({}_1i_2)]$. Using the decomposition in (3.34), we have

$$E_0(\tilde{m}_2) = E_0({}_0\tilde{m}_1 \cdot {}_1\tilde{m}_2) = E_0({}_0\tilde{m}_1)E_0({}_1\tilde{m}_2) + \text{Cov}_0({}_0\tilde{m}_1, {}_1\tilde{m}_2)$$

where, by arbitrage,

$$\frac{1}{(1+i_1)(1+{}_1f_2)} = \frac{1}{(1+i_1)(1+E_0({}_1i_2))} + \text{Cov}_0({}_0\tilde{m}_1, {}_1\tilde{m}_2). \tag{3.37}$$

The covariance term is a risk premium, referred to as the *term premium*, that captures any differences in aggregate consumption risk from holding long- rather than short-term bonds. When the *pure expectations hypothesis* holds the short- and long-term bonds are prefect substitutes, with $\text{Cov}_0({}_0\tilde{m}_1, {}_1\tilde{m}_2) = 0$ and ${}_1f_2 = E_0({}_1i_2)$.

Most empirical tests of the *expectations hypothesis* try to find a constant risk premium that is independent of the bond's term to maturity. There are a number of explanations for the risk premium. Long-term real bonds provide a less risky way of funding future consumption than rolling over a sequence of short-term real bonds as forward spot rates are known with certainty while expected spot rates are not beyond the first period. On the other hand, long-term bond returns are more volatile than short-term bond returns, particularly for nominal bonds which are affected by uncertainty about the future rate of general price inflation.

The presence of a risk premium makes it difficult to solve short-term interest rates using the yield curve. In the absence of a full set of long-term bonds they can be obtained from computable general equilibrium models, where most adopt assumptions to make short-term interest rates functions of a small number of factors (state variables). One approach adopts power utility in the CBPM and assumes security returns are lognormally distributed with the stochastic discount factor. Changes in the interest rate are then determined by the set of factors that cause aggregate consumption risk to change over time. Cochrane (2001) provides examples of these models and examines their properties.

Problems

1 Suppose there are three states of nature where the vector of prices for the primitive (Arrow) securities is

$$\varphi = \{0.25, 0.34, 0.38\}.$$

i Compute the price of a risk-free bond that pays \$1 in every state.

ii Compute the normalized probabilities (π^*) in the martingale pricing model. (These were explained in Section 3.2.4.) Explain how they are used to compute the values of capital assets. Why are they referred to as risk-neutral probabilities?

2 Consider a competitive capital market in a two-period setting where two financial securities have the following state-contingent payouts:

State	*Security A*	*Security B*
1	20	60
2	40	20

The securities currently trade at market prices $p_{aA} = \$16$ and $p_{aB} = \$18$, respectively.

i Compute the current market prices for the primitive (Arrow) securities.

ii Calculate the risk-free interest rate using your answers in part (i), then calculate the rate of return in each state for the respective probabilities $\pi_1 = 0.57$ and $\pi_2 = 0.43$.

iii What is the current price of an asset that pays \$10 in the first state and \$15 in the second state?

iv Compute the normalized probabilities (π^*) used in the martingale pricing model and then use them to price the securities in part (iii). When are these the true probabilities?

3 Consider the following payouts to three risky securities in a two-period setting with three states of nature:

Security	*Prices ($) (t = 0)*	*Payouts ($)*		
		State 1	*State 2*	*State 3*
A	5	15	0	8
B	10	0	18	4
C	8	20	0	16

i Derive the price of the primitive (Arrow) securities from this data. Explain how they relate to the probabilities when consumers are risk-neutral.

ii Compute the risk-free interest rate using the Arrow prices in part (i). Is it equal to the rate of time preference in a frictionless competitive capital market?

iii Compute the normalized probabilities (π^*) in the martingale pricing model and show how they are used to price the three securities.

4 Asset pricing models

When traders value capital assets they include a risk premium in their discount factors as compensation for any market risk in the net cash flows. This adjustment is made for projects undertaken by the public and private sectors, and for securities they sell to finance them. In a competitive capital market where the no arbitrage condition holds, traders face the same risk premium, but they may not compute it in the same way. Indeed, consumers with different information can measure and price risk differently, where asset pricing models are agent–specific. A key objective in finance research is to derive an asset pricing model where consumers measure and price risk in the same way. Ideally it should also be straightforward to use by isolating risk with a small number of state variables that are reported as aggregate data in national accounts. In this chapter we examine four equilibrium asset pricing models that do this – the *capital asset pricing model* (CAPM) developed by Sharpe (1964) and Lintner (1965), the *intertemporal capital asset pricing model* (ICAPM) by Merton (1973a), the *arbitrage pricing theory* (APT) by Ross (1976) and the *consumption-beta capital asset pricing model* (CCAPM) by Breeden and Litzenberger (1978) and Breeden (1979).

Following Cochrane (2001) we derive these models as special cases of the consumption-based pricing model (CBPM) obtained earlier in (3.17). It can be summarized as $E_t(\tilde{m}\tilde{R}_k) = p_{ak}$, where $E_t(\cdot)$ is the common expectations operator conditioned on information available at time $t, \tilde{m}$ the stochastic discount factor, with $\tilde{m}_\tau = \delta U'(\tilde{I}_\tau)/(I_t)$ for each period τ, $\tilde{R}_k$ the stochastic payouts to security k, and p_{ak} its price at time t. Since consumers ultimately derive utility from bundles of goods, they value securities by their contribution to final consumption, and with common $E_t(\cdot), \tilde{R}_k$ and p_{ak} they have the same stochastic discount factor ($\tilde{m}$) when they can trade in a frictionless competitive capital market. As the discount factors are determined by consumption in each period, consumers therefore have the same consumption risk in the CBPM. Thus, we can solve them as functions of variables that determine aggregate consumption risk. Unfortunately, however, they are in general quite complex non-linear functions that are difficult to solve and estimate empirically.

The four pricing models overcome this problem by placing restrictions on preferences, wealth and/or the stochastic properties of security returns and aggregate consumption. They all have a linear stochastic discount factor in the state variables (factors) used to isolate aggregate consumption risk. The return on the risky (market) portfolio is the only factor in the CAPM because consumer wealth is confined to portfolios of securities. And expected security returns are linearly related to their covariance with this factor because they are jointly normally distributed. The ICAPM extends the CAPM to allow consumption risk to change over time due to shifts in the investment opportunity set and changes in relative commodity prices. Additional state variables are used to account for these changes in aggregate consumption risk, thereby increasing the covariance terms in the linear pricing equation. In the CCAPM consumers have the same constant coefficient of relative risk aversion (CRRA) when security returns are lognormally distributed with aggregate consumption. This provides a one-to-one mapping between changes in wealth and consumption in each time period where expected security returns are linear in their covariance with aggregate consumption. The APT adopts a different approach by using a linear factor analysis to isolate risk in security returns. The factors themselves are not necessarily the source of consumption risk, but rather they are macro-variables used to identify any common component of changes in security returns – that is, to identify their systematic risk. There is no requirement for the returns to be jointly normally distributed in the APT as the linearity is imposed through the factor analysis.

All of these models have strengths and weaknesses. For example, the single factors in the CAPM and the CCAPM are identified by the models themselves, while the additional factors in the ICAPM and the factors in the APT are not specified by the models. Unfortunately consumers have no risky income from labour or other capital assets in the CAPM and the ICAPM, as income is confined to payouts on portfolios of securities. Wages and salaries are a significant source of income for most consumers and it can also be stochastic, particularly in sectors of the economy that experience regular fluctuations in activity. While labour and other income are included in the CCAPM, consumers must have the same constant coefficient of relative risk aversion for the variance in aggregate consumption to be the single risk factor. There are also problems measuring aggregate consumption flows as figures reported in the national accounts omit leisure and other non-marketed goods, and they include some items that should really be included in capital expenditure. In practice, the CAPM is widely used because of its simplicity and accessibility to data. Most use a broadly based index of stocks trading on the national stock exchange as their market portfolio. They are a value-weighted index, like the Standard Poor's 500 in the United States and the All Ordinaries Index in Australia.

Initially the CAPM was derived as the solution to the portfolio choice problem of consumers. Most textbook presentations follow this approach by deriving the efficient mean–variance frontier for risky securities in a frictionless competitive capital market to demonstrate the *diversification effect*. When security returns are less than perfectly correlated some of their variability can be eliminated by holding them in portfolios. Any risk that cannot be diversified in this way is market (non-diversifiable) risk that someone in the economy must bear. Thus, it is the only risk that attracts a premium in security returns. The CAPM is examined in Section 4.1 below by following the approach used in Copeland and Weston (1988) where the *efficient mean–variance frontier* for risky securities is derived in a number of steps.[1] The analysis begins with two risky securities to demonstrate the diversification effect identified by Markowitz (1959) and Tobin (1958). Consumers are then allowed to hold portfolios that combine a risky security with a risk-free security along a linear budget constraint called the *capital market line*. The APT is also examined separately in Section 4.2 to demonstrate the role of arbitrage in removing diversifiable risk from consumption expenditure, and the role of mimicking portfolios to price market (non-diversifiable) risk. These are common features of the consumption-based models examined in this chapter. Another reason for analysing the APT separately is to demonstrate a linear factor analysis which isolates market risk empirically by identifying the common component in security returns. We then follow Cochrane (2001) and derive the four consumption-based pricing models – the CAPM, the ICAPM, the APT and the CCAPM – as special cases of the CBPM in Section 4.3. These derivations are slightly more formal because they focus on the direct link between consumption and security returns, with portfolio choices and arbitrage pushed into the background of the analysis. For that reason we start the analysis by deriving the CAPM as the solution to the portfolio choices of consumers in Section 4.1, and the APT model as the solution to arbitrage portfolios in Section 4.2.

As noted above, the most attractive feature of the CBPM is that every consumer measures and prices risk in the same way, where in equilibrium the return on each asset (k) is equal to the risk-free interest rate (i) plus a risk premium (Θ_k) for the market risk in the asset, with $i_k = i + \Theta_k$. Conveniently, investors compute this risk premium by measuring the same quantity of market risk (q_{Rk}), which they value at the same price (p_R), with $\Theta_k = p_R q_{RK}$. The task is further simplified by the fact that market risk is the non-diversifiable variance in an asset's return. In more general models, however, the equilibrium risk premium will not be measured and priced identically by consumers, where more information than just the variance in the asset return may be required to isolate market risk. For example, with trading costs consumers can have different consumption risk, where the pricing models become agent-specific.

To see how the pricing models are used in practice, consider an asset (k) with random net cash flows of $\tilde{R}_k$ in the second period. Using one of the four consumption-based pricing models, we can compute its current price as

$$P_{ak} = \frac{\bar{R}_k}{1 + i + \Theta_k},$$

where $\bar{R}_k$ is the expected payout to the security. The discount rate $i + \Theta_k$ compensates asset holders for the opportunity cost of time (i) and the market (non-diversifiable) risk in the net cash flows (Θ_k) on each dollar of capital invested in the asset. Even though the risk premium is isolated using different state variables in the four models it is computed in the same way because every consumer has the same consumption risk.

4.1 Capital asset pricing model

As noted earlier, the CAPM is a popular pricing model because it is relatively straightforward to use. But it relies on a number of important assumptions that may not hold in practice. For that reason it is important to know the role they play so that users can assess the integrity of CAPM estimates. Financial analysts frequently use the model to approximate the risk premium on capital assets in a systematic way, rather than making a rough guess. Then, by choosing a range of values around this estimate, they undertake a sensitivity analysis to see what difference other assumptions make in the evaluation process. In this section we derive the CAPM by analysing the portfolio choices of consumers. The analysis commences with a summary of consumer preferences and the consumption space, before deriving the investment opportunity set. Then the pricing equation is obtained by bringing these two components together in the optimization problem for consumers. Finally, we relax the assumptions in the CAPM to see what role they play.

4.1.1 Consumption space and preferences

All the consumption risk in the CAPM originates from the risk in the returns to portfolios of securities held by consumers. We capture this by writing the consumer problem in the two-period Arrow–Debreu asset economy as

$$\max\left\{ v(I) \middle| \begin{array}{l} X_0 \leq \bar{X}_0 - V_0 + \eta_0 \ \equiv I_0 \\ X_S \leq R_S \ \equiv I_S, \forall s \end{array} \right\},^2 \tag{4.1}$$

where $R_s = \Sigma_k a_k R_{ks}$ is the payout to the portfolio of securities in each state s.[3] Consumers have no labour income in the second period, and no income from capital assets such as houses and land. Thus, in the first period they allocate their wealth to current consumption expenditure (X_0) and save the rest by purchasing a portfolio of securities with payouts to fund future consumption expenditure (X_s). This allows us to write the indirect utility function over future consumption expenditure, as $v(R_1, \ldots, R_S)$.[4] In the model, consumers are assigned the time-separable von Neumann–Morgenstern expected utility function in (3.13), and security returns are jointly normally distributed. This allows us to summarize their preferences for future consumption using the means and variances in the returns on their portfolios, with $V(\bar{i}_P, \sigma_P)$, where $\bar{i}_P$ is the expected return on portfolio (P) and σ_P its standard deviation.[5] The indifference schedules for this utility function are illustrated in Figure 3.10.

Box 4.1 Average annual returns on securities with different risk

By comparing the differences in the expected returns to stocks and bonds we can see how large the risk premium on equity is and how much it varies over time. The following data summarizes the average premium paid to equity over long-term (10-year) US government bonds and short-term (six-month) US Treasury bills for the period 1951–2001. There are eight separate countries plus Europe, Australasia and the Far East (EAFE) Index and the Morgan Stanley Capital International (MSCI) World Index, where the equity returns are measured for the broadest index available in each country. Based on these comparisons shares are riskier than bonds, and long-term bonds are riskier than short-term bonds.

Country	*Equity-bond premium (%)*	*Equity-bill premium (%)*
Australia	4.57	5.75
Canada	2.29	3.23
France	3.85	5.21
Germany	3.11	5.30
Italy	1.38	2.42
Japan	4.57	6.52
United Kingdom	4.79	5.79
United States	5.25	6.28
Europe	5.24	6.17
EAFE	4.78	5.71
MSCI	4.52	5.45

But these differences are somewhat misleading as they are based on nominal (geometric) returns and therefore do not account for the different effects of inflation on stocks and bonds. Real risk premiums are summarized below for a subset of these countries over the period 1925–2001. Notice how bonds outperform equity in Canada and Japan in the period 1979–2001. In some years equity and bonds paid negative real returns.

Country	*1925–1949*	*1949–1979*	*1979–2001*
Australia	3.74	7.00	0.98
Canada	—	7.00	–1.74
France	8.38	5.72	2.94
Germany	8.58	5.01	3.13
Italy	9.42	1.91	1.45
Japan	7.12	11.02	–1.80
United Kingdom	0.94	4.89	5.01
United States	2.94	7.62	3.99

Data source: Taylor (2007).

4.1.2 Financial investment opportunity set

Now we examine the investment opportunity set for investors with mean–variance preferences. This identifies the largest expected return that can be achieved at each level of risk by bundling together traded securities. As noted above, we follow Copeland and Weston by developing this budget constraint in the CAPM in stages to provide insight into the role of diversification, and to clarify the reason why all investors ultimately measure and price risk identically. The budget constraint is derived separately for:

i two risky securities;
ii one risky security and one risk-free security;
iii many risky securities;
iv many risky securities and one risk-free security.

The last of these steps provides the budget constraint in the CAPM, which is referred to as the capital market line

Two risky securities

The random payouts on two risky securities (A and B) are summarized in Table 4.1, together with their corresponding probabilities. The mean–variance consumption opportunities from holding one or other of the securities are illustrated in Figure 4.1.

Since the returns on these assets do not move together, it will be possible to diversify risk by bundling them together in portfolios, where the diversification effect determines the shape of the consumption opportunity set which must pass through points A and B in Figure 4.1. We determine the shape of the mean–variance frontier by marginally increasing the portion of asset A held in the portfolio and computing the change in its expected return ($\bar{i}_p$) over the resulting change in its standard deviation (σ_p). If we define a as the portion of asset A held in the portfolio (P) and $1 - a$ as the remaining portion held in asset B, the expected return on the portfolio is

Table 4.1 Random returns on securities A and B

States	*Probability*	$\tilde{i}_{Aj}$	$\tilde{i}_{Bj}$
1	0.30	−0.15	0.15
2	0.20	0.50	0.25
3	0.40	0.10	−0.15
4	0.10	0.50	0.10
Expected returns (%)		14.5	4.5
Variance (%)		6.5	2.7
Standard deviation (%)		25.4	16.5

$$\bar{i}_P = a\bar{i}_A + (1-a)\bar{i}_B. \tag{4.2}$$

It has a variance of:

$$\sigma_P^2 = a^2\sigma_A^2 + (1-a)^2\sigma_B^2 + 2a(1-a)\sigma_{AB}, \tag{4.3}$$

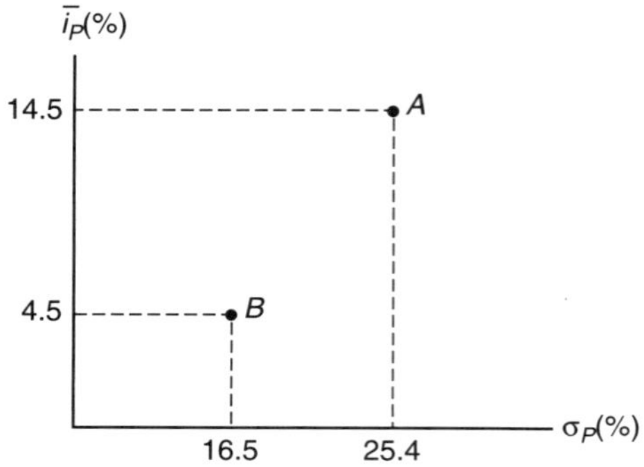

Figure 4.1 Investment opportunities with two risky securities.

with $\sigma_{AB} = \text{Cov}(\tilde{i}_A, \tilde{i}_B) = E\left((\tilde{i}_A - \bar{i}_A)(\tilde{i}_B - \bar{i}_B)\right)$ being the *covariance* of the asset returns. The diversification effect from bundling the securities together is determined by their *coefficient of correlation*, which is

$$\rho_{AB} = \text{Corr}(\tilde{i}_A, \tilde{i}_B) = \frac{\sigma_{AB}}{\sigma_A \sigma_B}. \tag{4.4}$$

If the asset returns are perfectly positively correlated, with $\rho_{AB} = +1$, there is no diversification effect, while at the other extreme, if they are perfectly negatively correlated, with $\rho_{AB} = -1$, complete diversification is possible. Thus, there is a diversification effect whenever this coefficient is less than +1, and it increases as the coefficient approaches −1.

We now derive the mean–variance frontier at each of these bounds to establish its shape in Figure 4.1 for more realistic interim values of the coefficient of correlation. We start with the case of no diversification ($\rho_{AB} = +1$).When asset returns move perfectly together they do not offset each other, where an example is given in Figure 4.2. The returns are plotted over the random outcomes in the left hand panel, and against each other in the right-hand panel. The positive linear relationship in the right-hand panel indicates they are perfectly positively correlated.

Notice how in the left-hand panel the returns always move in the same direction even though they do not have the same deviation from their normalized common mean return ($\bar{i}$). This makes the relationship between them in the return space linear with a positive slope that is less than unity as the returns on asset B are always larger. In these circumstances we can use the definition of the coefficient of correlation in (4.4) to write the variance on the portfolio in (4.3) as

$$\sigma_P^2 = (a\sigma_A + (1-a)\sigma_B)^2, \tag{4.5}$$

where the standard deviation in the return on the portfolio is the weighted sum of the standard deviations of the two asset returns, with $\sigma_P = a\sigma_A + (1 - a)\sigma_B$. Thus, the slope of the mean–variance frontier is constant, with

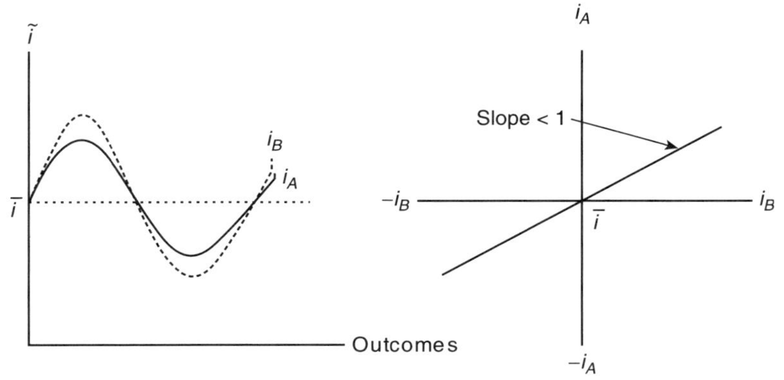

Figure 4.2 Perfectly positively correlated returns.

$$\frac{d\bar{i}_P / da}{d\sigma_P / da} = \frac{\bar{i}_A - \bar{i}_B}{\sigma_A - \sigma_B} > 0.$$

This is a line that passes through points *A* and *B*, as shown in Figure 4.3. Between these points the consumer is holding positive combinations of both assets, while above point *A* security *B* is sold to fund additional purchases of security *A*, and below point *B* security *A* is sold to fund the additional purchases of security *B*. Eventually, by going short in asset *A*, the standard deviation on the portfolio can be driven to zero. Further borrowing causes the standard deviation to rise along the dashed line, but this part of the frontier is dominated by points on the line vertically above where for each level of risk the expected return on the portfolio is higher. Thus, the dashed line is not part of the *efficient mean–variance frontier* which maximises the expected return at each level of risk.

We now turn to the case of complete diversification with $\rho_{AB} = -1$. Since the asset returns move perfectly against each other, it is possible to construct a bundle with positive holdings

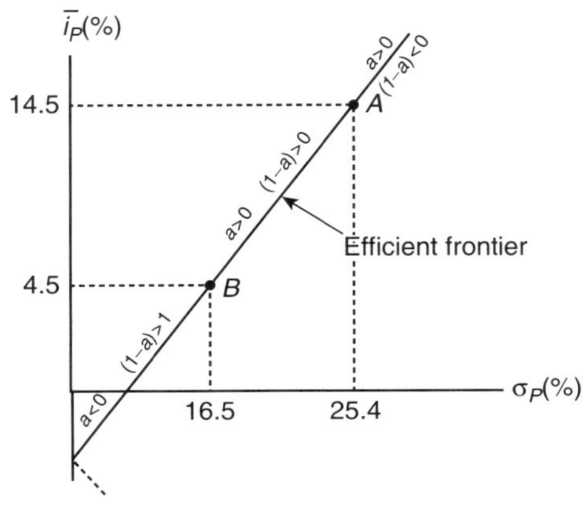

Figure 4.3 Efficient mean–variance frontier with $\rho_{AB} = +1$.

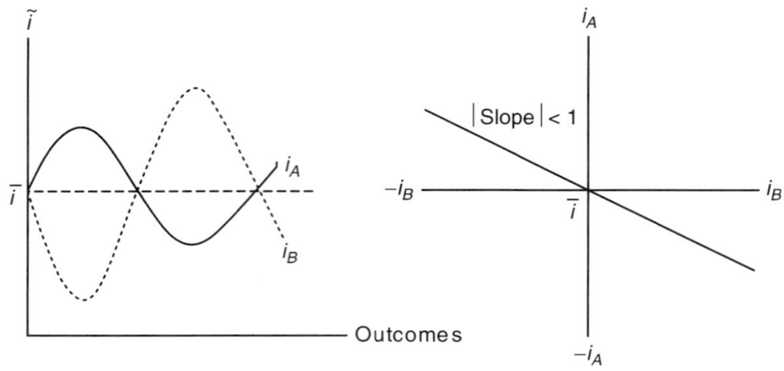

Figure 4.4 Perfectly negatively correlated returns.

of the two assets that eliminates the risk on the portfolio. In Figure 4.4 the random returns are plotted over, all possible outcomes in the left-hand panel and against each other in the right-hand panel. Once again, the returns on asset B deviate more from the normalized common mean return ($\bar{i}$) than the returns on asset A, except that now they move in opposite directions. There is a linear relationship between them in the return space and it has a negative slope with an absolute value less than unity due to the larger deviations in the returns on asset B.

With $\rho_{AB} = -1$, we can write the variance on the portfolio in (4.3) as

$$\sigma_P^2 = \left(a\sigma_A - (1-a)\sigma_B\right)^2, \tag{4.6}$$

where the return on the portfolio has a standard deviation which is the weighted difference in the standard deviations of the returns on the two assets. Since the returns move perfectly against each other it is possible to eliminate risk in the portfolio by choosing, $\hat{a} \approx 0.61$. This is the *minimum variance portfolio (MVP)* which has an expected return of 10.6 per cent, where the slope of the efficient mean–variance frontier is constant and changes sign either side of this bundle:

$$\frac{d\bar{i}_P / da}{d\sigma_P / da} = \begin{cases} \dfrac{\bar{i}_A - \bar{i}_B}{\sigma_A + \sigma_B} > 0, & \text{for } a > \hat{a}, \\ -\dfrac{\bar{i}_A - \bar{i}_B}{\sigma_A + \sigma_B} < 0, & \text{for } a < \hat{a}. \end{cases}$$

The efficient mean–variance frontier is illustrated in Figure 4.5 by the line with intercept 10.6 that passes through point A; it isolates the largest expected return on the portfolio at each level of risk.

Partial diversification with $-1 = \rho_{AB} \leq +1$ is more realistic as there is normally some market risk in the economy that cannot be eliminated by the diversification effect. Examples of negatively and positively correlated returns are illustrated in the left- and right-hand panels, respectively, of Figure 4.6. The efficient frontier is non-linear in these circumstances

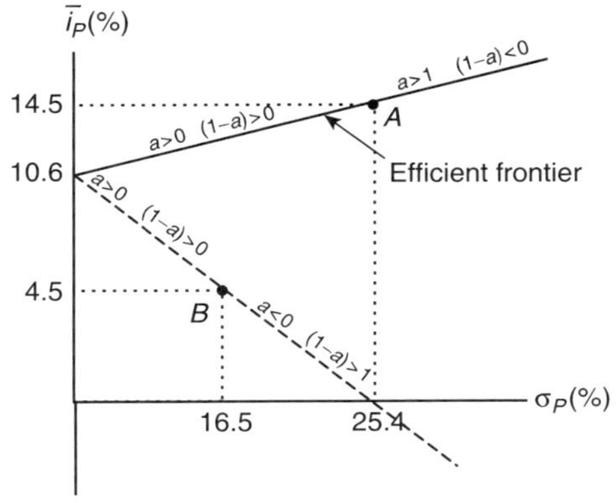

Figure 4.5 Efficient mean–variance frontier with $\rho_{AB} = -1$.

because its slope is a function of the asset share, and it lies within the bounds established by the frontiers for the two extremes considered above. An example is shown in Figure 4.7 as the solid line from the MVP through point *A*.

The returns summarized in Table 4.1 have a covariance of $\sigma_{AB} = 0.010725$, and coefficient of correlation of $\rho_{AB} = 0.002555$. The minimum variance portfolio ($\hat{a}$) is obtained using the portfolio variance for the securities in (4.3), as $\hat{a} \approx 0.234$.[6] In other words, the variance in the portfolio is minimized by holding approximately 23.4 per cent of each dollar in security *A* and the remaining 76.6 per cent in security *B*.

Now we are in a position to consider how consumers value risky assets *A* and *B*, when:

a they have homogenous expectations (which gives them the same mean–variance frontier); and
b there are no short-selling (borrowing) constraints (so they can trade along the efficient frontier beyond point *A* by selling asset *B*.

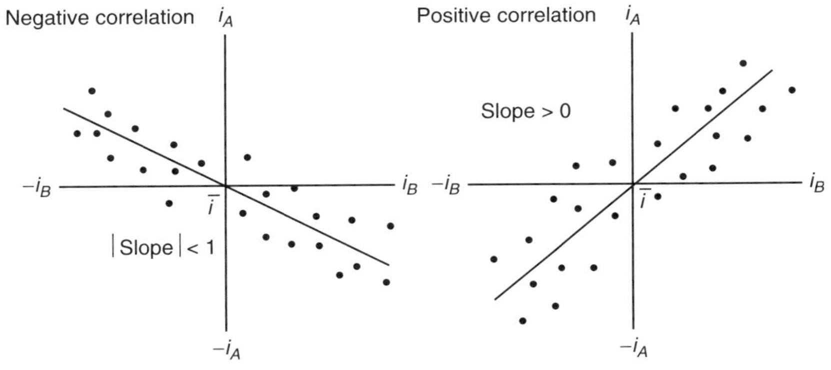

Figure 4.6 Partially correlated returns.

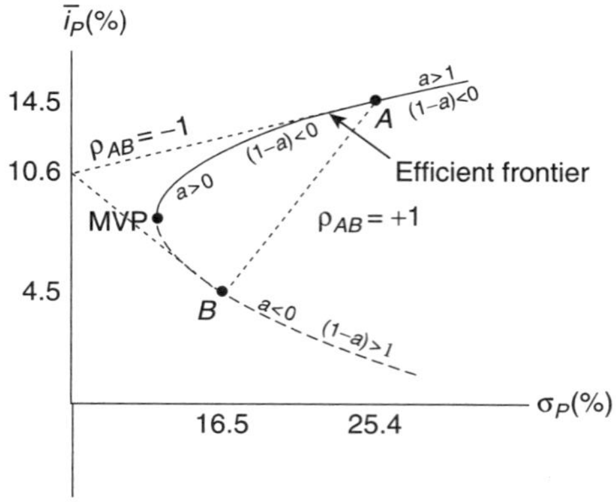

Figure 4.7 Efficient mean–variance frontier with $-1 < \rho_{AB} < +1$.

Figure 4.8 illustrates the portfolios chosen by two investors 1 and 2 in these circumstances, where investor 1 is relatively more risk-averse and therefore chooses a more risky portfolio (σ_{P1}) with a higher expected return $\bar{i}_{P1}$ than does investor 2. Since they trade along a non-linear frontier here they measure and price the risk in assets *A* and *B* differently. Investor 1 measures the risk each asset contributes to σ_{P1} and prices it using the slope of the indifference curve at point 1 on the efficient frontier. In contrast, investor 2 measures the risk each asset contributes to σ_{P2} and prices it using the slope of the indifference curve at point 2 on the efficient frontier. The standard deviations in the returns on the market portfolios determines the market (non-diversifiable) risk in their future consumption expenditure. When investors are risk-averse they must be compensated for bearing this risk, where the risk premium is determined by the slope of the indifference curves at their optimally chosen portfolios, and since the efficient frontier is non-linear, they will measure and price risk differently. In these circumstances the asset pricing model is agent-specific.

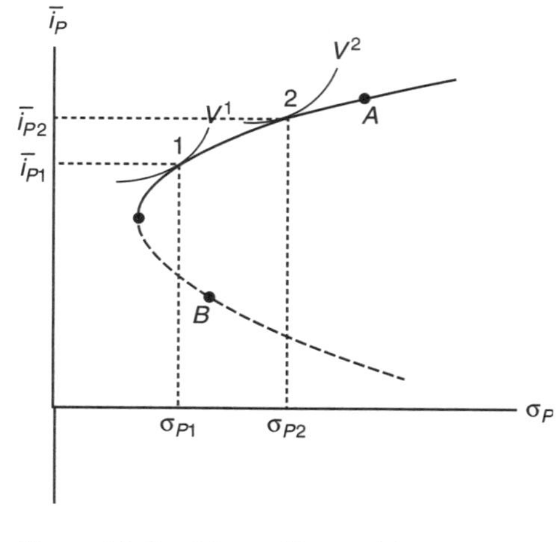

Figure 4.8 Portfolios with two risky securities.

One important reason why consumers measure and price risk identically in the CAPM is that they can trade a risk-free security. This is demonstrated by the next derivation of the mean–variance frontier.

One risky security and one risk-free security

The expected returns and variances on the one risky security (A) and risk-free security (F) are summarized in Table 4.2.

Table 4.2 Means and variances on securities A and F

Securities	*A*	*F*
Expected returns (%)	14.5	3
Variance	0.064725	0
Standard deviation (%)	25.4	0

In practice, it may not be possible for investors to purchase a pure risk-free security. Indeed, there is some risk in most government bonds because they pay nominal interest when expected inflation is uncertain. Very few governments issue bonds that pay a real risk-free return. Moreover, there can also be sovereign risk that results from the probability (in some cases fairly small) that the government will default on its debt. When a consumer bundles security A with a risk-free security the expected return on their portfolio is

$$\bar{i}_P = a\bar{i}_A + (1-a)i, \tag{4.7}$$

where $1 - a$ is the proportion of each dollar invested in risk-free security F. Since $\sigma_F = \sigma_{AB} = 0$ the variance on the portfolio collapses to

$$\sigma_P^2 = a^2\sigma_A^2. \tag{4.8}$$

Now the slope of the efficient frontier is linear, with:

$$\frac{d\bar{i}_P/da}{d\sigma_P/da} = \frac{\bar{i}_A - i}{\sigma_A} > 0. \tag{4.9}$$

This is illustrated by the line with intercept 3.0 passing through point A in Figure 4.9. As investors move away from security A into risk-free security F, the risk in their portfolio approaches zero. This not a diversification effect, but rather a reduction in the share of the risky security in the portfolio. Someone in the economy must bear the market risk in asset A, where the equilibrium security returns must equate the aggregate demands and supplies for both securities. The risk premium of 11.5 per cent for asset A is sufficient compensation to attract enough consumers to bear its market risk of 25.4 per cent.

Now we consider how consumers measure and price the risk in security A, when they:

a have homogenous expectations (and evaluate the means and variances on the two assets identically);
b can trade a risk-free security;[7] and
c face no short-selling (borrowing) constraints (so they can trade along the efficient frontier beyond point A by selling the risk-free asset).

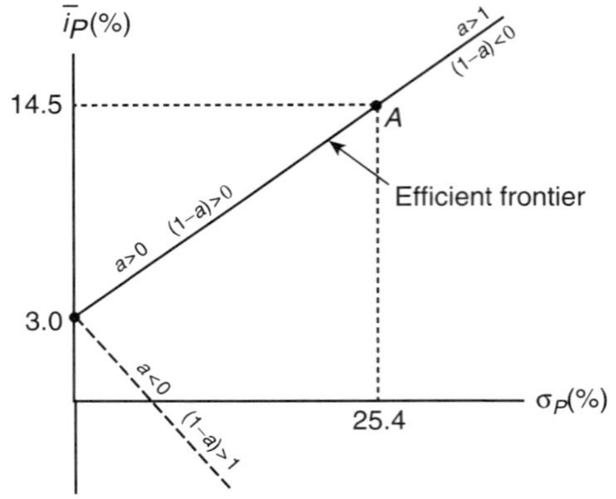

Figure 4.9 Portfolios with a risk-free security (*F*).

Since consumers face the same linear efficient frontier they will price and measure the risk in security *A* in the same way. In fact, the only risk they face is determined by the variance in the return on asset *A* which they combine with the risk-free security according to their risk preferences. Examples of portfolios for two investors 1 and 2 with different risk preferences are shown in Figure 4.10, where individual 1 holds relatively more of the risk-free security. Some investors may trade beyond point *A* on the efficient frontier by borrowing at the risk-free rate.

The consumption risk for each consumer is determined by the proportion of asset *A* they hold in their portfolio, with $\sigma_{P1} = a^1\sigma_A$ and $\sigma_{P2} = a^2\sigma_A$.[8] As they face the same market risk ($\sigma_A = 25.4$) and have indifference curves with the same slope along the linear efficient frontier they will measure and price risk in the same way. Thus, there is a common asset pricing model for all consumers in the economy, where the price of risk is determined by the slope of the frontier, with $(\bar{i}_A - i)/\sigma_A \approx 0.45$. This simple example provides considerable insight into the CAPM which is derived with many risky securities. Before taking that final step we examine the efficient mean–variance frontier with many risky securities and no risk-free security to analyse the diversification effect in a more realistic setting.

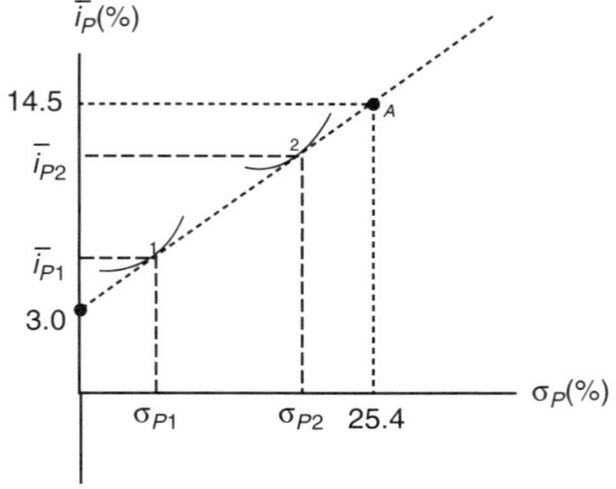

Figure 4.10 Efficient mean–variance frontier with risky security *A* and risk-free security *F*.

Many risky securities and no risk-free security

In practice many risky securities are sold by firms that bring different production risk to the capital market. An important role of the capital market is to allow investors to trade this risk and, where possible, to eliminate that part of it that is diversifiable by bundling securities in portfolios. In the absence of a risk-free security, the expected return on a risky portfolio drawn from K traded securities is

$$\bar{i}_P = \sum_{k=1}^{K} a_k \bar{i}_k, \tag{4.10}$$

where a_k is the proportion of each dollar of saving allocated to security $k = 1, \ldots, K$, with $\Sigma_k a_k = 1$. The variance in this portfolio return is:

$$\sigma_P^2 = \sum_{k=1}^{K} \sum_{j=1}^{K} a_k a_j \sigma_{kj}. \tag{4.11}$$

Clearly, the number of covariance terms has expanded from the example considered earlier with two risky securities A and B. This is best illustrated by writing the variance on the portfolio return, using the variance–covariance matrix, as:

$$\sigma_P^2 = \begin{bmatrix} a_1 & \ldots & a_K \end{bmatrix} \begin{bmatrix} \sigma_1^2 & \cdots & \sigma_{1K} \\ \vdots & \ddots & \vdots \\ \sigma_{K1} & \cdots & \sigma_{KK}^2 \end{bmatrix} \begin{bmatrix} a_1 \\ \vdots \\ a_K \end{bmatrix}. \tag{4.12}$$

There are as many variance terms as assets (K) along the diagonal of the variance–covariance matrix, but $K^2 – K$ covariance terms off the diagonal. The covariance terms determine the size of the diversification effect, and empirical estimates using stock market data suggest that most of the diversifiable risk can be eliminated from portfolios by bundling 15–20 securities together. This is illustrated in Figure 4.11, where the variance on the returns to optimally chosen portfolios approaches the non-diversifiable (market) risk as the number of securities in the portfolio rises.

Ultimately market risk is the risk in aggregate consumption, and securities pay investors a risk premium as compensation for bearing it. In an equilibrium this premium equates the aggregate demand for and supply of market risk, which emanates from the production activities

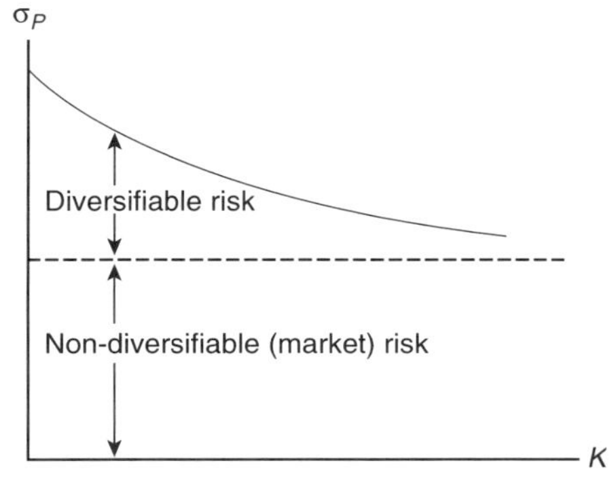

Figure 4.11 Portfolio risk and number of securities.

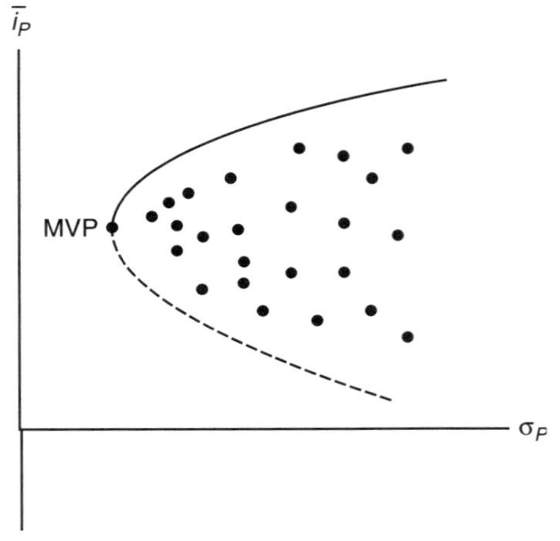

Figure 4.12 Efficient mean–variance frontier with many (N) risky securities.

of firms. In the absence of a risk-free security the efficient mean–variance frontier for K risky securities with partial diversification is illustrated by the solid curve starting at the *MVP* in Figure 4.12. Expected returns and standard deviations for all traded securities must lie on or inside the mean–variance frontier.

In the CAPM setting investors have homogenous expectations and face the same efficient mean–variance frontier. However, they will measure and price the risk in traded securities differently when they hold different portfolios. Two representative investors are illustrated in Figure 4.13, where individual 2 has a more risky portfolio, with $\sigma_{P2} > \sigma_{P1}$.

As was the case previously with two risky securities A and B, consumers compute the risk premium for any risky security k by its contribution to the risk in their portfolio. They then value this risk using the slopes of their indifference curves at consumption points 1 and 2 in Figure 4.13. Since they have different market portfolios and different marginal valuations

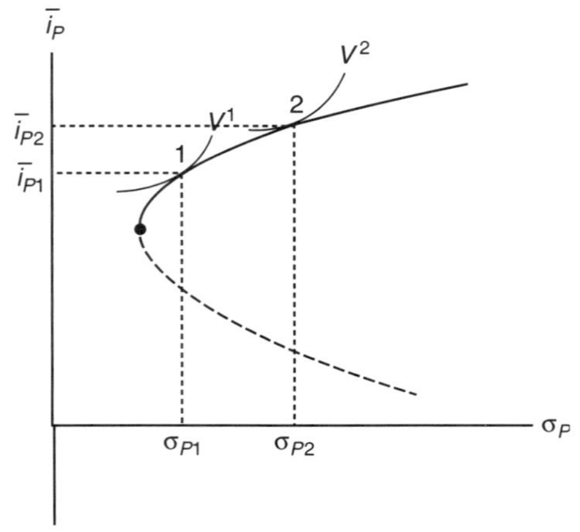

Figure 4.13 Portfolios with many risky securities.

for risk, the asset pricing model is agent-specific. Even though consumers see the same risk premium on each security they do not decompose it in the same way.

Many risky securities and one risk-free security

These are the trading opportunities in the CAPM, where expected returns on security portfolios are

$$\bar{i}_P = a_M \bar{i}_A + (1 - a_M) i, \tag{4.13}$$

with a_M being the proportion of saving invested in a bundle of risky securities (M) and $1 - a_M$ the remaining proportion invested in risk-free security F. The market portfolio is a derivative security constructed from positive combinations of the (K) risky traded securities. Since the return on the risk-free security is certain, we have $\sigma_F = \sigma_{FM} = 0$, where the variance on the returns to investor portfolios becomes

$$\sigma_P^2 = a_M^2 \sigma_M^2 + (1 - a_M)^2 \sigma_F^2 + 2a_M (1 - a_M) \sigma_{MF} = a_M^2 \sigma_M^2. \tag{4.14}$$

By combining risky bundle M with the risk free security, the slope of the mean–variance consumption opportunity frontier is constant, with:

$$\frac{d\bar{i}_P / da_M}{d\sigma_P / da_M} = \frac{\bar{i}_M - i}{\sigma_M} > 0. \tag{4.15}$$

This is referred to as the *capital market line (CML)*, and is illustrated in Figure 4.14.

In the CAPM every investor faces the same CML where:

- a they have homogenous expectations (and therefore see the same risky efficient mean–variance frontier);
- b there are no short-selling (borrowing) constraints (so they can trade along the CML beyond point M by selling the risk-free security);
- c they can trade a risk-free security; and,
- d there are no taxes or transactions costs.

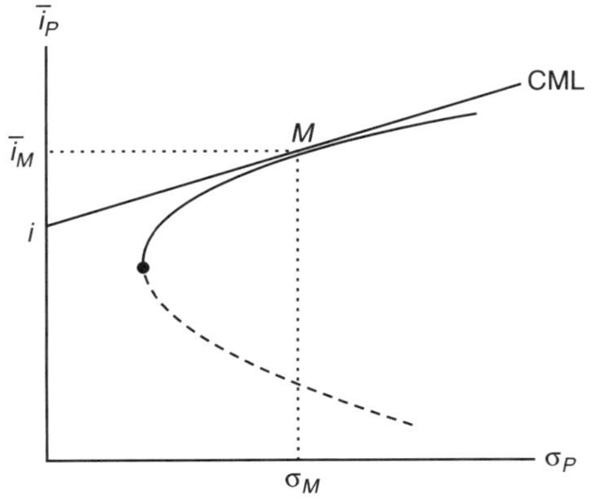

Figure 4.14 Capital market line.

Since investors face the same linear efficient mean–variance frontier they all choose the same risky bundle, called the market (M) portfolio, and have the same marginal valuation for risk. Thus, they measure and price risk identically. In particular, they measure risk by the standard deviation in the return on the market portfolio (σ_M), and price it using the slope of the CML, which is

$$\frac{d\bar{i}_P}{d\sigma_M} = \frac{\bar{i}_M - i}{\sigma_M}. \tag{4.16}$$

It is the premium that equates the aggregate demand for and supply of every traded security in the capital market. Suppose every investor in the economy becomes marginally *less* risk-averse where this moves their consumption bundles up along the CML. This creates an excess demand for risky bundle M and an excess supply of risk-free security F. A plausible outcome would see a higher interest rate and a flatter CML as the risk premium falls. In fact, the efficient mean–variance frontier for risky securities would fall when investors are willing to bear the same market risk at a lower risk premium. As a consequence, the market portfolio is likely to change as firms adjust their investment choices in response to the lower cost of capital. In the new equilibrium these adjustments would once again equate the demands for and supplies of all the traded securities in the economy. That is why the CAPM is frequently referred to as an equilibrium asset pricing model.

Two-fund separation holds in the CAPM because every investor bundles risky securities into the same derivative asset (M) which they combine with the risk-free security (F). They choose different amounts of market risk based on their risk preferences where relatively less risk-averse investors hold more of risky bundle M in their portfolio. Indeed, some investors may even choose to borrow at the risk-free rate to increase their holding of the derived risky bundle to trade beyond point M along the CML in Figure 4.14. But they all face the same market risk (σ_M). In other words, they have the same consumption risk.

The final step is to price each risky traded security held in the market portfolio. In the CAPM no risky security is held outside it, and all risk emanates from the underlying production risk in the economy, which attracts a risk premium when consumers are risk-averse.

4.1.3 Security market line – the CAPM equation

The asset pricing equation in the CAPM was derived independently by Sharpe (1964) and Lintner (1965). We provide an informal derivation here to draw out the economic intuition. A formal derivation is provided later in Section 4.2.1. Consider a portfolio which combines one of the risky securities (k) with the market portfolio, where the expected return on this portfolio is

$$\bar{i}_P = a_k \bar{i}_k + (1 - a_k) i_F. \tag{4.17}$$

It has a variance of

$$\sigma_P^2 = a_k^2 \sigma_k^2 + (1 - a_k)^2 \sigma_M^2 + 2a_k(1 - a_k)\sigma_{kM}. \tag{4.18}$$

Think of a_k as the excess demand for security k, and then raise it marginally to evaluate its impact on the slope of the efficient mean–variance frontier for risky securities with $a_k = 0$. This experiment tells us how much risk security k contributes to risky bundle M; it is the slope of the efficient mean–variance frontier for the risky securities at point M in Figure 4.14, where

$$\frac{d\bar{i}_P / da_k}{d\sigma_P / da_k} = \frac{\bar{i}_k - \bar{i}_M}{(\sigma_{kM} - \sigma_M^2) / \sigma_M}. \tag{4.19}$$

When every asset k is optimally held inside the market portfolio its contribution to market risk is equal to the premium for market risk, which is the slope of the CML:

$$\frac{\bar{i}_k - \bar{i}_M}{(\sigma_{kM} - \sigma_M^2)/\sigma_M} = \frac{\bar{i}_M - i}{\sigma_M}. \tag{4.20}$$

Slope of risky efficient frontier = Slope of CML

By rearranging these terms, we obtain the CAPM pricing equation,

$$\bar{i}_k = i + (\bar{i}_M - i)\beta_k, \tag{4.21}$$

where $\beta_k = \sigma_{kM}/\sigma^2_M$ is the beta coefficient that measures the amount of market risk in security k. It is referred to as the *security market line* (SML) and is based on two sets of assumptions. The first set relates to preferences:

- Consumers are risk averse, have homogeneous expectations and maximize NMEU functions in a two-period setting.
- Future consumption is funded solely from returns to portfolios of securities.
- Security returns are jointly normally distributed.

The second set are concerned with the budget constraint (CML):

- Consumers have homogeneous expectations.
- There are no borrowing constraints.
- A risk-free security exists.
- The capital market is competitive and frictionless (to rule out taxes and transactions costs).

It is easy to see why the CAPM is a popular model. The risk premium is based on the return to the common market portfolio which is normally estimated from time series data for a broadly based (value-weighted) price index of publicly traded stocks. In other words, consumption risk is identified by a single factor in the model. If any security k is a perfect substitute for the market portfolio, then $\beta_k = 1$ and the pricing equation in (4.21) collapses to $\bar{i}_k = \bar{i}_M$. Notice how the market risk in the return to security k is determined by its covariance with the return on the market portfolio. Using the coefficient of correlation defined in (4.4), we can write the beta coefficient as $\beta_k = \rho_{kM}\, \sigma_k/\sigma_M$. When the return on security k is perfectly correlated with the return on the market portfolio, with $\rho_{KM} = 1$, then we must have $\sigma_K = \sigma_M$. But assets with a higher standard deviation ($\sigma_k > \sigma_M$) can also have $\beta_k = 1$ if the extra risk is diversifiable. The SML in (4.21) is illustrated in Figure 4.15.

By arbitrage, all expected security returns must lie on the SML. In other words, the *no arbitrage condition* holds in the CAPM, where the only differences in expected security

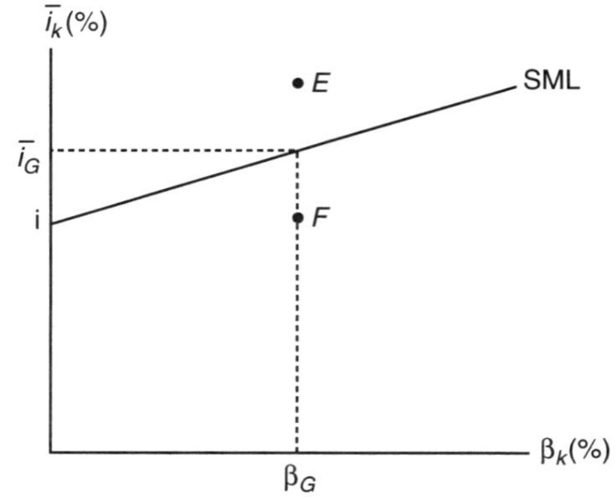

Figure 4.15 Security market line.

returns must be due solely to differences in market risk. To see this, consider the risky security G with beta coefficient β_G. If its expect return lies above the SML at point E it pays economic profit. As investors increase demand for this security its price rises until the expected return is driven down onto the SML. Conversely, if investors expect the return to be at point F where no risk premium is being paid, the fall in demand for the security drives down its price until its expected return rises onto the SML.

Box 4.2 The CAPM pricing equation (SML): a numerical example

The following financial data is taken from an imaginary economy where the CAPM holds. We use the share price index as the market portfolio held by all consumers, where its return in each year is computed by summing capital gains to the dividend yield. This index is a broadly based value-weighted index with weights equal to the market value of each firm's equity as a proportion of the total value of equity traded.

Year	*Share price index*	*Price change (%)*	*Dividend yield (%)*	*Market return (%)*	*Treasury bill rate (%)*	*Deadlock return (%)*
2006	5821.00	18.2	2.5	20.70	6.2	7.55
2005	4924.70	14.3	3.0	17.30	6.0	6.29
2004	4308.57	12.5	4.5	17.00	5.8	9.12
2003	3829.84	−6.4	1.5	−4.90	5.4	1.76
2002	4091.71	−8.8	0.0	−8.80	5.6	2.39
2001	4486.52	10.3	2.0	12.30	5.6	9.59
2000	4067.56	15.6	2.8	18.40	5.4	11.57
1999	3518.65	—	—	—	—	—
Mean		7.96	2.33	10.29	5.71	6.90
Variance		102.37	1.66	123.93	0.08	11.65

Using this data we find that the CAPM pricing equation is:

$$i_k = 5.71 + 4.58\beta_k,$$

with $i \approx 5.71$, $\bar{i}_M - i \approx 4.58$ and $\beta_k = \text{Cov}(\tilde{i}_M, \tilde{i}_k)/\text{Var}(\tilde{i}_M)$. Since the return on a Deadlock share has a covariance with the return on the market portfolio of $\sigma_{DM} \approx 32.12$, we can decompose its expected return, using the pricing equation, as

$$\bar{i}_D = 5.71 + 1.19 \approx 6.90 \text{ per cent},$$

where $\beta_D = \sigma_{DM}/\sigma^2_M = 32.12/123.93 \approx 0.26$ is the amount of market risk it contributes to consumption expenditure. Thus, Deadlock shares pay a risk premium of $4.58\beta_D \approx 1.19$ per cent.

Box 4.3 Numerical estimates of beta coefficients by sector

Beta books can be purchased in most countries. They provide estimates of the beta coefficients for all publicly listed companies where the return on the market portfolio is normally computed using time series data for a broadly based value-weighted share price index such as the Standard & Poor's 500 in the United States or the All Ordinaries Index in Australia. The following table summarizes average beta coefficients for publicly listed companies trading on the Australian Securities Exchange. They are reported as average coefficients for 20 sectors in the economy. The food, beverages and tobacco sector has the lowest beta coefficient at 0.57, while the highest is 1.37 in the insurance sector.

	Sector	β
1	Banks	0.78
2	Capital goods	0.99
3	Commercial services and supplies	1.21
4	Consumer durables and apparel	1.35
5	Consumer services	0.91
6	Diversified financials	0.78
7	Energy	1.15
8	Food and staples retailing	0.61
9	Food beverage and tobacco	0.57
10	Health care and equipment services	0.96
11	Insurance	1.37
12	Materials	1.16
13	Media	0.98
14	Real estate	0.91
15	Retailing	0.93
16	Software and services	1.28
17	Technology hardware and equipment	0.85
18	Telecommunication services	0.35
19	Transportation	0.91
20	Utilities	0.35
	Market	1.00

Source: Based on financial data taken from Aspect Financial Analysis on 17 May 2007. This database is produced by Aspect Huntley Pty Ltd.

4.1.4 Relaxing the assumptions in the CAPM

Two important features of the CAPM make it popular:

i Expected security returns are linear in a single risk factor.
ii All investors measure and price risk identically.

The beta books that are published in most countries are evidence of its popularity. They provide estimates of the beta coefficients for securities listed on the stock exchange. But it is important that financial analysts understand the assumptions in the CAPM and what role they play. We do this here by relaxing some of the main assumptions one at a time, while the results from empirical tests of the model are summarized later in Section 4.5.

With *risk-neutral investors* the indifference schedules are horizontal lines in the mean–variance space as no additional compensation is required for increases in risk. The equilibrium outcome is illustrated in Figure 4.16 where the CML is also horizontal at the risk-free return. All securities pay the risk-free return (i), where the SML in (4.21) collapses to $\bar{i}_k = i$ for all k. There is considerable evidence to suggest that risk aversion is a robust assumption in the CAPM.

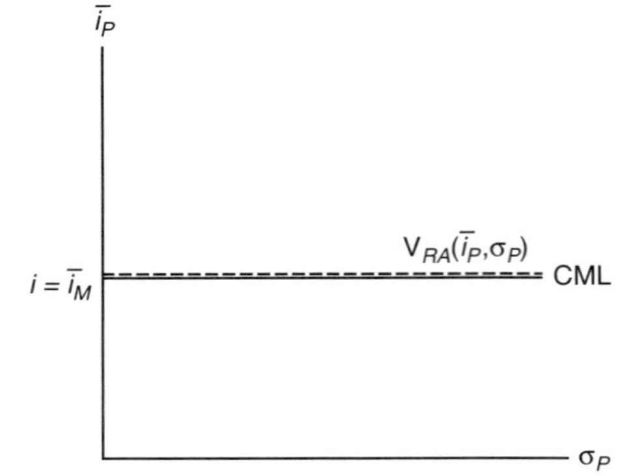

Figure 4.16 Risk-neutral investors.

When security returns are *not joint-normally distributed* we cannot, in general, describe the distributions of returns on portfolios solely by their means and variances. Indeed, it may take additional moments for the distribution to fully describe the returns on portfolios, and risk may not be linearly related to them. One way to rescue the CAPM is to adopt quadratic preferences, where investors only care about the means and variances in their portfolio returns. But placing restrictions on preferences is much less appealing. A number of empirical studies have tested security returns on portfolios to see whether they are jointly normality distributed. Fama (1965) did so for securities traded on the New York Stock Exchange and found they were symmetric with fat tails. In other words, they are approximately bell-shaped with infinite variances.

If investors have *heterogeneous expectations* they will not observe the same mean–variance frontier for risky securities. This is illustrated in Figure 4.17, where two consumers have different capital market lines and choose different market portfolios. Thus, they measure and price risk differently, with:

$$\bar{i}_k^h = i_F + (\bar{i}_{M^h} - i_F)\beta_k^h, \text{ for } h \in 1,2.$$

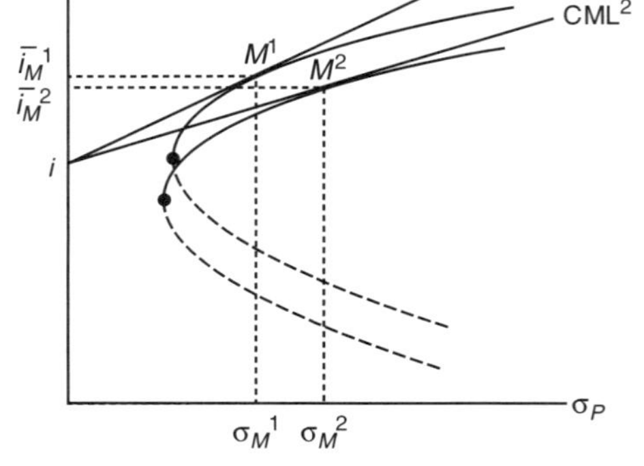

Figure 4.17 Heterogeneous expectations.

Differences in expectations normally result from costly information where that can compromise the competition assumption and the mutuality principle which both apply in the CAPM.

With *borrowing constraints* that restrict sales of the risk-free security the CML becomes non-linear at the point where the constraint binds. The efficient mean–variance frontier is illustrated in Figure 4.18 where no borrowing is allowed at the risk-free rate. It is the CML up to the market portfolio, then it becomes the efficient mean–variance frontier for risky securities. Once investors locate beyond point M on the efficient frontier they hold different risky bundles and therefore measure and price risk differently. All other investors measure and price risk identically as they hold risky bundle M and have the same marginal valuation for risk along the linear segment of the frontier between points i and M in the diagram. Borrowing constraints may also limit arbitrage activities that drive profits from security returns. In a competitive capital market a perfect substitute can be created for every security by bundling together existing traded securities, where arbitrage equates the expected return on the security with the return on its derivative. When borrowing constraints restrict the ability of traders to create these derivative securities the competition assumption may fail to hold, and there may be profits in security returns, which is not consistent with the CAPM pricing equation in (4.21).

In the absence of a *risk-free security*, investors hold different risky bundles on the non-linear efficient mean–variance frontier. Thus, they measure and price risk differently. Black (1972) argues the CAPM can be rescued in these circumstances when investors create derivative securities with no market risk in them as replacements for the risk-free security. They are referred to as *zero-beta securities* because they have $\beta_Z = 0$. These derivatives are normally created by shorting some securities and going long in others, where the CAPM pricing equation becomes

$$\bar{i}_k = \bar{i}_Z + (\bar{i}_M - \bar{i}_Z)\beta_k.$$

Unfortunately the Z security is not unique. Indeed, there are different ones for each market portfolio on the risky efficient mean–variance frontier. An example with two market portfolios is given in Figure 4.19.

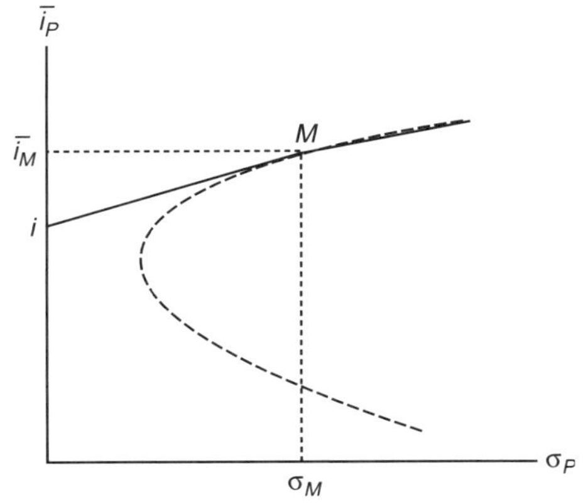

Figure 4.18 No borrowing.

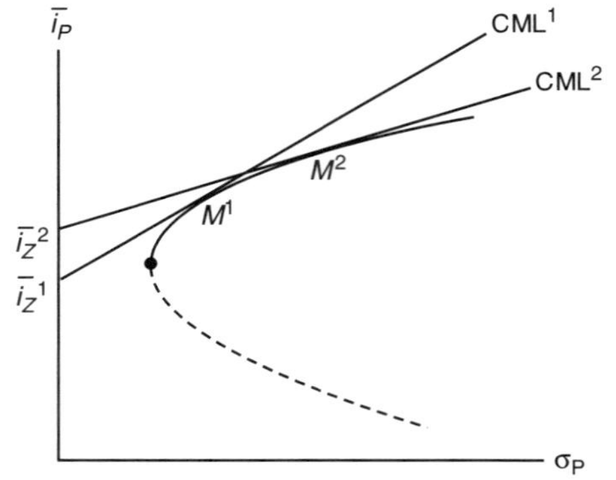

Figure 4.19 Zero beta securities.

Elton and Gruber (1995) manage to derive an aggregated CAPM pricing equation under these circumstances where the market portfolio and the Z security are the weighted sum of the individual investor market portfolios and Z securities which are both drawn from the same set of risky traded securities. Clearly, it is a much more difficult pricing equation to estimate and use in applied work.

When there are *taxes* on security returns, investors choose the same risky market portfolio when they face the same after-tax CML. They can have different tax rates on different types of securities, but they must be the same for all investors. An example is given in Figure 4.20, where the tax rate on interest is higher than the tax rate on returns to all the risky securities held in the market portfolio.

Since investors face the same before-tax (BT) and after-tax (AT) capital market lines they choose the same market portfolio. However, when they face different marginal tax rates on the same security returns they have different after-tax capital market lines and choose different market portfolios. Elton and Gruber (1995) and Brennan (1970) derive an aggregated CAPM pricing equation where the market portfolio is determined by the weighted after-tax returns on the risky portfolios chosen by investors. Clearly, it is much harder to compute than the simple CAPM pricing equation without taxes in (4.21).

The effects of *transactions costs* on the CAPM are similar to income taxes when they distort security returns, but they differ by using resources rather than transferring them as tax revenue. They also make it costly to eliminate diversifiable risk, where any marginal costs

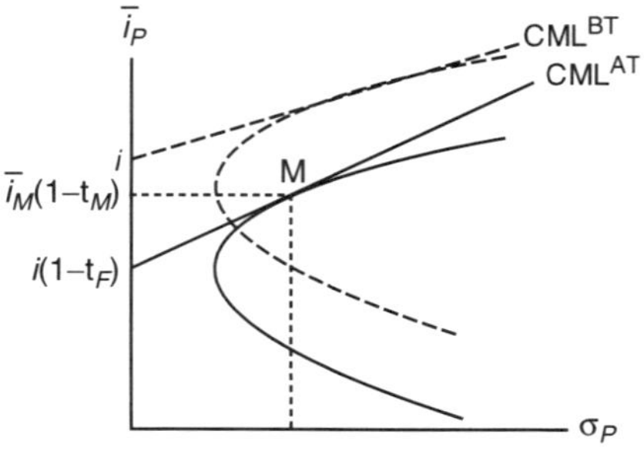

Figure 4.20 Income taxes.

incurred must be included in the asset pricing equation. Asymmetric information is much more likely when information is costly to acquire, where investors with different costs will likely have different information and form different expectations about security returns. Most popular asset pricing models assume there are no transactions costs, based largely on the view that institutional investors, who are specialist traders in the capital market, have low marginal transactions costs. In these circumstances they create risky mutual funds for individual consumers facing higher costs due to the relatively small value of their security trades.

A number of interesting puzzles arise in finance when equilibrium outcomes are examined in models without trading costs. For example, firms pay no dividends to fully taxable shareholders in economies with a classical corporate tax system. This so-called *dividend puzzle* is examined later in Chapter 7 where one of the explanations relies on differential trading costs on paying dividends and capital gains.

The CAPM holds when there are more than two time periods if the interest rate and relative commodity prices are constant and security returns are independently and identically distributed over time. This leaves consumers facing the same efficient mean–variance frontier, and the same real income, in every time period. Once consumption risk changes over time the CAPM fails to hold. Merton (1973a) extends the CAPM to the intertemporal setting by adding additional factors in the pricing equation to explain changes in market risk. This is the intertemporal CAPM which we examine later in Section 4.3.2.

4.2 Arbitrage pricing theory

One of the less attractive features of the CAPM is that it predicts every consumer will hold the same risky portfolio. It also relies on security returns being jointly normally distributed and consumers holding all their net wealth in financial securities. In response to these concerns Ross (1976) derives a pricing equation by isolating the common component of changes in security returns using a linear factor analysis.

As the name suggests, the APT relies crucially on arbitrage to eliminate any profits from security returns and to provide investors with the ability to eliminate idiosyncratic risk from their portfolios. An important starting point is the assumption that security returns can be fully described by a linear factor model, where the random return on any traded security k is related to $g = 1, \ldots, G$ factors and noise, with:

$$\tilde{i}_k = \bar{i}_k + \beta_{k1}\tilde{f}_1 + \cdots + \beta_{kG}\tilde{f}_G + \tilde{\varepsilon}_k \quad \forall k \in K,^9 \tag{4.22}$$

where β_{kg} is the sensitivity of the return on security k to the risk isolated by factor g, $\tilde{f}_g$ the deviation in the value of factor g from its mean value (with $\tilde{f}_g = \tilde{F}_g - \bar{F}_g$ and $E(\tilde{f}_g) = 0$ for all g), and $\tilde{\varepsilon}_k$ an error term (with $E(\tilde{\varepsilon}_k) = 0$ for all k). When (4.22) is used as a regression equation the factor deviations are uncorrelated with each other ($\text{cov}(\tilde{f}_g, \tilde{f}_j) = 0$ for all $g \neq j$)), and the model describes the returns to securities, and not just any arbitrary set of returns, when the error terms are uncorrelated across securities (with $E(\tilde{\varepsilon}_k, \tilde{\varepsilon}_j) = 0$ for all k, j).[10] To simplify the analysis, we report the factor deviations as rates of return on their *mimicking factor portfolios* (with $\tilde{f}_g = \tilde{i}_g - \bar{i}_g$ for all g). This makes the sensitivity coefficients in (4.22) standard beta coefficients, with $\beta_{kg} = \text{cov}(\tilde{i}_k, \tilde{i}_g)/\text{var}(\tilde{i}_g)$. Each mimicking portfolio is a derivative security with unit sensitivity for one factor and zero sensitivity for all others. Thus, their risk premiums are market premiums for the risk isolated by each factor.

It is important to note that (4.22) is not a functional relationship as the factors are not necessarily the source of aggregate uncertainty in security returns. Rather, they are correlated with it, and are typically macroeconomic variables such as industrial production and inflation, where deviations in security returns from their expected values are due to deviations in the values of these common factors from their means plus noise. Since factor risk is non-diversifiable it attracts a premium, while the noise, which can be diversified away inside portfolios with a large number of securities, attracts no premium.

A pricing equation for the APT is derived by first estimating the beta coefficients in (4.22) using a statistical analysis and then pricing the factor risk using the law of one price in a frictionless competitive capital market where the no arbitrage condition holds. The risk premium for each factor g is obtained by constructing a mimicking portfolio and deducting the risk-free interest rate from its expected return, with $\bar{i}_g - i$ for all g. A formal derivation of the pricing equation is provided below in Section 4.3.3 where it is obtained as a special case of the CBPM in (3.17). An intuitive derivation is provided here by demonstrating the properties and assumptions in the model, in particular the role of arbitrage. We begin by creating a risk-free arbitrage portfolio (A) with no initial wealth, where:

$$\sum_{k=1}^{K} a_k^A = 0. \tag{4.23}$$

Using the linear factor model in (4.22) the random return on this portfolio is

$$\tilde{i}_A = \sum_k a_k^A \tilde{i}_k = \sum_{k=1}^{K} a_k^A \bar{i}_k + \sum_{g=1}^{G}\sum_{k=1}^{K} a_k^A \beta_{kg} \tilde{f}_g + \sum_{k=1}^{K} a_k^A \tilde{\varepsilon}_k. \tag{4.24}$$

For it to be risk-free the security weights must be chosen to eliminate the factor risk in the second term, with $\Sigma_k a_g^A \beta_{kg} = 0$ for each factor g, and there must be enough securities (K) in the portfolio to eliminate idiosyncratic risk in the third term, with $\Sigma_k a_k^A \tilde{\varepsilon}_k = 0.$ As the number of securities in the arbitrage portfolio increases, the weight for each security becomes smaller, thereby eliminating the diversifiable risk. In these circumstances the return on the arbitrage portfolio is non-stochastic, with

$$i_A = \sum_{k=1}^{K} a_k^A \bar{i}_k = 0. \tag{4.25}$$

Thus, when the no arbitrage condition holds all profits are eliminated from security returns, where the return on the arbitrage portfolio, which is constructed with no initial wealth, must be zero.[11] By using the properties of linear algebra, the three orthogonality conditions, $\Sigma_{k=1} a_k^A = 0, \Sigma_k a_k^A \beta_{kg} = 0$ and $\Sigma_k a_k^A \tilde{\varepsilon}_k = 0,$ impose a linear relationship on the coefficients for the portfolio weights, with

$$\bar{i}_k = \lambda_0 + \sum_g \lambda_g \beta_{gk},^{12} \tag{4.26}$$

where λ_0 and λ_g are non-zero constants. And the constants are themselves rates of return, which is confirmed by using (4.26) for the risk-free security (F), with $\beta_{Fg} = 0$, where $\lambda_0 = i$, and the mimicking factor portfolios, with $\beta_{kg} = 1$ for all $k = g$ and $\beta_{kg} = 0$ for all $k \neq g$, where $\lambda_g = \bar{i}_g - i$. After substitution, we have the APT pricing equation,

$$\bar{i}_k - i = \sum_g \lambda_g \beta_{gk} \;\; \forall k, \tag{4.27}$$

where $\lambda_g = (\bar{i}_g - i)$ is the risk premium for factor g risk and $\beta_{gk} = \text{Cov}(\tilde{i}_g, \tilde{i}_k) / \text{Var}(\tilde{i}_g)$ the beta coefficient that measures its contribution to the market risk in security k. It is based on the following assumption:

- Consumers are risk–averse with homogeneous expectations.
- Security returns are described by a linear factor model.
- The law of one price holds.
- There is a risk free security.

Notice that this pricing equation has a similar structure to the CAPM equation in (4.21). Investors with homogenous expectations measure and price risk identically and therefore use the same factors (state variables) to identify market risk. The difference between the models is that the APT does not require jointly normally distributed asset returns, and risk is isolated using more than one factor. Unfortunately, however, the factors are not identified in the model. Instead, they are identified empirically by using data to find the best fit for the linear factor model in (4.22). Some analysts find the APT model more appealing as the risk factors are normally macroeconomic variables that investors monitor to evaluate economic activity. Chen *et al.* (1986) use US data to find four suitable candidates in the index of industrial production, changes in default risk premiums, differences in the yields on short- and long-term government bonds, and unanticipated inflation. Without a common set of factors the APT equation becomes an agent-specific pricing model.

Box 4.4 The CAPM as a special case of the APT

When the return on the market portfolio is the single factor that isolates market risk in the APT model, we have from (4.27) that, for any security k,

$$\bar{i}_k = i + (\bar{i}_M - i)\beta_{Mk},$$

with $\beta_{kM} = \text{Cov}(\tilde{i}_k, \tilde{i}M)/\text{Var}(\tilde{i}_M)$. This is the CAPM pricing equation in (4.21) where the linearity comes from the linear factor model and not from assuming security returns are jointly-normally distributed. The single factor is much more likely when consumers fund all their future consumption from returns to portfolios of risky securities.

If, in a two-period setting, asset returns are jointly normally distributed and consumer income is restricted to the returns on portfolios of securities, the APT equation in (4.27) collapses to the CAPM model in (4.21) where the variance in the return to the market portfolio is the sole factor in the model.

4.2.1 No arbitrage condition

Arbitrage plays an important role in the derivation of the APT model. But it is no less important in the CAPM, or, for that matter, any of the other equilibrium asset pricing models we examine later. They all rely on arbitrage to eliminate profits from expected security

Box 4.5 The APT pricing equation: a numerical example

Suppose we undertake an empirical analysis and find security returns are isolated using two factors – an index of industrial production (*Y*) and unanticipated inflation (*P*). The state-contingent returns on factor mimicking portfolios and two securities, Alpha (*A*) and Bastion (*B*), are summarized below.

		Returns (%)			
		Factor portfolios		*Shares (k)*	
States	*Probabilities*	*Y*	*P*	*A*	*B*
1	0.25	–5.00	34.50	35.0	5.0
2	0.30	25.00	3.90	18.0	25.0
3	0.20	–15.00	–5.00	–24.0	–10.0
4	0.25	35.00	18.16	28.0	40.0
	Mean	12.00	13.34	16.35	16.75
	Variance	401.00	211.75	447.33	333.19
	σ_{YP}	0	σ_{kY}	212.05	360.25
	i	6.25	σ_{kP}	256.03	40.61
			β_{kY}	0.53	0.90
			β_{kP}	1.21	0.19

Since each factor portfolio isolates the risk for a single factor, with $\beta_{YY} = \beta_{PP} = 1$ and $\beta_{YP} = \beta_{PY} = 0$, their returns have zero covariance with each other, where $\text{Cov}(\tilde{f}_Y, \tilde{f}_P) = E(\tilde{f}_Y \tilde{f}_P) = \text{Cov}(\tilde{i}_Y, \tilde{i}_P) = \sigma_{YP} = 0$. When these factors isolate all the market risk there are no residuals in the expected returns to securities, where the APT pricing equation becomes:

$$\bar{i}_k = 6.25 + (12.00 - 6.25)\beta_{kY} + (13.34 - 6.25)\beta_{kP}.$$

The premium for market risk isolated by the index of industrial production is 5.75 per cent, while it is 7.09 per cent for unanticipated inflation. After substituting the beta coefficients for the two shares, Alpha and Bastion, we find they have expected returns, of:

$$\bar{i}_A = 6.25 + (12.00 - 6.25)\ 0.53 + (13.34 - 6.25)\ 1.21 \approx 1787,$$
$$\bar{i}_B = 6.25 + (12.00 - 6.25)\ 0.90 + (13.34 - 6.25)\ 0.19 \approx 12.77.$$

Based on these calculations, traders could make arbitrage profits by selling security *A* and buying security *B* when the APT equation above correctly predicts their expected returns, as we have $\bar{i}_A$>16.35 and $\bar{i}_B$>16.75.

returns where any differences are explained by risk. This can be illustrated for the arbitrage trader (*A*) who maximizes profit $\pi^A = \bar{R}_k a_k^A + \bar{R}_D a_D^A$ by constructing a risk-free portfolio with no cost to initial wealth, where $P_{ak} a_k^A + P_{aD} a_D^A = 0$. It combines a risky security (*k*) with its perfect substitute (*D*) created by bundling together other traded securities. The optimization problem is illustrated in Figure 4.21 when security *D* initially has a higher expected return.

The budget constraint (W^A) is the solid line with slope $-p_{aD}/p_{ak}$ where every dollar allocated to one security must be financed by selling the other one. The iso-profit lines (illustrated as dashed lines) isolate combinations of securities *k* and *D* that hold profit constant at $\pi^{A'}$. Initially they have a steeper slope (in absolute value terms) than the slope of the budget constraint, where profits are obtained by going long in security *D* and short in security *k*. When the consumer holds portfolio *A′* by selling $a_k^{A'}$ dollars of security *k* to fund the purchase of $a_D^{A'}$ dollars of security *D*, the profit $\pi^{A'}$ is illustrated as distance 0*B* in Figure 4.21. In the absence of transactions costs the trader would maximize profit by being

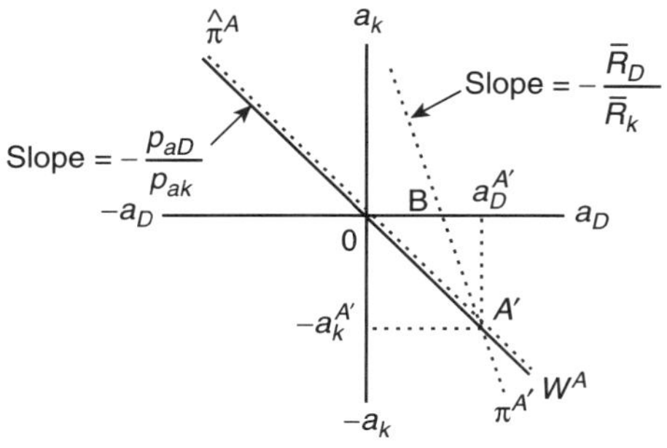

Figure 4.21 Arbitrage profits.

infinitely long in security D and infinitely short in security k. This process eliminates the excess return on security D by equating their expected returns, with $\bar{R}_k = \bar{R}_D$ and $p_{ak} = p_{aD}$. It is the *no arbitrage condition* where the iso-profit lines $(\hat{\pi}^A)$ have the same slope as the budget constraint.

4.3 Consumption-based pricing models

As noted in the introduction to this chapter, the CAPM and the APT are special cases of the consumption-based pricing model (CBPM) in (3.17). In a multi-period setting, the *consumption-based pricing model* (CBPM) is

$$E(\tilde{m}\tilde{R}) = p_a \tag{4.28}$$

where $E(\cdot) = {}_s\pi_s(\cdot)$ is the expectations operator conditioned on information at the beginning of the first period $(t), \tilde{m} = \delta U'(\tilde{I}_\tau)/U'(I_t)$ the stochastic discount factor over period t to τ, $\tilde{R}_\tau$ the payouts to the K securities at τ and p_a the vector of current security prices at t. It is based on the following important asumptions:

i Consumers have time-separable NMEU functions with a constant rate of time preference.
ii They have common expectations and conditional perfect foresight.
iii The capital market is competitive, frictionless and complete.

Since consumers can trade in a frictionless competitive capital market they have the same stochastic discount factor and face the same consumption risk.[13] Thus, the risk premiums in expected security returns are determined by their covariance with aggregate consumption. That means we can solve the discount factors as functions of the variables that determine aggregate consumption risk. We follow Cochrane (2001) in this section by deriving the CAPM and the APT, together with the ICAPM and the consumption-beta capital asset pricing model CCAPM, as special cases of the CBPM in (4.28). This is an effective way of comparing their strengths and weaknesses.

When there are *multiple time periods*, (4.28) is derived using a time-separable NMEU function with a constant rate of time preference (ρ), where, for an infinitely lived consumer, we have

$$EU_t = E_t \sum_{j=0}^{\infty} \delta^j \{U(\tilde{I}_{t-j})\},^{14} \tag{4.29}$$

with $0<\delta = 1/(1 + \rho) \leq 1$ being a measure of impatience for future consumption. It is convenient to define *a value function* that maps utility over wealth by writing the consumer problem in the Arrow–Debreu asset economy as

$$V(W_t) = \max_{(I_t, a_t)} \{U(I_t) + \delta E_t V(\tilde{W}_{t+1}) \mid \tilde{W}_{t+1} \leq (1+\tilde{i}_{W,t+1})(W_t - I_t)\}, \tag{4.30}$$

where $\tilde{W}_t$ is the discounted value of consumption expenditure at time t, and $\tilde{i}_{W,\, t+1}$ the rate of return on wealth over period t to $t + 1$. This can be collapsed into a two-period problem by including a vector of additional factors ($\tilde{z}_t$) in the value function at each time t to isolate shifts in the investment opportunity set and changes in relative commodity prices, where

$$V(W_t, z_t) = \max_{\{I_t, a_t\}} \left\{U(I_t) + \delta E_t V(\tilde{W}_{t+1}, \tilde{z}_{t+1}) \middle| \tilde{W}_{t+1} \leq (1+\tilde{i}_{W,t+1})(W_t - I_t)\right\}.^{15} \tag{4.31}$$

By using this value function we can write write the stochastic discount factor as

$$\tilde{m}_{t+1} = \delta \frac{V_W(\tilde{W}_{t+1}, \tilde{z}_{t+1})}{V_W(W_t, z_t)}.^{16} \tag{4.32}$$

All of the following pricing models start from this point and make different assumptions about the composition of wealth and the state variables that describe how it changes over time. The additional factors in (4.32) disappear when the interest rate and relative commodity prices are constant, and security returns are independently and identically distributed (i.i.d.) over time.

4.3.1 Capital asset pricing model

Recall from Section 4.1 that risk is isolated by a single factor in the CAPM. It is obtained from the CBPM in (4.28) in a multi-period setting by making the following additional assumptions:

i At the beginning of each period t, consumer wealth is confined to a portfolio of financial securities a_t^w with market value $p_{at} a_t^w = W_t - I_t$, and a stochastic net return over the next period of $\tilde{i}_{W,\, t+1}$.[17]
ii Security returns are jointly normally distributed.
iii The interest rate is constant and security returns are i.i.d. over time.[18]
iv Relative commodity prices do not change over time.

In a two-period setting the CAPM holds by adopting assumptions (i) and (ii), where (i) rules out income from labour and other capital assets by restricting consumer income to returns on portfolios of securities, while (ii) makes expected security returns linear in their covariance with the return on the risky portfolio. For the CAPM to hold in a multi-period setting, we need to add assumptions (iii) and (iv), where (iii) rules out shifts in the investment opportunity set over time and (iv) holds real income constant.

On the basis of these assumptions we can write the stochastic discount factor for each time period in (4.32), omitting time subscripts, as

$$\tilde{m} = \delta \frac{V_W[(1+\tilde{i}_W)p_a a^W]}{V_W[W]}. \tag{4.33}$$

In the absence of changes in consumer preferences it is independent of time, where $p_a a^W$ and W are the values of the wealth portfolio and consumer wealth, respectively, at the beginning of each period, and $\tilde{i}_W$ the return on wealth at the end of each period. When $\tilde{i}_W$ and $\tilde{R}_k$ are jointly normally distributed we can use *Stein's Lemma* to decompose the CBPM in (4.28) as:

$$p_{ak} = E(\tilde{m})E(\tilde{R}_k) + E\left\{\delta \frac{p_a a^W V_{WW}(\tilde{W})}{V_W(W)}\right\}\text{Cov}(\tilde{i}_W, \tilde{R}_k),$$ [19]

with $\tilde{W}=(1+\tilde{i}_w)W$. Using $\tilde{R}_k=(1+\tilde{i}_k)p_{ak}$ to isolate the return on security k, and $E(\tilde{m}) = 1/(1+i)$ for the price of the risk-free bond, we have

$$\bar{i}_k - i = -(1+i)E\left\{\delta \frac{p_a a^W V_{WW}(\tilde{W})}{V_W(W)}\right\}\sigma_{Wk},$$

where $\sigma_{Wk} \equiv \text{Cov}(\tilde{i}_W, \tilde{i}_k)$ is the non-diversifiable risk in the return on the wealth portfolio.

Since this relationship must also hold for the return on the risky market portfolio M, we have

$$\frac{\bar{i}_M - i}{p_{aM} a_M^W \sigma_M^2} = -(1+i)E\left\{\frac{p_a a^W V_{WW}(\tilde{W})}{V_W(W)}\right\},$$

with $\sigma_{WM} = p_{aM} a_M^W \sigma_M^2$ being the covariance in the returns on the wealth and market portfolios, $p_{aM} a_M^W$ being the wealth invested in risky market portfolio M, and $p_{aW} a^W = p_{aF} a_F^W + p_{aM} a_M^W$. After substitution, and using $\sigma_{Wk} = p_{aM} a_M^W \sigma_{Mk}$, we obtain the CAPM pricing equation in (4.21).

Box 4.6 The CAPM has a linear stochastic discount factor

Linear pricing models are equivalent to a linear stochastic discount factor. This can be demonstrated for the CAPM by writing (4.21) as

$$1+\bar{i}_k = 1+i+\text{Cov}\left(\frac{c}{b}+\tilde{i}_M - \bar{i}_M, 1+\tilde{i}_k\right)\frac{\bar{i}_M - i}{\text{Var}(\tilde{i}_M)},$$

with the constants $c>0$ and $b<0$. Since the price of market risk is

$$\frac{\bar{i}_M - i}{\text{Var}(\tilde{i}_M)} = -(1+i)b,$$

we can use $E(\tilde{m}) = c = 1/(1+i) \neq 0$ to write the pricing equation as

$$1+\bar{i}_k = (1+i)\{1 - E[(c+b\tilde{i}_M - b\bar{i}_M)(1+\tilde{i}_k)] + E(c+b\tilde{i}_M - b\bar{i}_M)E(1+\tilde{i}_k)\}.$$

This collapses to the CBPM in (4.28), where $E[\tilde{m}(1+\tilde{i}_k)] = 1$, with the linear discount factor $\tilde{m} = c + b(\tilde{i}_M - \bar{i}_M)$.

While there are two time periods in the CAPM derived by Sharpe and Lintner, it also holds for multiple time periods when the interest rate and relative commodity prices are constant and security returns are i.i.d. over time. In effect, consumers are in a steady-state equilibrium facing the same aggregate risk in each period, where the market risk in security returns in every period is described by a single factor, which is how they covary with the return on the market portfolio. Based on this derivation, we find two important features of the CAPM model. First, all the aggregate consumption risk comes through security returns, thereby limiting the ability of the CAPM to explain how consumers measure risk when they also have income from labour and other capital assets. Second, changes in aggregate consumption risk are not accommodated by the CAPM. The ICAPM addresses this problem by extending the CAPM to multiple time periods by including additional factors to describe changes in the investment opportunity set and relative commodity prices.

4.3.2 *Intertemporal capital asset pricing model*

As noted above, the popularity of the CAPM stems from its simplicity – in particular, the way it isolates consumption risk with a single state variable using mean–variance analysis. And this state variable is specified by the model as the variance in the return on the market portfolio which every consumer combines with a risk-free bond. In applied work the market portfolio is normally derived as a value-weighted index of the securities trading on the stock exchange. While the CAPM is frequently used by analysts in a multi-period setting, there is evidence to suggest aggregate consumption risk changes over time. Merton (1973a) extends the CAPM to accommodate changes in the investment opportunity set using a continuous-time analysis. The model maintains most of the assumptions in the CAPM – in particular, that consumers with homogeneous expectations maximize state-independent time-separable expected utility functions, they hold all their wealth in portfolios of securities, and can trade a risk-free bond (but with a return that can vary over time).[20] We derive the ICAPM as a special case of the CBPM in (4.28) using a discrete-time analysis of the consumer problem summarized by the value function in (4.31) where vectors of additional state variable (z) are included to describe changes in aggregate consumption risk. To obtain the model in Merton we make the following additional assumptions:

i At the beginning of each period t consumer wealth is confined to a portfolio of financial securities a_t^W with market value $p_{at}a_t^W = W_t - I_t$ and a stochastic net return over the next period of $\tilde{i}_{W,t+1}$.[21]
ii Security returns are jointly-normally distributed.

Relaxing assumptions (iii) and (iv) in the CAPM allows aggregate consumption risk to change over time. Following Merton, we restrict the analysis to a single consumption good and assume changes in aggregate risk can be described by a single state variable. When security returns and the state variable are multi-variate normal we use Stein's lemma (see note 19) to decompose the pricing equation in (4.28), with the stochastic discount factor in (4.32), as:

$$\bar{i}_k - i = A\,\mathrm{Cov}(\tilde{i}_M, \tilde{i}_k) + B\,\mathrm{Cov}(\tilde{z}_1, \tilde{i}_k),^{22} \tag{4.34}$$

where

$$A = -(1+i)\delta E\left\{\frac{V_{WW}(\cdot)p_a a^W}{V_W(\cdot)}\right\} \text{ and } B = -(1+i)\delta E\left\{\frac{V_{Wz}(\cdot)}{V_W(\cdot)}\right\}.$$

Merton assumes the interest rate is the sole factor needed to describe changes in the investment opportunity set, where a security n is identified with returns that are perfectly negatively correlated with changes in the interest rate, so that $\rho_{ni} = -1$. This security is used as a proxy for the single factor (z_n) that describes future changes in market risk, where the expected excess return on any security $k \neq n$ in (4.34) becomes

$$\bar{i}_k - i = A\sigma_{Mk} + B\sigma_{nk}. \tag{4.35}$$

After multiplying the excess return on each security in the market portfolio by their portfolio shares and summing them, we obtain the risk premium in the market portfolio:

$$\bar{i}_M - i = A\sigma_M^2 + B\sigma_{nM}. \tag{4.36}$$

Setting $k = n$ in (4.35), and using the risk premium in (4.36) to solve the variables A and B in (4.34), we have the ICAPM pricing equation,

$$\bar{i}_k - i = \frac{\sigma_k(\rho_{kM} - \rho_{nM}\rho_{nk})}{\sigma_M(1-\rho_{nM}^2)}(\bar{i}_M - i) + \frac{\sigma_k(\rho_{nk} - \rho_{nM}\rho_{kM})}{\sigma_n(1-\rho_{nM}^2)}(\bar{i}_n - i), \tag{4.37}$$

where M is the wealth portfolio and n the derivative security that is perfectly negatively correlated with changes in the interest rate. It is based on assumptions (i) and (ii) in the CAPM, but relaxes (iii) and (iv) by allowing changes in the investment opportunity set and in relative commodity prices over time.

The additional covariance terms make it slightly more complex than the CAPM equation in (4.21), where the first term is compensation for non-diversifiable risk in the market portfolio, and the second term compensation for non-diversifiable risk due to changes in the interest rate over time. There are additional terms in (4.37) when changes in the investment opportunity set are described by more than one state variable. Long (1974) shows how this is much more likely with multiple consumption goods, where additional factors describe changes in their relative prices.[23]

There are a number of special cases where the pricing equation in (4.37) can be simplified. When the returns on the market portfolio and security n are uncorrelated (with $\rho_{nM} = 0$) the pricing equation in (4.37) collapses to a multi-beta model, where

$$\bar{i}_k - 1 = \frac{\sigma_{kM}}{\sigma_M^2}(\bar{i}_M - i) + \frac{\sigma_{kn}}{\sigma_n^2}(\bar{i}_n - i).$$

Merton identifies two situations where the ICAPM becomes the CAPM – the first is where the interest rate is non-stochastic, with $\sigma_n = 0$, and the second is where all traded security returns are uncorrelated with changes in the interest rate, with $\rho_{ki} = 0$ for all k.[24]

4.3.3 Arbitrage pricing theory

In both the CAPM and ICAPM consumer preferences can be summarized by the mean and variance of the return on their wealth, which is confined to a portfolio of securities, as security returns are jointly normally distributed. The arbitrage pricing theory (APT) is more general because it makes no assumption about the distributions of the returns on securities and allows consumers to receive other types of income, including income from labour. Instead it assumes the security returns can be fully described by the linear factor model in (4.22). Using the CBPM in (4.28) for each security k, with $\tilde{R}_k = (1 + \bar{i}_k + \beta_k\tilde{f} + \tilde{\varepsilon}_k)p_{ak}$, we have

Box 4.7 The ICAPM pricing equation: a numerical example

The following data will be used to compute the expected return on Homestead (*H*) shares when the ICAPM in (4.37) holds. The market return is for a broadly based share price index that contains all risky traded securities, while security *n* is perfectly negatively correlated with the Treasury Bill rate.

Year	*Market return (%)*	*Security n return (%)*	*Treasury bill rate (%)*
2006	20.70	4.2	6.2
2005	17.30	4.6	6.0
2004	17.00	5.2	5.8
2003	–4.90	6.0	5.4
2002	–8.80	5.6	5.6
2001	12.30	5.7	5.6
2000	18.40	6.1	5.4
Mean	10.29	5.34	5.71
Variance	123.93	0.44	0.08
Standard deviation	11.13	0.66	0.28
ρ_{HM}	0.97	ρ_{ni}	–1.00
ρ_{nM}	–0.51	ρ_{nH}	–0.51

Based on this data the expected return on any risky security *k* solves:

$$\bar{i}_k = 5.71 + \frac{\sigma_k(\rho_{kM} + 0.51\rho_{nk})}{11.13[1-(-0.52)^2]}(10.29 - 5.71) + \frac{\sigma_k(\rho_{nk} + 0.51\rho_{kM})}{0.66[1-(-0.51)^2]}(5.34 - 5.71).$$

When the return on Homestead shares has a variance of $\sigma_H = 6.94$ per cent and correlation coefficients of $\rho_{HM} = 0.97$ and $\rho_{nH} = -0.51$.

$$\bar{i}_H = 5.71 + 0.60(10.29 - 5.71) - 0.28(5.34 - 5.71) \approx 8.56 \text{ per cent.}$$

Thus, the share contains consumption risk of 0.60 due its positive covariance with the return on the market portfolio, and consumption risk of –0.28 due changes in the risk-free interest rate. The negative sensitivity coefficient for the interest rate risk indicates the return on Homestead shares is positively correlated with the return on security *n*, which is negatively correlated with the interest rate. It means Homestead shares contain interest rate risk, and since there are risk benefits from holding security *n* its expected return is less than the risk-free rate. Once the sensitivity coefficients for the two factors are priced, the premium for the risk in the market portfolio is 0.60 (10.29–5.71) ≈ 2.75 percentage points, while for the interest rate risk it is – 0.28 (5.34 – 5.71) ≈ 0.10 percentage points. Together they constitute a total risk premium of approximately 2.85 percentage points. The contribution by each risk factor can be determined by computing their beta coefficients, where

$$\beta_{nH} = \sigma_{nH}/\sigma_n^2 = -2.35/0.44 \approx -5.3 \quad \text{and,} \quad \beta_{MH} = \sigma_{MH}/\sigma_M^2 = 75.09/123.93 \approx 0.61.$$

Thus, if we set $\rho_{nM} = 0$ we find $\bar{i}_H = 10.47$ per cent, where the correlation coefficient of $\rho_{nM} = -0.51$ reduces the expected share return by 1.91 percentage points.

$$E[\tilde{m}(1 + \bar{i}_k + \beta_k \tilde{f} + \tilde{\varepsilon}_k)] = 1,$$[25]

where β_k is a $(1 \times G)$ vector of beta coefficients, with $\beta_{kg} = \text{Cov}(\tilde{i}_k, \tilde{i}_g)/\text{Var}(\tilde{i}_g)$ for all g, and $\tilde{f}$ a $(G \times 1)$ column vector of deviations in factor returns from their means, with

$\tilde{f}_g = \tilde{i}_g - \bar{i}_g$ for all g. The factor returns are returns on mimicking portfolios with unit sensitivity to one factor and zero sensitivity to all others. These factor securities are derivatives created by bundling securities together from the K traded securities in the capital market. Using the decomposition for covariance terms, and noting that $E(\tilde{m}) = 1/(1+i)$, we can rewrite this pricing equation as

$$1 + \bar{i}_k = (1+i)\{1 - \beta_k E(\tilde{m}\tilde{f}) - E(\tilde{m}\tilde{\varepsilon}_k)\}.$$

When the residuals are eliminated from the mimicking factor portfolios through the diversification effect (with $\beta_g = 1$) they have a zero price, with $E(\tilde{m}\tilde{\varepsilon}_k) = 0$ for all k, where the risk premium for each factor g is

$$\bar{i}_g - i = -(1+i)E(\tilde{m}\tilde{f}_g).$$

After substituting this into the previous equation we obtain the APT pricing equation in (4.27).[26]

The model can be used in a multi-period setting by including additional factors to isolate changes in aggregate consumption risk. Unfortunately, however, actual security returns do not display an *exact factor structure* as there are residuals in estimates of their expected values. Since the APT model uses statistical analysis to identify the set of factors that isolate common movements in security returns, it relies on all the idiosyncratic risk being eliminated inside large factor portfolios. But most estimates of the beta coefficients in the linear factor model have R^2 values less than unity. Cochrane (2001) shows that these residuals have non-unique positive prices which undermine the APT model. The larger the number of traded securities that can be bundled into factor portfolios, the closer the R^2 values get to unity. The smaller the error terms become, the better the APT model gets at pricing risky securities.

4.3.4 Consumption-beta capital asset pricing model

One of the main deficiencies of the ICAPM and the APT is that they do not specify all the factors that isolate aggregate consumption risk. None are specified in the APT because the factors are macro variables chosen to provide the best fit in a linear factor analysis (with the highest R^2). In the ICAPM the variance in the market portfolio isolates consumption risk, but none of the factors used to explain changes in market risk over time are specified by the model. Thus, both models are more difficult to use than the CAPM. The CAPM can be used in a multi-period setting if real aggregate consumption expenditure is constant over time. Breeden and Litzenberger (1978) and Breeden (1979) derive the CCAPM in a single-good, multi-period setting. Breeden extends the analysis to accommodate multiple goods, and does so in a continuous-time setting where aggregate uncertainty follows a Markov process of the Ito type.[27] However, data on aggregate consumption is not reported at point in time, but rather for quarterly periods. Breeden and Litzenberger (1978) derive the CCAPM for discrete time periods by making the following assumptions:

i There is a single consumption good.
ii The interest return is constant and security returns are independently and identically distributed over time.

iii Consumers have preferences with the same constant coefficient of relative risk aversion.

iv Aggregate consumption and security returns are jointly lognormally distributed.

Assumptions (i) and (ii) make consumption risk the same in each future time period, while assumptions (iii) and (iv) make the stochastic discount factor linear in aggregate consumption risk. It should be noted that, unlike the CAPM and the ICAPM, wealth is not confined to returns on portfolios of securities in the CCAPM.[28]

There is a one-to-one mapping between wealth and aggregate consumption in each time period when consumers have a constant coefficient of relative risk aversion (γ), while the stochastic discount factor is linearly related to aggregate consumption risk when security returns and consumption growth are jointly lognormally distributed.[29] This is confirmed by using the CBPM in (4.28) with the power utility function in (3.20) to isolate the return on security k as

$$E_t[(1+\tilde{g}_{t+1})^{-\gamma}(1+\tilde{i}_{k,t+1})] = 1+\rho, \tag{4.38}$$

where ρ is the rate of time preference, γ the CRRA and $\tilde{g}_{t+1} = (\tilde{I}_{t+1} - I_t)/I_t$ the growth rate in consumption expenditure. Notice how the stochastic discount factor is now a function of the growth rate in consumption in the same period, with $\tilde{m}_{t+1} = (1+\tilde{g}_{t+1})^{-\gamma}$. When security returns and consumption growth are lognormally distributed we can decompose (4.38), with time subscripts omitted, as

$$E[\ln(1+\tilde{i}_k)] - \ln(1+i) = \gamma \operatorname{Cov}[\ln(1+\tilde{g}), \ln(1+\tilde{i}_k) - \tfrac{1}{2} \operatorname{Var}[\ln(1+\tilde{i}_k)].^{30} \tag{4.39}$$

For small enough values of $\tilde{i}_k$, i and $\tilde{g}$, this can be approximated as

$$\bar{i}_k - i = \gamma \operatorname{Cov}(\tilde{g}, \tilde{i}_k).^{31} \tag{4.40}$$

The premium for aggregate consumption risk is obtained by creating its mimicking portfolio (I) with stochastic return $\tilde{i}_I$, where from (4.40) we have $\gamma = (\bar{i}_I - i)/\operatorname{Var}(\tilde{i}_I)$. After substitution, this leads to the CCAPM pricing equation

$$\bar{i}_k - i = (\bar{i}_I - i)\beta_{Ik} \tag{4.41}$$

where $\beta_{Ik} = \operatorname{Cov}(\tilde{i}_I, \tilde{i}_k)/\operatorname{Var}(\tilde{i}_I)$ is the beta coefficient that measures the aggregate consumption risk in any risky security k.

Like the CAPM, this is a linear pricing model with a single beta coefficient. But it too relies on a number of simplifying assumptions that may restrict the ability of the model to explain the observed risk premiums in security returns. First, consumers have a common and constant CRRA, and aggregate consumption and security returns are lognormally distributed. CRRA preferences provide a one-to-one mapping between changes in aggregate consumption and wealth, while lognormality generates a linear relationship between security returns and the beta coefficients used to isolate aggregate consumption risk. Ruling out shifts in the investment opportunity set and adopting a single commodity makes aggregate consumption risk constant in real terms over time. That makes current aggregate consumption risk the sole factor in the model.[32] Also, with constant consumption risk the pricing equation in (4.41) holds unconditionally. Allowing consumption risk to change over time would add additional beta coefficients to the pricing equation. The CCAPM is more general than both the CAPM and ICAPM because it also allows income from labour and other capital assets.

Box 4.8 The CCAPM pricing equation: a numerical example

The aggregate consumption data summarized below is for an economy where the CCAPM in (4.41) holds. Over the period 1990–2006 the 2 per cent annual interest rate and relative commodity prices are both constant over time. Since the rate of return on the mimicking portfolio I is perfectly correlated with the growth rate in aggregate consumption expenditure, with $\text{Corr}(\tilde{g}, \tilde{i}_I) = 1$, the risk premium for consumption risk is $\bar{i}_I - i = 0.06$.

Year	*Level (\$bn)*	*Growth rate (g)*	*Return portfolio I*	*Return Security A*
2006	2.04	0.07	0.16	0.11
2005	2.04	0.04	0.09	0.08
2004	1.91	0.06	0.14	0.07
2003	1.83	0.05	0.11	0.06
2002	1.73	–0.01	–0.02	0.00
2001	1.65	0.04	0.09	–0.03
2000	1.67	0.05	0.11	–0.04
1999	1.60	–0.03	–0.07	–0.12
1998	1.52	0.04	0.09	0.16
1997	1.57	0.09	0.21	0.09
1996	1.51	–0.05	–0.11	0.03
1995	1.39	0.04	0.09	0.12
1994	1.46	0.07	0.16	0.03
1993	1.40	0.06	0.14	0.04
1992	1.31	–0.01	–0.02	–0.03
1991	1.24	0.05	0.11	0.19
1990	1.25	—	—	—
Mean	1.59585	0.03500	0.08000	0.04719
Variance	0.05992	0.00144	0.0075102	0.00603
Standard deviation	0.24479	0.03791	0.08666	0.07766

After computing the covariance between the returns on the mimicking portfolio I and security A, with $\sigma_{IA} = 0.034036$, we can use (4.41) to confirm the expected return on security A is

$$\bar{i}_A = i + (\bar{i}_I - i)\beta_{IA} = 0.02 + (0.06 \times 0.45319) \approx 0.04719,$$

with $\beta_{IA} = \sigma_{IA}/\sigma_I^2 = 0.0034036/0.0075102 = 0.45319$.

With multiple consumption goods, changes in their relative prices can affect the composition of investor consumption bundles, which can change utility, even without changing future consumption expenditure. In the ICAPM the relative price changes are identified by additional beta coefficients in the pricing equation. Recall that the single-good version of the ICAPM already has two beta coefficients – one for the risk in the market (wealth) portfolio and another for changes in it over time. Breeden extends the single-beta CCAPM to multiple consumption goods in a continuous-time setting by measuring expected security returns and consumption expenditure in real terms, where the pricing equation becomes

$$\bar{i}_k^* = i^* + \left(\bar{i}_j^* - i^*\right)\frac{\beta_{Ik}^*}{\beta_{Ij}^*},$$

with i^*, $\bar{i}_k^*$ and $\bar{i}_j^*$ being the real returns on a risk–free bond and securities k and j, respectively, and β_{Ik}^* and β_{Ij}^* the real consumption betas for securities k and j. The price index used to discount security returns is constructed with marginal weights as they provide the correct valuation for goods purchased from an additional dollar of income, while the price index for computing real aggregate consumption is constructed with average weights as they are used in the calculation of average real consumption, which is inversely related to the marginal utilities of consumption goods.

4.4 A comparison of the consumption-based pricing models

Four equilibrium asset pricing models were derived in the previous section as special cases of the consumption-based pricing model in (4.28). All of them

i use set factors to isolate the risk in aggregate consumption; and
ii have pricing equations that are linear in these risk factors.

Their important assumptions are summarized in Figure 4.22. As special cases of the CBPM they are all based on consumers having time-separable NMEU functions with homogeneous expectations. With state independence, consumers care about the statistical distribution of their consumption expenditure in each future time period, while time separability makes the stochastic discount factor between any two periods independent of consumption expenditure in other time periods; it means the growth in marginal utility will depend only on consumption expenditure in that time period.[33] Under these circumstances

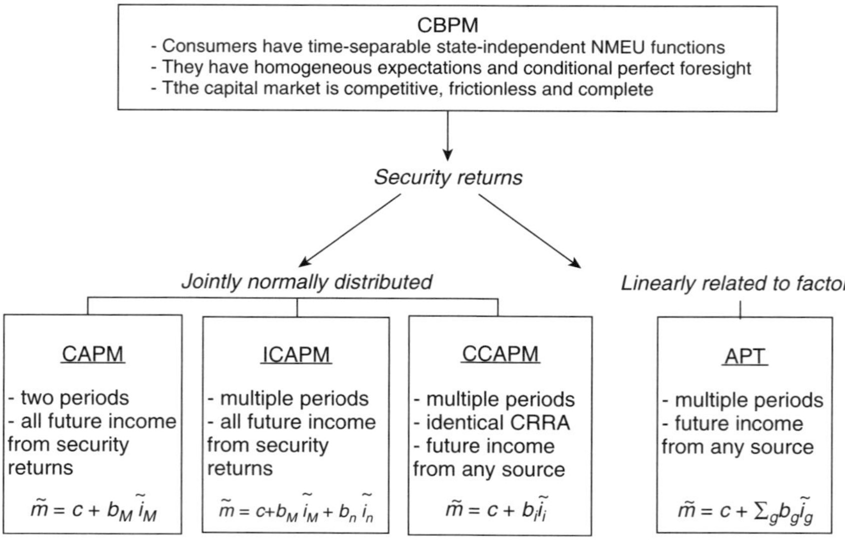

Figure 4.22 Main assumptions in the consumption-based asset pricing models.

consumers with homogeneous expectations have the same stochastic discount factor and, as a consequence, the same changes in marginal utility. Given the inverse relationship between marginal utility and consumption, they must also have the same consumption risk. Thus, the stochastic discount factor in the CBPM can be solved as a function of aggregate consumption risk.

Any differences in the models arise from the additional assumptions they make to isolate the aggregate consumption risk. All of them use mean–variance analysis, where it results from consumption risk being normally distributed in the CAPM, ICAPM and CCAPM, while it results from a linear factor analysis in the APT.[34] For the CAPM and the ICAPM future consumption is funded solely from payoffs to securities. And since consumers can trade a risk-free security they combine it with the same bundle of risky securities (M) whose variance determines changes in their future consumption expenditure. In the two-period CAPM there is a single beta coefficient that measures how much security returns covary with the return on M, while there are additional beta coefficients in the multi-period ICAPM that summarize changes in the investment opportunity set (and relative commodity prices). The multi-period CCAPM also has a single beta coefficient because consumers have the same constant coefficient of relative risk aversion that makes consumption expenditure a constant coefficient fraction of wealth in each time period. The APT model is also a multi-period model which, like the ICAPM, uses a number of factors to isolate changes in aggregate consumption risk.

On the plus side, the single factors in the CAPM and CCAPM are specified by each model, while the multiple factors in the ICAPM and the APT are variables that investors frequently monitor when assessing the returns to securities. Also, ICAPM, CCAPM and APT can be used in a multi-period setting. On the minus side, the CAPM cannot be used in a multi-period setting unless security returns are i.i.d. and the interest rate and relative commodity prices are constant over time. But consumers need to have the same constant coefficient of relative risk aversion in the CCAPM, while the additional factors used to isolate changes in consumption risk are not specified in the ICAPM or the APT.

A criticism that is common to all models is that they are based on the CBPM in (4.28) where consumers have time-separable NMEU functions. Arguably, the most restrictive assumption is that of homogeneous expectations. If we allow consumers to have different subjective expectations they will, in general, measure and price risk differently, where pricing models are based on individual, rather than aggregate data. Another extension would allow state-dependent preferences, but again consumers would likely measure and price risk differently, even with homogeneous expectations, as they would no longer have the same changes in consumption expenditure over time. Thus, we cannot solve the discount factors in (4.28) as functions of aggregate consumption expenditure. Indeed, the problem is further compounded when consumers have both state-dependent preferences and subjective expectations.

4.5 Empirical tests of the consumption-based pricing models

Given the nature of the assumptions made in the consumption-based pricing model in (4.28), it should not be surprising that the asset pricing models derived from it perform poorly when confronted with data. There are good practical reasons for wanting to derive pricing models where consumers measure and price risk identically using a small number of state variables that can be accessed in reported data. Models based on individual consumption data are impractical because it is costly data to obtain.

One problem for empirical tests of these pricing models is the absence of appropriate data – in particular, the expected values of the risk factors and the means and variances on security returns. Most studies assume that ex-post time series data provides a true reflection of the statistical attributes of their distributions when observed by consumers ex ante. Another problem arises when the reported data does not provide all the information needed. For example, consumers in the CCAPM measure market risk in security returns by their covariance with aggregate real consumption expenditure. It must include consumption flows to capital, as well as non-marketed consumption such as leisure and other home-produced goods. Most countries measure their national accounts on a quarterly basis where aggregate consumption expenditure excludes expenditure on major capital items and includes the rental value of housing consumed by owner-occupiers. However, some capital expenditure is included, while a considerable proportion of non-marketed consumption is omitted. These discrepancies may not be a significant problem if they are closely correlated with measured aggregate real consumption, particularly when on average they are relatively small.[35]

Early empirical studies tested the pricing models, in particular the CAPM, to see whether they could successfully explain the risk premiums in security returns without considering whether the resulting consumption risk was consistent with measures of risk aversion obtained from observed consumer behaviour. That link was made later by Mehra and Prescott (1985) who tested the CCAPM using a computable general equilibrium model where they identified equity premium and low risk-free real interest rate puzzles. We summarize these empirical findings in the following two subsections.

4.5.1 *Empirical tests and the Roll critique*

Using time series data Black *et al.* (1972) divide all the securities traded on the New York Stock Exchange (NYSE) over the period 1931–1965 into 10 portfolios and estimate the coefficients on the CAPM pricing equation:

$$\bar{i}_k - \bar{i} = \lambda_0 + \lambda_1 \beta_k + \varepsilon_k,$$

where $\lambda_0 = 0$ and $\lambda_1 = \bar{i}_M - i$ when the CAPM holds. Their main findings are as follows:

i $\lambda_0 > 0$ and $\lambda_1 < \bar{i}_M - i$, which implies securities with low (high) beta coefficients pay higher (lower) returns than the CAPM would predict.
ii β dominates other terms as a measure of risk.
iii The simple linear model fits best.

Blume and Friend (1973) draw similar conclusions using cross-sectional returns. They construct 12 portfolios with approximately 80 different stocks listed on the NYSE over three separate periods between 1955 and 1968. Fama and MacBeth (1973) extend the analysis in Black *et al.* and find omitted variables in the CAPM. Their findings support the multi-factor ICAPM that accounts for changes in aggregate consumption risk.

Roll (1977a) was critical of these (and other) empirical tests of the CAPM, arguing that the only true test is whether the market portfolio is ex ante mean–variance efficient, where the linearity of the model follows by implication. There are an infinite number of mean–variance efficient market portfolios where by construction the expected returns on the individual securities in each portfolio must be linearly related to their beta coefficients.

Fama and French (1992, 1993) include firm size and book-to-market equity ratios as additional factors to explain a cross-section of average returns to securities traded on the NYSE not explained by the CAPM or the CCAPM. Lettau and Ludvigson (2001) derive conditional versions of these models by allowing the stochastic discount factor to change over time. But instead of including additional factors to describe changes in consumption risk they scale the parameters in the discount factor with a proxy for the log consumption–wealth ratio, and find the conditional models perform about as well as the three-factor pricing model used by Fama and French.[36] Their findings are supported by Campbell and Cochrane (2000) who test the conditional versions of the CAPM and CCAPM. Using US data, Hansen and Singleton (1982, 1983) find the unconditional CCAPM performs poorly in explaining the time variation in interest rates and the cross-sectional pattern of average returns on stocks and bonds, while Wheatley (1988) also rejects the model using international data. In fact, Mankiw and Shapiro (1986), Breeden *et al.* (1989), Campbell (1996) and Cochrane (1996) find it performs no better than, and in most cases worse than, the unconditional CAPM in explaining cross-sectional differences in average returns. Campbell and Cochrane (2000) argue the market return in the CAPM captures time variations in risk premiums much better than consumption growth in the CCAPM because the market return is affected by dividend–price ratios while consumption growth is not. This view is supported by Campbell (1993) based on empirical tests of a discrete-time version of the ICAPM.

4.5.2 Asset pricing puzzles

As noted by Cochrane (2001), early tests of the CAPM and ICAPM focused on their ability to explain the risk premiums in expected security returns without considering how much risk was being transferred into real consumption expenditure. When testing the CCAPM, Mehra and Prescott looked at whether the implied values of the (constant) coefficient of relative risk aversion and the (constant) rate of time preference were consistent with the risk in aggregate real consumption. Using US data, they discovered the equity premium and low risk-free real interest rate puzzles, where the premium puzzle finds the need to adopt a coefficient of relative risk aversion in the CCAPM that is approximately five times larger than its estimated value in experimental work, while the low risk-free rate puzzle finds the observed real interest rate much lower than the CCAPM would predict when the coefficient of relative risk aversion is set at its estimated value. Once it is set at the higher values required to explain the observed equity premium the predicted real interest rate is even higher.

We demonstrate these puzzles using the Hansen and Jagannathan (1991) bound on the price of risk in security returns. It is an adaptation of the *Sharpe ratio* (Sharp 1966) which measures the equilibrium price of risk, for any security *k*, as $(\bar{i}_k - i)/\sigma_k$. Using the CBPM equation in (4.28) when consumers have a power utility function and security returns are jointly log normally distributed with aggregate consumption, we have the following definition.

Definition 4.1 The *Hansen-Jagannathan bound* on the equilibrium price of risk in the CCAPM is

$$\frac{\bar{i}_k - i}{\sigma_k} \leq (1+i)\,\sigma_m \approx (1+i)\,\gamma\sigma_g, \tag{4.42}$$

where σ_m is the variance in the pricing kernel, γ the constant coefficient of risk aversion and σ_g the growth rate in aggregate real consumption expenditure, with $\tilde{I}/I_0 = 1 + \tilde{g}$ and $\tilde{g} = (\tilde{I} - I_0)/I_0$.

Table 4.3 The asset pricing puzzles in US data

	Mehra and Prescott (1985)	*Cochrane (2001)*
σ_g	3.57%	1%
$\bar{i}_M$	6.98%	9%
σ_M	16.54%	16%
i	0.80%	1%

This bound on the Sharp ratio is obtained by setting the coefficient of correlation between the stochastic discount factor and the real return on the security k at its upper bound of unity, with $Corr(-\tilde{m}, \tilde{i}_k) = 1$.[37] Since (4.42) conveniently relates the risk premium to the CRRA (γ), it can be used to demonstrate the equity premium puzzle identified by Mehra and Prescott, where they add dividends to the US Standard & Poor's 500 Index and divide it by the consumer price index to obtain a measure of its real return over the period 1889–1978. The real risk-free return is computed using short-term Treasury bills over the same period. Similar data is collected by Cochrane (2001) for the value-weighted index of stocks trading on the NYSE over the post-war period in the US. The relevant statistics for the two data sets are summarized in Table 4.3, where M denotes the index of stocks used in each study.

We compute the Sharpe ratio and the coefficient of relative risk aversion using these data. The results are summarized in Table 4.4 for $Corr(-\tilde{m}, \tilde{i}_k) = 1$ which is the upper bound used in (4.42), and $Corr(-\tilde{m}, \tilde{i}_M) = 0.2$ which is used by Cochrane.

The implicit values for γ are much larger than those obtained from empirical estimates, which fall within the range 0 to 2. Friend and Blume (1975) obtain an estimate of 2 using household data in the US, while Fullenkamp *et al.* (2003) obtain values ranging from 0.6 to 1.5 using data from a television game show. Clearly, the value of γ in the CCAPM pricing equation is 5 times larger than 2 using the Mehra–Prescott data, and 25 times larger using Cochrane's data when $Corr(-\tilde{m}, \tilde{i}_M) = 1$. They are significantly higher for $Corr(-\tilde{m}, \tilde{i}_M) = 0.2$.

To demonstrate the low interest rate puzzle identified by Mehra and Prescott, we use (4.28) with the power utility function in (3.20) to compute the expected price of the risk-free bond as

$$E(\tilde{m}) = \delta E(1+\tilde{g})^{-\gamma} = \frac{1}{1+i},$$

where $\tilde{g} = (\tilde{I} - I_0)/I_0$ is the growth rate in aggregate real consumption expenditure. An approximate relationship between the interest rate, the rate of time preference and the growth rate in consumption expenditure is obtained by expressing this bond price in logarithmic form as

Table 4.4 Equity premium puzzle

	Mehra and Prescott (1985)	*Cochrane (2001)*
Sharpe ratio:	37%	50%
RRA(γ)		
$Corr(-\tilde{m}, \tilde{i}_M) = 1$	10	50
$Corr(-\tilde{m}, \tilde{i}_M) = 0.2$	52	248

$$\ln(1+i) \approx \gamma E(\tilde{g}) - \ln \delta.^{38} \qquad (4.43)$$

There is good intuition for this relationship. Consumers need a higher return on consumption transferred to the future as saving when they are more risk-averse, and when they expect a higher growth rate in consumption expenditure. Similarly, a higher rate of time preference (which lowers δ) reduces saving and drives up the interest rate (with $\ln \delta < 0$ for $0 < \delta < 1$). Table 4.5 applies the data in Table 4.3 to the relationship in (4.43) for different values of γ and δ. In both data sets in Table 4.3 the average real interest rate was approximately 1 per cent, which is much lower than the rate predicted by the CCAPM with power utility. Indeed, it is almost three times higher using Mehra and Prescott's data and twice as high using Cochrane's data, with $\gamma = 1$. And this difference is even larger for higher values of γ and δ.

4.5.3 Explanations for the asset pricing puzzles

There are essentially two ways to explain these puzzles – one modifies consumer preferences in the CCAPM, while the other finds more risk in individual consumption than there is in aggregate consumption.[39] This subsection summarizes the intuition for these extensions, along with their ability to explain the two puzzles identified by Mehra and Prescott.[40]

Preference modifications

As noted in previous sections, a number of important restrictions are placed on consumer preferences in the CCAPM. Most extensions relax time separability and state independence in the following ways.

Habit theory. This makes utility for a representative agent depend on one or a combination of past own consumption (*internal habit*), past consumption of others, and the current consumption of others (*external habit*). These models add a habit variable to the utility function at each point in time, where its equilibrium effects are determined by the way habits are formed and how they change over time. For example, Abel (1990) models habit as a multiplicative function of past consumption by others, together with past own consumption

Table 4.5 Low risk-free interest rate puzzle

RRA(γ)	*Mehra and Prescott data* $E(\tilde{g}) = 1.83\%$	*Cochrane data* $E(\tilde{g}) = 1\%$
For $\delta = 0.99$		
1	2.88%	2.03%
2	4.78%	3.05%
10	21.29%	11.63%
50	152.20%	66.54%
For $\delta = 0.94$		
1	8.35%	7.45%
2	10.35%	8.53%
10	27.75%	17.57%
50	165.61%	75.40%

to capture internal habit, Constantinides (1990) makes habit an exponential function of past own consumption, and Campbell and Cochrane (1999) make it an additive function of past consumption by all other consumers.[41]

With internal habit consumers become attached to a particular level of consumption which they prefer to maintain, while external habit is based on past consumption of others, reflecting a concern for relative consumption levels. The benefits most people get from consumption at any point in time depend on their past consumption as well as the amount consumed by neighbours or their social peers. Internal habit extends standard preferences by relaxing time separability, while external habit introduces consumption externalities. Both approaches provide an explanation for the risk-free rate puzzle by raising aggregate saving. For internal habit consumers save more when consumption is habit-forming, while for external habit they save more due to their sensitivity to aggregate consumption risk.[42] Both approaches explain a large equity premium if, in the case of internal habit, consumers are highly sensitive to their own consumption risk, or, in the case of external habit, they are highly sensitive to aggregate consumption risk. But high sensitivity to own consumption risk requires a high degree of risk aversion, whereas aggregate consumption is fairly smooth. Thus, in both cases a high degree of risk aversion is required to explain why consumers are indifferent between bonds and equity. In other words, habit formation cannot successfully explain the equity premium puzzle identified by Mehra and Prescott.[43]

Separating risk aversion from intertemporal substitution. There is an inverse relationship between the CRRA and the elasticity of intertemporal substitution when consumers have standard preferences. Indeed, for the power utility function $U(I_t) = I_t^{1-\gamma}/(1-\gamma)$ the elasticity of intertemporal substitution is $1/\gamma$.[44] Thus, highly risk-averse consumers view consumption in different time periods as more complementary. And when they are reluctant to substitute consumption intertemporally in a growing economy the equilibrium interest rate has to be higher. Epstein and Zin (1989) suggest using the generalized expected utility preferences of Kreps and Porteous (1978) and Selden (1978) that separate the coefficient of relative risk aversion from the elasticity of intertemporal substitution. They write the utility function as

$$U\left(I_t, E_t(U_{t+1})\right) = \left[(1-\delta)I_t^{1-\gamma/\theta} + \delta\left(E_t(I_{t+1}^{1-\gamma})\right)^{1/\theta}\right]^{\theta/(1-\gamma)},$$

where $\theta = (1-\gamma)/(1-1/\Omega)$ with Ω being the elasticity of intertemporal substitution. This collapses to the time-separable power utility function when $\gamma = 1/\Omega$. While relaxing this inverse relationship provides a solution to the risk-free rate puzzle, it does not solve the equity premium puzzle. Ultimately, a relatively high value for the CRRA is required to explain the large equity premium in the presence of low consumption risk.

Behavioural experiments and loss aversion. Benartzi and Thaler (1995) and Barberis *et al.* (2001) use evidence from behavioural studies to justify the inclusion of a state variable in the utility function to capture additional welfare effects from financial gains and losses on security portfolios. They argue that utility falls more when there are losses than it rises when there are gains, where these welfare effects are not captured as direct benefits derived from their consumption flows. In effect, they suffer from loss aversion which drives up the risk premium on equity. Thus, the equity premium in the data can be explained with a lower CRRA. While this approach can successfully explain the equity premium and risk-free rate puzzles, it does so in a somewhat ad hoc fashion. In fact, it may provide evidence that consumer preferences are state-dependent.

Heterogeneous consumption risk

Consumers have the same individual consumption risk in the consumption-based pricing models because they can costlessly eliminate diversifiable risk. A number of studies extend these models by allowing individuals to face different consumption risk. This personalizes the asset pricing equation and impacts on the equilibrium risk premium. There are a number of reasons for incomplete insurance, including (i) incomplete markets and borrowing constraints and (ii) transactions costs.

Incomplete markets and borrowing constraints can stop consumers from eliminating diversifiable risk from their consumption expenditure. In particular, they may not be able insure against variations in labour income when human capital cannot be used as collateral, and private insurance may be restricted by moral hazard and adverse selection problems in the presence of asymmetric information. Weil (1992) is able to explain the equity premium and risk-free rate puzzles in a two-period setting with incomplete financial markets. Consumers who cannot fully insure against idiosyncratic risk will save more to offset increases in future consumption risk. The extra saving drives down the risk-free rate, while the extra individual consumption risk drives up the equilibrium premium on returns to equity over debt. However, the ability of incomplete markets to explain these pricing puzzles is mitigated in an multi-period setting by dynamic self-insurance where consumers can offset low (transitory) consumption shocks by borrowing. This provides them with a substitute for insurance unless there are borrowing constraints. Heaton and Lucas (1996) make numerical simulations in a computable general equilibrium model where they find that incomplete markets and borrowing constraints have a small effect on the risk-free interest rate in an infinite horizon setting.[45]

Constantinides and Duffie (1996) extend the analysis of incomplete financial markets by making idiosyncratic labour income shocks permanent. For example, when labour income falls and stays low for ever, dynamic self-insurance cannot overcome the inevitable fall in consumption, even in the absence of borrowing constraints. When these income shocks are sufficiently large and persist they can raise individual consumption risk above aggregate consumption risk sufficiently to explain the low interest rate and high equity premiums in the data. However, Heaton and Lucas estimate idiosyncratic shocks to labour income using US data and find it has an autocorrelation of approximately 0.5 that reduces the risk-free rate by only a small amount.

Transactions costs explain the equity premium when equity is much more costly to trade than debt. Based on turnover rates for equity traded on the NYSE, Fisher (1994) finds that the bid–ask spread on equity needs to be as high as 9.4 to 13.6 percentage points. There are a range of different costs that traders face, including broking fees, taxes and a range of processing costs, that create the spreads between buyer and seller prices. But these costs do not appear to be large enough to explain the equity premium puzzle.

In an infinite horizon setting, Aiyagari and Gertler (1991) include differential transactions costs on debt and equity used by consumers to smooth idiosyncratic shocks to labour income in the absence of formal insurance. When equity is relatively costly to trade, consumers use debt to offset these income shocks. And this is consistent with the high turnover rates for debt and the low turnover rates for equity in financial markets. Aiyagari and Gertler find that debt in the US turns over on average between three and seven times each year, depending on the type of debt instrument, while equity turnover is negligible. Since self-insurance relies on trading both debt and equity, relatively large transactions costs on equity leave consumers with higher individual consumption risk. This is similar to the explanation for the pricing puzzles in Constantinides and Duffie where dynamic self-insurance cannot eliminate persistent shocks to labour income. The higher risk in individual consumption explains the equity premium, while the demand for debt to smooth the variance in future consumption reduces the interest rate.

Swan (2006) finds one-way transactions costs as small as 0.5 percentage point on equity can explain both pricing puzzles due to the (invisible) costs of forgone equity trades at 5.7 per cent of value. These marginal costs arise from inefficient risk sharing in the presence of differential trading costs, and are approximately 15 times higher than the observed trading costs. Debt turnover rises significantly, due to its lower transactions costs, to match the lower net marginal gain from spreading risk with equity, but without the same risk-sharing benefits. Thus, individual consumption risk is higher than aggregate consumption risk, and there is a lower interest.

As noted earlier, explanations for the equity premium and low interest rate puzzles can be divided between those that seek to extend the CCAPM by modifying consumer preferences, and those that allow different individual consumption risk. Grant and Quiggin (2004) argue there are potentially large differences in the welfare and policy implications of these explanations. Whenever the observed risk premium and the low risk-free rate are equilibrium outcomes in an efficient capital market, there are no potential welfare-improving policies. Habit formation, transactions costs and preferences that separate risk aversion from intertemporal substitution are explanations that fall into this category. In contrast, explanations based on market failure or investor irrationality may provide opportunities for welfare-improving policies if governments can overcome market failure or improve on irrational private outcomes.

Grant and Quiggin argue that, whenever governments can eliminate idiosyncratic risk in labour income at lower cost than private traders using the tax system, the discount rate on public sector projects is marginally higher than the risk-free interest rate.[46] As a consequence, welfare can be raised through tax-funded public investment. Similarly, if private financial markets for trading aggregate risk are incomplete, then, consistent with proposals by Arrow and Lind (1970), the cost of capital for investment in the public sector will be lower than it is for the private sector undertaking the same projects when the government can spread aggregate risk more efficiently. Indeed, Grant and Quiggin link the implications of the equity premium puzzle to the arguments made by Arrow and Lind to identify potentially large welfare gains from macroeconomic stabilization policies that reduce fluctuations in aggregate income.

There are, however, good reasons to be cautious about this claim. First, the scope for governments to diversify risk more efficiently than private markets seems rather optimistic.[47] It is difficult to find circumstances where agents in the public sector are better informed and better placed to overcome asymmetric information, or trade at lower transactions costs, than private agents. But even in circumstances where they can, governments have difficulty implementing stabilization policies to counteract the effects of the business cycle on economic activity. Indeed, they have trouble identifying turning points in the business cycle, as well as problems implementing the appropriate tax-spending changes in a timely manner. Additionally, there are principal–agent problems in the public sector that make it a notoriously inefficient operator, where any potential welfare gains from a lower cost of capital can be offset by a lower marginal productivity of investment in the public sector. For example, managers of public enterprises face soft budget constraints and frequently succumb to excessive union-backed wage demands, particularly when politicians are sensitive to disruptions that impact adversely on their voter support.

A logical implication of explanations for the large equity premium that gives the public sector a lower cost of capital, is that all aggregate investment should be financed through the public sector. Indeed, this would also be the case when loss aversion explains the large equity premium. By using taxes to finance investment we avoid the financial losses on privately issued securities. But that is unlikely to lower the cost of capital when taxpayers suffer loss aversion from the risk transferred into their taxes.

4.6 Present value calculations with risky discount factors

There are a number of important issues to address when valuing capital assets with risky net cash flows. Frequently, they have revenues and costs with different risks that can change over time. Moreover, aggregate consumption risk itself can change over time. This section looks at how the consumption-based pricing models examined earlier in Section 4.3 are used to value assets in these circumstances. Since consumers have common information they measure and price risk identically, and by employing mean–variance analysis there is a linear relationship between expected security returns and market risk premiums. While these properties simplify the task of computing risk-adjusted discount factors, it is not straightforward to use them in present value calculations over multiple time periods, particularly when consumption risk can change over time.

4.6.1 Different consumption risk in the revenues and costs

It is not uncommon for assets, and projects more generally, to have revenue streams with more or less risk than the costs of generating them. Indeed, these differences are identified by managers of statutory monopolies when regulatory agencies impose ceilings on their prices to restrict monopoly profits. When revenues are more risky than costs, managers seek less restrictive price caps so they can pay a risk premium to their capital providers.

Consider share k which pays a random dividend $\widetilde{DIV}_k$ in 12 months' time when the share expires. It is funded from net cash flows $(\widetilde{NCF})$ generated by the firm who issued the share, and is the difference between its risky revenues $(\widetilde{REV})$ and costs $(\widetilde{CST})$ per share. When the CAPM holds we can compute the current value of the share by discounting its expected net cash flows, with $\widetilde{NCF}_k = \widetilde{REV}_k - \widetilde{CST}_k$, as

$$p_{ak} = \frac{E(\widetilde{NCF}_k)}{1+i+\left(E(\tilde{i}_M)-i\right)\beta_k}, \tag{4.44}$$

where $\beta_k = \beta_{NCF_k}/p_{ak}$ is the *project risk* per dollar of capital invested in the share, with $\beta_{NCF_k} = \text{Cov}(\widetilde{\text{NCF}}_k, \tilde{i}_M)/\text{Var}(\tilde{i}_M)$. After solving the current share price, we have

$$p_{ak} = \frac{CE_k}{1+i}, \tag{4.45}$$

with $CE_k = E(\widetilde{NCF}_k) - (\bar{i}_M - i)\beta_{NCF_k}$ being the *certainty-equivalent* net cash flows. After deducting a premium for project risk, the remaining net cash flows provide shareholders with consumption benefits equal to the value of their initial capital plus compensation for the opportunity cost of time at the risk-free interest rate i. We can also value the share by discounting its revenues and costs separately as:

$$p_{ak} = \frac{E(\widetilde{REV}_k)}{1+i+\left(E(\tilde{i}_M)-i\right)\beta_{REV_k}/PV_{REV_k}} - \frac{E(\widetilde{CST}_k)}{1+i+\left(E(\tilde{i}_M)-i\right)\beta_{CST_k}/PV_{CST_k}}, \tag{4.46}$$

where β_{REV_k}/PV_{REV_k} and β_{CST_k}/PV_{CST_k} are, respectively, the market risk per dollar of revenue and cost in present value terms. After rearranging this expression, we have

$$p_{ak} = \frac{E(\widetilde{REV}) - E(\widetilde{CST}) - (\bar{i}_M - i)(\beta_{REV_k} - \beta_{CST_k})}{1+i}.$$

Box 4.9 Valuing an asset with different risk in its revenues and costs

Consider share B that makes one dividend payout in 12 months' time when the CAPM holds. It is paid from the random net cash flows ($\widetilde{NCF}$) of a firm on $S_0 = 500$ shares issued at the beginning of the period ($t = 0$). The firm's expected revenues ($E(\widetilde{REV})$) and costs ($E(\widetilde{CST})$) for the period are summarized below, together with their covariance with the return on the market portfolio.

	$E(\widetilde{NCF})$	$E(\widetilde{REV})$	$E(\widetilde{CST})$	i_M	i
Mean	800	1540	740	0.15	0.03
Covariance with i_M	0.5	0.87808	0.37808	0.0016	0

Using the net cash flows to compute the current share price, we have

$$P_{aB} = \frac{E(\widetilde{NCF})/S_0 - (\bar{i}_M - i)\beta_{NCF}/S_0}{1+i} = \frac{800/500 - (0.12)(0.5/0.0016)/500}{1.03} \approx 1.48.$$

This can be decomposed by computing the present values of the revenues and costs as:

$$PV(REV) = \frac{E(\widetilde{REV})/S_0 - (\bar{i}_M - i)\beta_{REV}/S_0}{1+i}$$
$$= \frac{1540/500 - (0.12)(0.87808/0.0016)/500}{1.03} \approx 2.86$$

and

$$PV(CST) = \frac{E(\widetilde{CST})/S_0 - (\bar{i}_M - i)\beta_{CST}/S_0}{1+i}$$
$$= \frac{740/500 - (0.12)(0.37808/0.0016)/500}{1.03} \approx 1.38.$$

By deducting the current value of the costs from the revenues, we have

$$P_{aB} = \frac{\{E(\widetilde{REV}) - E(\widetilde{CST})\}/S_0 - (\bar{i}_M - i)(\beta_{REV} - \beta_{CST})/S_0}{1+i}$$
$$= \frac{(1540-740)/500 - (0.12)(548.8-236.3)/500}{1.03} \approx 1.48.$$

The risk in the revenues and costs is related to the project risk through the covariance between the net cash flows and the return on the market portfolio, with:

$$\sigma_{MY_k} = E\left\{\left(\tilde{i}_M - E(\tilde{i}_M)\right)\left([\widetilde{REV}_k - E(\widetilde{REV}_k)] - [\widetilde{CST}_k - E(\widetilde{CST}_k)]\right)\right\} = \sigma_{M\,REV_k} - \sigma_{M\,CST_k},$$

leading to $\beta_{NCF_k} = \beta_{REV_k} - \beta_{CST_k}$. After substitution we obtain the asset value in (4.45), where $p_{ak} = PV(\widetilde{REV}_k) - PV(\widetilde{CST}_k)$.

While it sounds counter-intuitive, more market risk in the costs, all other things constant, will make the share more valuable. In effect, the costs transfer consumption flows to other agents in the economy. If market risk in the costs (with $\beta_{CST_k} > 0$) exceeds market risk in the revenues (with $\beta_{REV_k} > 0$) the project risk becomes negative (with $\beta_{Y_k} = \beta_{REV_k} - \beta_{CST_k} < 0$), where the expected discount rate for the net cash flows $E(\tilde{i}_k)$ is less than the risk-free rate i and less than the discount rates for both the revenues $E(\tilde{i}_{REV_k})$ and costs $E(\tilde{i}_{CST_k})$.

4.6.2 Net cash flows over multiple time periods

Most capital assets have risky net cash flows over a number of future time periods, and there are two main reasons why their market risk can change over time – one is due to investor reassessments of the project risk, while the other is from changes in aggregate consumption risk. Both make present value calculations more complex, and we demonstrate this by computing the present value of a security (k) with net cash flows $(\widetilde{NCF}_t)$ over T periods. With constant *aggregate consumption risk* we use the CAPM to compute its current price as:

$$p_{ak} = \sum_{t=1}^{T} \frac{E(\widetilde{NCF}_{kt})}{\Pi_{j=1}^{t}[1 + i_j + (\bar{i}_{Mj} - i_j)\beta_{kt,j}]} \tag{4.47}$$

where $\beta_{kt,j} = \text{Cov}[\tilde{V}_{kt,j}/E(\tilde{V}_{kt-j}), \tilde{i}_{Mj}]/Var(\tilde{i}_{Mj})$ is the market risk in the discount rate at time j on net cash flows realized at t with a market value of $\tilde{V}_{kt,j}$. In the period when the net cash flows are realized ($j = t$) the beta coefficient is the normalized project risk, with $\beta_{kt,t} = \text{Cov}(\widetilde{NCF}_{kt}, \tilde{i}_{Mt})/E(\tilde{V}_{kt,t-1})$. In all prior periods the beta coefficients are compensation for reassessments of the risk in the net cash flows. But while the discount factors in (4.47) can have different expected values in each time period they must be non-stochastic when computed using the CAPM. That is, the potentially different values of the risk-free rate, the return on the market portfolio and the beta coefficient in each period are known with certainty at time 0.

Fama (1977) argues that *intermediate uncertainty* is admissible in the CAPM if it contributes no uncertainty to the beta coefficients in the discount factors. When uncertainty is partially resolved with the passing of time, investors may expect to get new information that will lead them to revise their assessment of the risk in the net cash flows in periods prior to the date they are realized. Fama introduces multiplicative uncertainty by allowing expectations of net cash flows realized at t to evolve in each prior period τ (omitting subscript k) as:

$$\tilde{E}_\tau(\widetilde{NCF}_t) = E_{\tau-1}(\widetilde{NCF}_t)(1+\tilde{\varepsilon}_\tau), \tag{4.48}$$

where $\tilde{\varepsilon}_\tau$ is a random variable with zero mean and constant covariance with the return on the market portfolio. This process imparts uncertainty to $\text{Cov}(\tilde{V}_{t,\tau}, \tilde{i}_{M\tau})$ and $E_{\tau-1}(\tilde{V}_{t,\tau})$, but without imparting uncertainty to the discount rates in (4.47). Fama demonstrates this by using (4.48) to write the discounted value at $\tau - 1$ of the net cash flows realized at date t as:

$$V_{\tau-1} = E_{\tau-1}(\tilde{V}_\tau)\left\{\frac{1-\lambda_\tau \text{Cov}(\tilde{V}_\tau, \tilde{i}_{M\tau})/E_{\tau-1}(\tilde{V}_\tau)}{1+i_\tau}\right\} = E_{\tau-1}(\tilde{V}_\tau)\left(\frac{1}{1+E(i_\tau)}\right), \tag{4.49}$$

with $\lambda_\tau = (\bar{i}_{M\tau} - i_\tau)/\text{Var}(i_{M\tau})$.[48] Notice how the normalized covariance $\text{Cov}(V_\tau, i_{M\tau})/E_{\tau-1}(V_\tau)$ here is not the same as the normalized covariance used to determine the beta coefficients in the discount rates of (4.47), where they are $\text{Cov}(\tilde{V}_\tau, \tilde{i}_{M\tau})/E(\tilde{V}_{\tau-1})$. Starting in the period prior to realization ($t - 1$) and using (4.48) to iterate back in time to the current period (0), with $V_t = \widetilde{NCF}_t$, we have

$$V_0 = E_0(\widetilde{NCF}_t)\prod_{j=1}^{t}\left\{\frac{1-\lambda_j \text{Cov}(\tilde{V}_j, \tilde{i}_{Mj})/E_{j-1}(\tilde{V}_j)}{1+i_j}\right\} = E_0(\widetilde{NCF}_t)\prod_{j+1}^{t}\left(\frac{1}{1+E(i_j)}\right). \tag{4.50}$$

It is clear from this expression that the ratio $\text{Cov}(\tilde{V}_\tau, \tilde{i}_{M\tau})/E_{\tau-1}(V_\tau)$ must be non-stochastic for the expected discount rate $E(i_\tau)$ to be non-stochastic, which is the case for the multiplicative uncertainty in (4.48), as the two variables are perfectly correlated, with:

$$\frac{\text{Cov}(\tilde{V}_\tau, \tilde{i}_{M\tau})}{E_{\tau-1}(V_\tau)} = \frac{\text{Cov}[E_\tau(\widetilde{NCF}_t), \tilde{i}_{M\tau}]}{E_{\tau-1}(\widetilde{NCF}_t)} = \text{Cov}(\tilde{\varepsilon}_\tau, \tilde{i}_{M\tau}).$$ [49]

Clearly, the discount factors for each net cash flow in (4.47) can change over time due to changes in the risk-free rate, the return on the market portfolio and the beta coefficients. But, as noted above, all of these variables are known with certainty at time 0. While the risk-free and market returns in each time period are the same for all other net cash flows, they can have different beta coefficients in each time period due to differences in their contribution to market risk and in their intermediate uncertainty. We could also decompose the net cash flows in these valuation formulas by separating the revenues and costs in each period using the analysis illustrated in the previous section by noting $\beta_{NCF_\tau} = \beta_{REV_\tau} - \beta_{CST_\tau}$ in each time period τ.

Fama (1977) identifies circumstances where the present value calculations using (4.50) are less complex, and we demonstrate them here by computing the current value of security D with a single net cash flow in period t of $\widetilde{NCF}_t$.

i *No intermediate uncertainty.* All the beta coefficients in periods prior to realization are zero when investors do not expect to revise their assessments of the project risk, where the current value of security D in (4.50) becomes

$$p_{aD} = E_0(\widetilde{NCF}_t)\prod_{j=1}^{t-1}\left(\frac{1}{1+i_j}\right)\left\{\frac{1-\lambda_t \text{Cov}(\widetilde{NCF}_t, \tilde{i}_{Mt})/E_{t-1}(\widetilde{NCF}_t)}{1+i_t}\right\}.$$

It is the expected value of the net cash flows at $t-1$ discounted at the risk-free interest rate to the current period. A risk premium is only paid in period t when the net cash flows are realized because that is when they impact on the consumption risk of investors. We can also write this expression, as:

$$p_{aD} = E_0(\widetilde{NCF_t})\prod_{j=1}^{t-1}\left(\frac{1}{1+i_j}\right)\left(\frac{1}{1+E(\tilde{i}_t)}\right),$$

where $E(\tilde{i}_t)$ is the only risk-adjusted discount rate.

ii *Constant discount factors.* When the risk-free interest rate, the return on the market portfolio and the beta coefficients in the discount rates are constant over time the current value of security D in (4.50) can be written as

$$p_{aD} = E_0(\widetilde{NCF_t})\left\{\frac{1-\lambda\Omega_t}{1+i}\right\}^t = \frac{E_0(\widetilde{NCF_t})}{\left(1+E(\tilde{i}_D)\right)^t},$$

where $\Omega_t = \mathrm{Cov}(\tilde{V}_j, \tilde{i}_M)/E_{j-1}(\tilde{V}_j)$ is the same in each period j. Now investors expect the net cash flows to become more uncertain as time passes, where the extra expected project risk in each period generates the same risk premium. Since $\mathrm{Cov}(\tilde{V}_j, \tilde{i}_M)/E_{j-1}(\tilde{V}_j)$ is constant, $\mathrm{Cov}(\tilde{V}_j, \tilde{i}_M)$ must rise over time to offset the increase in $E_{j-1}(\tilde{V}_j)$. This increase in project risk is confirmed by writing the current value of the security in these circumstances as

$$p_{aD} = \frac{E_0(\widetilde{NCF_t})}{\left(1+E(\tilde{i}_D)\right)^t} = \frac{CE(\widetilde{NCF_t})}{(1+i)^t},$$

where $CE(\widetilde{NCF_t})$ is the certainty-equivalent value of the net cash flows at realization date t. Based on this relationship we can see that the risk premium grows by $\left(1+E(\tilde{i}_D)\right)(1+i)-1$ in each period. Thus, using the CAPM (or one of the other consumption-based pricing models) to value capital assets with a constant expected discount rate includes intermediate uncertainty in periods prior to the date net cash flows are realized. In other words, uncertainty is expected to increase over time, where the longer the time to realization the greater the uncertainty. It is important to emphasize the point made earlier that a single risk premium is paid to investors in period t for bearing the project risk. They are not paid a risk premium in prior periods to compensate them for bearing this project risk, but rather they are paid compensation for revisions made to their expectations of the project risk.

Finally, when *aggregate consumption risk changes over time* we can use one of the three multi-period consumption-based asset pricing models with G additional risk factors to isolate changes in the investment opportunity set, where the valuation formula in (4.47), becomes

$$p_{ak} = \sum_{t=1}^{T}\frac{E_0(\widetilde{NCF_t})}{\prod_{j=1}^{t}\{1+i_j+\Sigma_{g_j\in G}(E(\tilde{i}_{g_j})-i_j)\beta_{g_j,j}\}}. \tag{4.51}$$

If we allow *admissible intermediate uncertainty* using (4.48) we can write the current value of the security as

$$p_{ak} = \sum_{t=1}^{T} E_0(\widetilde{NCF}_t) \prod_{j=0}^{t} \left\{ \frac{1 - \Sigma_{g_j} \lambda_{g_j} \operatorname{Cov}(\tilde{V}_j, \tilde{i}_{g_j}) / E_{j-1}(\tilde{V}_j)}{1 + i_j} \right\}, \tag{4.52}$$

where $\lambda_{g_j} = (E(\tilde{i}_{g_j}) - i_j)/\operatorname{Var}(i_{g_j})$ is the normalized premium for risk isolated by factor g in time period j, $E(\tilde{i}_{gj})$ being the expected return on its mimicking portfolio. A numerical example is provided in Box 4.10 using the two-factor version of the ICAPM in equation (4.37) above. In the ICAPM, APT and CCAPM, the additional factors isolate changes in aggregate consumption risk over time. Even with intermediate uncertainty the risk-free interest rate, the returns on the mimicking factor portfolios and the beta coefficients for the factor risk in the discount rates in each time period are known with certainty. There is empirical evidence that suggests security returns depend on trading rules over longer time periods where investors condition expected returns on information about variables such as the dividend–price ratio and firm size. Investors predict different expected returns on capital assets based on (possibly private) information they have about these variables which they use as signals. As noted earlier in Section 4.5.1, Fama and MacBeth (1973) find that the CAPM performs better empirically when additional factors such as firm size and book-to-market values are added to the model. Campbell and Cochrane (2000) and Lettau and Ludvigson (2001) get similar results by deriving conditional versions of the CAPM and CCAPM. Instead of including additional factors, however, they scale the parameters in the linear discount factors using the log consumption-wealth ratio.

In practical situations financial analysts frequently use the consumption-based pricing models as though they are unconditional models by assuming the current information investors use to value assets is fully reflected in their risky discount factors. Others assume aggregate consumption risk is constant over time and use the CAPM to compute an expected one-period simple return which they use as the discount rate in every time period. As noted above, this assumes there is intermediate uncertainty in time periods prior to the realization of the cash flows. Those who allow the consumption risk to change do so by adding additional factors to the CAPM, using the ICAPM, or by scaling the parameters in the linear discount factors in the CAPM and CCAPM.

Box 4.10 Using the ICAPM to compute the present value of a share

We use the ICAPM in a multi-period setting to compute the value of a share D which is expected to pay a dividend (*DIV*1) of \$1.44 in 12 months' time, and a final dividend (*DIV*2) of \$2.30 in 24 months time when there is no intermediate uncertainty. Both dividends have the same aggregate consumption risk, and to simplify the analysis we compute the return on a mimicking portfolio (n) which is perfectly correlated with the stochastic interest rate ($\rho_{ni} = 1$) and uncorrelated with the return on the market (M) portfolio ($\rho_{nM} = 0$). This makes the coefficients in the ICAPM pricing equation in (4.37) standard beta coefficients. We assume the expected return on the market portfolio and the expected risk-free rate are constant over time, where the covariance between the dividends and the returns on the market and mimicking portfolios are summarized below, together with the variance in their returns.

	i_M	i_n	i
Mean	0.18	0.04	0.03
Variance	0.25	0.08	—
Covariance with DIV	0.30	0.06	—

Using the ICAPM, we compute the present value of the dividends in each period and sum them to obtain the current price of share *D*:

$$PV(DIV_1) = \frac{E_0(DIV_1) - (\bar{i}_M - i)\beta_{MDIV} - (\bar{i}_n - i)\beta_{nDIV}}{1+i}$$
$$= \frac{1.44 - (0.15)(0.3/0.25) - (0.01)(0.06/0.08)}{1.03} \approx 1.22,$$

and

$$PV(DIV_2) = \frac{E_0(DIV_2) - (\bar{i}_M - i)\beta_{MDIV} - (\bar{i}_n - i)\beta_{nDIV}}{(1+i)^2}$$
$$= \frac{2.30 - (0.15)(0.3/0.25) - (0.01)(0.06/0.08)}{1.0609} \approx 1.99.$$

Thus, the current share is

$$p_{aD} = PV(DIV_1) + PV(DIV_2) \approx \$3.21.$$

We can now compute the risk-adjusted discount factors for the dividends in each period. For the dividends paid in the second period, we have

$$PV(DIV_2) = \frac{E_0(DIV_2)}{(1+i)\{1+i+(\bar{i}_M - i)\beta_{MB} + (\bar{i}_n - i)\beta_{nB}\}} \approx 1.99,$$

with $\beta_{MB} = \beta_{MDIV}/PV_1(DIV_2) \approx 0.59$, $\beta_{nB} = \beta_{nDIV}/PV_1(DIV_2) \approx 0.37$ and $E(\tilde{i}_B) \approx 0.12$.

If there is intermediate uncertainty that makes the risk-adjusted discount rate constant over time, the present value of the dividends in the second period will fall by approximately 16 cents to \$1.83. This additional consumption risk reduces the current share price to \$3.05.

Problems

1 The returns on shares *A* and *B* in four equally likely states at the end of next year are summarized below.

State	*Probability*	*Rates of return (%)*	
		Share A	*Share B*
1	0.3	–25	30
2	0.4	50	25
3	0.2	5	–40
4	0.1	40	30

i Calculate the expected return, variance and standard deviation for each share.
ii Compute the coefficient of correlation for the returns to these shares.

iii Calculate the expected return, variance and standard deviation on a portfolio with 60 per cent invested in share *A* and 40 per cent in share *B*. Compute the diversification effect for this portfolio.

iv Derive the standard deviation for the return to the minimum variance portfolio and compute the diversification effect.

v Explain what factors determine the risk premium paid on any security.

2 In a capital market where the CAPM holds the expected return on a portfolio (*G*) that combines the risk-free asset (*F*) and the market portfolio (*M*) is 25 per cent. (This is based on a risk-free rate of 5 per cent, an expected return on the market portfolio of 20 per cent, and a standard deviation in the return on portfolio *G* of 4 per cent. This information is summarized in the diagram below.)

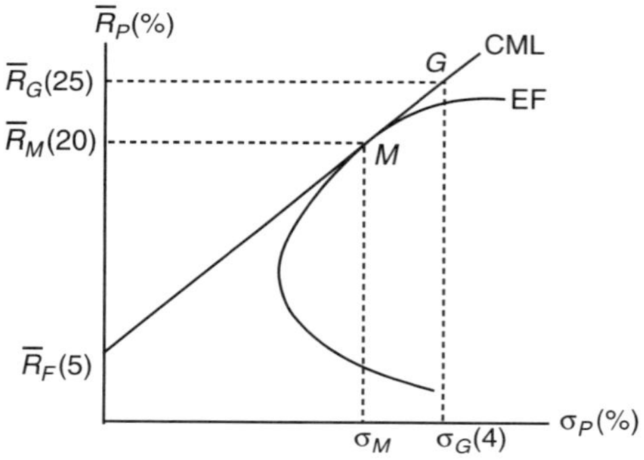

i What is the expected rate of return on a risky security that has a correlation coefficient with the market portfolio of 0.5 and a standard deviation of 2 per cent?

ii What is the correlation coefficient between the returns on portfolio *G* and the market portfolio?

3 Assume a mean–variance opportunity set is constructed from two risky shares, *A* and *B*, with the variance–covariance matrix for their returns of

$$\begin{pmatrix} 0.0064 & 0 \\ 0 & 0.0016 \end{pmatrix}.$$

Share *A* has an expected return of 25 per cent and share *B* an expected return of 15 per cent. Suppose investor *I* chooses a 'market portfolio' which consists of 80 per cent in share *A* and 20 per cent in share *B*, whereas investor *J* chooses a different 'market portfolio' with 50 per cent in each share. Calculate the beta coefficient (β_A) of share *A* for each investor. Explain why they differ.

4 Security prices are determined, in part, by the non-diversifiable risk in their expected net cash flows. Suppose investors can construct a portfolio by combining two risky securities *A* and *B* with expected returns and standard deviations summarized below.

	A	*B*
$\tilde{i}$	0.08	0.12
σ	0.4	0.6

Consider whether it is possible to diversify risk by bundling these assets together when the covariance on their returns is 0.08, and identify the factors that determine the size of the diversification effect. Explain how investors would choose their risky bundle when there is a risk-free security and the returns on assets *A* and *B* are jointly normally distributed. How would they compute the risk premium for each asset *A* and *B*? (Assume investors have homogeneous expectations, and assets *A* and *B* are the only risky securities that trade. You are not required to compute their risky portfolios or the risk premiums on the assets.)

5 Two shares *A* and *B* trade in a capital market where the CAPM holds and they have current prices of \$50 and \$25, respectively. They are not expected to pay dividends over the next 12 months and at that time their prices in each of the three possible states of the world are summarized below.

State	*Probability*	*Share A*	*Share B*
1	0.1	\$40	\$28
2	0.7	\$55	\$30
3	0.2	\$60	\$20

Other information about the market includes $\sigma_M = 0.10$, $\rho_{AM} = 0.8$ and $\rho_{BM} = 0.2$.

i Calculate the beta coefficient for each share when the standard deviation in the return to the market portfolio is $\sigma_M = 0.10$, and the coefficients of correlation between the returns on each share and the market portfolio are $\rho_{AM} = 0.8$ and $\rho_{BM} = 0.2$, respectively.

ii Derive the expected return and standard deviation of a portfolio consisting of 40 per cent invested in share *A* and 60 per cent invested in share *B*. What is the beta coefficient of this portfolio?

6 Traders in the capital market where the CAPM holds expect the return on the market portfolio to be $\bar{i}_M = 0.16$ with a standard deviation of $\sigma_M = 0.20$ when the risk-free interest rate is $i = 0.08$. They also compute a covariance between the returns on risky security *k* and the market portfolio of $\sigma_{kM} = 0.01$.

i If you obtain new information that indicates the expected return on security *k* is 6 per cent (with $\sigma_{kM} = 0.01$) should you purchase it?

ii If security *k* actually pays 15 per cent over the year, has the CAPM failed?

7 Show how the intertemporal CAPM pricing equation in (4.37) becomes the CAPM pricing equation in (4.21) when the interest rate is non-stochastic, with $\sigma_n = 0$. Repeat the exercise when traded security returns are uncorrelated with changes in the interest rate, with $\rho_{ki} = 0$ for all *k*. Provide economic intuition for these outcomes.

8 Use the consumption-based pricing model in (4.28) to solve the wealth of a consumer with the power utility function $U(I_t) = I_t^{1-\gamma}/(1-\gamma)$. Solve the coefficient of relative risk aversion for this function and then show that it is inversely related to the rate of time preference.

9 This question asks you to examine the consumption-based asset pricing model.

i Representative agent pricing models in the financial economics literature are special cases of the CBPM. Explain how consumers measure risk in the CBPM and why it is a representative agent model. In particular, summarize the assumptions that make it a representative agent model. How would allowing state-dependent preferences change the CBPM?

ii The CAPM, ICAPM, APT and CCAPM are special cases of the CBPM where in each model the stochastic discount factor (pricing kernel) has a linear relationship with the factors that isolate aggregate consumption risk using mean–variance analysis.

Explain what the stochastic discount factor measures and how it is affected by risk aversion, then examine the way the factors used to isolate aggregate consumption risk are determined in each of the four models. Derive the coefficient of relative risk aversion and the stochastic discount factor for the utility function $U(I_t) = I_t^{1-\gamma}/(1-\gamma)$, where I_t is consumption expenditure at time t. Why do consumers need to have preferences with a constant and identical coefficient of relative risk aversion in the single-good, single-beta coefficient version of the CCAPM? How does it differ from the CAPM and the single-beta coefficient version of the ICAPM?

10 This question looks at the mutuality principle and its implications for consumption risk faced by individual consumers.

i In all the representative agent pricing models the mutuality principle holds. Explain this principle using the insurance problem for a large number of identical consumers who maximize expected utility over given income (M) facing loss (L) with probability π. Identify the important assumptions for it to hold, then show why idiosyncratic risk is costless to trade when it does.

ii Constantinides and Duffie (1996) explain the equity premium and low risk-free rate puzzles identified by Mehra and Prescott (1985) in the consumption-based asset pricing model by relaxing the requirement for the mutuality principle to hold. Outline the two puzzles and then provide an intuitive explanation for the solution offered by Constantinides and Duffie. (As you are unlikely to be familiar with their formal analysis you need only conjecture an intuitive explanation.)

iii Summarize two of the extensions made in the finance literature to the consumption-based pricing model that attempt to explain the pricing puzzles identified by Mehra and Prescott (1985) without moving outside the representative agent model framework. Provide intuitive explanations for the extensions and comment on their ability to explain the puzzles.

5 Private insurance with asymmetric information

There are a number of different sources for the risk in consumption expenditure. Consumers hold securities with risky returns and have variable income from labour and other capital assets. *Diversifiable risk* in security returns is eliminated by bundling them together in portfolios, whereas most of the diversifiable risk in their labour and other income is eliminated by purchasing insurance. We examined the *diversification effect* inside portfolios of securities earlier in Chapter 3. In this chapter we look at the role of insurance where consumers pool individual risk that can be eliminated across the population by the law of large numbers. *Individual risk* is where a portion of the population incurs income losses that do not affect aggregate consumption. The only uncertainty is over the identity of the consumers in the group incurring losses. In a frictionless competitive market where insurance trades at prices equal to the probability of incurring losses, consumers with state-independent preferences fully insure to eliminate individual risk from their consumption expenditure. In effect, consumers pay premiums into a pool of funds that cover the insurance claims made by the proportion of the population incurring losses. When insurance trades at these *actuarially fair prices* there is no expected cost to consumers from removing individual risk from their consumption expenditure so they fully insure. When individual risk can be costlessly eliminated in this way it attracts no premium, where the only premium in expected security returns is determined by aggregate non-diversifiable risk. This is referred to as the *mutuality principle* that holds in all the consumption-based asset pricing models examined earlier in Chapter 4.

We look at insurance with *common (symmetric) information* in Section 5.1 and then extend the analysis by introducing *asymmetric information* in Section 5.2. Consumers will fully insure against individual risk in a frictionless competitive equilibrium when traders have common information and state-independent preferences. We use this as a benchmark to identify the effects of trading costs and asymmetric information. Consumers choose not to fully insure when trading costs raise the price of insurance above the probability of incurring losses. When they are minimum necessary costs of trade the competitive equilibrium outcome is Pareto efficient, where expected security returns rise to compensate consumers for the cost of eliminating individual risk from their consumption expenditure.

A number of government policies, including price stabilization schemes and publicly funded insurance, are justified as ways to overcome the effects of asymmetric information on private insurance. Moral hazard and adverse selection are the most widely cited problems. With *moral hazard* consumers have the ability to reduce their individual risk by undertaking costly self-protection. Whenever marginal effort, which cannot be observed by insurers, is not reflected in the price consumers pay for insurance, they less than fully insure. *Adverse selection* occurs when there are consumers with different probabilities of incurring losses that insurers cannot costlessly identify and separate. Low-risk types suffer from high-risk types buying low-risk policies. This imposes externalities on low-risk consumers. At one extreme high-risk types may prove too big a problem for the existence of a private insurance market. These are the most common reasons cited for incomplete insurance markets. Newbery and Stiglitz (1981) argue that moral hazard and adverse selection problems are especially severe in developing countries and they recommend the use of price stabilization policies to reduce the risk in consumer incomes. Dixit (1987, 1989) argues, however, that these stabilization policies should be evaluated in the presence of the moral hazard and adverse selection problems. Unless governments have better information than private traders, or can trade risk more efficiently, the stabilization policies are unlikely to be socially beneficial.

Before we commence the formal analysis it is helpful to illustrate the difference between aggregate uncertainty and individual risk.[1] *Aggregate uncertainty* is economy-wide non-diversifiable risk which agents trade according to their differing risk preferences, while *individual risk* is diversifiable across the economy by the law of large numbers. The difference between them can be illustrated in consumer budget constraints. Consider a situation where every individual has the same endowment of money income, $\bar{M}(s)$, in each state of nature s. Since it can vary across states of nature they face aggregate uncertainty. Now suppose they can also suffer a loss L with probability π in each state s, where the income for each consumer becomes

$$M_B(s) = \bar{M}(s) - L$$

for the bad (B) outcome, and

$$M_G(s) = \bar{M}(s)$$

for the good (G) outcome without the loss with probability $1 - \pi$.

When a large number of consumers (H) have the same probability of loss π, aggregate income in each state will be equal to their expected income multiplied by the number of consumers,

$$\left(\pi M_B(s) + (1-\pi) M_G(s)\right) H = \left(\bar{M}(s) - \pi L\right) H.$$

Within each state aggregate income is non-stochastic as a fixed proportion π of the population always has low income, while the remaining proportion $1 - \pi$ of the population always has high income. Thus, there is scope in this setting for mutual insurance among consumers to eliminate their individual risk. The combined effects of aggregate uncertainty and individual risk on consumer income are illustrated in a two-period setting with three states of nature in Figure 5.1, where individual risk doubles the number of random outcomes for consumers. In each state of nature bad outcomes occur with probability $\pi_s \times \pi$, and good outcomes in each state with probability $\pi_s \times (1 - \pi)$.[2] The analysis could be generalized by allowing loss L and its probability to both be state-dependent, but that would complicate things without providing much additional insight into the following results.

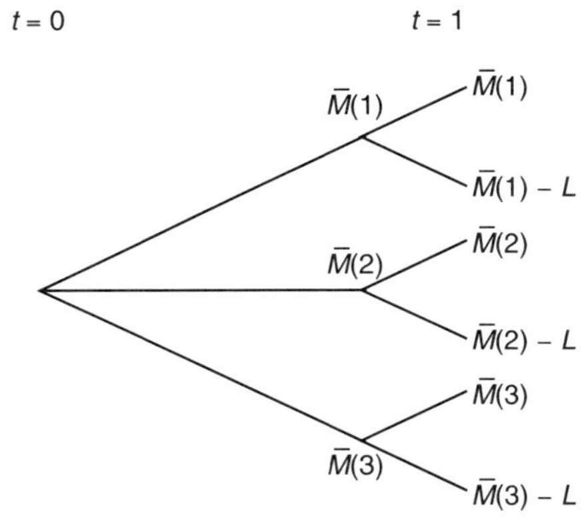

Figure 5.1 Aggregate uncertainty and individual risk.

We focus on individual risk in this chapter as it is where asymmetric information problems arise. Since aggregate uncertainty is common to consumers it is possible for them to negotiate Pareto optimal intertemporal resource transfers whenever they agree on the true state and can trade in competitive markets. We examined the effects of aggregate uncertainty in detail in Chapters 3 and 4, so it is removed from the following analysis.

5.1 Insurance with common information

It is useful to establish the full insurance equilibrium outcome as a benchmark for understanding how trading costs and asymmetric information affect private insurance. This benchmark occurs in a frictionless competitive economy where consumers have common information and maximize von Neumann–Morgenstern expected utility functions. Since these preferences are state-independent, consumers have the same marginal utility of income in states with the same consumption expenditure. Thus, they fully insure against individual risk when the marginal cost of insurance is equal to the probability of bad state outcomes. This benchmark is derived in Section 5.1.1 before trading costs are included in Section 5.1.2.

5.1.1 No administrative costs

Consider an economy with $h = 1, \ldots, H$ identical consumers who choose a single good to maximize an NMEU function when income is subject only to individual risk. In the absence of insurance (0) the problem for each consumer is

$$\max\left\{EU_0 = \pi U(X_B) + (1-\pi)U(X_G) \left| \begin{matrix} X_B \le M - L \equiv I_B \\ X_G \le M \equiv I_G \end{matrix} \right.\right\}^3, \tag{5.1}$$

with M being a fixed endowment of money income, X_B consumption expenditure in the bad state (B) when a dollar loss of L is incurred with probability π, and X_G consumption expenditure in the good state (G) without the loss.[4] There is no discount factor in the expected utility function as we assume uncertainty is resolved the instant consumption choices have been made. In effect, no time elapses between the consumption choice and the resolution of uncertainty. By the *law of large numbers* there is certain aggregate income of $(M - \pi L)H$. Consumers face individual risk where a fixed proportion of the population incurs loss L. The only uncertainty is whether or not they are in that group.

Clearly, individuals consume their income endowments in the absence of insurance. After substituting the budget constraints in (5.1) into the expected utility function, we have

$$EU_0 = \pi U(M-L) + (1-\pi)U(M).$$

At the endowment point the slope of the indifference curve measures the marginal valuation of bad to good state consumption expenditure, with

$$MRS_{B,G} = \left.\frac{dX_G}{dX_B}\right|_{dEU_0=0} = \frac{-\pi U_B'}{(1-\pi)U_G'},$$

where $U_B' = \partial U/\partial x_B$ and $U_G' = \partial U/\partial x_G$ are, respectively, the marginal utility in the bad and good states. Consumption without insurance is illustrated at point E in Figure 5.2. Along the 45° line where consumption expenditure is constant every indifference schedule has the same slope,

$$MRS_{B,G} = \frac{dX_G}{dX_B} = \frac{-\pi}{(1-\pi)},$$

with $U_B' = U_G'$ at point A in the diagram. Indeed, the indifference schedules have this slope for all consumption bundles in the commodity space for risk-neutral consumers, while

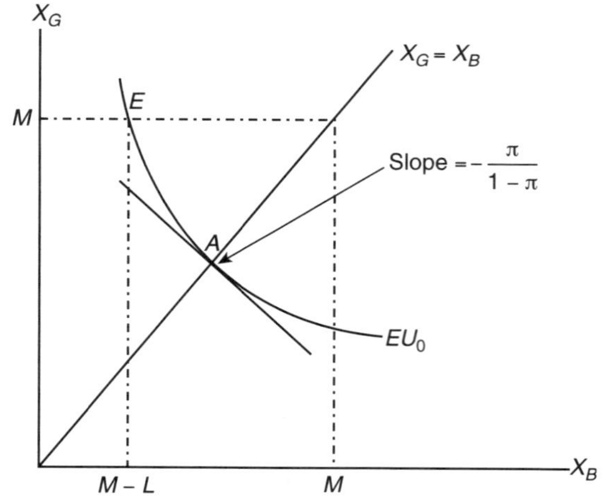

Figure 5.2 Consumption without insurance.

it only holds for bundles on the 45° line for risk-averse consumers. In effect, risk averse consumers are marginally neutral to risk on the 45° line where they have no consumption risk.

Consumers use insurance to transfer income from the good to the bad state, where Q is the dollar value of insurance they purchase for premium P. By pooling the premiums they create a mutual fund to cover claims made by those who incur the income loss, where the consumer problem with insurance can be summarized as

$$\max\left\{EU_Q = \pi U(X_B) + (1-\pi)U(X_G) \left| \begin{matrix} X_B \le M - L + Q - P \equiv I_B \\ X_G \le M - P \equiv I_G \end{matrix} \right.\right\}. \tag{5.2}$$

Optimally chosen insurance (at an interior solution with $Q > 0$) satisfies

$$\pi U_B'\left(1 - \frac{\partial P}{\partial Q}\right) - (1-\pi)U_G'\frac{\partial P}{\partial Q} = 0, \tag{5.3}$$

where $\partial P/\partial Q$ is the marginal cost of additional cover. In a frictionless competitive market this price of insurance is obtained from the solution to the problem

$$\max \eta = (P - \pi Q)\, H \tag{5.4}$$

for insurers, where η is the profit from selling insurance to H consumers in the population, with total revenue of PH and total cost of $\pi Q \alpha H$ where πH is the number of people who incur the loss.[5] Since the optimal supply of insurance solves:

$$\frac{d\eta}{dQ} = \left(\frac{dP}{dQ} - \pi\right)H = 0,$$

a dollar of insurance trades at price $dP/dQ = \pi$, where each consumer pays premium $P = \pi Q$. After substituting this price into the optimality condition in (5.3), we have

$$\pi U_B'(1-\pi) - (1-\pi)U_G'\pi = 0. \tag{5.5}$$

For this to hold we must have the same consumption in each state, with $U_B' = U_G'$, where full cover is chosen with $Q = L$.

This outcome is illustrated in Figure 5.3 where consumers trade from their endowment point at E to point Q on the 45° line where they have the same consumption expenditure of $M - P$ in each state. Whenever income can be transferred from the good to the bad state at a price equal to the probability of loss, consumers with state-independent preferences fully insure. In effect, they can transfer consumption expenditure to the bad state at the same rate nature deals

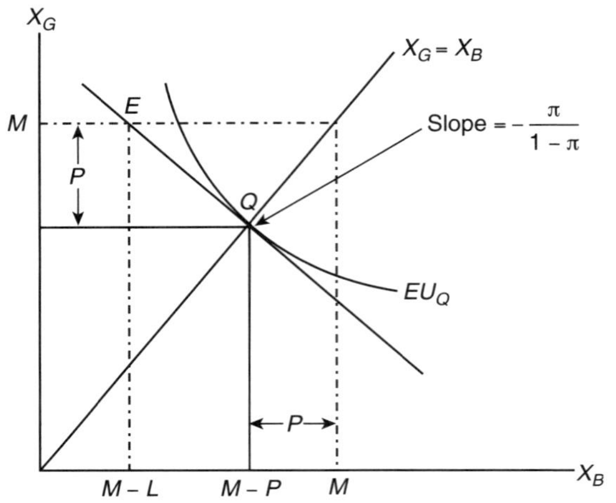

Figure 5.3 Full insurance.

Box 5.1 Full insurance: a numerical example

Leonard has a fixed income endowment of \$500 which he allocates to consumption expenditure to maximize expected utility $EU_0 = 0.4 \ln X_B + 0.6 \ln X_G$, where X_B is consumption in the bad state when he loses \$200 from theft with probability $\pi = 0.4$, and X_G consumption in the good state without the loss. In the absence of insurance (or other financial securities), Leonard consumes his endowment and gets expected utility of $EU_0 \approx 6.0102$, where his marginal valuation for income in the bad state is

$$MRS_{BG} = -\left.\frac{dX_G}{dX_B}\right|_{dEU_0=0} = \frac{\pi X_G}{(1-\pi)X_B} = \frac{0.4 \times 500}{0.6 \times 300} = \frac{200}{180} \approx \$1.11.$$

If the marginal cost of transferring a dollar of income from the good to the bad state is less than this amount he will insure against the risk of theft. Since he has a diminishing marginal valuation for income in the bad state he is risk-averse, with $d(dX_G/dX_B)/dX_B > 0$. (There is no aggregate uncertainty in this example and individual risk is diversifiable across the population by the law of large numbers.)

When Leonard can purchase insurance (Q) in a frictionless competitive market (with common information) at a marginal cost of $c = \$0.40$ his budget constraints for bad and good state consumption expenditure are, respectively, $X_B = 300 - 0.4Q + Q$ and $X_G = 500 - 0.4Q$. His optimal insurance choice solves

$$\frac{dEU_Q}{dQ} = 0.4\frac{\partial EU_Q}{\partial X_B}(1-c) - 0.6\frac{\partial EU_Q}{\partial X_G}c = \frac{0.24}{X_B} - \frac{0.24}{X_G} = 0,$$

with $X_B = X_B = \$420$ and $Q^* = \$200$. Thus, Leonard fully insures and gets expected utility of $EU_{Q^*} :\approx 6.0403$, which is approximately 0.50 per cent higher than expected utility without insurance.

the income loss to them, so they fully insure. While they are worse off in the good state, the gain in the bad state is largly due to risk aversion that makes their indifference schedules concave to the origin in the consumption space. Their consumer surplus is the change in utility $(EU_Q - EU_O)$ in the move from endowment point E to point Q on the 45° line in Figure 5.3. This is the most consumers would pay to have access to a competitive insurance market.

As noted earlier, we use the full insurance outcome as a benchmark for identifying the effects of trading costs and asymmetric information on private insurance in the rest of this section and the next.

5.1.2 Trading Costs

In practice insurers employ labour, invest capital and incur other operating expenses when they trade insurance. While some costs arise from gathering information, others arise from writing policies and processing claims. These administrative costs may be fixed for each policy sold or may change with the amount of cover purchased. With a constant cost of τ_C to process each dollar of cover claimed, the problem for competitive insurers becomes

$$\max \eta = (P - \pi(1 + \tau_C)Q)H, \tag{5.6}$$

where $\tau_C \pi QH$ is the total cost of processing the insurance claim Q. The optimal supply of insurance solves

$$\frac{d\eta}{dQ} = \left\{\frac{dP}{dQ} - \pi(1+\tau_C)\right\}H = 0,$$

where the price of each dollar of insurance is $dP/dQ = \pi(1 + \tau_C)$. Thus, consumers pay a premium of $P = \pi(1 + \tau_C)Q$, which includes trading costs of $\tau_C \pi Q$ to cover the administrative costs of processing claims. We obtain the optimal insurance cover by substituting $dP/dQ = \pi(1 + \tau_C)$ into (5.3), where, for an interior solution (with $Q > 0$), we have

$$\pi U_B'(1-\pi) - (1-\pi)U_G'\pi - \tau_C(\pi^2 U_G' + (1-\pi)\pi U_G') = 0.$$

The positive marginal trading costs in the third term must be offset by higher marginal utility in the bad state, with $U_B' > U_G'$, where this requires lower consumption expenditure $M - L + Q - P < M - P$ and $L > Q$. Consumers choose not to insure at all when $\pi U_B'(1-\pi) - (1-\pi)U_G'\pi < \tau_C(\pi^2 U_B' + (1-\pi)\pi U_G')$. The equilibrium outcome for partial insurance is illustrated at Q' in Figure 5.4. Once administrative costs push the market price of insurance above the probability of loss the indifference curve must be tangent to the budget constraint at bundles located above the 45° line.

If insurers incur a constant administrative cost of τ_Q for writing each dollar of insurance, its market price is higher at $\partial P/\partial Q = \pi/(1 - \tau_Q)$, where consumers pay a premium of $P = \pi Q/(1 - \tau_Q)$. These costs raise the slope of the budget constraint to $-\pi/(1 - \tau_Q)/[1 - \pi/(1-\tau_Q)]$, and consumers only partially insure (if they insure at all).

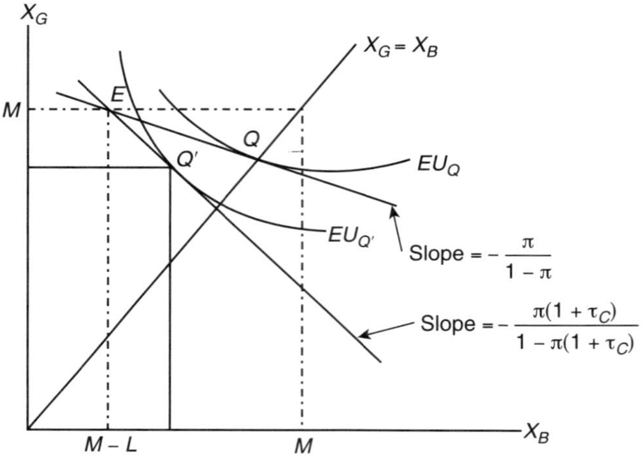

Figure 5.4 Partial insurance with processing costs.

Private insurance is unaffected by fixed trading costs when insurers can fund them using access fees (*AF*) that do not exceed consumer surplus. An access fee shifts the endowment point for consumers from *E* to *E′* along the dashed line that is parallel to the 45° line in Figure 5.5. It is the most consumers would pay to trade in the insurance market at a price equal to the probability of loss. At this price they fully insure at point Q^{AF}. If the access fee rises above this amount consumers do not insure at all because it makes them worse off. When firms cannot use access fees or price-discriminate along consumer demand schedules they pass the fixed costs into a higher price of insurance and consumers partially insure (if they insure at all). Access fees can be problematic due to leakage in demand, but that is unlikely in the insurance market as policies are verifiable legal contracts between individual consumers and insurers.

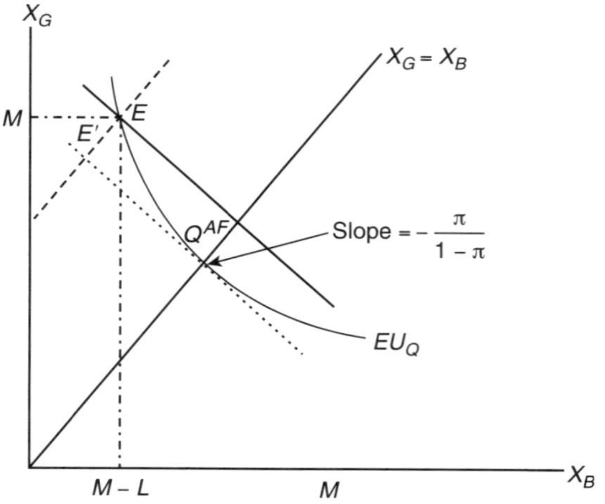

Figure 5.5 Insurance with fixed administrative costs.

Box 5.2 Administrative costs and insurance: a numerical example

Suppose insurers incur a constant marginal cost of $\tau_P = 0.2$ on each dollar of insurance they sell to Leonard in Box 5.1, where the price he must now pay rises from \$0.40 to $c = \pi/(1 - \tau_P) =$ \$0.50. His budget constraints for bad and good state consumption expenditure are, respectively, $X_B = 300 - \frac{1}{2}Q + Q$ and $X_G = 500 - \frac{1}{2}Q$, where his optimal insurance choice solves

$$\frac{dEU_Q}{dQ} = \frac{\pi}{X_B}\left(1 - \frac{0.4}{1-\tau_P}\right) - \frac{1-\pi}{X_G}\frac{0.4}{1-\tau_P} = 0,$$

with $X_B = \frac{2}{3}X_G$. Using the budget constraints we find Leonard purchases insurance of $Q^* = \$50$, and consumes $X_G^* = \$475$ and $X_B^* = \$316.67$. He has expected utility of 6.0116, which is approximately 0.475 per cent lower than his expected utility without trading costs. Since the trading costs raise the relative cost of each dollar of bad state consumption expenditure from $\pi/(1 - \pi) = \frac{2}{3}$ to $\pi/(1 - \pi - \tau_P) = 1$, Leonard no longer fully insures. Recall from Box 5.1 that his marginal valuation for bad state consumption is $\frac{2}{3}$ of a dollar of good state consumption expenditure when he has the same consumption in each state, which is less than the marginal cost of insurance.

It is tempting to automatically conclude trading costs are a source of inefficiency when they change the relative cost of good and bad state consumption expenditure and restrict private insurance. But while they are minimum necessary costs of trade they do not distort private activity. If regulatory or other barriers restrict entry into the market the price of insurance can rise above marginal cost and cause allocative inefficiency. Throughout the following analysis we assume trading costs are zero, or if they are positive they are fixed and less than consumer surplus. Hence, any equilibrium outcome with less than full insurance will result from market failure.

5.2 Insurance with asymmetric information

Insurers need to know the probability of income losses for consumers. In many situations consumers can change these probabilities and/or the size of any losses by expending effort. Moreover, they can have different loss probabilities. For example, drivers have different skills and other attributes that give them different accident probabilities, and the probability of having a car accident can be reduced by driving more carefully and in good weather conditions. When information is costly to obtain insurers can have incomplete (asymmetric) information about these probabilities, and this can lead to equilibrium outcomes where some consumers have less than full insurance. Two cases are considered in this section, moral hazard and adverse selection.[6]

5.2.1 Moral hazard

In most practical situations consumers can take actions to reduce expected losses in income from individual risk. They take precautions to reduce the probability of loss through *self-protection*, or the size of the loss incurred through *self-insurance*. We look at how they impact on the demand for market insurance using the analysis in Ehrlich and Becker (1972). When competitive insurers can costlessly observe marginal reductions in the probability of income losses they adjust their insurance premiums accordingly, and consumers fully insure.

However, with costly monitoring and asymmetric information, the price of insurance will not reflect the marginal effort expended by individual consumers who have a diminished incentive to self-protect and choose to partially insure.

We make the probability of loss a function of effort, with $\pi(e)$, where it is assumed $d\pi/de = \pi_e < 0$ and $d^2\pi/de^2 = \pi_{ee} > 0$. This relationship links the levels of effort and insurance together, where the more consumers insure, the less effort they expend on self-protection (with $de/dQ = e_Q < 0$), so that $d\pi / dQ = \pi_Q = \pi_e\, e_Q > 0$.

The consumer problem with *self-protection and insurance* becomes

$$\max_{\{Q,e\}}\left\{EU_Q = \pi(e)U(X_B) + [1-\pi(e)]U(X_G) - e \;\middle|\; \begin{matrix} X_B \leq M - L + Q - P \\ X_G \leq M - P \end{matrix}\right\}, \tag{5.7}$$

where the cost of effort e is measured as a dollar cost to expected utility. To demonstrate moral hazard and identify its consequences for the amount of insurance traded, we consider two extremes – no monitoring and complete monitoring. With no monitoring the insurance premium is determined by $P = \pi(Q)\,Q$, and with complete monitoring it is determined by $P = \pi(e)Q$.

No Monitoring ($P = \pi(Q)\,Q$) is the extreme form of asymmetric information where monitoring is prohibitively costly, and the price of insurance is not directly affected by individual changes in effort. Instead, effort has an indirect effect on the premium when insurers observe a reduction in the probability of income losses at the aggregate level. They see the amount of insurance purchased and can anticipate the level of self-protection, but without observing its marginal effects. Thus, the price of insurance is determined by the amount purchased, with $\partial P/\partial Q = \pi(Q)$. Using (5.7), the optimal level of effort solves

$$\frac{\partial EU}{\partial e} = \pi_e\big(U(X_B) - U(X_G)\big) - 1 = 0, \tag{5.8}$$

where the first term is the marginal benefit from self-protection and the second term its marginal cost. Since $\pi_e < 0$, utility in the good state must exceed utility in the bad state to make the first term positive and equal to unity, with $U(X_B) < U(X_G)$. Thus, consumers less than fully insure. In the absence of monitoring there is no reduction in the price of insurance from marginal increases in effort in (5.8). Any benefits flow indirectly through the insurance decision where insurers identify the probability of loss from the amount of insurance purchased. Using (5.7), the optimal insurance choice solves:

$$\frac{\partial EU}{\partial Q} = \pi(1-\pi)(U_B' - U_G') - \pi_Q Q(\pi U_B' + (1-\pi)U_G') = 0, \tag{5.9}$$

where the first term is the net marginal consumption benefit from insurance, and the second term the change in the insurance premium, with $\pi_Q > 0$. Notice that the first term is the same as the condition for optimally chosen insurance in the absence of self-protection in (5.3), while the second term is the higher price of insurance due to the fall in self-protection; it is an externality that spills over from the effort choice. Thus, consumers partially insure, with $U'_B > U'_G$ and $X_B < X_G$.

Complete monitoring ($P = \pi(e)Q$) is the opposite extreme where monitoring is assumed to be costless, so that insurers observe marginal effort and adjust the price of insurance accordingly, with $\partial P/\partial Q = \pi(e)$. At an interior solution to the consumer problem in (5.7) the optimal effort choice solves

$$\frac{\partial EU}{\partial e} = \pi_e\left(U(X_B) - U(X_G)\right) - 1 - \pi_e Q\left(\pi U'_B + (1-\pi)U'_G\right) = 0, \tag{5.10}$$

where the last term isolates the reduction in the price of insurance from marginal effort that leads to more self-protection than the solution in (5.8) without monitoring. In these circumstances the optimal insurance choice solves

$$\frac{\partial EU}{\partial I} = \pi(1-\pi)(U'_B - U'_G) = 0, \tag{5.11}$$

which is the same as the optimal condition in (5.3) with common information where consumers fully insure, with $U'_B = U'_G$.[7]

In summary, consumers only partially insure when they are not compensated for their marginal effort with costly monitoring. The lack of monitoring imposes an externality on consumers that affects their effort and insurance choices.

5.2.2 Adverse selection

Another externality arises from asymmetric information when insurers cannot distinguish between consumers with different individual risk. Low-risk types suffer from the presence of high-risk types who purchase insurance at low-risk prices.

We demonstrate this externality using the analysis in Rothschild and Stiglitz (1976) where consumers are divided into those with either a high (H) or low (L) probability of loss – a proportion λ have the same high probability π_H and remaining proportion $1 - \lambda$ the same low probability π_L. In every other respect they are identical because they have the same preferences, income and dollar loss. We rule out moral hazard by assuming they cannot change their risk type through self-protection.

With different risk types the consumer problem becomes

$$\max_{\{Q^h\}}\left\{ EU_{Q^h} \left| \begin{array}{l} X_B^h \leq M - L + Q^h - \sigma_h Q^h \\ X_G^h \leq M - \sigma_h Q^h \end{array} \right. \right\} \text{for } h \in \{H, L\}, \tag{5.12}$$

where $EU_{Q^h} = \pi_h U(X_B^h) + (1-\pi_h)U(X_G^h)$, and σ_h is the price of insurance for each risk type $h \in \{H, L\}$. The optimal insurance decision for an interior solution solves

$$\pi_h U_B^{\prime h}(1-\sigma_h) - (1-\pi_h)U_G^{\prime h}\sigma_h = 0 \quad \text{for } h \in \{H, L\}. \tag{5.13}$$

Box 5.3 Self-protection with costless monitoring: a numerical example

The impact of self-protection on private insurance will be demonstrated here by allowing Leonard (in Box 5.1) to reduce his probability of losing income through theft, with $\pi = 1 - \sqrt{e}$ for $0 \le e \le 1$, where e is the cost to expected utility from expending effort. Notice how effort has a positive and diminishing marginal product, with $\pi_e < 0$ and $\pi_{ee} > 0$. With costless monitoring Leonard will

$$\max \left\{ \pi(e)\ln X_B + [1-\pi(e)]\ln X_G + e \,\middle|\, \begin{matrix} X_B \le 300 - \pi(e)Q + Q \\ X_G \le 500 - \pi(e)Q \end{matrix} \right\}$$

In the absence of insurance (with $Q = 0$) he consumes his income endowment in each state, with $X_B = 300$ and $X_G = 500$, where optimal self-protection (at an interior solution) must satisfy the condition

$$-\frac{1}{2\sqrt{e_0}}(\ln X_B - \ln X_G) - 1 = 0.$$

This leads to $e_0^* \approx 0.0652$ and $\pi_0^* \approx 0.75$, with expected utility of $EU_0 \approx 5.7691$. When Leonard can purchase insurance in a frictionless competitive market (with complete information), the optimal insurance choice satisfies

$$\frac{\pi}{X_B}(1-\pi) - (1-\pi)\frac{\pi}{X_G} = 0,$$

and the optimal effort level

$$-\frac{1}{2\sqrt{e_Q}}(\ln X_B - \ln X_G) + \frac{Q}{2\sqrt{e_Q}}\left(\frac{\pi}{X_B} + \frac{1-\pi}{X_G}\right) - 1 = 0.$$

Based on the insurance condition Leonard fully insures, with $X_B^* = X_G^*$ and $Q^* = 200$, where this allows us to write the condition for optimal effort as

$$3\sqrt{e^*_Q} + 2e_Q^* - 1 = 0,$$

with $e_Q^* = 0.0788354$ and $\pi^* \approx 0.72$. The ability to transfer income from the good to the bad state at a marginal cost equal to the probability of loss raises his expected utility by almost 0.5 per cent from $EU_0 \approx 5.7691$ to $EU_Q \approx 5.7965$.

By rearranging this expression we find that indifference curves over good and bad state consumption have slope equal to the relative cost of insurance, with

$$\left.\frac{dX_G^h}{dX_B^h}\right|_{dEU^h=0} = \frac{-\pi_h U_B'^h}{(1-\pi_h)U_G'^h} = \frac{-\sigma_h}{(1-\sigma_h)} \quad \text{for } h \in \{H, L\}. \tag{5.14}$$

Equilibrium in the insurance market can take a number of forms. Insurers may personalize the contracts for high-and low-risk types in a *separating equilibrium*, or they may sell a

Box 5.4 Self-insurance without market insurance

At the beginning of this section we noted the possibility of consumers being able to self-insure against income losses. Suppose Leonard can reduce the size of his loss from theft by expending effort to secure it in a safe place, with $L = 200 - 200\sqrt{e}$, where this effort reduces expected utility by $e/4$. To simplify the analysis we assume he cannot self-protect and faces a given probability of loss of $\pi = 0.4$, where his optimization problem becomes

$$\max\left\{0.4\ln X_B + 0.6\ln X_G + \frac{e}{4}\left|\begin{matrix} X_B \le 500 - L \\ X_G \le 500 \\ L = 200 - 200\sqrt{e} \text{ for } 0 \le e \le 1\end{matrix}\right.\right\}.$$

In the absence of market insurance, the optimal effort level solves

$$-\frac{0.4}{X_B}\frac{100}{\sqrt{e}} - \frac{1}{4} = 0.$$

By using the constraint on consumption expenditure in the bad state when it binds, with $X_B = 300 + 200\sqrt{e}$, we have $e_0^* = 0.234103$, which results in loss $L_0^* \approx \$103.23$ and consumption expenditure of $X_B^* \approx \$396.77$ and $X_G^* \approx \$500$. In these circumstances Leonard's expected utility is $EU_0 \approx 6.0636$, which is approximately 0.9 per cent higher than his expected utility without self insurance in Box 5.1. The additional consumption opportunities with self-insurance are illustrated below. In the absence of insurance the consumption opportunities are constrained by the frontier *BEC*, and with self-insurance they are constrained by frontier *BE′C′*. As Leonard expends effort to reduce the income loss it has two competing effects on his expected utility. It rises with the extra bad state consumption and falls with the extra effort, where the extra consumption moves him to a new indifference schedule with higher utility while the extra effort reduces the utility on each indifference schedule (a relabelling effect). Thus, his expected utility is maximized at an outcome like point *A* along segment *EE′* of the consumption frontier, where at the margin the move to a new indifference schedule is offset by the relabelling effect.

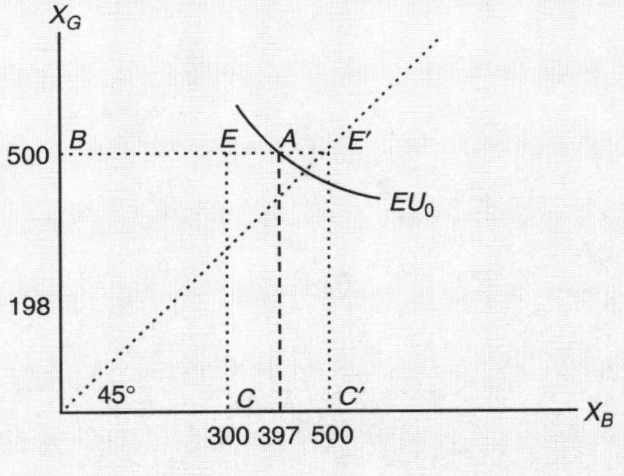

Box 5.5 Self-insurance with competitive market insurance

When Leonard can self-insure and purchase market insurance he has additional consumption opportunities if market insurance is less costly at the margin than self-insurance. In this setting his optimization problem becomes

$$\max\left\{0.4\ln X_B + 0.6\ln X_G + \frac{e}{4}\left|\begin{array}{l} X_B \le 500 - L - 0.4Q + Q \\ X_G \le 500 - 0.4Q \\ L = 200 - 200\sqrt{e}\ \text{for}\ 0 \le e \le 1 \end{array}\right.\right\}.$$

At an interior optimum the demand for market insurance satisfies

$$\frac{\pi}{X_B}(1-\pi) - \frac{(1-\pi)}{X_G}\pi = 0,$$

where Leonard fully insures, with $Q^* = 200$ and $X_B^* = X_G^*$. His optimal effort level satisfies

$$-\frac{0.4}{X_B}\frac{100}{\sqrt{e_Q^*}} - \frac{1}{4} = 0.$$

By using the budget constraint for bad state consumption, with $X_B = 420 + 80\sqrt{e}$, we can write the optimality condition for effort as $21\sqrt{e_Q^*} + 4e_Q^* - 8 = 0$, where $e_Q^* = 0.127246$. Leonard expends less effort when he can purchase market insurance than he did previously in its absence in Box 5.4. Even though the income loss rises to $L_Q^* \approx \$128.66$, market insurance increases his consumption expenditure in each state to $X_B^* = X_G^* \approx \$448.54$, where expected utility rises by approximately 0.2 per cent to $EU_Q \approx 6.0742$. The new equilibrium outcome is illustrated in the diagram below at point F which is on an indifference schedule with higher expected utility than consumption at point A in the absence of market insurance. The larger income loss moves him to the left of point A, while market insurance allows him to trade along the solid line with slope $\pi/(1-\pi)$ onto the 45° line.

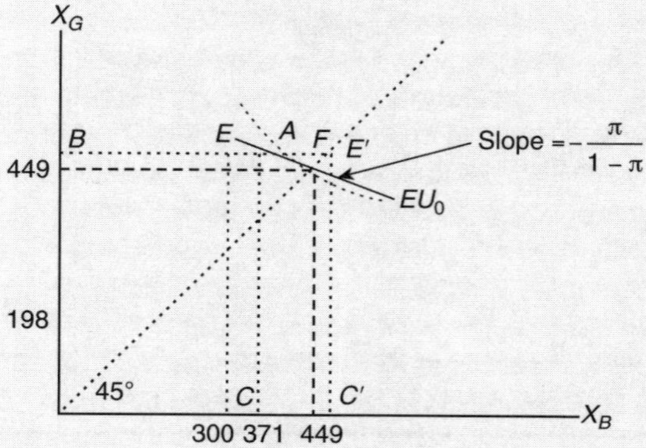

single contract to all risk types in a *pooling equilibrium*.[8] Both are examined to see whether they are robust to competition.

With *complete information*, insurers can separate the risk types, so they offer insurance at actuarially fair odds, with $\sigma_H = \pi_H$ and $\sigma_L = \pi_L$. Thus, from (5.13) both risk types fully insure, with $U_B'^h = U_G'^h$ for $h = H, L$. This separating equilibrium is illustrated in Figure 5.6 where high-risk types locate at point H on budget constraint P_H, and low-risk types locate at point L on budget constraint P_L. The slopes of their budget constraints are equal to the ratio of the bad to good state probabilities.

Once again, the price of insurance is determined by competitive insurers who

$$\max \eta = \sum_h \left((1-\pi_h)\sigma_h - \pi_h(1-\sigma_h)\right)Q^h H^h, \text{for } h \in \{H, L\}.$$

with $H^H = \lambda H$ and $H^L = (1-\lambda)H$. From the first-order condition on this problem, we have $\pi_h/(1-\pi_h) = \sigma_h/(1-\sigma_h)$ for $h \in \{H, L\}$, where insurers break even when the risk types are correctly screened. When insurers cannot separate the risk types, the high-risk consumers try and locate at L by declaring themselves to be low-risk types.[9] Thus, insurers make losses as they raise insufficient revenue to cover the cost of their insurance claims. Therefore, with asymmetric information, the contracts L and H cannot be equilibrium contracts.

In a *pooling equilibrium*, insurers sell a single contract to both risk types. This is illustrated in Figure 5.7 as contract P_P on price line $\bar{P}$ that lies between the separating price lines P_L and P_H. This price line has slope $\bar{\sigma}/(1-\bar{\sigma})$, where $\bar{\sigma}$ is the average price of insurance, with $\sigma = \lambda\pi_H + (1-\lambda)\pi_L$ and $\lambda = N^H/(N^H + N^L)$. Along $\bar{P}$ insurers make losses on high-risk policies, but they are cross-subsidised by profits on low risk policies. But the pooling equilibrium is not stable as new entrants to the insurance market can offer low-risk type contracts in the cross-lined region in Figure 5.7 that makes them better off without attracting the high-risk types who remain at P_P. However, the pooling contract P_P is no longer

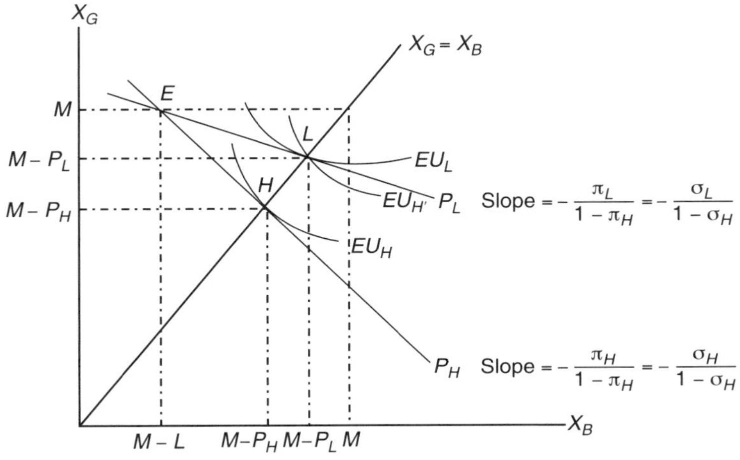

Figure 5.6 Insurance with complete information.

Box 5.6 A separating equilibrium

Consider an insurance market where 20 per cent of consumers are high-risk types (*H*) with probability $\pi_H = 0.6$ of incurring a \$200 loss, while the remainder are low-risk types (*L*) with probability $\pi_L = 0.4$ of incurring the same size loss. They all maximize the expected utility function $\pi_h \sqrt{X_B^h} + (1-\pi_h)\sqrt{X_G^h}$, for $h \in H$, L, where X_B^h and X_G^h are consumption expenditure in the bad and good states, respectively. When they have the same fixed money income of \$500 we can summarize their optimization problem as

$$\max\left\{\pi_h \sqrt{X_B^h} + (1-\pi_h)\sqrt{X_G^h} \middle| \begin{matrix} X_B^h \leq 500 - 200 - \sigma_h Q^h + Q^h \\ X_G^h \leq 500 - \sigma_h Q^h \end{matrix}\right\} \forall h \in H, L,$$

with σ_h being the marginal cost of insurance Q^h. There is no aggregate uncertainty here because 60 per cent of high-risk types and 40 per cent of low-risk types suffer the \$200 loss in income with certainty. The only uncertainty is over the identity of the consumers that incur the losses in each group.

In the absence of insurance (with $Q^h = 0$ for all h) everyone consumes their endowment, with $X_B^h = \$500 - \$200 = \$300$ and $X_G^h = \$500$ for $h \in H$, L, where high-risk types get expected utility of $EU_0^H = 19.34$ and low risk types $EU_0^L = 20.35$. When they can purchase insurance against the income loss their optimal choice satisfies:

$$\frac{\pi_h}{2\sqrt{X_B^h}}(1-\sigma_h) - \frac{1-\pi_h}{2\sqrt{X_G^h}}\sigma_h = 0 \quad \forall h \in H, L.$$

In a frictionless competitive market with common information each risk type is offered an insurance contract that allows them to purchase insurance at a marginal cost equal to their probability of loss, with $\sigma_h = \pi_h$ for all h. Thus, in this separating equilibrium (*SE*) every consumer fully insures, where high-risk types pay a premium of 0.6 × \$200 = \$120, and low risk types a premium of 0.4 × \$200 = \$80. The high-risk types consume $X_B^H = X_G^H = \$380$ and raise their expected utility by 0.78 per cent to $EU_{SE}^H = 19.49$, while the low risk types consume $X_B^L = X_G^L = \$420$ and raise their expected utility by 0.69 per cent to $EU_{SE}^L = 20.49$.

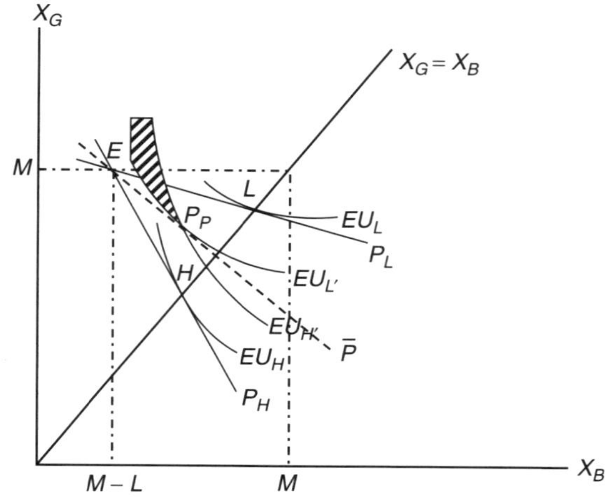

Figure 5.7 Pooling equilibrium.

Box 5.7 A pooling equilibrium

We reconsider the numerical example provided earlier in Box 5.6 by introducing asymmetric information. Consumers know whether they are high (*H*) or low (*L*) risk types, but insurers do not. If all high-risk types purchase low-risk policies in a separating equilibrium (without restrictions on the level of cover), insurers incur losses of $(\sigma_L - \pi_H)\$200 = -0.2 \times \$200 = \$40$ on every policy. If insurers have no way of separating the risk types and offer a (break even) pooling contract (*P*) the marginal cost of insurance becomes $\bar{\sigma} = \lambda\pi_H + (1-\lambda)\pi_L = 0.44$, where $\lambda = 0.2$ is the proportion of high-risk consumers in the population. The insurance cover in a pooling equilibrium is determined by the insurance chosen by low-risk types, which satisfies

$$\frac{\pi_L}{2\sqrt{X_B^L}}(1-\bar{\sigma}) - \frac{1-\pi_L}{2\sqrt{X_G^L}}\sigma = 0.$$

By using their budget constraints, $X_B^L = 300 + 0.44\,Q_P$ and $X_G^L = 500 - 0.44\,Q_P$, we can rewrite this condition as

$$\pi_L(1-\bar{\sigma})\sqrt{(500-0.44\,Q_p)} = (1-\pi_L)\bar{\sigma}\sqrt{(300+0.44Q_P)} = 0.$$

where the optimal insurance choice is $Q_P^* \approx \$79.24$, which is less than full cover. Clearly, the high-risk types prefer to insure fully at the pooling price as it is lower than their probability of loss, $\bar{\sigma} < \pi_H$. But any attempt to purchase more cover would allow insurers to identify them. Thus, when both risk types purchase pooling contracts they choose the same level of cover and have consumption expenditure of $X_B \approx \$333.21$ and $X_G \approx \$436.79$, where high-risk types have expected utility of $EU_P^H = 19.61$, which is 0.62 per cent higher than expected utility in the separating equilibrium, while expected utility for low-risk types falls by 1.12 per cent to $EU_P^L = 20.26$. This loss in utility for low-risk types is a measure of the negative externality imposed on them by the high-risk types not being truthful.

profitable because low-risk types cross-subsidize the high-risk types. Therefore, a pooling equilibrium will not exist in these circumstances.

A *constrained separating equilibrium* can exist when insurers cannot screen the risk types by restricting cover on low-risk policies. An example is illustrated in Figure 5.8 by low-risk policy L' on price line P_L, where the high-risk types are indifferent between L' and policy H on price line P_H. Clearly, low-risk types prefer full insurance at L, but the unconstrained separating equilibrium is unstable.

Insurers break even when they sell contracts L' and H because consumers separate according to their risk type. It now remains to show that these policies are robust to competition from other types of contracts. Indeed, there are circumstances where pooling contracts can make both risk types better off than they are with contracts L' and H. It depends on the location of the pooling price line relative to the indifference curves of low-risk types.

Two pooling price lines, $\bar{P}_1$ and $\bar{P}_2$, lie between the separating price lines P_L and P_H in Figure 5.9. The slope of the break-even pooling price line is determined by the proportion of consumers in each risk type, where a larger proportion of high-risk types makes it steeper. Consider price line $\bar{P}_1$, which has a low proportion of high-risk types than $\bar{P}_2$. Since it cuts the indifference curve of low-risk types a pooling contract can make both risk types better

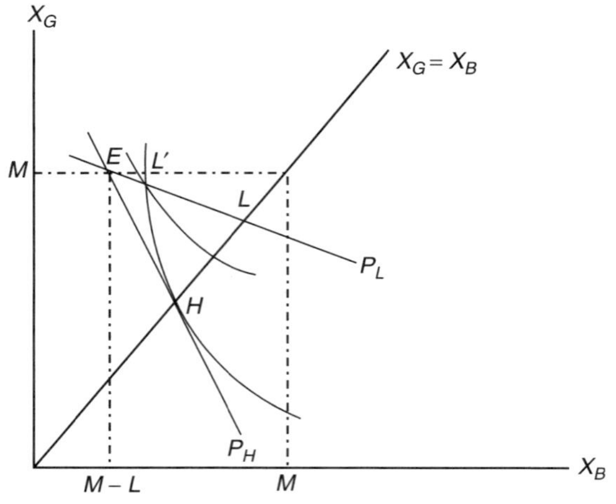

Figure 5.8 Separating equilibrium.

off in the cross-lined region. While these contracts undermine the constrained separating equilibrium, as we saw earlier, the pooling equilibrium cannot exist either. Thus, the insurance market closes down and no contacts are traded in these (extreme) circumstances.

If the pooling price line lies below the indifference curves of the low-risk types through point L' in Figure 5.9 a pooling contract cannot undermine the constrained separating equilibrium. For example, no contract along price line $\bar{P}_2$ can attract low-risk types where this allows the constrained separating equilibrium at L' and H to exist.

In summary, high-risk types impose externalities on low-risk types when insurers cannot separate them due to asymmetric information. The unconstrained separating equilibrium and the pooling equilibrium are unstable as high-risk types attempt to trade low-risk policies.

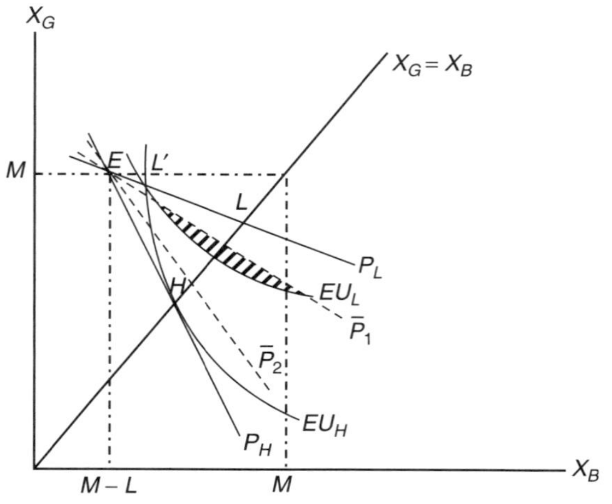

Figure 5.9 Non-existence of separating equilibrium.

Box 5.8 A constrained separating equilibrium

In Boxes 5.6 and 5.7 we solved the insurance outcomes in separating and pooling equilibria, respectively. Since these equilibrium outcomes are unstable, insurers offer high- and low-risk policies with a constraint on the cover offered to low-risk types. We find the constraint on them by isolating the consumption bundle where the indifference curve for high-risk types (tangent to price line P_H) cuts the low-risk price line P_L at point L' in the diagram below. All the insurance contracts along P_L between endowment points E and L' make low-risk types better off, while high-risk types prefer full cover at point H along price line P_H.

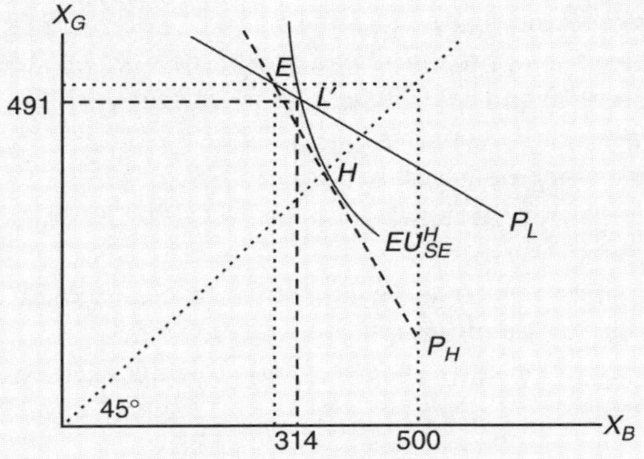

We isolate L' by solving the consumption bundle where the high-risk type indifference curve for bundle H, $0.6\sqrt{X_B} + 0.4\sqrt{X_G} = 19.49$, cuts the price line for low-risk policies, $X_G = 700 - \frac{2}{3}X_G$, where $X_G^{L'} \approx \$490.65$ and $X_B^{L'} \approx \$313.86$. Thus, the insurance cover on low-risk policies in the constrained separating equilibrium solves $X_G^{L'} = 500 - 0.4\,Q_{L'} \approx \$490.65$, with $Q_{L'} \leq 23.375$, where low-risk consumers get expected utility of $EU_{CE}^{L} \approx 20.38$. This equilibrium outcome is stable because the low-risk indifference schedule through L' lies above the pooling price line. Thus, their expected utility is higher in the constrained separating equilibrium than it is in the pooling equilibrium, with $EU_{CE}^{L} \approx 20.38 > EU_P \approx 20.26$.

A constrained separating equilibrium exits when a pooling contract cannot attract low-risk types. But low-risk types are worse off because they cannot fully insure, and this welfare loss is due to actions by high-risk types.

5.3 Concluding remarks

We have examined the role of competitive insurance in economies with individual risk. Consumers with state-independent expected utility functions fully insure when there is common information and no marginal trading costs. They deviate from this equilibrium outcome when there are marginal trading costs or asymmetric information with costly monitoring. When insurers cannot observe effort by consumers to reduce their probability of loss they do not adjust the insurance premium for marginal effort where consumers choose less than full insurance. And when they cannot separate different risk types they restrict insurance cover on low-risk policies to deter higher-risk types from taking them.

Problems

1 Jeremy purchases insurance (Q measured in dollars), at a price equal to the probability (π) of incurring income loss (L), in order to

$$\max\left\{EU = \pi\frac{I_B^{1-\gamma}}{1-\gamma} + (1-\pi)\frac{I_G^{1-\gamma}}{1-\gamma}\middle| \begin{matrix} I_B \leq \bar{X} - L + Q - \pi Q \\ I_G \leq \bar{X} - \pi Q \end{matrix}\right\},$$

where $\bar{X}$ is an endowment of income and $0 \leq \gamma < 1$.

i Derive the first-order condition for optimally chosen insurance (when he is non-satiated in consumption expenditure) and determine whether Jeremy partially or fully insures. Does your answer depend on how risk-averse he is?

ii Will Jeremy purchase insurance when he is risk neutral (with $\gamma = 1$)?

iii Illustrate your answers to parts (i) and (ii) in the good–bad (G–B) state consumption expenditure space.

iv Re-do parts (i), (ii) and (iii) above when there is also an access fee for trading insurance (which is less than Jeremy's consumer surplus in part (i)).

2 Consider an economy with a large number (h = 1, ... , H) of consumers who each consume a single good x in order to

$$\max\left\{EU = \pi_i\sqrt{x_B} + (1-\pi_i)\sqrt{x_G}\middle| \begin{matrix} x_B \leq M - L \\ x_G \leq M \end{matrix}\right\}, \forall h \in \{H, L\},$$

where the bad state (B) occurs with probability π_h and the good state (G) with probability $1-\pi_h$. The price of the single consumption good is numeraire, so all values are expressed in units of good x. Each individual has the same income M = 10,000 (units of good x), and faces the same size loss L = 5100 (units of good x). They differ only by their risk type, where a proportion λ of consumers are high-risk types (H) with a probability of incurring the loss L of $\pi_H = 0.4$, and the remaining proportion 1 – λ of consumers are low-risk types with $\pi_L = 0.2$. All the risk in the economy is fully diversifiable across consumers so aggregate income is constant. (Notice that preferences are state-independent, and the probabilities of incurring the loss are unaffected by the amount of insurance chosen – i.e., there is no moral hazard.)

i Calculate the gain in welfare for the representative risk types when they can purchase insurance in a complete information setting. (Assume the insurance market is competitive with no transactions costs.) Illustrate your answer in the state-contingent consumption space. What are their respective marginal rates of substitution between good and bad state consumption when they purchase insurance?

ii Calculate the price per unit of insurance in the pooling equilibrium under asymmetric information when 60 per cent of consumers are high-risk types. Explain what determines the amount of insurance in a pooling contract. (Assume insurers have no access to information that allows them to separate the risk types.) Illustrate this outcome in the state-contingent consumption space and explain why it cannot exist as an equilibrium. Consider how insurers distinguish between different risk types in practice.

iii Explain how you determine the amount of insurance that would be sold to low-risk types in a separating equilibrium under asymmetric information. Derive an expression from which you would solve this level of cover. (You are not required to find its numerical value, but rather to provide an expression that could be solved.) Illustrate this outcome in the state-contingent consumption space and identify circumstances where it cannot exist as an equilibrium. What happens in such circumstances?

3 A large number of individuals each consume a single good x (which is numeraire) in order to

$$\text{maximize } EU_i = \pi_i \sqrt{x_B} = (1 - \pi_i)\sqrt{x_G}, \quad i \in \{H, L\},$$

where a quarter of them are high-risk types (H) with a probability of bad state consumption of $\pi_H = 0.7$ and the remainder are low-risk types (L) with a probability of bad state consumption of $\pi_L = 0.3$. Good and bad state consumption are $x_G = 10{,}000$ and $x_B = 8100$, respectively.

i Compute the expected utility of the representative high- and low-risk types in the absence of insurance. Derive an expression for their marginal valuation for bad state consumption and compute its value. Illustrate your answers in the commodity space.

ii Compute the expected utility of the representative high- and low-risk types when they can purchase insurance sold in a frictionless competitive market with common information. Calculate their marginal valuations for bad state consumption in this equilibrium and illustrate your answer in the commodity space. Describe the insurance contracts that trade in the equilibrium. Explain how a fixed transactions cost of writing insurance contracts would affect the outcome. Illustrate your answer in the commodity space.

iii Calculate the per unit cost of insurance in the pooling equilibrium when there is asymmetric information and insurers have no ability to screen the risk types. Describe the insurance contract and illustrate the equilibrium in the commodity space. Derive a relationship between good and bad state consumption for the low-risk types when they can purchase insurance at this price. Consider whether it is possible for this equilibrium to exist.

iv Can a constrained separating equilibrium exist when there is asymmetric information? Illustrate the equilibrium outcome and describe the insurance contracts that will trade if it exists.

v Use diagrams to identify the externality that arises in the asymmetric information outcomes in parts (iii) and (iv) above. Identify circumstances where this externality arises in practice and indicate ways insurers mitigate its effects. Compare the welfare outcomes in parts (i) and (ii) above with the equilibrium outcome when there is asymmetric information and insurers cannot screen the risk types or sell them different types of contracts.

4 Consider an economy with a large number of identical consumers (H) who each maximise their expected utility

$$EU = \pi U(x_B) + (1 - \pi)U(x_G),$$

where π is the probability of bad state consumption (x_B) and $1 - \pi$ the probability of good state consumption (x_G). (Assume there is complete information.)

i Suppose each consumer can self-insure by expending effort (e) to reduce the size of a loss L (where $L_e < 0$) so that consumption in each state is $x_B = M - L(e) - e$ and $x_G = M - e$. Derive the necessary condition for positive effort and draw the consumption opportunity set in the commodity space when $L_{ee} > 0$. (Start from the endowment point with $e = 0$ and then increase effort.) Derive the marginal cost of increasing bad state consumption (measured in units of good state consumption) and isolate the circumstances where optimally chosen self-insurance eliminates the variability in consumption across the two states.

ii Now suppose consumers can self-insure and purchase insurance (Q) in a competitive market at price p per dollar. (Assume there are no transactions costs.) This makes their consumption in each state $x_B = M - L(e) - e + Q - pQ$. and $x_G = M - e - pQ$. Derive the first-order conditions for optimally chosen insurance when self- and market insurance are both positive. What is the marginal cost of increasing bad state consumption (measured in units of good state consumption) with market insurance, and how does it compare with the marginal cost of bad state consumption through self-insurance when they are optimally chosen? Use this cost comparison to explain how self-insurance changes when transactions costs raise the dollar cost of market insurance p. (Assume changes in effort do not affect p.)

6 Derivative securities

Financial securities are used to fund investment in future consumption flows. As noted in Chapter 3, these flows are subject to aggregate uncertainty and individual risk – aggregate uncertainty must ultimately be borne by consumers, while individual risk can be eliminated through the diversification effect from holding securities in portfolios and by trading private insurance. In a complete capital market where the no arbitrage condition holds consumers costlessly eliminate individual risk. In previous chapters no distinction was made between primary financial securities, such as shares and bonds, and the derivative securities written on them, such as options and futures contracts. Derivatives have values that derive from underlying assets, both financial and physical, because they represent claims to them at predetermined prices and times. Derivatives are normally thought of as financial securities whose values derive from one or a bundle of other financial securities, but the term is used more widely here to include options and futures contracts for commodities. There has been a large growth in derivative trades in recent years. Micu and Upper (2006) report a combined turnover in fixed income, equity index and currency contracts (including both options and futures) on international derivatives exchanges of $US344 trillion in the fourth quarter of 2005. Most financial contracts were for interest rates, government bonds, foreign exchange and stock indexes, while the main commodity contracts were for metals (particularly gold), agricultural goods and energy (particularly oil).

Derivative securities play a key role in facilitating trades in aggregate risk and allowing investors to diversify individual risk by completing the capital market. They also provide valuable information about the expectations investors have for future values of the underlying assets. An *option contract* gives the bearer the right to buy or sell an underlying asset at predetermined price on or before a specified date – a *call option* is the right to buy the asset and a *put option* the right to sell it. They are not obliged to exercise these rights, and do so only if it increases their wealth. In contrast, a *forward contract* is an obligation to buy an underlying asset at a specified price and time. They are frequently implicit contracts, where, for example, consumers commit to purchase a house or car at a future time at an agreed price, and most employers commit to pay wages and salaries for labour services rendered to them. A *futures contract* is a standardized forward contract that trades at official stock exchanges, such as the New York Stock Exchange and the Australian Securities Exchange. They can be traded repeatedly up to the settlement date, where the gains and losses made on them are settled daily through a clearing house. To ensure they are liquid markets, traders are required to maintain deposits with them to cover expected daily gains and losses, and price limits are employed to restrict the size of daily changes in futures prices. Standardized options contracts also trade on formal exchanges.

A key objective in this chapter is to price these derivative securities. One approach would be to adopt an economic model that allows us to solve the stochastic discount factor in the consumption-based pricing model in (4.28) and use it to value the payouts to derivatives. This is the approach adopted in the asset pricing models examined earlier in Chapter 4 where restrictions were imposed on consumer preferences and the distributions of returns to securities to make the stochastic discount factor linear in a set of state variables reported in aggregate data. But the preferred approach obtains pricing models for derivatives as functions of the current values of the underlying asset prices, together with conditions specified in the contracts. Since the assets already trade we can use their current prices as inputs to the pricing model without trying to compute them. In effect, this approach works from the premise that markets price assets efficiently and all we need to do is work out how the derivatives relate to the underlying assets themselves.

In Section 6.1 we summarize the peculiar features of options contracts and then present the Black and Scholes (1973) option pricing model. This values share options using five variables – the current share price, its variance, the expiry date, exercise price and the risk-free interest rate. It is a popular and widely used model because this information is readily available, but it does rely on a number of important assumptions. For example, the variance on the underlying share is constant and the option is a European call option which cannot be exercised prior to expiration as is permissible for American options. There is evidence that the variances in share prices change over time, and it may be optimal to exercise an American option early when shares pay dividends.

After summarizing the defining features of futures contracts in Section 6.2 we look at how they are priced. Once again, their values are determined by the current price of the underlying asset, the settlement date, margin requirements, price limits and storage costs when the goods are storable. Commodity futures trade for agricultural commodities, metals and oil, while financial futures trade for interest rates, stock indexes, shares, bonds and foreign currencies. It is rare for the underlying assets to be delivered at settlement, and cash settlements are much more common. Traders who buy a futures contract commit to pay the contract price for the underlying asset at settlement. When the future spot price is less than the contract price the buyer pays the difference to the seller by way of cash settlement, while the reverse applies when the future spot price is higher. Physical commodities may actually be delivered at settlement when they are used as inputs to production.

6.1 Option contracts

In this section we focus on formal options contracts, but it is also important to recognize the role of informal contracts in the allocation of resources. For example, firms may buy land that gives them the option of expanding activities in locations where availability of land in the future is uncertain. If there are fixed sunk costs from undertaking activities with uncertain future payouts, there may be gains from delaying them until the uncertainty is partially resolved. There are welfare gains when the benefits from waiting exceed the costs of creating the option.[1] In other circumstances options raise welfare by allowing a more efficient allocation of risk between consumers. For example, share options allow consumers to truncate the payouts on shares, as the contracts give them the right, but not the obligation, to trade them at (or before) a specified time and price. Specialized options contracts trade over the counter while standardized contracts trade on formal exchanges.

6.1.1 Option payouts

There are two types of options – a call that gives the buyer the right to purchase an underlying asset, and a put that gives the buyer the right to sell it. These contracts specify the following conditions:

- The *underlying asset* that can be traded at the discretion of the buyer. Most of the standardized financial contracts are for a fixed quantity of financial securities, such as individual shares, bonds, stock indexes and foreign exchange, while standardized commodity contracts specify quantities of goods with defined qualities. Usually quality is determined by setting bounds on their physical attributes.
- The *expiration date* when the contract lapses.
- The *exercise (strike) price* for the underlying asset when the contract lapses.

European options can only be exercised when they expire, while American options can be exercised any time up to or at expiration. Later we identify realistic circumstances where the American options will not be exercised early because the expected payouts are higher from waiting. For that reason we examine European options in the following analysis and do so for an individual ordinary share (S) in a publicly listed company. Holders of call options on shares receive no dividends or voting rights until they exercise the option. Thus, the payouts (at expiration, time T) from holding a *European call option* are

$$C_T = \max\left(\tilde{S}_T - \hat{S}_T, 0\right) \tag{6.1}$$

where S_T is the random share price at time T and $\hat{S}_T$ the exercise price. Since the option is only exercised when $\tilde{S}_T > \hat{S}_T$ the buyer pays no more than $\hat{S}_T$ for the share. A *European put option* gives the buyer the right to sell the share at time T, where the payouts are

$$P_T = \max(\hat{S}_T - \tilde{S}_T, 0). \tag{6.2}$$

Since it is exercised when $\tilde{S}_T < \hat{S}_T$, the buyer receives no less than $\hat{S}_T$ from selling the share. The payouts to both contracts at time T are summarized in Figure 6.1 by the solid lines, while the dashed lines summarize the corresponding liabilities incurred by sellers. Trading costs would shift down the solid lines and shift up the dashed lines. These payouts are not profits because buyers pay a price for option contracts. There are expected profits when the discounted value of the option payouts exceed the option price. And this occurs when traders have different information about the share price at the expiration date. In a frictionless competitive market with common information, arbitrage eliminates profit by equating option prices to the discounted value of their payouts. When European share options are written the exercise price is usually set near the market price of the share (when it pays no dividends). If, at any time prior to expiration, the share price exceeds the exercise price the call option is *in the money*, it is *out of the money* when the share price is lower, and *at the money* when it is the same. This also applies to put options when the relationships between the market and exercise prices are reversed. Options have a positive market value even when, prior to

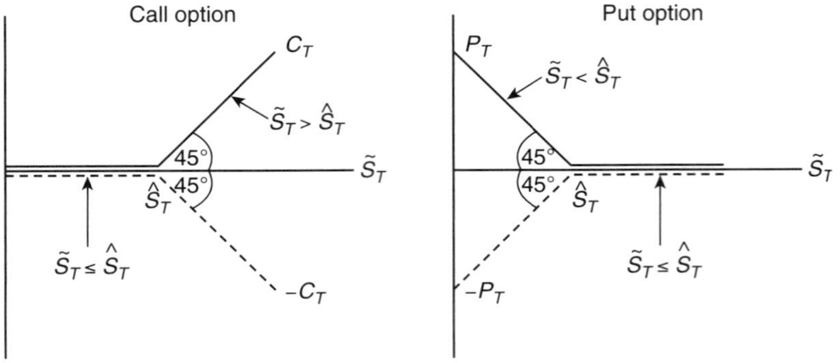

Figure 6.1 Payouts on options contracts at expiration date (T).

expiration, they are out of the money if the variance in the share price creates the possibility of their being in the money at expiration.

Traders use options contracts to exploit any profits from having different information and to spread risk. They combine options with other assets to create perfect substitutes for all existing traded securities. By bundling securities with their perfect substitutes they can create risk-free arbitrage portfolios to exploit any profits in security returns. Options can also be used to complete the capital market so that consumers can trade in every state of nature.

Before demonstrating these roles we summarize the payouts (at date T) to the underlying share ($\tilde{S}_T$), and to a risk-free zero coupon bond (B_T) with a payout equal to the exercise price ($\hat{S}_T$). These are illustrated in Figure 6.2, where payouts to buyers of both securities are solid lines and payouts by their sellers are dashed lines.

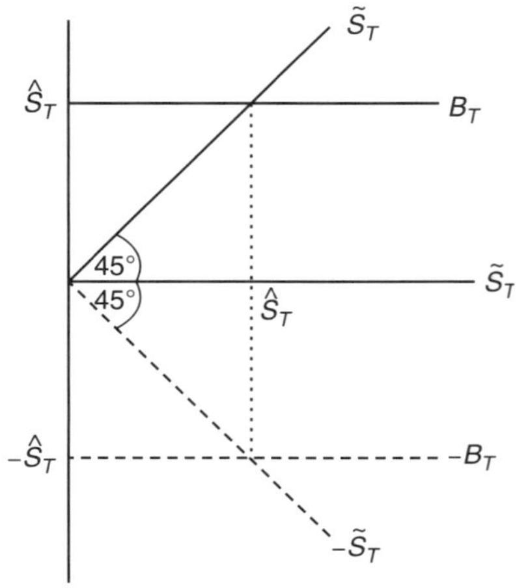

Figure 6.2 Payouts at time T on shares and risk-free bonds.

Based on the law of one price, the payouts to a call option on this share can be replicated by purchasing the share and a put option on it, and selling a zero coupon bond with a payout equal to the exercise price on the option, where

$$\tilde{C}_T = \tilde{S}_T + \tilde{P}_T - B_T.^2 \tag{6.3}$$

The combined payouts to these three securities are illustrated in Figure 6.3. There are potential arbitrage profits when the current price of the option is not equal to the discounted value of the payouts to the three securities that replicate it. In a competitive capital market there are perfect substitutes for all new securities where options play an important role in making this possible.

To see how options can be used to shift risk between traders with different information, we consider three strategies for combining put and call options:

- *spread*, where a put and call are combined with the exercise price on the put set below the exercise price on the call at a common expiration date;
- *straddle*, which combines a put and call on a share with the same exercise price and expiration date;
- *strip* and *strap*, which combine two puts with a call and two calls with a put, respectively.

The payouts for a straddle are illustrated in Figure 6.4, together with two probability distributions for the share price with the same mean value. Clearly, the payouts to the straddle rise with the variance in the share price. When traders have common information and see the same probability distribution for the share price the straddle pays a normal return. But traders can make profits from holding the straddle when they have different information than the market that indicates there is greater volatility in the share price (around an unchanged mean). The dashed curve is a distribution where the variance in the share price is larger than the variance observed by market traders in the solid curve. Thus, traders with different information expect

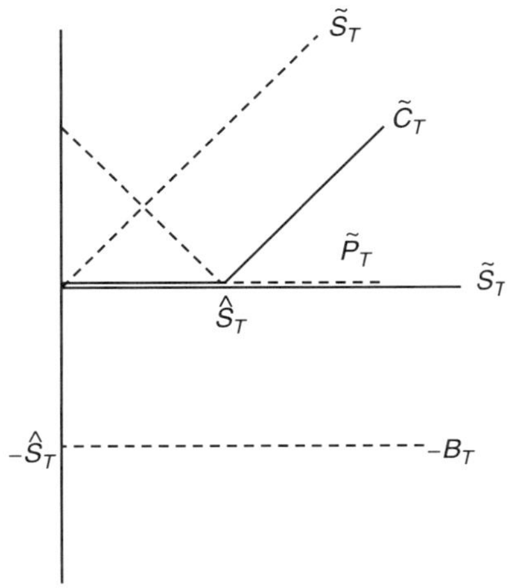

Figure 6.3 Replicating payouts on a call option.

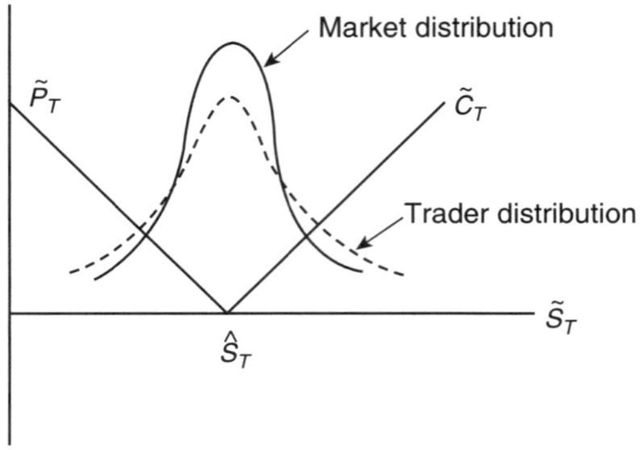

Figure 6.4 Payouts to a straddle.

the two option contracts to have higher expected payouts and therefore value them above their current market prices. Clearly, if the volatility turns out to be smaller than what the market believes then traders make losses when they are long in the straddle. Those with better information make profits by taking the appropriate positions in the market, and this provides them with an incentive to become better informed.

A spread allows traders to access payouts located in the tails of the probability distribution for the share price. Thus, it becomes more attractive than the straddle when the largest difference between the trader and market expectations occurs in the extremities of the distribution. Traders can make profits by constructing a *butterfly* when they expect less volatility in the share price (with an unchanged mean) than the rest of the market. This is a strategy that goes long in a call in the money (with strike price $\hat{S}_T + a$), long in a call out of the money (with strike price $\hat{S}_T - a$) and short in two calls at the money (with strike price $\hat{S}_T$). The payouts at expiration (T) are illustrated in Figure 6.5, together with the different market and trader probability distributions.

6.1.2 Option values

Up to this point we have summarized the payouts for short and long positions on call and put options at their expiry dates. The next important step is to compute the market prices

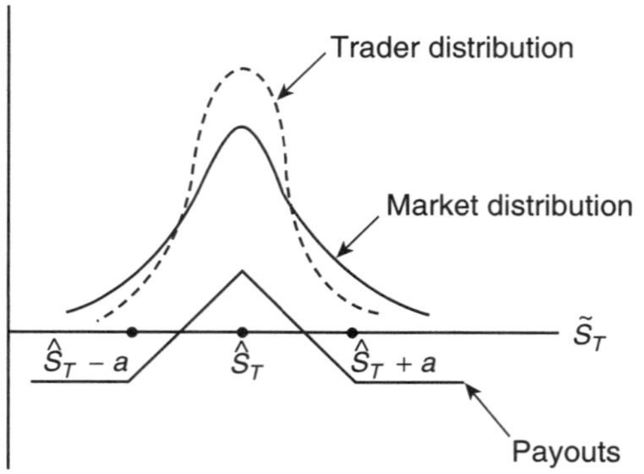

Figure 6.5 Payouts to a butterfly.

in time periods prior to expiration, that is, to compute the discounted present value or their payouts at any time $t < T$. To simplify the analysis we focus on share options and then consider how the pricing model changes for options on other assets.

In a competitive capital market where the law of one price holds, Stoll (1969) uses (6.3) to obtain the *put–call parity* relationship for European share options, given by

$$\tilde{C}_T - \tilde{P}_T = \tilde{S}_T - B_T,$$

where the option contracts have the same exercise price, which is also the payout to the risk-free bond, with $B_T = \hat{S}_T$. This is confirmed by using the option payouts in (6.1) and (6.2), where

$$\max\left(\tilde{S}_T - \hat{S}_T, 0\right) - \max\left(\hat{S}_T - \tilde{S}_T, 0\right) = \tilde{S}_T - \hat{S}_T.$$

Since this parity relationship holds at expiration in every state of nature, it also holds for the current values of the assets, with:

$$C_0 - P_0 = S_0 - B_0, \tag{6.4}$$

where $B_0 = \hat{S}_T/(1 + i)^T$ is the value of risk-free debt that pays $\hat{S}_T$ with certainty at the expiry date. This means there is no need to separately compute the prices of call and put options. Once we know the value of a call option we can use it, together with the share price and the risk-free interest rate, to compute the value of the put option. For that reason we will focus on pricing call options on shares in the following analysis. The same model can be used to price European and American call options when shares pay no dividends as American options are not exercised early in these circumstances. This is demonstrated by comparing the payouts on two portfolios of securities – one long in a share that pays no dividends and the other long in a call on the share and a zero coupon bond with a payout equal to the exercise price on the call option ($\hat{S}_T$). At expiration the payout on the share ($\tilde{S}_T$) is less than the combined payout on the call and bond ($\max(\tilde{S}_T, \hat{S}_T)$), which means the market value of the share cannot exceed the market value of the call and bond at any time $t < T$:

$$\tilde{S}_t \le \tilde{C}_t + \frac{\hat{S}_T}{(1+i)^{T-t}}.$$

On rearranging this expression, we can see why at any time $t < T$ the market value of the call must be strictly greater than the payout from exercising the option early, with:

$$\tilde{C}_T \ge \tilde{S}_t - \frac{\hat{S}_T}{(1+i)^{T-t}} > \tilde{S}_t - \hat{S}_T,$$

where traders maximize profit by holding options until they expire, or by selling them rather than exercising early. But the following pricing models will not in general apply to American options when shares pay dividends, unless all traders expect the same dividend payments and compute their impact on the future share prices in the same way.

As noted earlier, we could use the consumption-based pricing model in (4.28) to value the call option in any time period $t < T$, as:

$$C_t(S,T) = E(\tilde{m}_T\,\tilde{C}_T) = E[\tilde{m}_T \cdot \max(\tilde{S}_T - \hat{S}_T, 0)].$$

But additional restrictions need to be imposed on consumer preferences and/or the distributions of security prices before this model can be estimated using financial data. In general circumstances the stochastic discount factor ($\tilde{m}_T$) is a non-linear function of a potentially larger number of variables that are difficult to solve. Before taking a different approach, however, we can use this pricing model to place upper and lower bounds on the option value using the current share price, the risk-free interest rate, the exercise price and the exercise date. This is illustrated in Figure 6.6, where the option value is measured against the share price at time $t < T$ along curve AB.

Since the payout on the option approaches the current share price as T goes to infinity, $A\tilde{S}_t$ sets the upper bound on the option value. In fact, it will be slightly lower when shareholders have valuable voting rights that do not accrue to option holders. The lower bound is determined by the current value of the payouts to the option, which is the difference between the current share price and the discounted value of the exercise price, where:

$$\tilde{C}_T \geq \tilde{S}_T - \hat{S}_T \quad \text{and} \quad C_t \geq S_t - \frac{\hat{S}_T}{(1+i)^T}.$$

On that basis, the option value must lie inside the shaded region in Figure 6.6, where curve AB is an example of the valuation schedule. When the current share price is zero the call option has no value as traders are expecting no future net cash flows. Even when the current share price is equal to the discounted value of the exercise price it still has a positive value because the variance in the share price means there is a positive probability

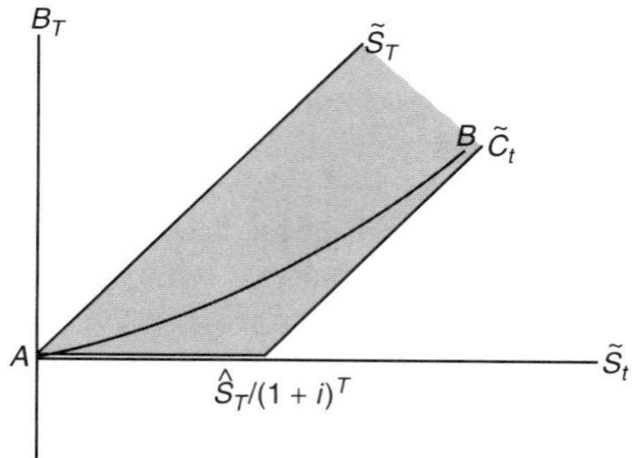

Figure 6.6 Bounds on call option values

it will be in the money at time T. The vertical distance between the lower bound and schedule AB is a measure of the *time value* of the option due to the variance in the share price. As the current share price rises above the discounted value of the exercise price the option value approaches the lower bound in the diagram because the share price is less

Box 6.1 Valuing options with Arrow prices: a numerical example

Consider the European call and put options written on Purple Haze Ltd. shares. They expire in 3 months' time and have an exercise price of \$19.25. The current share price is \$19.10, while its future value at expiration in each of six possible states of nature are summarized below, together with the full set of Arrow prices.

	States						
Prices	*t = 0*	*1*	*2*	*3*	*4*	*5*	*6*
Share	19.10	25.80	12.50	16.20	26.40	8.90	22.00
Arrow	0.990	0.18	0.22	0.16	0.19	0.09	0.15

Since the current value of a three-month risk-free bond that pays one dollar in each state is the sum of the Arrow prices (\$0.99), the interest rate for the period is approximately 1 per cent, with $i = 1/\$0.99 - 1 \approx 0.01$. The payouts to the call and put options in each state are summarized below in the absence of transactions costs, with $C_s = S_s - \$19.25$ and $P_s = \$19.25 - S_s$, respectively.

	Payouts					
States	*1*	*2*	*3*	*4*	*5*	*6*
Call	6.55	0.00	0.00	7.15	0.00	2.75
Put	0.00	6.75	3.05	0.00	10.35	0.00

Using the Arrow prices the current value of the call option is

$$C_0 = (0.18 \times \$6.55) + (0.19 \times \$7.15) + (0.15 \times \$2.75) = \$2.95,$$

while the current value of the put option is

$$P_0 = (0.22 \times \$6.75) + (0.16 \times \$3.05) + (0.09 \times \$10.35) = \$2.90.$$

We can use these prices to confirm the put–call parity relationship in (6.4) by computing he current value of a risk-free bond that pays \$19.25 in 3 months' time, as $B_0 = (\$19.25 \times \$0.99) = \$19.0575$, where:

$$\begin{aligned} C_0 - P_0 &= S_0 - B_0 \approx \$0.05. \\ \$2.95 - \$2.90 &= \$19.10 - \$19.05 \end{aligned}$$

Arrow prices are not used in practice as they are not observable. In general, they are difficult to compute using reported data as they are potentially complicated functions of the exogenous variables that determine a competitive equilibrium outcome. That is why the popular pricing models in finance compute Arrow prices by placing restrictions on consumer preferences and/or security returns.

likely to rise much further in the future. In other words, higher share prices are located further to the right-hand side of the probability distribution. As the exercise price rises the option value approaches the share price because there is a greater chance of it being in the money at expiration, but a higher exercise price lowers the option value by reducing the payouts at expiration.

As noted earlier, we could derive an option pricing model that solves the share price by adopting the approach used to derive the CAPM, ICAPM, APT and CCAPM in Chapter 4. But that makes the model more difficult to use in practice because it solves the underlying value of the asset subject to the restrictions imposed by the options contracts. Since share prices are functions of variables that are difficult to measure, even with minimal restrictions placed on preferences and security returns, the pricing models perform poorly in empirical tests. Indeed, we saw earlier in Chapter 4 how poorly they perform in a number of empirical studies. Black and Scholes (1973) adopt a different approach by using the current share price to determine the market value of the options written on them. As they do not attempt to solve the price of the underlying asset their pricing model is much easier to use because it is a function of a small number of variables that are readily obtained from reported financial data.

6.1.3 Black–Scholes option pricing model

Black and Scholes price a European call option on a share by constructing a replicating portfolio that combines the share with a risk-free bond, where the portfolio is continually adjusted over time to make its payoffs the same as the option. They invoke the law of one price and set the option value equal to the value of its perfect substitute, the replicating portfolio. Unlike the consumption-based pricing models examined in Chapter 4, no restrictions are placed on consumer preferences in their model. They make the following important simplifying assumptions:

1 The share price follows a random walk in continuous time, which is consistent with it being lognormally distributed in discrete time, and it has a constant variance.
2 It is a European option on a share that pays no dividends.
3 The risk-free interest rate is constant.
4 There are no frictions such as taxes and transactions costs in the capital market, where the no arbitrage condition holds (as a basis for invoking the law of one price).

Rather than provide a complete derivation of the model we focus on providing intuitive explanations for the steps taken. Based on the put–call parity relationship in (6.4), we construct a continuous risk-free hedge portfolio (H) which combines the share with *a* call option on it, and which at each time t (omitting time subscripts to avoid notational overload) has a market value of

$$H = a_s S + a_C C, \tag{6.5}$$

where a_S and a_C are the number of shares and call options held in the portfolio, respectively. Over time the share price and option value change, with

$$dH = a_S dS + a_C dC. \tag{6.6}$$

To see how the share and call are combined in the risk-free hedge portfolio at each point in time, consider the situation illustrated in Figure 6.7 where the value of the option is 7.5 cents when the current share price is 40 cents. (The positively sloped line is tangent to a point G located on the call option valuation schedule AB illustrated in Figure 6.6.) If, over the next very small interval of time, the share price can be either 35 cents or 45 cents, the slope of the valuation schedule is $\partial C/\partial S = 0.5$. The hedge portfolio is kept risk-free by selling $\partial C/\partial S = 2$ call options, which is one over the slope of the valuation schedule at point G. When the share price is 45 cents the investor loses 2.5 cents on each option sold due to the increase in its market valuation. But this 5 cent loss is offset by the 5 cent gain in the share price. In contrast, when the share price is 35 cents the investor gains 5 cents on the two options, offsetting the 5 cent loss on the share. Since $\partial S/\partial C$ options are short-sold with every share purchased in the hedge portfolio, set $a_S = 1$ and $a_C = -1/(\partial C/\partial S)$ in (6.6), where:

$$dH = dS + \frac{\partial S}{\partial C} dC. \tag{6.7}$$

The next step is to specify how the share and option values change over time. Since the option value derives from the underlying share price, we need only explain how the share price changes. Black and Scholes assume the rate of return on the share follows a geometric Brownian motion in continuous time, which over a small time interval (dt) is described by:

$$\frac{dS}{S} = \mu_S dt + \sigma_S dz, \tag{6.8}$$

with μ_S being the instantaneous expected rate of return on the share (which measures the drift in the random walk over the time interval dt), σ_S the instantaneous standard deviation in the rate of return on the share, and dz a Wiener process.[3]

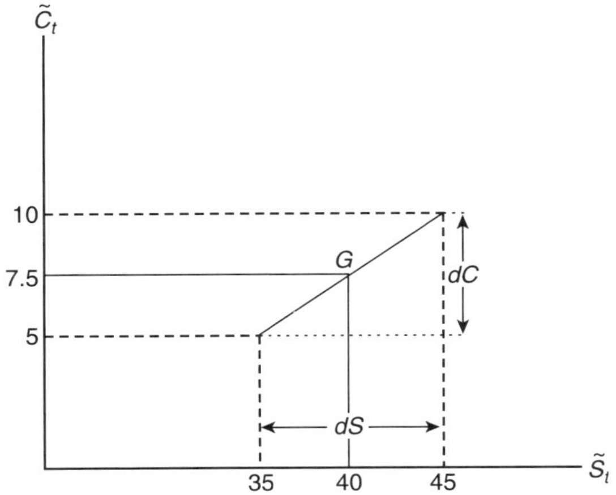

Figure 6.7 Constructing a risk-free hedge portfolio.

A Wiener process of Brownian motion is the continuous-time limit of a random walk with independent increments having mean zero and variance proportional to the time interval.[4] Thus, we can interpret $\mu_S dt$ as the expected rate of return from holding the share over the next small interval in time (dt), and $\sigma_S dz$ as the unexpected change in the return (with $E(dS/S) = \mu_S$), where the unexpected change is the product of the instantaneous standard deviation (σ_S), which is positive, and the stochastic deviation (or white noise, dz), which can be positive or negative. Thus, the proportionate change in the share price can be positive or negative over each small time interval. Since z is purely random it is non-differentiable so standard calculus cannot be used to integrate the stochastic differential equation in (6.8). Instead, Ito's lemma is used to obtain a differential equation for changes in the value of the call option, of

$$dC = \frac{\partial C}{\partial S} dS + \frac{\partial C}{\partial t} dt + \frac{1}{2}\frac{\partial^2 C}{\partial S^2}\sigma_S^2 S^2 dt.^5 \tag{6.9}$$

After substituting this into (6.7), and noting that the rate of return on the hedge portfolio is by construction risk-free, with $dH/H = i\,dt$, we obtain a differential equation for changes in the current value of the call option:

$$\frac{\partial C}{\partial t} = iC - i\frac{\partial C}{\partial S}S - \frac{1}{2}\frac{\partial^2 C}{\partial S^2}\sigma_S^2 S^2.^6 \tag{6.10}$$

The most notable feature of this equation is that it is non-stochastic due of the absence of dS, which results from pricing the call option inside the continuously adjusted hedge portfolio to make it risk-free. Black and Scholes solve this differential equation subject to the boundary condition on the payouts at expiry date T in (6.1) (and also requiring $C = 0$ when $S = 0$), which leads to the *Black–Scholes option pricing model,*

$$C_t(S_t, T) \quad = \quad S_t N(d_1) \quad - \quad \hat{S}_T e^{-i\tau} \quad N(d_2), \tag{6.11}$$

where

$$d_1 = \frac{\ln(S_t/\hat{S}_T) + (i + \sigma_S^2/2)\tau}{\sigma_S\sqrt{\tau}} \text{ and } d_2 = d_1 - \sigma_S\sqrt{\tau}, \text{ for } \tau = T - t.$$

It is based on the following assumptions:

- Changes in the share price are described by a Wiener process with a constant variance.
- It is a call option that pays no dividends.
- The interest rate is constant.
- There are no frictions in the capital market and the no arbitrage condition holds.

As noted above, the striking feature of this model is that it is a function of five variables we can obtain from reported financial data. Four of them are directly observable in reported financial data (the current share price, exercise price, expiration date, and interest rate), while the fifth (the variance in the share price) can be estimated from historical data. Also, the model does not depend on investor risk preferences because they determine

Box 6.2 The Black–Scholes option pricing model: a numerical example

We use the Black–Scholes model here to compute the current value of a European call option written on an AutoGrand share. The current share price is \$12.50, while the exercise price on the option is \$9.50 when it expires in 3 months' time. Using past data, we find the share price has a standard deviation of 25 per cent, and the risk-free interest rate is 5.5 per cent. If no dividends are expected on the share over the next 3 months we can compute the current value of the option by substituting S_0 = \$12.50, S_T = \$9.50 $\sigma_S = 0.25$, $i = 0.055$ and $\tau = 0.25$ into the Black–Scholes model in (6.11),

$$C_0 = 12.50N(d_1) - 9.5e^{-(0.055\times 0.25)}N(d_2),$$

with

$$d_1 = \frac{\ln(12.5/9.5) + (0.055 + 0.25^2/2)}{0.25\sqrt{0.25}} \approx 2.367994766,$$

and

$$d_2 = d_1 - 0.25\sqrt{0.25} \approx 2.242994766.$$

Using the cumulative standard normal distribution function we find the inverse value of the hedge ratio is $N(d_1) \approx 0.991057605$, and the probability the option will be in the money at expiration is $N(d_2) \approx 0.987551424$. After substituting these into the valuation equation above, and using $e^{-(0.055\times 0.25)} = 0.986344099$, the option value is $C_0 \approx \$3.13$. These workings are summarized below as the base case, together with the recalculation of the option value for a different expiration date, standard deviation, interest rate, exercise price and current share price, respectively.

	Base	$\tau = 0.5$	$\sigma = 0.35$	$i = 0.08$	$S_T = 12.50$	$S_0 = 9.50$
S_0	12.5	12.5	12.5	12.5	12.5	[9.5]
S_T	9.5	9.5	9.5	9.5	[12.5]	9.5
τ	0.25	[0.5]	0.25	0.25	0.25	0.25
i	0.055	0.055	0.055	[0.08]	0.055	0.055
σ	0.25	0.25	[0.35]	0.25	0.25	0.25
d_1	2.3680	1.7964	1.7343	2.4180	0.1725	0.1725
d_2	2.2430	1.6196	1.5593	2.2930	0.0475	0.0475
$N(d_1)$	0.9911	0.9638	0.9586	0.9922	0.5685	0.5685
$N(d_2)$	0.9876	0.9473	0.9405	0.9891	0.5189	0.5189
$e^{-i\tau}$	0.9863	0.9729	0.9863	0.9802	0.9863	0.9863
C_0	3.13	3.29	3.17	3.19	0.71	0.54
Change (%)	—	5.01	1.10	1.84	−77.42	−82.84

The option value rises for increases in the time to maturity, the standard deviation in the share price and the interest rate, while it falls for increases in the current share and exercise prices.

the current value of the share price which is not solved in the model. Despite its apparent complexity, there is good intuition for the functional relationships in (6.11). $N(.)$ is the standard cumulative normal distribution function over the random variable z with mean zero and unit standard deviation. It is the stochastic process that generates the variance in the share price, where $N(d_1)$ is the inverse of the hedge ratio (with $N(d_1) = \partial C/\partial S$) and $N(d_2)$ the probability the option will be in the money at expiration. On that basis we can interpret the value of the call in (6.11) as the market value of the shareholding required to replicate the call $S_t N(d_1)$ less the present value of the implicit amount borrowed $\hat{S}_T e^{-i\tau} N(d_2)$.

We can confirm the earlier conjecture about the way the five variables in (6.11) affect the value of the option. It increases with a higher share price, interest rate, variance in the share price and expiration date. A larger variance and later expiration date both raise the value of the option by increasing the likelihood of it being in the money at expiration. Indeed, the time value of the option derives from the variance in the share price which increases over time. To see why this happens, consider the term $\sigma_S \sqrt{\tau}$. It measures the standard deviation in the rate of return on the share price over the life of the option ($\tau \equiv T - t$), and is a property of the Wiener process that generates the uncertainty in the share price. In each infinitesimally small time interval over the life of the option the share price can rise or fall proportionally by σ_S around the expected increase of μ_S. Since it can rise (or fall) by σ_S around this expected trend in every period, the variance over the life of the option contract (τ) becomes $\sigma_S^2 \tau$, so that the standard deviation is $\sigma_S \sqrt{\tau}$. Thus, the later the expiration date the larger is the variance in the return on the underlying share. A higher interest rate also increases the option value because it reduces the current value of paying the exercise price, while a higher exercise price reduces the option value.

Merton (1973b) modifies the Black–Scholes option pricing model by including continuous dividend payments on the share and finds it is not optimal for traders to exercise early. Roll (1977b) achieves the same result by assuming dividend payments are known beforehand. Beyond these restrictions, however, the impact of dividends on the valuation of American call options is unclear. Similar problems arise for the valuation of American put options when the share price falls below the exercise price. As it gets closer to zero traders can eventually do better by exercising early and investing the proceeds in bonds for the remaining time to expiration. Merton was also able extend the Black–Scholes model by allowing a stochastic interest rate, but not a stochastic variance in the share price or a random maturity date. Cox *et al.* (1979) derive the Black–Scholes model using binomial distributions, while Cox and Ross (1976) extend it by allowing the variance in the share price to change in a constant elasticity of variance model.

6.1.4 Empirical evidence on the Black–Scholes model

Black and Scholes test their pricing model using data for over-the-counter options on securities traded in the Unites States between 1966 and 1969. They use their model to estimate the expected prices of these contracts and compare them to the actual prices. Any differences between them did not provide significant expected profit when combined inside the hedge portfolio. In particular, the profit could not be eliminated with transactions costs as low as 1 per cent. Galai (1977) and Bhattacharya (1983) also find evidence supporting the ability of the Black–Scholes model to predict option prices using data from the Chicago Board of Options Exchange. However, Macbeth and Merville (1979) and Beckers (1980) obtained better estimates of in-the-money options using the constant elasticity of variance model than the constant variance Black–Scholes model. Rubinstein (1985) concluded the extensions to the Black–Scholes model could not explain all the bias in its estimates all the time.

6.2 Forward contracts

It is common for consumers to make commitments to buy and sell commodities in future time periods. For example, they agree to trade major items like houses and cars in this way. Firms also contract to buy inputs ahead of time to ensure uninterrupted future production flows and to reduce the variance in their costs, while others contract to sell their outputs ahead of time to reduce the variance in their sales revenue. The seller of a forward contract agrees to deliver an underlying asset at a specified date (or, for commodity contracts, within a specified period of time) at a specified price. Many of these exchanges are implicit forward contracts while others are official, and the official contracts take one of two forms. The first are *specialized forward contracts* that trade between specified sellers and buyers in *over-the-counter* trades, while the second are *standardized futures contracts* that trade on official futures exchanges run by most stock exchanges.[7] Over-the-counter contracts match individual buyers and sellers and are rarely traded between the time they are written and the date they are settled. They are used by traders of assets where differences in quality are important to buyers. In contrast, buyers and sellers of futures contracts trade them frequently over this period but through an official futures exchange. There is no matching of buyers and sellers in futures markets because there is less variability in the quality of the underlying assets or their quality can be summarized in sufficient detail in standardized contracts. The underlying assets can be physical commodities, such as wheat, wool and metals, or financial securities, including individual shares, bonds, share indexes and foreign currencies. Clearly, financial securities are likely to be less variable in quality than commodities, and as a consequence are more easily accommodated in standardized futures contracts. Quality differences in some commodities can be summarized fairly accurately in standardized contracts as well. For example, wool can be described by a comprehensive set of characteristics such as colour, fibre length, fibre width, vegetable matter content, weight and yield, which are measured and reported at all the wool auctions in Australia. For that reason, wool futures are actively traded in Australia.

Futures contracts are highly liquid markets where gains and losses from movements in futures prices are settled daily through clearing houses operated by futures exchanges. In other words, the gains and losses are *marked to the market* each trading day. The main reason for doing this is to stop traders defaulting on their contracts, or at least, to limit the losses when default occurs. To that end, futures traders are required to make initial deposits and maintain them at *margins* that are expected to cover any daily losses. Additionally, bounds are set to limit the daily price changes on futures contracts, where the price limits are normally raised when they bind for a number of consecutive days. Without margins and *price limits*, futures traders can be exposed to very large losses because they pay no price when the contract is initially written. This is a problem when *speculators* trade futures contracts solely for the purpose of making expected profits by exploiting different information from the market. They make profits by combining the underlying asset with its futures contract when they expect a future spot price for the commodity at settlement different from the rest of the market. For example, if the market expects a lower future spot price the speculator can make profits by selling the futures contract and buying the underlying asset.

Forward contracts play a number of important roles that facilitate the efficient allocation of resources over time. Their prices are important signals about the expectations market traders have for future prices of the underlying assets, where speculators can profit from accessing new information. Another role is that of *hedging*, where traders use futures to transfer aggregate risk and eliminate individual risk. Farmers sell wool futures to reduce the variance in their income, where they trade aggregate risk to agents who specialize in risk bearing, and diversify individual risk across wool growers with uncorrelated production risk. Futures contracts are used to perform these functions when they do so at lower cost than other alternatives such as purchasing explicit insurance contracts.

6.2.1 Pricing futures contracts

We now turn to the pricing of futures contracts, noting that prices of non-standarized forward contracts can be obtained as special cases. As stated earlier, no price is paid for a futures contract at the time it is written, where the contract price is the expected spot price of the underlying asset at the date of settlement. In prior time periods the asset price normally changes, thereby causing the futures price to change. For the most part, the underlying asset is not traded at settlement, but rather the difference between the contract and spot price is paid in cash. If the contract price is higher, the buyer pays the difference to the futures exchange which transfers it to the seller, while the reverse applies when it is lower. This ensures the seller always ends up being paid the contract price for the underlying asset at settlement. However, rather than wait until then, traders settle their gains and losses at the end of the each trading day based on the closing price of their contract. This is where the gains and losses are marked to market against deposits lodged at the futures exchange by traders. In time periods closer to the settlement date the contract price approaches the underlying asset price. Since there are fundamental differences between the payouts to commodity and financial futures contracts, we consider then separately.

A *commodity futures* contract that delivers a *storable commodity* (N) at settlement date T has a current price (${}_0F_{NT}$) equal to the current spot price of the commodity plus the opportunity cost of time and *storage costs*:

$$
{}_0F_{NT} = p_{N0}(1+i_T)^T + {}_0Q_{NT}(1+i_T)^T, \tag{6.12}
$$

where i_T is the average annual yield on a risk-free bond that matures at time T, and ${}_0Q_{NT}$ the present value of the marginal cost of storing commodity N over the period. As a way to understand this relationship, consider a situation where storage is costless, so that ${}_0F_{NT} = p_{N0}(1 + i_T)^T$. A trader who sells a futures contract commits to sell the commodity at time T for price ${}_0F_{NT}$. By arbitrage in a frictionless capital market this price must be equal to the cost of borrowing funds at the risk-free rate to buy the good now at price p_{N0} and to hold it until time T when the contract expires. At this time the trader receives certain revenue of ${}_0F_{NT}$ and retires the debt by paying $p_{N0}(1 + i_T)^T$. Marginal storage costs raise the futures price because they increase the cost of transferring the commodity into the future. Hicks (1939) and Keynes (1923) refer to this arbitrage activity as *hedging*, while Kaldor (1939) also includes a marginal *convenience yield* in the commodity futures contract price when stocks provide positive benefits (by way of lower costs) for users. For example, a steel producer can minimize disruptions to its production run by holding (or having access to) stocks of coal, iron and other raw material inputs, where the benefits lower the futures price, so that

$$_0F_{NT} = \left(p_{N0} + {}_0Q_{NT} - {}_0Y_{NT}\right)(1+i_T)^T,^8 \tag{6.13}$$

where ${}_0Y_{NT}$ is the present value of the marginal convenience yield from storing a unit of the commodity until time T. In practice, it is useful for traders to know whether futures prices are accurate predictors of expected spot prices because it provides them with valuable information for making intertemporal consumption choices. In a certainty setting (or with risk-neutral consumers) the futures price in (6.13) is also the expected spot price for the commodity at time T, with ${}_0F_{NT} = E_0(\tilde{p}_{NT})$. However, when the return from holding the commodity is uncertain the expected spot price becomes

$$E_0(\tilde{p}_{NT}) = p_{N0}[1+E(\tilde{i}_{NT})]^T,^9 \tag{6.14}$$

where $E(\tilde{i}_{NT})$ is the expected annual yield from holding commodity N until time T. Any storage costs and convenience yield are included in this expected return. When the commodity contributes to consumption risk, and consumers are risk-averse, a risk premium will drive the futures price below the expected spot price. Indeed, some commodity producers use futures contracts to reduce their consumption risk by transferring it to speculators who are specialists at risk bearing, and they pay a risk premium to them as compensation by discounting futures prices. This can be demonstrated by using one of the consumption-based asset pricing models examined earlier in Chapter 4 to isolate the risk premium embedded in the expected holding return to commodity N in (6.14). If, for example, the CCAPM in (4.41) holds, the expected spot price in (6.14) can be decomposed as

$$E_0(\tilde{p}_{NT}) = (p_{N0} + {}_0Q_{NT} - {}_0Y_{NT})\,(1+i)^{T-1}\left(1+i+(\bar{i}_I - i)\,\beta_{IN}\right), \tag{6.15}$$

where β_{IN} is commodity N's contribution to aggregate consumption risk, and $\bar{i}_I - i$ is the market premium paid for this risk. Notice the risk premium $(\bar{i}_I - i)\beta_{IN}$ is only paid in the last period. Thus, there is no intermediate uncertainty where consumers revise their expectations about the commodity risk in prior periods.[10] It is clear from (6.13) and (6.15) how the risk premium drives the futures price below the expected spot price. Keynes refers to this as *normal backwardation*, and it can be illustrated by considering the futures contract that matures in 1 year, with $T = 1$, where

$$_0F_{NT} = E_0\,(\tilde{p}_{NT}) - p_{N0}\,(\bar{i}_I - i)\,\beta_{IN}. \tag{6.16}$$

Dusak (1973) finds no evidence of any discount in the futures prices for wheat, corn and soybeans in US data. In other words, all the commodity price variability was diversifiable risk and attracted no risk premium.

Futures prices for *financial securities* do not include the last two terms in (6.13) because they trade in highly liquid markets with (almost) no storage or other trading costs and no convenience yield. Thus, the current price of a *futures contract* for share S that *pays no dividends* and is settled at date T is:

$$ {}_0F_{ST} = S_0(1+i_T)^T, \tag{6.17}$$

where S_0 is the current share price and i_T the average annual yield to maturity (T) on a long-term bond. There are two ways of acquiring share S at time T – one is to purchase it now by paying price S_0 and then holding it until time T, while the other is to purchase a futures contract which allows the holder to pay the price ${}_0F_{ST}$ for the share at time T. Arbitrage in a frictionless competitive capital market will equate the present value of these options, with $S_0 = {}_0F_{ST}/(1+i_T)^T$. Once again, the futures price will be less than the expected spot price when the economic return on the share contains market risk. To see this, we compute the expected share price at settlement date T in the absence of intermediate uncertainty as

$$E_0(\tilde{S}_T) = S_0(1+i_T)^{T-1}[1+\bar{i}_{ST}], \tag{6.18}$$

where $\bar{i}_{ST}$ is the expected return to share S in period T. When the CCAPM in (4.41) holds we can decompose (6.18) as

$$E_0(\tilde{S}_T) = S_0(1+i_T)^{T-1}[1+i-(\bar{i}_I - i)\beta_{IS}], \tag{6.19}$$

where $(\bar{i}_I - i)\beta_{IS}$ is the premium for the share's contribution to aggregate consumption risk. Clearly, this risk premium drives the futures price in (6.17) below the expected spot price in (6.19), with ${}_0F_{ST} < E_0(\tilde{S}_T)$. When *dividends* are paid in periods prior to settlement the futures price in (6.17) falls as they are not received by the holder of the futures contract, so that

$$ {}_0F_{ST} = [S_0 - PV_0(\widetilde{DIV_{ST}})](1+i_T)^T, \tag{6.20}$$

with $PV(\widetilde{DIV_{ST}})$ being the discounted present value of the dividends paid to share S over periods 0 to T. Since share S has a lower market value when it pays dividends prior to settlement the futures price also falls.

Futures prices for discount bonds (D) are described by (6.17) as all their payouts occur at maturity:

$$ {}_0F_{DT} = D_0(1+i_T)^T. \tag{6.21}$$

This can differ from the expected spot price when the interest rate changes over time. Long (1974) uses the ICAPM to compute the forward price of a discount bond that matures at time T when the interest rate and relative commodity prices are stochastic, and finds that the expectations hypothesis can fail in the presence of the no arbitrage condition. As a way to demonstrate this point, we allow changes in aggregate consumption risk through changes in the interest rate (β_{iD}) and relative commodity prices ($\beta_{\pi D}$), where the expected spot price for the discount bond becomes

$$E_0(\tilde{D}_T) = D_0[1 + i_1 + (\bar{i}_M - i_1)\beta_{MD} + (\bar{i}_i - i_1)\beta_{iD} + (\bar{i}_\pi - i_1)\beta_{\pi D}]^T, \qquad (6.22)$$

Box 6.3 Prices of share futures: a numerical example

Long-grain brown rice (R) is a storable commodity that is harvested twice a year on Equatorial Island – once in March and then again in September. It is stored by traders at each harvest and then released to the market before the next harvest. Traders incur wastage and other storage costs with a present value of ${}_0Q_{RT}$ = \$0.10 per kilo of rice, while consumption demand for rice and the annual risk-free interest rate (of 6 per cent) are constant over time. When the current price of long-grain brown rice is p_{R0} = \$1.20 per kilo, then, in the absence of a convenience yield, the price of a futures contract that promises to deliver 1 kg in 3 months' time (with $T = 0.25$), is

$${}_0F_{RT} = (p_{R0} + {}_0Q_{RT})(1+i)^T = (\$1.20 + \$0.10)1.015 \approx \$1.32.$$

If storage provides retail outlets with a convenience yield of ${}_0Y_{RT}$ = \$0.05 per kilo of rice in present value terms, the futures price falls to

$${}_0F_{RT} = (p_{R0} + {}_0Q_{RT} - {}_0Y_{RT})(1+i)^T = (\$1.20 + \$0.10 - 0.05)1.015 \approx \$1.27.$$

In the absence of uncertainty, arbitrage equates the expected spot price to the futures price, with ${}_0F_{RT} = E_0(\tilde{p}_{RT}) \approx \$1.27$ If ${}_0F_{RT} > E_0(\tilde{p}_{RT})$ traders can make profits by going short in (selling) rice futures and long in (buying) rice, while the reverse applies when ${}_0F_{RT} < E_0(\tilde{p}_{RD})$. However, commodity futures also allow producers to transfer risk to speculators when rice price variability cannot be costlessly diversified from their income. In these circumstances the futures price sells at a discount to compensate speculators for bearing the risk. Suppose the ICAPM holds with two risk factors – one to isolate consumption risk in the return on the market portfolio (M), and the other interest rate risk (i) that isolates changes in consumption risk over time. If the risk premiums for the these factors are $\bar{i}_M - i = 0.08$ and $\bar{i}_i - i = 0.05$, and the beta coefficients for the return generated by holding rice are $\beta_{MR} = 1.2$ and $\beta_{iR} = 0.4$, the expected spot price at settlement date T is

$$E_0(\tilde{p}_{RT}) = p_{R0}[1 + i_1 + (\bar{i}_M - i_1)\beta_{MR} + (\bar{i}_i - i_1)\beta_{iR}]^T = \$1.20 \times (1.176)^{0.25} \approx \$1.25,$$

which is 2 cents (1.6 per cent) lower than the futures price above.

with i_1 being the interest rate in the first period and β_{MD} the aggregate consumption risk in the return to the market portfolio (M) which every investor holds in the ICAPM. The three beta coefficients isolate aggregate consumption risk in the expected return on the bond, and they are each multiplied by a risk premium that is determined by computing the expected returns on their mimicking factor portfolios.[11]

Based on the expectations hypothesis, the forward price of the bond should be less than or equal to its expected spot price at settlement. There is normal backwardation, with ${}_0F_{DT} < E_0(\tilde{D}_T)$, when changes in short-term interest rates and relative commodity prices both add a risk premium to the yield on a long-term bond, with $\beta_{iD} > 0$ and $\beta_{\pi D} > 0$. However, it is possible that ${}_0F_{DT} > E_0(\tilde{D}_T)$ when the bond provides a hedge against aggregate consumption risk, with $\beta_{iD} < 0$ and $\beta_{\pi D} < 0$.

All these pricing relationships are obtained in a competitive capital market where the no arbitrage condition holds. When the futures price is higher than the expected spot price of the underlying asset at settlement there are arbitrage profits from going long in the futures contract and short in the asset, while the reverse applies when the contract price is lower. By taking equal and opposite positions in the share and the futures contract, the portfolio is risk-free.

6.2.2 Empirical evidence on the relationship between futures and expected spot prices

Houthakker (1968), Cootner (1960) and Bodie and Rozansky (1980) find evidence to support normal backwardation, while Telser (1981), Gray (1961), Rockwell (1967) and Dusak (1973) find that futures prices are unbiased predictors of spot prices without any risk premium. Despite their different findings on normal backwardation, Bodie and Rosansky (1980) and Dusak (1973) find the CAPM does poorly at explaining commodity returns because commodity prices are negatively correlated with inflation while stock returns are positively correlated with it. Fama and French (1987) find marginal evidence of a risk premium in futures prices when commodity contracts are bundled into portfolios, as well as a convenience yield in the prices of some commodity futures, which both appear to vary over time. In that case the risk premium should be measured using the ICAPM or APT, both of which allow aggregate consumption risk to change over time. Fama and French also find evidence that futures prices are good predictors of expected spot price when commodities are stored at relatively low cost. Any demand and supply shocks are transferred into prices across time periods in these circumstances. Roll (1984) examined frozen orange juice futures where most of the variation in price is explained by changes in weather, and found futures prices predicted the weather better than did the US National Weather Service.

In summary, there is mixed evidence on normal backwardation in futures prices, and when there is a risk premium it appears to vary over time. Also, futures prices are good predictors of expected spot prices when storage costs are low.

Problems

1 Options contracts are actively traded derivative securities. Examine the factors that determine the value of a European put option written on an individual share at time (t)

prior to its expiration date (T). Compare its value at $t < T$ to its value at T for each possible share price. Consider how the value of the option at $t < T$ is affected by increases in the variance in the share price, the expiration date, the interest rate and the exercise price. Identify reasons why investors would purchase put options on shares.

2 European call options trade on shares in Linklock Roofing Pty Ltd. These shares have a current price of \$1.05 and pay no dividends over the life of the option.

i Calculate the current value of a call option on a Linklock share when there is a standard deviation of 30 per cent in the share price on the expiration date in 6 months' time. The exercise price at that time is \$1.00 and the annual risk-free interest rate is 5 per cent.

ii Identify the number of call options that must be combined with each Linklock share in a risk-free hedge portfolio.

iii Recalculate the option value in part (i) above when:

a the maturity date is increased to 1 year;
b the standard deviation in the share price at maturity rises to 45 per cent;
c the interest rate rises to 8 per cent;
d the current share price falls to \$1.00;
e the current share price rises to \$1.10.

Explain the reasons for the changes in the option value in each of these cases.

3 Compute the current value of a European put option on a Fleetline share that pays no dividends over the life of the option contract when the vector of Arrow prices for the five possible states of nature, is φ: = {0.18, 0.08, 0.35, 0.10, 0.25}. The option has an exercise price of \$2.50 at the expiration date when the state-contingent share prices are:

State	*Share price at the expiration date (\$)*
1	2.8
2	2.5
3	3.4
4	1.2
5	2.3

7 Corporate finance

A significant proportion of capital investment is financed through security sales. While consumers borrow funds to purchase homes, cars and other capital assets, most private investment is undertaken by corporate firms who sell a range of securities that are classified in general terms as debt and equity instruments. Many of these securities are purchased by large institutional investors, such as insurance companies and mutual funds, who convert them into derivative securities. As specialist finance institutions they facilitate resource flows at lower cost, which has the potential to simultaneously raise the expected returns received by consumers at each level of risk and to reduce the cost of capital for firms financing risky investments. Consumers bundle securities together into portfolios to determine their future consumption risk, while institutional investors create derivative securities to satisfy consumer risk preferences and to earn profits from private information about the net cash flows of firms which are ultimately paid as security returns. By exploiting profitable opportunities they provide firm managers with a greater incentive to operate in the interest of their shareholders and bondholders, but these ideals may be compromised when there are trading costs and asymmetric information.

Before analysing the financial policy choices of firms we summarize the different ways they can raise funds for investment in Section 7.1. Many of the primary assets they sell are used by financial institutions to create a vast array of derivative securities that perform a number of important wealth-creating roles, including the provision of risk-spreading services and transfers of information through arbitrage activity. The range of financial decisions made by firms can be separated into the capital structure choice, which determines the debt–equity mix for a given level of investment, and dividend policy, which determines how income is distributed to investors as dividends, interest or capital gains. We examine capital structure choices in Section 7.2 and dividend policy in Section 7.3. In both sections the analysis starts in a classical finance model where investors with common information trade in frictionless competitive markets. In this setting the *Modigliani–Miller (MM) financial policy irrelevance theorems* hold, so that real equilibrium outcomes in the economy are independent of the types of financial securities used to fund investment and of the way securities distribute their income. It provides a simple framework that can be extended to a more realistic setting in stages to identify the separate factors that determine the optimal financial policy choices made by consumers and firms. These factors are difficult to isolate in a general model where taxes, trading costs and asymmetric information are included from the outset. By introducing them one at a time to the classical finance model we obtain a much clearer understanding of the likely real effects of different financial policy choices.

7.1 How firms finance investment

Most private investment is undertaken by corporate firms who acquire separate legal identity under corporate law. They are created to exploit, among other things, any economies of scale from large production runs. As institutions they have no initial wealth of their own, so they sell financial securities to finance their investment. Firms have three main sources of funds: they can sell new shares, including ordinary (or common) shares, preference shares, publicly listed shares and proprietary shares; retain earnings on existing shares; and, sell debt, including short- and long-term, secured and unsecured, debt with fixed and variable interest rates, accounts payable and bank overdrafts.

In a certainty setting without taxes and transactions costs these sources of finance are perfect substitutes and will therefore pay the same rate of return in a competitive capital market. However, they are not in general perfect substitutes in the presence of risk, taxes and transactions costs. Most new share issues are publicly listed common shares with limited liability that trade on stock exchanges. When companies list their shares on a stock exchange they must fulfil a number of important legal obligations. In particular, they must publish information at prescribed times each year and issue a prospectus with new share issues that provides important information to investors about the management of the finance and production activities of firms. Limited liability shares restrict the legal claims that can be made against the wealth of shareholders to the value of their invested capital. This is important because it limits the risk firm managers can impose on shareholders when they have less information. But limited liability shares force bondholders to bear risk when losses exceed the capital of shareholders, which is why there are default provisions in corporate law that allow bondholders to file to have firms declared bankrupt when they cannot make their interest payments. Once bankruptcy claims are granted administrators are appointed to restrict the actions of managers.

These important institutional features distinguish debt from equity, particularly in the presence of uncertainty and asymmetric information. Even though bondholders have prior claims to the net cash flows of firms, they face default risk when losses exceed the invested capital of shareholders, while shareholders face risk, which is bounded by limited liability, because they have a residual claim on the net cash flows. But most shareholders have voting rights that allow them to influence the investment choices made by firm managers. Indeed, majority shareholders can take firms over by changing managers, merging them with other firms, or liquidating them. Another important difference between debt and equity arises from the different taxes on their returns. For example, share income is taxed twice, while interest payments on debt are subject only to personal tax under a classical corporate tax system. Moreover, there are higher personal taxes on cash income paid as dividends and interest than there are on capital gains in most countries.

We examine the effects of these important institutional features on the financial policy choices of firms in the following sections.

7.2 Capital structure choice

As owners, shareholders have the ability to affect the way firms operate, but without providing all the capital, as debt allows them to leverage their control over firms. The factors that impact on this leverage policy can be isolated by first establishing conditions under which the *Modigliani–Miller leverage irrelevance theorem* holds. This identifies important equilibrium forces at work in a frictionless competitive capital market where consumers have common information. In particular, it emphasizes the role of arbitrage that equates the expected returns to securities in the same risk class. In this setting leverage policy is irrelevant to the market value of firms. By extending the analysis to accommodate *taxes* and *asymmetric information*, it is possible to identify circumstances where changes in leverage have real effects.

When Modigliani and Miller (1958) proved their irrelevance theorems they did not explicitly identify the need for *common information*. Indeed, it was implicit in much of the analysis of financial policy at that time. More recently, however, greater emphasis has been placed on the role of asymmetric information. If investors have less information than managers about the net cash flows of firms, their financial structure choices can have real effects by signalling new information, or by changing the incentives facing managers and the decisions they make. In these circumstances leverage policy can change the cost of capital and affect a firm's market valuation.

Modigliani and Miller (1963) extended their earlier analysis by including a classical corporate tax. Since it falls on income paid to shareholders by making interest payments tax-deductible expenses, it drives equity out of the corporate capital market in a classical finance model without *leverage–related costs*. In a competitive capital market all corporate income is paid to consumers through the lowest tax channel as interest. Thus, no tax revenue is raised by the corporate tax as firms issue only debt in these circumstances. Clearly, other factors must offset this tax advantage of debt to explain the significant amount of equity that trades in most capital markets. Prior to the irrelevance theorems of Modigliani and Miller (1958, 1961) the finance literature examined the role of leverage-related costs, and, in particular, that of default costs, in determining the optimal debt–equity choices of firms. As they increase leverage there is a greater probability of defaulting on interest payments when shares have limited liability. And this occurs because there is variability in the firms' net cash flows which must eventually spill over onto debt at high levels of leverage. When bondholders know how risky the debt becomes, its price sells at a discount to compensate them for the default risk, where leverage is irrelevant to the cost of capital and the market valuation of the firm. But when bondholders have less information than firm managers about this risk, bond prices may not discount sufficiently to properly compensate them. Most countries write bankruptcy provisions in their corporate laws as a way to protect bondholders in these circumstances. The associated default costs are third party claims on firm net cash flows that reduce the value of the firm to its capital providers. Once marginal expected default costs offset the interest tax deduction on debt, corporate firms also sell equity, where an optimal capital structure trades off marginal leverage-related costs against the interest tax deductions.

Clearly, *bankruptcy costs* rely on asymmetric information, but that was not recognized explicitly until the more recent literature identified other forms of leverage-related costs. Most studies examine the role of agency costs when firm financial policy alters the incentives facing capital providers and firm managers in an asymmetric information setting. For example, there can be principal–agent problems when it is costly for bondholders and shareholders to monitor the actions of firm managers, where higher leverage increases interest payments and reduces the free cash flows that can be used by managers for private gain. Harris and Raviv (1991) provide a comprehensive summary of the agency costs that change with leverage.

Lost corporate tax shields are another source of leverage-related costs, but they can arise in a common information setting. In most countries profits and losses are not treated symmetrically by the classical corporate tax, which taxes profits without making tax refunds on losses. Tax losses occur when tax-deductible expenses, including interest and depreciation, exceed the net cash flows. When firms cannot sell their tax losses to other firms or carry them forward at interest, they lose the real value of their tax deductions. And since tax losses occur when firms default, the expected value of these lost corporate tax shields rises with leverage.

Earlier empirical work by Warner (1977) and Altman (1984) showed that the default costs were considerably less than the interest tax deductions on debt. This led people to seek other explanations for use of equity in the presence of a classical corporate tax. Miller (1977) likened them to the rabbit in a horse and rabbit stew, and responded by including personal taxes on security returns. Prior studies focused on factors affecting firms and ignored those affecting investors – in particular, the role of personal taxes. This is probably because they (perhaps implicitly) adopted a partial equilibrium analysis to examine the financial decisions made by firms. Miller recognized the importance of including demand-side factors and exploited two important features of personal tax codes to explain the presence of equity: first, marginal cash tax rates are progressive where different consumers have different tax rates on security returns; and second, taxes on capital gains are lower than taxes on cash income. Thus, it is possible for high-tax consumers (with cash tax rates above the corporate rate) to prefer equity that pays capital gains, even though they are taxed twice, once at the corporate rate and then again at the personal tax rate. Since low-tax investors must have a tax preference for debt both securities trade in the Miller equilibrium, where investors form strict tax clienteles. When both securities trade leverage irrelevance holds for individual firms in this setting. The analysis is general enough to accommodate uncertainty because there is common information and no trading costs in a competitive capital market.

Subsequent empirical studies by Graham (2000) and Molina (2005) find evidence of larger expected default costs when indirect bankruptcy costs are also taken into account. They use information provided by debt rating agencies to get estimates of the default probabilities which they apply to their estimates of the costs of default.

In the following subsections we examine the important role of taxes and risk in firm capital structure choices, starting with the results obtained by Modigliani and Miller.

7.2.1 Certainty with no taxes

We begin by proving the Modigliani–Miller leverage policy irrelevance theorem in a certainty setting without taxes. While the outcome is fairly obvious in this setting, the analysis provides an ideal opportunity to establish a simple methodology for analysing more complicated cases in following sections. As a way to identify the factors impacting on equilibrium outcomes we obtain separate relationships between security returns that would make consumers and firms indifferent to debt and equity. (These are the demand and supply conditions, respectively, discussed below.) Much of the early analysis in corporate finance focused on factors affecting firms without explicitly recognizing the important role of factors affecting consumers. And this is especially important when taxes are included in the analysis. The approach we use is formalized by the demand and supply conditions, as well as the equilibrium condition, which identifies the relationship between the market returns to debt and equity in a competitive capital market equilibrium.

The two-period certainty model of an asset economy in Section 2.2.5 is extended here by allowing consumers and firms to trade two risk-free securities, debt (B) and equity (E), where the current market value of the portfolio held by each consumer (h) is $p_{aB}\, a_B^h + p_{aE}\, a_E^h$,

Box 7.1 Debt–equity ratios by sector

As a way to illustrate the financial structure choices of firms we report the debt–equity (*B*/*E*) ratios for publicly listed companies on the Australian Securities Exchange in 15 sectors of the economy. There is no debt issued in the energy sector, while transportation has the highest ratio at 60.7 per cent.

No.	*Sector*	*B/E(%)*
1	Capital goods	34.1
2	Commercial services and supplies	28.4
3	Consumer durables and apparel	43.6
4	Consumer services	32.5
5	Energy	0
6	Food and staples retailing	60
7	Food, beverages and tobacco	49.4
8	Health care & equipment services	6.9
9	Materials	0
10	Media	22.7
11	Retailing	35.6
12	Software and services	1.4
13	Technology hardware and equipment	0
14	Telecommunications services	5.8
15	Transportation	60.7
	Market	37.2

Source: Based on financial data reported by Aspect Financial Analysis on 17 May 2007. This database is produced by Aspect Huntley Pty Ltd.

with payouts of $a^h_B p_{aB}(l + i_B) + a^h_E p_{aE}(1 + i_E)$ in the second period. Thus, their optimal security trades satisfy

$$\varphi^h_1 (1 + i_k) \leq 1, \quad k = B, E,^1 \tag{7.1}$$

where φ^h_1 is the primitive (Arrow) price of security that pays one dollar in the second period; it is the discount factor used by the consumer to compute the current value of income in the second period.[2]

Proposition (*Demand condition*). Consumers are indifferent to debt and equity in a certainty setting without taxes, when the securities pay the same return, with:

$$i_B = i_E.^3 \tag{7.2}$$

Proof. In a competitive equilibrium without taxes, transactions cost or borrowing constraints, consumers trade both securities until, using (7.1), we have

$$\varphi^h_1 \, (1 + i_B) = \varphi^h_1 \, (1 + i_E).$$

Whenever $i_B \neq i_E$ they will hold the security paying the highest return, preferring debt if $i_B > i_E$ and equity if $i_B < i_E$. This arbitrage activity, which Modigliani and Miller refer to as *homemade leverage*, leads to (7.2).

□

Box 7.2 A geometric analysis of the demand condition

Useful insights can be obtained from a geometric analysis of the demand condition for an individual consumer whose optimal debt–equity choice is illustrated in the diagram below where the budget line (M^h) maps the largest combinations of debt and equity that can be traded from income transferred between the two periods. A saver chooses current consumption and then purchases a portfolio of securities from remaining current income, while a borrower sells securities to transfer future income to the current period. The slope of the budget line is determined by the relative cost of debt ($-p_{aB}/p_{aE}$), and is constant for a price-taker. The indifference schedules (v^h), which are illustrated as dashed lines, isolate the bundles of debt and equity that provide the consumer with same utility, and are defined for optimally chosen consumption expenditure in each period. Thus, we are looking at the security trades with all other things held constant. Since consumers derive utility from consuming payouts to securities, the slopes of the indifference schedules are determined by the relative payout to debt ($-(1 + i_B)p_{aB}/(1 + i_E)p_{aE}$), and are linear because the two securities are equally risky and the consumer is a price-taker. When the demand condition (DC) holds, the indifference schedules have the same slope as the budget M^h. Since $i_B = i_E$ they are willing to hold any of the bundles along indifference schedule v^h_{DC}.

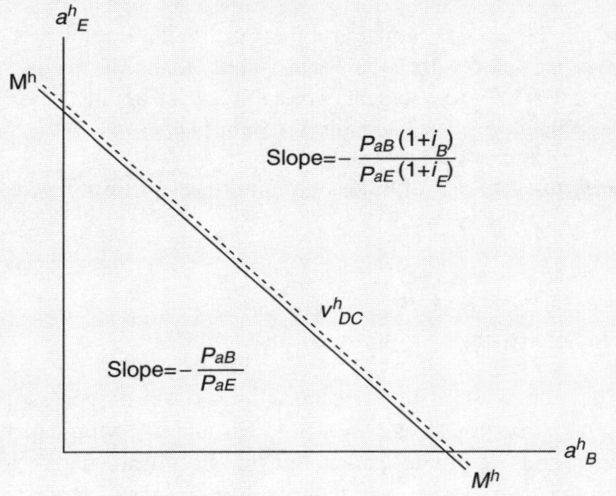

Whenever the indifference schedules and budget line have different slopes the consumer has unbounded demands for the security paying the highest return. For example, when the indifference schedule is flatter than the budget line (with $i_B < i_E$) the consumer has an infinite demand for equity funded by selling debt. The reverse applies when the indifference schedule is steeper. Thus, the consumer is willing to buy or sell both securities when the indifference schedules (v^h_{DC}) have the same slope as the budget constraint as confirmation of the demand condition (DC) in (7.2).

In a certainty setting where the Fisher separation theorem holds, firms maximize profit by choosing a portfolio of securities to minimize their cost of capital and a level of investment (Z_0) to maximize their current market value, with

$$V_0 = \frac{Y_1(Z_0)}{1+(1-b)i_E + bi_B},^4 \qquad (7.3)$$

where $Y_1(Z_0)$ is the market value of the net cash flows, b the portion of capital (V_0) financed with debt, and $1 - b$ the remaining portion financed with equity. When debt and equity are optimally traded by each firm (j), they satisfy

$$\varphi_1^j\,(1 + i_k) \leq 1, \quad \text{for } k \in B, E, \tag{7.4}$$

where φ^j is the price of a primitive (Arrow) security that pays one dollar in the second period; it is the discount factor used by firms to value their future net cash flows.

Proposition (*Supply condition*). Firms are indifferent to debt and equity in a certainty setting without taxes, when each security has the same marginal cost, with:

$$i_B = i_E. \tag{7.5}$$

Proof. In a competitive equilibrium without taxes, transactions cost or borrowing constraints, firms trade both securities until, using (7.4), we have

$$\varphi_1^j(1 + i_B) = \varphi_1^j(1 + i_E).$$

Whenever $i_B > i_E$ firms can reduce the cost of capital and increase their value by selling only equity. Indeed, they can make arbitrage profits by selling more equity than they need to finance their production investment by using it to purchase debt, while the reverse applies when $i_B < i_E$.[5] This arbitrage activity in a frictionless competitive capital market leads to (7.5). □

Proposition (*Equilibrium condition*). In a frictionless competitive equilibrium consumers and firms are indifferent to debt and equity, with

$$i_B = i_E, \tag{7.6}$$

and they have same discount factors, with $\varphi_1^h = \varphi_1^j = \varphi_1$ for all h, j.

Proof. In a competitive equilibrium without taxes, transactions costs or borrowing constraints the two securities must pay the same rates of return to eliminate arbitrage profits and bound the equilibrium demands and supplies. Consumers purchase only debt and firms supply only equity whenever $i_B > i_E$, while the reverse applies when $i_B > i_E$. Once the equilibrium condition in (7.6) holds firms cannot make profits, and consumers cannot increase their utility, by changing their debt–equity choice. Since (7.2) and (7.5) both hold, we have from (7.1) and (7.4), that

$$\varphi_1\,(1 + i_B) = \varphi_1\,(1 + i_E)\ \forall h, j.$$

Thus, consumers and firms use the same discount factors to value capital assets. □

The *Modigliani–Miller* (MM) *leverage policy irrelevance theorem* is a direct implication of (7.6). Since debt and equity are perfect substitutes for consumers and firms, the aggregate debt–equity mix is irrelevant. At the firm level, changes in leverage have no impact on their market valuation, where from (7.3) we have

$$\left.\frac{dV_0}{db}\right|_{dZ_0=0} = \frac{(i_E - i_B)V_0}{1 + bi_B + (1-b)i_E} = 0. \tag{7.7}$$

Box 7.3 A geometric analysis of the supply condition

The supply condition for each firm j is illustrated in the diagram below where the asset production frontier $R^j R^j$ isolates the bundles of debt and equity the firm can supply, while the iso-profit lines (η^j) are the bundles of debt and equity that provide the same profit. Asset supplies are ultimately constrained by the discounted value of the firm's net cash flows (Y_1^j), where the most debt it can issue is $\hat{a}_B^j = Y_1^j / [p_{aB}(1+i_B)]$, and the most equity $\hat{a}_E^j = Y_1^j / [p_{aE}(1+i_E)]$. The slope of the asset prodution frontier is the marginal cost of raising leverage, with $-p_{aB}(1+i_B)/p_{aE}(1+i_E)$, and it is constant for price-taking firms. The iso-profit schedules are also linear for the same reason, and their slope measures the net marginal revenue from raising leverage ($-p_{aB}/p_{aE}$) for a given level of investment. If they are steeper than the asset production frontier (with $i_B < i_E$) firms supply only debt, while the reverse applies when the iso-profit lines are flatter (with $i_B > i_E$). Indeed, firms have unbounded demands for the security paying the highest return because they can use the proceeds to sell the security with lowest return and make profits from arbitrage. These profits are eliminated when the securities pay the same rate of return (with $i_B = i_E$) because the iso-profit lines (η_{SC}^j) satisfy the supply condition (*SC*) and have the same slope as the asset production frontier.

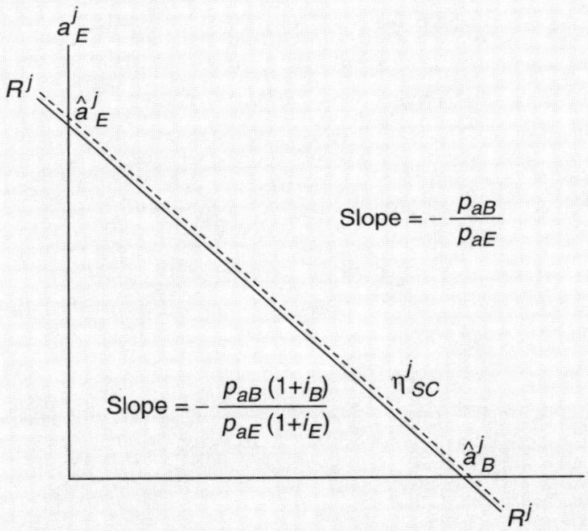

At the aggregate level the debt–equity mix is irrelevant to consumers because the securities are perfect substitutes. Indeed, there are no risk benefits from bundling them together as both produce the same future consumption flows.

As noted earlier, MM leverage irrelevance is straightforward in a certainty setting without taxes. There is really no need to have more than one security in this setting because there is no risk to diversify or taxes and other leverage related costs to minimize. But it is useful to demonstrate the leverage irrelevance theorem in these circumstances because it emphasizes the way arbitrage activity drives the equilibrium relationship between security returns with the same risk. Arbitrage is crucial in all the MM financial policy irrelevance theorems. Indeed, it is important in all the equilibrium asset pricing models we examined earlier in Chapter 4. In following subsections the leverage irrelevance theorem can hold for individual firms but not in aggregate when risk and taxes are introduced.

Box 7.4 Modigliani–Miller leverage irrelevance: a geometric analysis

It is possible to demonstrate MM leverage irrelevance by using the diagrams in Boxes 7.2 and 7.3 above. Since all firms face the same security prices and returns, we obtain the aggregate production frontier by summing the discounted value of their net cash flows. It is the line labelled *RR* in the diagram below where security trades are aggregated over firms, with $\Sigma_j \alpha_k^j = \alpha_k$ for $k = B, E$. All the bundles of securities along this frontier exhaust the net cash flows of firms. As consumers also face the same security prices and returns they have indifference schedules with the same slope, and we obtain aggregate indifference schedules (v) by summing the utilities they derive from the aggregate debt–equity bundles supplied by firms. Since firms pay out all their net cash flows the aggregate production frontier is also the aggregate budget constraint for consumers.

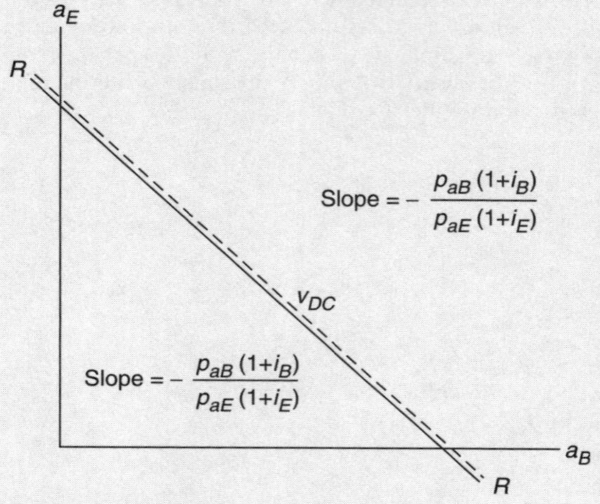

In a competitive equilibrium when the no arbitrage condition in (7.6) holds the aggregate indifference schedule lies (v_{DC}) along the aggregate production frontier. As a consequence, consumers get the same utility from every bundle of debt and equity along *RR*, which means the aggregate debt–equity ratio is irrelevant to them.

7.2.2 Uncertainty with common information and no taxes

Modigliani and Miller proved their irrelevance theorems in an uncertainty setting where traders have common information. Even though they placed little emphasis on the role of common information in their analysis, its importance has since been recognized. We initially demonstrate leverage irrelevance in an economy without taxes by using the CAPM pricing equation, and later generalize it in the Arrow–Debreu model outlined in Section 3.1.3.

Since investors have homogeneous expectations and trade in a frictionless competitive capital market in the CAPM, leverage simply redistributes given project risk between shareholders and bondholders without affecting the value of the firm. Investors know what the firm's project risk is, and how it is distributed by leverage policy between debt and equity, where changes in their expected security returns must reflect changes in risk bearing without altering the total risk premium firms pay. This also applies in the more general Arrow–Debreu state-preference model as the key requirements for leverage policy irrelevance are competition, no trading costs and common information. In this setting all profits are eliminated from expected security returns by arbitrage where they can only differ by the amount of project risk in them. Thus, changes in capital structure have no real effects on consumers because they do not alter their consumption opportunities. The analysis in the Arrow–Debreu economy is more general than the CAPM because no restrictions are placed on the distributions of security returns, or on the preferences and wealth of consumers. Instead, it identifies circumstances where the risk-spreading opportunities available to consumers are unaffected by the leverage policy choices of firms.

Leverage irrelevance using the CAPM

The security market line in the CAPM is an equilibrium asset pricing equation that combines the demand and supply conditions. Thus, it can be used to compute the market value of firms in (7.3) when they have random net cash flows, with $V\tilde{c} = \tilde{Y}(Z)$, where $\tilde{c} = 1 + b\tilde{i}_B + (1-b)\tilde{i}_E$ is the user cost of capital.[6] Now the returns to debt and equity can be different due to the non-diversifiable (project) risk in the net cash flows. To provide a benchmark for determining how asset values are affected by changes in leverage, consider the *unlevered firm (U)* which has an expected user cost of capital of $\bar{c}_U = 1 + \bar{i}_{E_U}$, where the expected return on its equity, using the CAPM, is

$$\bar{i}_{E_U} = i + (\bar{i}_M - i)\beta_{E_U}, \tag{7.8}$$

with $\beta_{E_U} = \text{Cov}(\tilde{i}_{E_U}, \tilde{i}_M)/\text{Var}(\tilde{i}_M) = \sigma_{E_U M} / \sigma_M^2$ being the market risk in each dollar of equity capital. Since shareholders bear all the project risk (β_Y) in the firm, we can decompose the beta coefficient for equity as

$$\beta_{E_U} = \frac{\beta_Y}{V_U}, \tag{7.9}$$

where $\beta_Y = \text{Cov}(\tilde{Y}, \tilde{i}_M)/\text{Var}(\tilde{i}_M)$ and V_U is the current market value of the firm.[7] Thus, the beta coefficient for unlevered equity is the market risk in the net cash flows (which is referred to here as project risk) per dollar of capital invested in the firm. Substituting the beta coefficient in (7.9) into (7.8), and applying the expectations operator to the market value of the unlevered firm, we have

$$V_U = \frac{\bar{Y} - (\bar{i}_M - i)\beta_Y}{1+i}. \tag{7.10}$$

This is the certainty-equivalent value of the firm, where the risk-adjusted expected net cash flows $\bar{Y} - (\bar{i}_M - i)\beta_Y$ are discounted by the risk-free user cost of capital. The risk premium $(\bar{i}_M - i)\beta_Y$ is compensation the firm must pay to risk-averse shareholders for bearing its project risk.

Now suppose the firm finances investment by selling risk-free debt and equity, where the expected user cost of capital for the *levered firm* (*L*) becomes $\bar{c}_L = 1 + bi + (1-b)\bar{i}_{E_L}$.

Box 7.5 The market value of an all-equity firm: a numerical example

Duraware Pty Ltd is a publicly listed company that produces sports clothing. It has no debt and the current market value of its shares is \$1.64 million. In 12 months' time Duraware is expected to have net cash flows of \$1.68 million, so its expected user cost of capital solves $V_U = \bar{Y}/\bar{c}_U$, as $\bar{c}_U = 1 + \bar{i}_{E_U} \approx 1.13$. If the net cash flows have a covariance with the return on the market portfolio of 12 per cent, when the variance in the return on the market portfolio is 9 per cent, the firm's project risk is $\beta_Y = \text{Cov}(\tilde{Y}, \tilde{i}_M)/\text{Var}(\tilde{i}_M) = 0.12/0.09 \approx 1.33$. Using the CAPM with a risk-free interest rate of 5 per cent, the risk premium in the expected return on equity (of 8 per cent) can be decomposed as

$$\bar{i}_{E_U} = 0.05 + (0.15 - 0.05)\beta_{E_U} \approx 0.13,$$

where the beta coefficient is $\beta_{E_U} = \beta_Y/V_U \approx 0.81$. This allows us to write the current value of the firm as

$$V_U = E = \frac{\bar{Y}}{1 + i + (\bar{i}_M - i)\beta_Y/V_U}$$

Rearranging terms, we have

$$V_U = E = \frac{\bar{Y} - (\bar{i}_M - i)\beta_Y}{1+i} = \frac{\$1.86\text{m} - \$0.133\text{m}}{1.05} \approx \$1.64\text{m},$$

with $(\bar{i}_M - i)\beta_Y = 0.10 \times \$1.33 = \$0.133\text{m}$ being the total risk premium paid to shareholders. Thus, the firm has risk-adjusted net cash flows of \$1.86m – \$0.133m = \$1.73m.

When bondholders bear no project risk they are paid a risk-free return that cannot be affected by price-taking firms. However, the expected return on equity will change with leverage now because shareholders are bearing all the project risk. By using the CAPM we can write the firms expected user cost of capital as $\bar{i}_{E_L} = i + (\bar{i}_M - i)\beta_{E_L}$, where the beta coefficient for each dollar of equity is

$$\beta_{E_L} = \frac{\beta_Y}{(1-b)V_L}, \tag{7.11}$$

with V_L being the current market value of the levered firm, and $(1 - b)V_L = E_L$ the current market value of its levered equity. When (7.11) is substituted into the expected user cost of capital we find the value of the levered firm is the same as the value of the unlevered firm in (7.10), with $V_L = V_U$. Thus, the market value of the firm is independent of leverage, even though debt pays a lower expected return, with $\bar{i}_{E_L} > i$. To see why, consider how the expected user cost of capital changes when leverage is raised marginally, where

$$\frac{d\bar{c}_L}{db} = i - \bar{i}_{E_L} + (1-b)\frac{d\bar{i}_{E_L}}{db} = 0.\text{[8]} \tag{7.12}$$

The lower return on debt reduces the cost of capital by $i - \bar{i}_{E_L}$, and it is offset by the increase in the expected return on each dollar of remaining equity due to the increase in its beta coefficient in (7.11) as $(1 - b)V_L$ falls. As confirmation of this result, Modigliani and Miller derive a linear relationship between the return on levered and unlevered equity by noting that

$$V_U = \frac{\bar{Y}}{1+\bar{i}_{E_U}} = V_L = \frac{\bar{Y}}{1+bi+(1-b)\bar{i}_{E_L}}.$$

Rearranging terms, we have

$$\bar{i}_{E_L} = \bar{i}_{E_U} + (\bar{i}_{E_U} - i)\frac{b}{1-b}, \tag{7.13}$$

where the change in the return on levered equity becomes

$$\frac{d\bar{i}_{E_L}}{db} = \frac{\bar{i}_{E_U} - i}{(1-b)^2} > 0. \tag{7.14}$$

Substituting (7.14) into (7.12), and using (7.13), we find that $d\bar{c}_L/db = 0$.

This derivation of MM leverage irrelevance makes the implicit assumption that there is no restriction on the amount of project risk that shareholders can be asked to bear when debt is risk-free. Thus, at high levels of leverage firms may need to collect additional funds from shareholders to pay a risk-free return to bondholders in bad states with low net cash flows. In practice, however, most shares have *limited liability* which restricts shareholder losses to the value of

Box 7.6 Leverage policy with risk-free debt: a numerical example

Suppose the unlevered company Duraware in Box 7.5 issues risk-free debt and retires equity without changing total investment. When the debt constitutes 75 per cent of the firm's current market value (V_L = \$1.64m), more risk is transferred to each dollar of equity, with

$$\beta_{E_L} = \frac{\beta_Y}{(1-b)V_L} = \frac{1.33}{0.25 \times 1.64} \approx 3.24,$$

where the risk premium in the expected return to equity must rise by 400 per cent to $(\bar{i}_M - i)\beta_{E_L} = 0.10 \times 3.24 \approx 0.32$. But the higher expected return to equity of 37 per cent does not raise the expected user cost of capital due to the lower cost of the risk-free debt, with

$$\bar{c}_L = 1 + bi + (1-b)\bar{i}_{E_L} = 1 + 0.04 + 0.09 = 1.13.$$

Thus, the market value of the firm is unchanged at \$1.64m.

their invested capital. Whenever the losses are greater than this some of the project risk is transferred to bondholders. In practice, a number of institutional arrangements have been adopted to protect bondholders from bearing more risk than they know about, including bankruptcy provisions, reporting requirements, and inviting large bondholders onto company boards.

But in a common information setting where shareholders and bondholders know how much project risk there is and who bears it, changes in leverage simply redistribute it between them without altering the aggregate risk premium firms must pay to the capital market. This is confirmed by noting that the expected user cost of capital with risky debt and equity becomes $\bar{c} = 1 + b\bar{i}_B + (1-b)\bar{i}_E$, where the respective beta coefficients are

$$\beta_B = \frac{\mu\beta_Y}{bV_L} \text{ and } \beta_E = \frac{(1-\mu)\beta_Y}{(1-b)V_L}, \tag{7.15}$$

with μ being the share of project risk borne by bondholders, and $1-\mu$ the share of project risk borne by shareholders. Default occurs when firms cannot meet their interest commitments, where the expected return on debt must rise to compensate bondholders for bearing project risk. But this shifts project risk from shareholders without changing the total risk premium paid by firms, with

$$\frac{d\bar{c}_L}{db} = \bar{i}_B - \bar{i}_E + b\frac{d\bar{i}_B}{db} + (1-b)\frac{d\bar{i}_E}{db} = 0.$$

By using the CAPM to solve the expected returns to debt and equity with the beta coefficients in (7.15) we obtain the value of the firm in (7.10), which is independent of b. Thus, leverage irrelevance holds with risky debt and equity in a common information setting.

Now a marginal increase in leverage can raise or lower the expected return on equity because there are two competing effects on its beta coefficient when debt is risky – the value of equity capital $(1-b)V_L$ and the amount of project risk borne by shareholders $(1-\mu)\beta_Y$ in (7.15) both fall. If debt is less risky at the margin the equity beta coefficient rises without changing the expected user cost of capital as the higher expected return on equity offsets the cost saving from issuing less costly debt (with $\bar{i}_E > \bar{i}_B$). But when the extra debt is more risky at the margin, higher leverage reduces the expected return on equity by lowering its beta coefficient, and this offsets the cost premium on the extra debt issued ($\bar{i}_E < \bar{i}_B$). While firms normally issue debt that is less risky than their equity, that is not always the case. Indeed, during the 1980s a number of firms funded large takeover bids using *junk bonds* which were riskier than their equity.

One advantage of using the CAPM to demonstrate leverage irrelevance is that it allows us to compute expected returns to debt and equity, and to demonstrate why the user cost of capital is unaffected by changes in capital structure. In this setting all traders measure and price market risk in the same way and they know who bears the project risk. All that leverage policy does is redistribute unchanged project risk between shareholders and bondholders. But the requirements for the CAPM to hold are more restrictive than the requirements for leverage irrelevance. It only requires common information in a frictionless competitive capital market. When Modigliani and Miller proved this theorem they emphasized the role of homemade leverage as a way for consumers to undo changes in capital structure by firms. This rebundling activity by consumers can be demonstrated much more clearly using the

Box 7.7 Leverage policy with risky debt: a numerical example

If we let the debt issued by Duraware in Box 7.6 bear 25 per cent of the project risk its beta coefficient becomes

$$\beta_B = \frac{\mu\beta_Y}{bV_L} = \frac{0.25\times 1.33}{0.75\times 1.64} \approx 0.27.$$

This introduces a risk premium of $(i_M - i)\,\beta_B = 0.10 \times 0.27 \approx 0.03$ to the expected return on debt, which rises to 8 per cent. Since shareholders bear less project risk the beta coefficient on equity falls from 3.24 to

$$\beta_{B_L} = \frac{(1-\mu)\beta_Y}{(1-b)V_L} = \frac{0.75\times 1.33}{0.25\times 1.64} \approx 2.43,$$

where the low-risk premium on equity of $(\bar{i}_M - i)\beta_{E_L} = 0.10\times 2.43 \approx 0.24$ reduces its expected return by 3 percentage points to 29 per cent. Since Duraware still pays the same total risk premium of

$$(\bar{i}_M - i)\beta_Y = (\bar{i}_M - i)[b\beta_B + (1-b)\beta_{E_L}] = 0.81,$$

it has the same expected user cost of capital, with

$$\bar{c}_L = 1 + b\bar{i}_B + (1-b)\bar{i}_{E_L} \approx 1 + 0.06 + 0.07 \approx 1.13.$$

As a consequence, Duraware's market value is unchanged at \$1.64m.

state-preference model of Arrow and Debreu in Section 3.4, which is more general than the CAPM.

Leverage irrelevance in the Arrow–Debreu economy

In a frictionless competitive capital market each traded security can be priced using the Arrow–Debreu model in (3.11) as

$$\sum_s \varphi_s p_{ak}(1+i_{ks}) = p_{ak}, \quad k \in K. \tag{7.16}$$

Since all consumers and firms face the same payout to each security k in each state s, with $p_{ak}(1+i_{ks}) = R_{ks}$, they use the same discount factors $\varphi_s = \varphi_s^h = \varphi_s^j$ for all h, j to compute the security prices. We follow conventional analysis and divide securities into one of two types – debt (B) and equity (E) – which traders can use to create a full set (K) of primitive (Arrow) securities. As noted above, there is no obvious way to distinguish between debt and equity in this common information setting without taxes. The standard approach is to give debt a prior claim on the net cash flows and equity the residual claim. But once investors know how risky the net cash flows are and how the risk is divided between debt and equity, a prior claim provides no real advantage to bondholders as they are compensated with the appropriate risk premium. Indeed, with limited liability, debt can be more risky than equity at high enough levels of leverage.

In a complete capital market where traders can create a full set of primitive securities arbitrage equates the rates of return on payouts in each state, with $i_{Bs} = i_{Es}$ for all s. When firms increase leverage, with investment held constant, they are transferring a given set of risky net cash flows to investors with debt instead of equity, where by the law of one price we have from (7.16) that

$$\sum_s \varphi_s (1 + i_{Bs}) = \sum_s \varphi_s (1 + i_{Es}). \tag{7.17}$$

It is important to emphasize that this relationship is derived for substitutions between equally risky debt and equity instruments. Whenever firms increase leverage, holding investment constant, the state-contingent payouts they make on the extra debt must come from payouts formerly made to equity. In other words, a change in leverage represents a constant risk rebundling of debt and equity securities. An example of this in a three-state world is

$$\begin{matrix} k = a_F & & k = a_{E_1} & & k = a_{E_2} \\ \begin{bmatrix} 1 \\ 1 \\ 1 \end{bmatrix} & = & \begin{bmatrix} 0 \\ 1 \\ 1 \end{bmatrix} & + & \begin{bmatrix} 1 \\ 0 \\ 0 \end{bmatrix} \end{matrix}$$

where the extra unit of risk-free debt (F) replaces two risky shares (E_1 and E_2). Clearly, the equilibrium condition $i_{Bs} = i_{Es}$ for all s does require every security to pay out in the same state. Indeed, individual debt and equity securities can pay in different states, but when they do make payouts in the same state they must pay the same rate of return. There is no optimal capital structure for individual firms or the aggregate economy in the Arrow–Debreu economy with common information. This is confirmed by writing the current market value of the firm as

$$V_0 = \frac{Y_s}{1 + (1 - b)i_{Es} + b i_{Bs}} \quad \forall s. \tag{7.18}$$

When the no arbitrage condition holds in a complete capital market with common information, we have $i_{Bs} = i_{Es}$ for all s where the value of the firm is independent of b. Thus, MM leverage irrelevance holds in the Arrow–Debreu economy.

There are a number of important ways to extend the models we have used to demonstrate leverage irrelevance. Taxes and leverage related costs are introduced next.

7.2.3 Corporate and personal taxes, leverage-related costs and the Miller equilibrium

One important difference between debt and equity results from the way they are taxed. Under a classical corporate tax system equity income of corporate firms is taxed twice, once

Box 7.8 Leverage irrelevance in the Arrow–Debreu economy: a geometric analysis

Equilibrium outcomes in the Arrow–Debreu economy with complete capital markets are equivalent to a certainty analysis. All agents have certain real income and can choose their consumption bundles in each state of the world, and the only uncertainty is over the state that actually eventuates. For that reason, we can use the same certainty analysis as in Box 7.4 to illustrate the capital market equilibrium under uncertainty. In the diagram below the aggregate production possibility frontier is linear because all the debt–equity bundles along *RR* make payouts from the same aggregate state-contingent net cash flows of firms. When the capital market is complete consumers can trade in every state, and constant risk debt–equity substitutions along *RR* are irrelevant to them when the demand condition holds, with $i_{Bs} = i_{Es} \forall s$. Since these debt–equity bundles are perfect substitutes, both in terms of risk and state-contingent returns, consumers have linear indifference schedules (v_{DC}) with the same slope as the aggregate production possibility frontier. For that reason the aggregate debt–equity ratio is irrelevant to them, and the market valuations of individual firms are unaffected by their debt–equity choices. Thus, MM leverage irrelevance holds for the aggregate capital market and for individual firms. Suppose, for example, that one or more firms raise their leverage and move the aggregate debt–equity mix from point *A* to point *D* along *RR* in the diagram. Then consumers simply adjust their portfolios to preserve their preferred real consumption in each state of nature without any change in their utility.

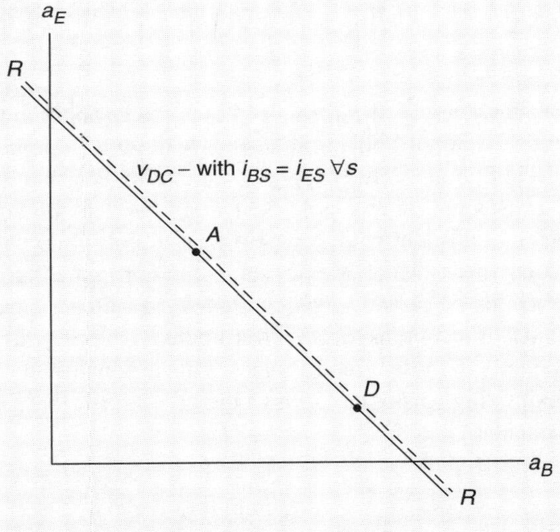

inside the firm at the corporate tax rate and then again at the personal rates of shareholders, while interest income is taxed once at the personal level. Modigliani and Miller (1963) extended their financial policy irrelevance theorems by including a classical corporate tax. As noted in the introduction to this chapter, personal taxes were not included because their analysis focused on factors directly impacting on firms. We isolate the role of *investor tax preferences* on security trades by using a certainty analysis, and then include uncertainty to account for the role of risk preferences.

The classical corporate tax discriminates against equity as capital gains are not taxed at the personal level until they are realized by investors. It is not, in general, feasible to tax capital gains as they accrue to investors because they are difficult to calculate. Often there are no markets where changes in the values of their assets can be objectively determined, so they are taxed at realization rather than as they accrue. This gives shareholders an incentive to delay realizing their capital gains to reduce the present value of their tax liabilities. In response, most governments levy a corporate tax on equity income when it accrues (on an annual or semi-annual basis) inside corporate firms. Income on unincorporated firms, such as partnerships and sole owners, is only subject to personal tax on the grounds that it is mostly realized in lieu of wages and salaries.

Just classical corporate tax

In a certainty setting the classical corporate tax (t_c) leads to an all-debt equilibrium. We can demonstrate this using the conditions for optimally traded debt and equity by corporate firms, with[9]

$$\begin{aligned} &\varphi(1+i_B)(1-t_C)\le 1, &&\text{for debt,}\\ &\varphi(1-t_C+i_E)\le 1, &&\text{for equity.} \end{aligned} \tag{7.19}$$

Since interest and the repayment of capital (V_0) are deductible expenses the tax falls solely on equity income.[10] By using these conditions we find that firms are indifferent to debt and equity when the *supply condition* is

$$i_B(1-t_C)=i_E. \tag{7.20}$$

Due to the absence of personal taxes the *demand condition* in (7.3) will also apply in this setting, with $i_B = i_E$. Since these conditions cannot hold simultaneously there is no equilibrium condition where debt and equity will both trade. If the supply condition holds consumers will only purchase debt as $i_B > i_E$, while firms will only supply debt when the demand condition holds as $i_B(1 - t_C) < i_E$. Thus, there is an all-debt equilibrium where all corporate income is transferred to consumers as interest payments which are not subject to corporate tax. Indeed, whenever firms pay income as dividends or capital gains on shares, consumers have lower future consumption due to the transfer of resources to the government as tax revenue.[11]

Clearly, MM leverage irrelevance fails in these circumstances. This is confirmed by using the payout constraint for profit-maximizing corporate firms in the presence of the corporate tax to write their current market value as

$$V_0=\frac{Y_1(1-t_C)}{1-t_C+bi_B(1-t_C)+(1-b)i_E}. \tag{7.21}$$

With $b = 1$ the value of the firm becomes $V_0 = Y_1/(1 + i_B)$, which is independent of the corporate tax. Notice how interest and the repayment of capital attract implicit tax refunds in (7.21). Since they shield the net cash flows from tax they are frequently referred to as *corporate tax shields*, which in total are equal to $bV_0(1 + i_B) + (1 - b)V_0$.

The all-debt equilibrium also arises in an uncertainty setting with common information when consumers can satisfy their risk preferences by just holding debt. To do so they need access to a full set of debt securities so they can trade in every set of nature. In the Arrow–Debreu economy with a complete capital market for firms and consumers, the demand condition is $i_{Bs} = i_{Es}$ for all s, while the supply condition is $i_{Bs}(1-t_C)=i_{Es}$ for all s. Once again, they cannot hold simultaneously and the equilibrium outcome is all debt. Risk preferences play a role when consumers need to bundle debt and equity together to trade

Box 7.9 The capital market with a classical corporate tax: a geometric analysis

The impact of the corporate tax on the debt–equity choice is illustrated in the capital market diagram below. By taxing the income paid to shareholders it reduces the net cash flows that firms can distribute to them, where the equity intercept of the aggregate asset production frontier contracts from $\hat{a}_E$ to $\hat{\alpha}_E^C$ as it rotates downwards around $\hat{a}_B$ to R_CR_C. This makes its slope flatter than the indifference schedules, where, in a competitive equilibrium, consumer utility is maximized by the all-debt outcome at $\hat{a}_B$.

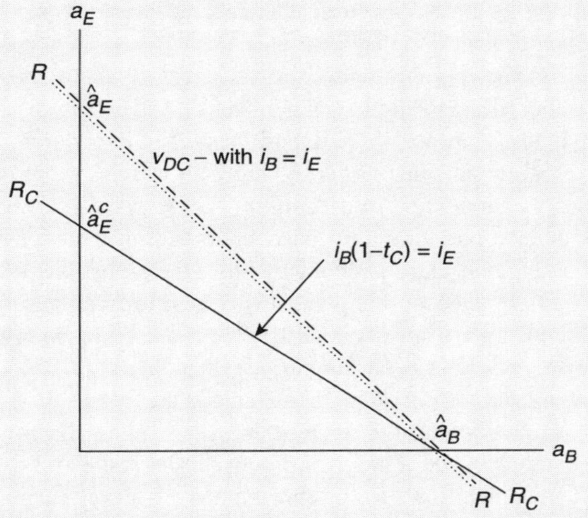

Since tax revenue is returned to consumers as lump-sum transfers the new debt–equity bundle on the asset frontier R_CR_C must also lie on the pre-tax frontier RR when there is no change in intertemporal consumption. Consumers have the same initial resources but are facing distorted security prices. If current consumption rises the new debt–equity bundle will lie inside RR, while the reverse applies when current consumption falls. As no tax revenue is raised in the all-debt equilibrium consumers have the same real income. And with unchanged intertemporal consumption the new asset frontier R_CR_C cuts the pre-tax frontier RR at $\hat{a}_B$.

across states of nature, and that happens when trading costs make it too costly for firms to create a full set of debt securities. In a frictionless setting, however, competition provides firms with the necessary incentive to create these securities.

At this point it is important to stress that the analysis in this section is not meant to be a realistic description of the capital market. Rather, it provides a very clear demonstration of the way that corporate tax discriminates against debt in favour of equity. In practice, there are a number of other factors that impact on the debt–equity choices of firms and consumers. At the time Modigliani and Miller presented their irrelevance theorems the conventional analysis obtained optimal debt–equity choices by including leverage-related costs with the corporate tax. We now examine these costs before summarizing the empirical evidence on their role.

Leverage-related costs

There are a number of reasons why firms incur leverage-related costs that impose third party claims on their net cash flows. These are claims by agents other than bondholders, shareholders and the government. Equity is supplied when marginal leverage-related costs offset the interest tax shield before reaching an all-debt equilibrium. Most early studies focus on bankruptcy costs, but there are also lost corporate tax shields and agency costs. Bankruptcy and agency costs both require asymmetric information, while lost corporate tax shields do not. Each of them is now considered in turn, beginning with *bankruptcy costs*.

When firms issue limited liability shares, their debt eventually becomes risky at high levels of leverage. Default occurs whenever their net cash flows fall below the risk-free interest payments on their debt. As leverage rises, the probability of default eventually becomes positive and increases. However, in a common information setting there are no default costs because bondholders know ex ante how much project risk they bear and bond prices sell at a discount to compensate them. They cannot, in these circumstances, make legal claims against firms when default occurs as they knew about risk at the time they purchased the debt. But with asymmetric information bondholders may not be aware of the default risk when they purchase debt. Once it occurs they can then make claims against firms by applying to have them declared bankrupt. Provisional administrators are appointed to determine whether the firms should be reorganized or liquidated. Any associated costs are third party claims on their net cash flows that reduce the funds available to bondholders and shareholders. Since the probability of default increases with leverage, expected bankruptcy costs are positively related to leverage.

Firms in *non-defaulting states* have sufficient net cash flows to meet their interest payments on debt, with $Y_s \geq (1 + i_{Bs})\, bV_0$, while in *defaulting states* they have $Y_s < (1 + i_{Bs})\, bV_0$. If default costs are incurred in every defaulting state firms have even less to distribute to bondholders, with $Y_s - h_s V_0 < (1 + i_{Bs})\, bV_0$, where h_s is the default cost per dollar of capital invested by the firm in defaulting state s.[12] The relationship between leverage and default is illustrated in Figure 7.1, where the net cash flows for a representative firm are mapped over states of nature. When leverage is set at or below $\hat{b}$ there is no default because the firm can pay a risk-free return on its debt. At $\hat{b}$ the net cash flows just cover the payouts to bondholders and there are no funds available for shareholders. Once leverage rises above $\hat{b}$,

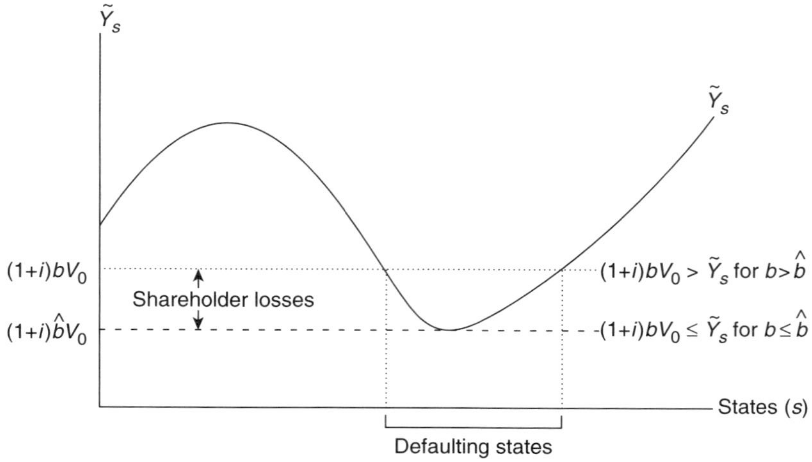

Figure 7.1 Default without leverage-related costs.

however, there are defaulting states where the net cash flows are not large enough to pay a risk-free return on debt.

In a common information setting bondholders know about the defaulting states and how much they will lose in them so that bond prices sell at a discount. Thus, there are no default costs and MM leverage irrelevance holds. However, with asymmetric information bondholders do not have complete information about the risk firm managers impose on them, where bankruptcy provisions act as a costly deterrent. This makes more sense in a multi-period setting where firm managers care about their reputations and want to avoid presiding over bankrupt firms. Constant default costs are illustrated by the shaded area in Figure 7.2, where it is assumed the firm is declared insolvent in every defaulting state.

These bankruptcy costs reduce the funds available to bondholders in defaulting states. They have an expected value of $\bar{h}(b) = \sum_s \pi_s h_s$, where h_s is the default cost in each state s per dollar of capital invested in the firm. Since the probability of default rises with leverage, we have $d\bar{h}/db > 0$. With costly default and the corporate tax we can write the expected user cost of capital as

$$\bar{c} = (1-t_C) + (1-b)\bar{i}_E + bi(1-t_C) + \bar{h}(b)(1-t_C),^{13} \tag{7.22}$$

where the bankruptcy costs are tax-deductible expenses along with capital and interest payments. Now an optimal interior debt–equity mix satisfies

$$\frac{d\bar{c}}{db} = i(1-t_C) - \bar{i}_E + (1-b)\frac{d\bar{i}_E}{db} + \frac{d\bar{h}}{db}(1-t_C) = 0. \tag{7.23}$$

When the expected return on equity rises to compensate shareholders for bearing the same project risk on less equity capital, with $i - \bar{i}_E + (1-b)(d\bar{i}_E/db) = 0$, firms equate the marginal default cost to the interest tax shield it generates, with

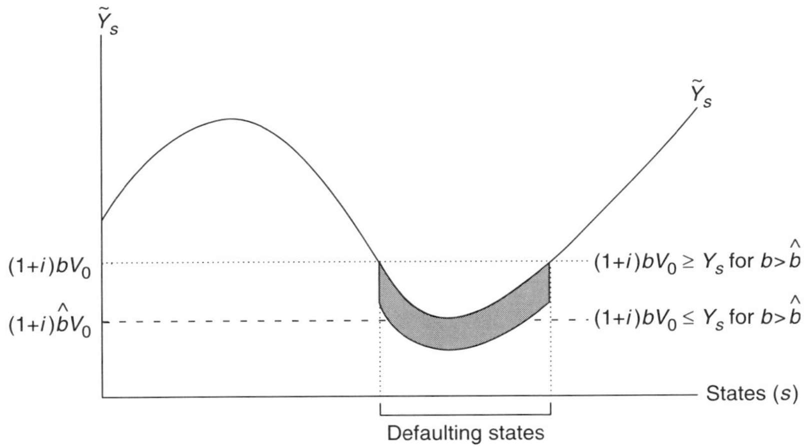

Figure 7.2 Default with leverage-related costs.

$$it_C = \frac{d\bar{h}}{db}(1-t_C). \tag{7.24}$$

A number of studies argue bankruptcy costs are insignificant. For example, Haugen and Senbet (1978) argue they are limited to the lesser of the costs of going bankrupt and the costs of avoiding it. When bankruptcy occurs ownership and control of the firm are transferred to bondholders, and firms can avoid this outcome by selling new shares and using the funds to repurchase fixed claims on their assets. This makes bankruptcy costs the lesser of the costs of transferring ownership and control to bondholders or new shareholders.

Two important issues are ignored by this analysis; the first is how default costs impact on consumption risk, while the second is the role of agency costs when there is asymmetric information. Notice how default costs increase the downside risk in the net cash flows in Figure 7.2. If this changes the non-diversifiable risk in the payouts to investors additional terms will appear in (7.24) to accommodate the resulting changes in the expected returns to debt and equity. Agency costs are examined later in this subsection.[14]

Lost corporate tax shields are examined by DeAngelo and Masulis (1980a) in an Arrow–Debreu economy with a full set of primitive securities and common information. In most countries corporate tax treats income and losses differently, where tax is collected on income but not refunded (in full) on losses. Table 7.1 summarizes the state-contingent returns paid to debt and equity after corporate tax, where the states of nature are assigned numbers that rise with the net cash flows. Default occurs in states $s \in [0, \hat{s})$ where at $\hat{s}$ the net cash flows just cover the payouts to debt, with $Y_{\hat{s}} = (1+i)bV_0$. The tax losses are equal to the amount by which the tax-deductible expenses exceed the net cash flows, with $[ibV_0 - V_0] - Y_s \geq 0$. No default occurs in states $s \in [\hat{s}, \bar{s})$, but there are tax losses because a fraction α_s of shareholder capital is not returned to them, with $0 \leq \alpha_s < 1$. At $\bar{s}$ there are no tax losses and no income is paid to shareholders, with $Y_{\bar{s}} - (1+i)bV_0 = (1-b)V_0$. In the final group of states $s \in (\bar{s}, S]$ shareholders are paid income of $Y_s - (1+i)bV_0 - (1-b)V_0 > 0$.[15] The lost corporate tax shields in states $s \in [0, \bar{s})$ reduce the value of the firm, and since they rise with leverage, MM leverage irrelevance fails. Indeed, there is an optimal capital structure for the firm in these circumstances because higher leverage increases the number of defaulting states.

There are three ways firms can get the full value of their tax deductions: through tax refunds from the tax office; by selling them to firms with tax profits; and by carrying them forward with interest. Governments rarely pay tax refunds or allow firms to sell their tax losses. Most, however, do allow firms to carry their tax losses forward, but without interest.[16] Thus, in periods when firms have tax losses, the present value of their tax deductions is eroded. And since interest payments are tax-deductible expenses lost corporate tax shields are related to leverage, where an increase in leverage raises the probability of default and reduces the present value of the tax shields.

Table 7.1 Payouts in the absence of tax refunds on losses

States	R_{Bs}	R_{Es}
$s \in [0, \hat{s})$	$Y_s < (1+i)bV_0$	0
$s \in [\hat{s}, \bar{s})$	$(1+i)bV_0$	$(1-t_C)[Y_s - (1+i)bV_0 - \alpha_s(1-b)V_0] = 0$
$s \in [\bar{s}, S]$	$(1+i)bV_0$	$(1-t_C)[Y_s - (1+i)bV_0 - (1-b)V_0] \geq 0$

Agency costs and information signalling arise when managers, shareholders and bondholders have different information about a firm's net cash flows.[17] Agency costs that arise from conflicts of interest between these groups can be constrained by capital structure decisions. Jensen and Meckling (1976) identify two sources of conflict. The first arises between shareholders and managers, while the second is between shareholders and bondholders. Since managers receive only a portion of the residual claim on the firm's net cash flows they do not reap the entire benefit from maximizing profit, whereas they bear the full cost of forgoing private benefits from perquisites, such as bigger offices and more personal staff. Thus, they have an incentive to consume private benefits at the expense of shareholder profit. Higher leverage can reduce this agency cost by absorbing *free cash flows* in higher interest payments and by raising the share of equity held by firm managers.

Conflicts arise between shareholders and bondholders due to limited liability, where shareholders have an incentive to invest in more risky projects when downside risk is shifted onto bondholders. But bondholders rationally anticipate this behaviour and discount the price of debt, thereby reducing the payouts to shareholders. This *asset substitution effect* is an agency cost of debt.[18]

Leverage can be used to convey private (or insider) information to the capital market. Myers and Majluf (1984) argue that when new investors have less information about the value of a firm's assets than existing investors they can discount the price of new equity below the present value of the profit from new investment. Existing shareholders avoid these losses by rejecting the projects so that firms are forced to use lower-cost internal funds and debt. Myers (1984) refers to this as a *pecking order theory*. Ross (1977b) argues that if managers benefit from shares having high values and lose when firms default they will have an incentive to use capital structure to convey private information to the capital market. Firm's with high-quality net cash flows (based on first-order stochastic dominance) will have a lower probability of default and can justify higher leverage than lower-quality firms. This leverage choice is a signal of quality to the capital market. Leland and Pyle (1977) argue that with managerial risk aversion managers are also less willing to hold a larger share of equity from increases in leverage unless the firm has high-quality projects.

In summary, leverage policy can affect the market valuation of firms when there are agency costs and information signalling, where optimally chosen leverage equates the marginal costs and benefits of reducing agency costs and providing valuable information to the capital market. Thus, the MM leverage irrelevance theorem fails to hold in these circumstances.

Most early *empirical estimates* of (ex-post) financial distress costs for bankrupt firms found they were less than the interest tax shield. Warner (1977) estimated the direct bankruptcy costs for 11 failed railroad firms in the US and found they averaged 1 per cent of market value 7 years prior to bankruptcy and rose to 5.3 per cent of market value just beforehand. Subsequent studies obtained higher estimates by including indirect bankruptcy costs, such as the loss of goodwill and other intangible assets in defaulting firms. Altman (1984) used data for 19 industrial companies in the US and obtained estimates of default costs that ranged from 11 to 17 per cent of market value 3 years prior to default. Alderson and Betker (1995) found they were 35 per cent of value at the time firms were being restructured, while Andrade and Kaplan (1998) obtained estimates of 10 to 23 per cent of value for a group of highly geared firms.

Graham (2000) used these estimates to compute expected default costs and found a typical firm could increase its market value by 7.5 per cent by raising leverage to its optimal level, where ex-post default costs were multiplied by estimates of the probability of default

Box 7.10 Optimal capital structure choices with leverage-related costs

The role of leverage related costs for an individual firm *j* are illustrated in the debt–equity space diagram below. Without default costs the firm's asset production frontier is the dotted line, which is flatter than the slope of the consumer indifference schedules due to the corporate tax. At low levels of debt the firm can supply the debt–equity bundles along this frontier as there is no probability of it defaulting. Once leverage is high enough to trigger default costs the asset production frontier becomes steeper. As these costs rise with leverage the frontier labelled $R_{CL}R_{CL}$ becomes concave to the origin. An optimal debt–equity ratio for the firm is illustrated at point â where the asset production frontier has the same slope as the indifference schedules.

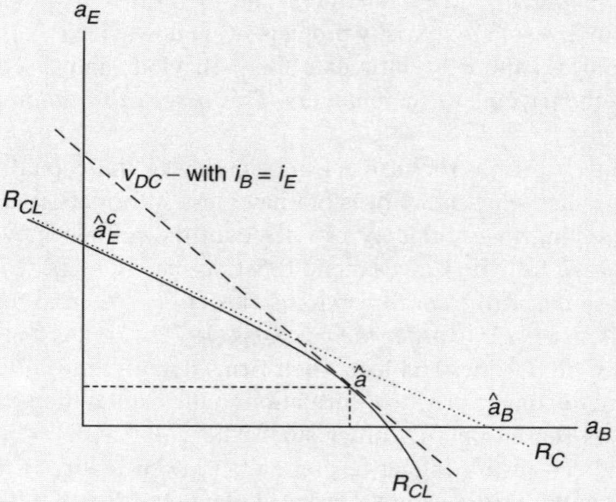

taken from information provided by debt ratings agencies. Molina (2005) argued that Graham underestimated the probability of default by failing to recognize its endogenous relationship with leverage. When changes in project risk cause ratings agencies to adjust their debt ratings firms respond by changing leverage, thereby affecting their probability of default. By taking this endogeneity into account Molina finds probabilities of default three times larger than those obtained by Graham, which are large enough to explain the leverage policies adopted by firms. In other words, they could not raise their market value by increasing leverage.

Based on Warner's findings, it was argued at that time that default costs were not large enough on their own to explain why firms use equity finance in the presence of a classical corporate tax. This led to the Miller equilibrium, to which we now turn.

The Miller equilibrium

In a widely cited paper delivered as a presidential address to the American Finance Association meetings, Miller (1977) portrayed leverage-related costs as the rabbit in the horse and rabbit stew and argued that demand-side factors – in particular, personal taxes – would play an important role in explaining firm capital structure choices in the presence of taxes. While corporate tax discriminates against equity, personal taxes can discriminate against debt for high tax bracket consumers. Most tax codes have progressive marginal personal tax rates that are lower for capital gains than dividends and interest. There are two reasons for the favourable tax treatment of capital gains:

i Capital gains are taxed on realization and not on accrual, and investors can reduce their effective tax rates on them by delaying realization.
ii Most countries have lower statutory personal tax rates on capital gains than income paid as cash distributions, such as dividends and interest. For example, the personal tax rate on capital gains in Australia is half the marginal personal tax rate on cash distributions for shares held more than 12 months.[19]

Due to the favourable tax treatment of capital gains, some high-tax investors can have a tax preference for shares that pay capital gains over debt, even though capital gains are taxed twice under a classical corporate tax system – once at the corporate rate and then again at the investor's personal tax rate. Since high-tax investors have cash tax rates above the corporate tax rate, those in the highest tax brackets are more likely to have a tax preference for equity. Table 7.2 summarizes the taxes levied on income generated by the corporate sector under a classical corporate tax system. For each investor (h) the marginal personal tax rate on cash distributions is t_B^h, while on capital gains it is t_E^h, with $t_B^h < t_E^h$ for all h.[20]

Most countries have progressive personal tax rates that increase with taxable income, and they are normally piecewise linear functions with three to four tax brackets. Table 7.2 makes it clear how equity income is taxed twice, and why no fully taxed investor would have a tax preference for dividends in the Miller equilibrium. This is referred to as the *dividend puzzle*. A number of solutions to this puzzle are examined in Section 7.3.

Typically the Miller equilibrium is explained in a certainty setting to highlight the role of consumer tax preferences. A number of studies argue it will not generalize to uncertainty – for examples, see Auerbach and King (1983) and Dammon (1988) – but that is not the case, as is demonstrated later in this section.[21] In the presence of the personal taxes summarized in Table 7.2 optimally chosen security demands will satisfy

$$\begin{aligned} &\varphi[1+i_B(1-t_B^h)] \le 1, && \text{for debt,} \\ &\varphi[1+i_D(1-t_B^h)] \le 1, && \text{for equity paying dividends,} \\ &\varphi[1+i_G(1-t_E^h)] \le 1, && \text{for equity paying capital gains,} \end{aligned} \tag{7.25}$$

where i_D and i_G are, respectively, returns to shares paying dividends and capital gains. In practice, shares pay a combination of dividends and capital gains, but we simplify the

Table 7.2 Income taxes on the returns to debt and equity

Taxpayer	*Debt (B)*	*Equity (E)*	
	Interest	*Dividends (D)*	*Capital Gains (G)*
Firms	—	t_C	t_C
Investor h	t_B^h	t_B^h	t_E^h

Box 7.11 Marginal income tax rates in Australia

Australia, like most countries, has progressive personal income tax rates. The rates in July 2007 are summarized below, and they include a 1.5 per cent Medicare surcharge used to (partially) fund publicly provided health care. Personal tax rates on capital gains are set at half these rates when assets have been held longer than 12 months, and the corporate tax rate is 30 per cent. Australia adopted the imputation tax system for company tax in 1989, where corporate tax is used as a withholding tax that is credited to shareholders when they receive the income as dividends.

Income range ($)	*Marginal tax rate (%)*
0–6000	0
6001–25,000	16.5
25,001–75,000	31.5
75,001–150,000	41.5
150,001+	46.5

It should be noted that most Australian taxpayers have higher effective tax rates because the government pays them family and other welfare payments that it withdraws as income rises.

analysis by separating shares into those that pay dividends and those that pay capital gains. In this setting some consumers can have a tax preference for debt and others a tax preference for equity. Once this happens they can raise their wealth through tax arbitrage, and they will have unbounded demands for their tax preferred securities when the tax rates are endowed on them. Miller bounds their security demands by imposing short-selling (borrowing) constraints on them. When these constraints bind one of the optimality conditions in (7.25) will hold with a strict inequality. Each consumer (h) is indifferent to debt and shares that pay dividends and capital gains, when the demand condition is

$$i_B(1-t_B^h) = i_D(1-t_B^h) = i_G(1-t_E^h). \tag{7.26}$$

Since every consumer has a lower personal tax rate on capital gains, the market rates of return must satisfy $i_B = i_D > i_G$ for all the three securities to trade. We can use the supply condition derived earlier in (7.20) because all equity income is treated in the same way by the corporate tax, with

$$i_B(1-t_C) = i_D = i_G,^{22} \tag{7.27}$$

where the relationship between the security returns must satisfy $i_B > i_D = i_G$. Clearly, this is incompatible with the demand condition in (7.26). Thus, when the demand and supply conditions are combined, we have an equilibrium relationship between the tax rates of

$$\begin{array}{ccccc} \text{interest} & & \text{dividends} & & \text{capital gains} \\ (1-t_B^h) & > & (1-t_C)(1-t_B^h) & < & (1-t_C)(1-t_E^h) \quad \forall h. \end{array} \tag{7.28}$$

This confirms the proposition made earlier based on the tax rates summarized in Table 7.2 that no consumer has a tax preference for dividends in the Miller equilibrium. Instead, they divide into strict *tax clienteles*, with:

$$\begin{aligned}&(1-t_B^h) > (1-t_C)(1-t_E^h), \text{ for debt specialists,}\\&(1-t_B^h) < (1-t_C)(1-t_E^h), \text{ for equity specialists,}\\&(1-t_B^h) = (1-t_C)(1-t_E^h), \text{ for marginal investors.}\end{aligned} \tag{7.29}$$

Equity specialists prefer shares that pay capital gains. They must be high-tax investors $(t_B^h > t_C)$ with marginal cash tax rates that are higher than the combined corporate and personal taxes on capital gains. While all low-tax investors $(t_B^h < t_C)$ are *debt specialists*, not all high-tax investors are equity specialists. In practice there may not be any *marginal investors*, but none are needed for both securities to trade.

Box 7.12 Tax preferences of high-tax investors in Australia

To demonstrate how plausible these tax relationships are in practice, consider Australian taxpayers in the top tax bracket with a marginal cash tax rate of 46.5 per cent when the corporate tax rate is 30 per cent. They will have a tax preference for equity that pays capital gains whenever their marginal tax rates on capital gains are less than 23.6 per cent, where:

$$\begin{aligned}&\left(1-t_B^h\right) \approx \left(1-t_C\right)\left(1-t_E^h\right),\\&\left(0.535\right) \quad \left(0.70\right)\left(0.754\right)\end{aligned}$$

for $t_E^h \approx 23.6$.

Whenever there are consumers with a tax preference for debt and others with a tax preference for equity they can increase their wealth through *tax arbitrage* by trading the two securities with each other. If debt specialists sell shares to equity specialists and use the proceeds to buy their debt, both groups generate net tax refunds which transfer revenue from the government budget.[23] Miller simplifies the analysis by endowing tax rates on consumers, but they will have unbounded demands for their tax preferred securities. Three studies examine different ways to bound security demands: Dammon and Green (1987) make personal tax rates increasing functions of income so that tax arbitrage eliminates investor tax preferences; Jones and Milne (1992) include a government budget constraint to bound the revenue consumers can extract through tax arbitrage;[24] and Miller (1988) imposes borrowing constraints on consumers.[25] While Miller's approach does simplify the analysis, it conceals potentially important endogenous relationships identified by Dammon and Green and by Jones and Milne that can have important welfare implications for the final equilibrium outcome.[26] With short-selling constraints, debt and equity specialists have bounded demands for securities in the Miller equilibrium and both securities trade. Due to the absence of any constraints on security trades by firms the market returns to debt and equity will satisfy the supply condition in (7.27) in a competitive capital market. When it does, MM leverage policy irrelevance holds for individual firms. This is confirmed by using the supply condition to write the current market value of the firm in (7.21) as

$$V_0 = \frac{Y_1(1-t_C)}{(1-t_C)+i_G} = \frac{Y_1}{1+i_B},$$

which is independent of b. But the aggregate debt–equity ratio does matter in the Miller equilibrium because there must be enough debt and equity to satisfy the security demands of debt and equity specialists. Whenever it lies within these bounds the aggregate debt–equity ratio is irrelevant to consumers if there are marginal investors who are willing to hold either security. If debt and equity specialists cannot satisfy their tax preferences they

Box 7.13 The Miller equilibrium: a geometric analysis

It is possible to see the peculiar attributes of the Miller equilibrium in the debt–equity space diagram below where the aggregate asset production frontier $R_C R_C$ maps the debt–equity bundles over the aggregate net cash flows of firms trading in the corporate sector of the economy. Its slope is determined by the supply condition in (7.27) without dividends. Since consumers face different personal tax rates their indifference schedules have different slopes. To simplify the analysis we assume the consumers in each tax clientele have the same tax preferences. Point A isolates the minimum debt $(\bar{a}_B)$ needed to satisfy debt specialists, while point B isolates the minimum equity $(\bar{a}_E)$ needed for equity specialists. Any additional debt and equity supplied between these points is held by marginal investors. Thus, points A and B and the distance between them are determined by the net wealth of the investors in each tax clientele. The slopes of the indifference schedules for each clientele reflect their different tax preferences, where they have larger (negative) slopes than frontier $R_C R_C$ for debt specialists (v^B_{DC}), a lesser (negative) slope for equity specialists (v^E_{DC}), and the same slope for marginal investors (v^M_{DC}). As long as the aggregate debt–equity bundle lies between points A and B along frontier $R_C R_C$ it is irrelevant to consumers. Since debt and equity specialists are holding their tax-preferred securities any differences between the bundles in this region are absorbed by marginal investors. Once the aggregate debt–equity ratio moves outside these bounds aggregate welfare falls. For example, bundles that lie above point A along $R_C R_C$ do not provide enough debt for debt specialists so they hold equity and are worse off due to the extra tax burden on them.

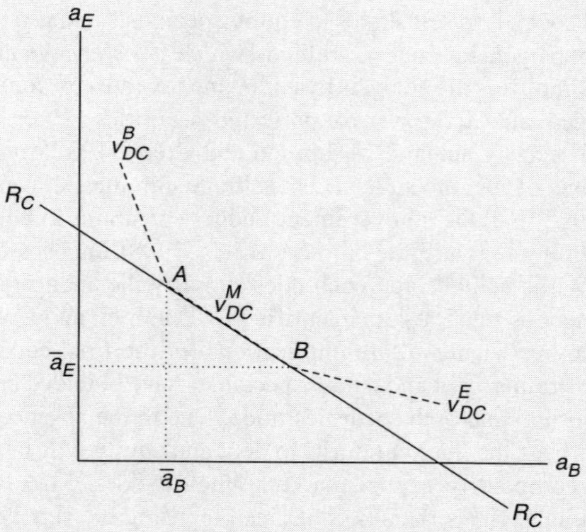

will have lower welfare due to the extra tax burden imposed on them from holding the higher-taxed security.

A number of commentators on the Miller equilibrium draw on the role played by home-made leverage in the original proofs of MM leverage irrelevance to argue there must be marginal investors and certainty for MM leverage irrelevance to hold in the presence of taxes. They claim marginal investors are needed in the model to absorb changes in firm capital structure, while certainty removes risk preferences from security demands so that consumers divide into strict tax clienteles.[27] But leverage irrelevance holds in the Miller equilibrium without marginal investors and with uncertainty.

Suppose there are *no marginal investors* in a certainty setting, so that all consumers are debt or equity specialists. If one firm raises its leverage (with investment held constant) there is an excess supply of debt and an excess demand for equity that puts upward pressure on the market price of equity and downward pressure on the market price of debt. Other firms respond to these price changes by substituting equity for debt until the aggregate debt–equity ratio is restored to its original level. Thus, the market value of individual firms is unaffected by changes in leverage as changes in security prices induce other firms to take offsetting positions so that consumers continue to hold their tax–preferred securities. In a frictionless competitive capital market where profit-maximizing firms respond to security price changes consumers get their tax-preferred securities.

Stiglitz (1974) recognized that rebundling by financial intermediaries (as agents of corporate firms) would make leverage policy irrelevant in a frictionless competitive capital market without taxes.[28] Even in the absence of personal taxes and short-selling constraints, homemade leverage is likely in practice to be more costly than rebundling on the supply side of the market by specialist traders with lower transactions costs. While there are no transactions costs in the Miller equilibrium, there are borrowing constraints on consumers to bound their security demands and rule out tax arbitrage. Thus, all the arbitrage activity must be undertaken by profit-maximizing firms.

Now suppose we introduce *uncertainty* to the earlier analysis of the Miller equilibrium. It is tempting to conclude consumers will not separate into strict tax clienteles in these circumstances as their security demands will be determined by a combination of risk and tax preferences. Auerbach and King argue consumers will forgo some of the benefits from holding tax-preferred securities and bundle debt and equity together to satisfy their risk preferences. In response, firms will form leverage clienteles to create different risky mutual funds for consumers with the same tax preferences. They argue these mutual funds are unlikely to satisfy the risk preferences of every consumer. Kim (1982) and Sarig and Scott (1985) argue there are no leverage clienteles in the Miller equilibrium because consumers can satisfy their risk preferences by holding just tax-preferred securities. There are two ways firms (or financial intermediaries) achieve this outcome: by providing a complete set of debt and equity securities so that consumers can create a full set of primitive equity and primitive debt securities; or by creating securities to satisfy the risk and tax preferences of consumers (in effect, they create personalized mutual funds constructed solely from tax-preferred securities).

While the outcome in Auerbach and King is more realistic, they are implicitly including transactions costs and asymmetric information to stop firms from creating personalized risky mutual funds for consumers. Clearly, they are trying to explain what actually happens in the capital market, but, in doing so, are moving outside the confines of the frictionless classical finance model of the Miller equilibrium. In a frictionless competitive economy with common information, firms know the risk and tax preferences of every consumer and are driven by the profit motive to satisfy them. Due to the absence of trading costs

Box 7.14 The Miller equilibrium without marginal investors

A geometric analysis helps to clarify the reason why marginal investors are not required in the Miller equilibrium. In their absence there is an optimal aggregate debt–equity bundle for the corporate sector of the economy at $\hat{a}$ on the asset production frontier $R_C R_C$ in the debt–equity space diagram below. Since consumers face borrowing constraints to restrict tax arbitrage they are unable to access any arbitrage profits when the after-tax security returns are not equal. Instead, that role is undertaken by profit-maximizing firms which equate the cost of debt and equity along the frontier $R_C R_C$, with $i_B(1 - t_C) = i_G$. Whenever changes in leverage by one or more firms moves the aggregate debt–equity bundle away from $\hat{a}$, other firms respond to the (incipient) changes in security prices and bring the bundle back to $\hat{a}$ where consumer tax preferences are satisfied. Profit-maximizing firms undertake this repackaging due to the absence of restrictions on their security trades, which is reflected in the linearity of the asset production frontier. Thus, the homemade leverage identified by Modigliani and Miller in their original proof of the leverage irrelevance theorem without taxes will not be possible in the Miller equilibrium with taxes when there are no marginal investors.

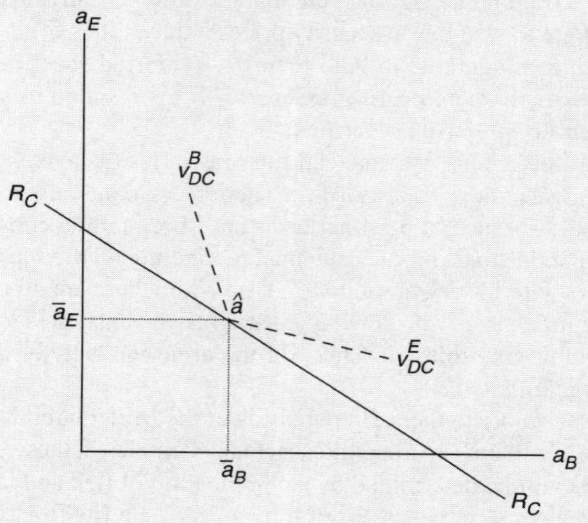

consumers are not required to trade off risk and tax preferences in these circumstances. In practice, consumers do purchase bundles of debt and equity, often as mutual funds, to satisfy their conflicting risk and tax preferences as firms cannot costlessly create their personalized risky tax-preferred securities.[29] Moreover, it is too costly for them to create a full set of primitive debt and equity securities to make the capital market *double complete*. This is confirmed by Kim *et al* (1979) who find empirical evidence of shareholder leverage clienteles, where firms choose capital structures to satisfy investors with different risk and tax preferences. Even though leverage clienteles are absent in the Miller equilibrium, it does, however, establish the important arbitrage activity by firms (or their agents financial intermediaries) in competitive capital markets. In practice, trading costs are likely to restrict homemade leverage, where consumers face higher trading costs than specialist financial intermediaries. As transactions costs fall and traders acquire better information about investor risk and tax preferences the actual capital market outcome will converge to the Miller equilibrium.

MM leverage irrelevance for individual firms in the Miller equilibrium with uncertainty can be confirmed by computing the market value of firms in the Arrow–Debreu economy as

$$V_0 = \frac{Y_s(1-t_C)}{(1-t_C)+bi_{Bs}(1-t_C)+(1-b)i_{Gs}} \quad \forall s,$$

where equity pays capital gains. When both securities trade in a complete capital market the supply condition in (7.27) holds, with $i_{Bs}(1 - t_C) = t_{Gs}$ for all s, where the value of the firm becomes $V_0 = Y_s/(1 + i_{Bs})$ for all s, which is independent of the debt–value ratio. And this also applies without marginal investors.

A growing number of countries have reformed their tax systems to remove the double tax on dividends. For example, governments in Australia, the United Kingdom, New Zealand and the United States have adopted tax imputation systems that give shareholders credit for corporate tax paid on dividends. This makes all investors indifferent to interest and dividends. We examine the impact of dividend imputation later in Section 7.3.3.

The Miller equilibrium in open economies

With perfect capital mobility the market returns to domestic debt and equity are determined by the returns on perfect substitutes in world markets, where the supply condition becomes $i_B(1-t_C^F)=i_G$, for the foreign corporate tax rate t_C^F.[30] In a certainty setting countries form supply clienteles where those with higher corporate tax rates supply only debt, with $i_B(1-t_C)<i_B(1-t_C^F)=i_G$, and those with lower rates supply only equity, with $i_B(1-t_C)>i_B(1-t_C^F)=i_G$. The country with the corporate tax rate that satisfies the supply condition is determined by the aggregate demand for debt and equity in the international capital market, which depends on the personal tax rates in each country. If there are tax agreements between countries that give domestic residents credits for any foreign personal tax payments, consumer income is subject only to domestic personal tax rates, where the demands for debt and equity in each country will be determined by the tax relationships; $(1-t_B^h)<(1-t_C^F)(1-t_E^h)$. The larger the aggregate demand for equity, the greater the number of countries supplying it, where the country with the highest corporate tax rate determines the supply condition for the returns to debt and equity.

7.2.4 The user cost of capital

In (7.22) we gave a general expression for the expected user cost of capital, which is the *weighted average cost of capital* (WACC) used to compute the market value of a firm in a two-period setting with risk and taxes. It is the average cost of raising and using each dollar of capital invested by bondholders and shareholders, where the total economic cost of capital is obtained by multiplying the market value of the firm by (7.22). When the no arbitrage condition holds it is equal to the firm's after-tax net cash flows, with $\bar{c}V_0=\bar{Y}_1$. In some circumstances the WACC in (7.22) is also the *marginal cost of capital* (MCC) used by firms to determine their level of investment, with

$$\left.\frac{d\bar{Y}_1}{dZ_0}\right|_{db=0} = \bar{c}.$$[31]

When the MCC is constant in the absence of fixed costs, we have MCC = WACC. This occurs in the following circumstances:

i In a certainty setting the last term in (7.22) disappears because there are no default costs, and the user cost of capital simplifies to:

$$c = (1 - t_C) + bi_B(1 - t_C) + (1 - b)i_E.$$

Since firms cannot affect the returns they pay to debt and equity in a competitive capital market, the user cost of capital is unaffected by their investment choices. When both securities trade, we have $i_B(1 - t_C) = i_E$, where MM leverage irrelevance holds, and profit-maximizing firms equate the value of the marginal product of investment to the MCC, which is also the WACC.

ii It unlikely for (7.22) to be the MCC when there is uncertainty, even with common information, as leverage-related costs and project risk on each dollar of capital are affected by additional investment. If investment has scaling effects on the net cash flows in each state of nature, nothing happens to the WACC in (7.22) because the probability of default and the project risk per dollar of capital are unchanged.

iii In a two-period setting there is depreciation in the WACC in (7.22) because firms liquidate in the second period and repay capital to investors from their net cash flows. This makes depreciation unity in the user cost of capital. In a multi-period setting, however, the first term in (7.22) is replaced by $-\bar{\Phi}_t(1-t_C) = -(\bar{V}_t - \bar{V}_{t-1})(1-t_C)/\bar{V}_{t-1}$, which is the rate of change in the market value of the firm over the period from $t - 1$ to t; it is the expected rate of economic depreciation when $V_t < V_{t-1}$. For most depreciating assets there is less than complete depreciation, with $0 \le -\bar{\Phi}_t < 1$. Frequently, however, firm values rise in some time periods. For example, there are firms which invest a significant portion of their capital in assets such as land, buildings and goodwill, and they can increase in value. In periods when capital gains on these assets are large enough to offset reductions in the market values of their depreciating assets, their market values will rise. The rate of appreciation or depreciation in the value of a firm will not change with investment when it has a scaling effect on the value of its outputs and inputs. When this happens the WACC in (7.22) is also the MCC that determines the optimal level of investment.

These cases tell us something about the circumstances where the WACC is not equal to the MCC:

i When the amount of project risk per dollar of capital changes with investment, firms must pay higher expected returns to shareholders and/or bondholders to compensate them for bearing this extra risk. In the absence of lost corporate tax shields, which eliminates the last term in (7.22), the condition for optimally chosen investment becomes

$$\left.\frac{d\bar{Y}_1}{dZ_0}\right|_{db=0} = \bar{c} + b(1-t_C)\frac{\partial \bar{i}_B}{\partial Z_0} + (1-b)\frac{\partial \bar{i}_E}{\partial Z_0} > \bar{c}.$$

While extra project risk raises the user cost of capital and reduces the market value of the firm, MM leverage irrelevance continues to hold when traders have common information. But once investment changes the project risk on each dollar of capital invested, the MCC deviates from the WACC in (7.22).[32]

ii Whenever profits and losses are not treated symmetrically by the corporate tax, there are expected default costs from lost corporate tax shields, even in a common information setting. If the extra project risk from additional investment changes the probability of default, it also changes the expected default costs in the last term of (7.22), where the condition for optimally chosen investment becomes

$$\left.\frac{d\bar{Y}_1}{dZ_0}\right|_{db=0} = \bar{c} + b(1-t_C)\frac{\partial \bar{i}_B}{\partial Z_0} + (1-b)\frac{\partial \bar{i}_E}{\partial Z_0} + \frac{\partial \bar{h}}{\partial Z_0}(1-t_C).^{33}$$

The last term is the change in expected default costs when investment affects the probability of default.

iii With more than two time periods the first term in (7.22) is replaced by $-\bar{\Phi}_t(1-t_C)$, which measures the rate of change in the market value of the firm over period from $t-1$ to t, where $\bar{\Phi}_t < 0$ when it declines, and $\bar{\Phi}_t > 0$ when it rises. It would seem reasonable to expect this term to be a function of the level of investment as firms are likely to change their input mix when they expand investment and production. In other words, it would seem unlikely, even in the long run when all inputs can be varied, that firms will simply scale their operations when they change investment, where the condition for optimally chosen investment, in the absence of changes in project risk and expected default costs, becomes

$$\left.\frac{d\bar{Y}_1}{dZ_0}\right|_{db=0} = \bar{c} - \frac{\partial \bar{\Phi}_1}{\partial Z_0}(1-t_C).$$

The second term is the change in the (average) rate of economic depreciation that causes the MCC to deviate from the WACC in (7.22). Ross (2005) derives an expression for the cost of capital in a multi-period setting with common information and finds that it differs from the standard WACC formula because shareholders and bondholders in bankrupt firms incur losses from recapitalization and reorganization costs. Recapitalization losses occur because investors are forced to exchange their initial debt and equity for securities with lower values. It therefore assumes the capital market is incomplete due to transactions costs. In a frictionless complete capital market where investors can trade in every future state, any recapitalization is costless and is already included in current security prices.

iv The WACC can deviate from the MCC when traders have asymmetric information. Additional investment that provides new information or affects the actions taken by firm managers can change the expected user cost of capital. For example, when traders get better information about a firm's project risk it changes the risk premium paid to debt and equity and the cost of capital.

Most governments estimate the user cost of capital for firms in different sectors of the economy to determine how their policies or other factors impact on private investment and employment. Private traders also estimate the user cost of capital to guide their investment decisions. It is reasonably clear from (7.22) and the subsequent discussion that depreciation allowances, the corporate tax, project risk and default costs all play an important role in determining the user cost of capital. Other factors can also play a role by impacting on the equilibrium returns paid to debt and equity, and on the prices that determine the net cash flows to investment. We conclude this section by considering three of them.

First, investor demands are affected by personal taxes on the returns to debt and equity. In the previous subsection we saw how the double tax on dividends makes interest and capital gains more attractive for all investors. Corporate and personal taxes affect the relative returns to debt and equity as well as their equilibrium levels. From the supply condition in (7.27), with $i_{Bs}(1 - t_C) = i_{Ds} = i_{Gs}$ for all s, we have $i_{Bs} > i_{Ds} = i_{Gs}$ due to the tax deductibility of interest. The combined corporate and personal taxes drive wedges between the pre- and post-tax returns to debt and equity, thereby raising the cost of capital for firms and lowering the after-tax income received by investors; the larger the tax wedges, the lower the aggregate level of saving and investment.

Investors divide into strict tax clienteles in the Miller equilibrium to minimize their tax payments. Recall from the previous subsection how this occurs in a common information setting without transactions costs where consumers effectively have access to a full set of primitive debt and primitive equity securities. However, investors may bundle debt and equity together and incur larger tax burdens to satisfy their risk preferences when there are trading costs and asymmetric information. This further reduces saving and investment by simultaneously raising the cost of capital for firms and reducing the after-tax returns to investors.

From time to time governments reform their spending and taxing policies to expand aggregate income and employment. Lower corporate and personal tax rates expand private investment and saving by reducing the cost of capital and raising the after-tax returns to investors. The final change in the cost of capital in (7.22) is ultimately determined by the interest elasticities of aggregate investment demand and aggregate saving.[34] A lower corporate tax rate reduces the value of interest tax deductions. When it falls below the lowest marginal cash tax rate every investor becomes a high-tax investor, with $t_B^h > t_C$ for all h, where this is likely to increase the number of equity specialists in the Miller equilibrium.

Second, governments in some countries allow firms in politically sensitive sectors of the economy to accelerate their depreciation deductions for tax purposes. While this provides an implicit subsidy by raising the present value of their tax deductions relative to firms in other sectors, it has efficiency effects that can reduce aggregate income. Concessions of this kind are fairly common in relatively new industries and for firms which undertake research and development. When the implicit subsidy from accelerated depreciation allowances corrects externalities in these activities it can raise aggregate income. But they too are frequently granted on political rather than efficiency grounds.

Third, fiscal and monetary policies can also impact on the user cost of capital by changing the equilibrium returns to debt and equity. For example, tighter monetary policy can drive up the cost of capital and discourage investment, at least in the short term when there are nominal price rigidities that allow changes in the money supply to have real effects in the economy. Extra government spending can also affect the user cost of capital when it reallocates resources inter-temporally. In recent years governments have been much less inclined to use fiscal and monetary policies to smooth economic activity through normal cyclical changes. They have difficulty identifying the cycles, and it also takes considerable time to legislate and implement their policy responses. Moreover, monetary policy is much less effective in economies with flexible nominal prices, while government spending may be ineffective when there are principal–agent problems between voters, politicians and bureaucrats that affect the provision of public services.

Box 7.15 The Miller equilibrium with a lower corporate tax rate

A lower corporate tax rate will reduce any tax preferences for equity. Indeed, it makes initial marginal investors debt specialists and some initial equity specialists marginal investors or even debt specialists. The effects of making debt specialists marginal investors are illustrated in the debt–equity space diagram below where initially debt and equity specialists have the same tax preferences within each group. Prior to the tax change there are no marginal investors and the aggregate debt–equity bundle $\hat{a}$ satisfies the security demands of debt and equity specialists in the corporate sector of the economy. As the corporate tax rate falls it rotates the aggregate asset possibility frontier upward around the debt axis. Since firms can distribute more of their net cash flows to shareholders they can issue more equity at each level of debt when they supply both securities. At the new lower tax rate t'_C former debt specialists become marginal investors along asset frontier $R'_C R'_C$, with $(1-t^h_B)=(1-t'_C)(1-t^h_E)$. All the aggregate debt–equity bundles along this frontier above $\hat{a}'$ are irrelevant to consumers. However, consumers are worse off when the aggregate debt–equity bundles are moved below $\hat{a}'$ along the frontier.

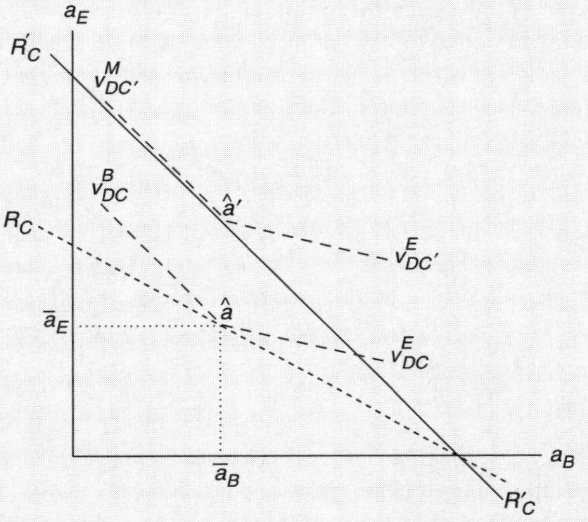

It should be noted that the lower corporate tax rate will increase the aggregate wealth of consumers by reducing allocative inefficiency. If that changes their intertemporal consumption choices it will affect their demands for the two securities, where that causes parallel shifts in the new asset frontier $R'_C R'_C$ and moves the new debt–equity bundle along it. If there is a rise in future consumption for all consumers the new frontier shifts out and the debt–equity bundle $\hat{a}'$ moves down the frontier.

Policy changes like these need to be evaluated formally using a model that incorporates the public sector in the economy. We do this in the next chapter where marginal policy changes are examined in a tax-distorted economy.

7.3 Dividend policy

Another important financing decision firms make is how to distribute equity income to shareholders. Most corporate debt has a fixed market value and pays variable interest, while the market value of equity can vary through time with income paid as dividends and capital gains. Dividend policy determines whether equity income is paid to shareholders as a cash dividend or retained by firms who repurchase shares to pay capital gains. Modigliani and Miller (1961) prove dividend policy is irrelevant to the market values of firms in a frictionless common information setting without taxes. Whenever firms use income to repurchase a dollar of equity the market value of their equity falls by a dollar, while shareholder wealth is unchanged as the cash they receive matches the fall in the market value of their shareholdings.

But dividend irrelevance fails in the presence of a classical corporate tax where personal taxes favour capital gains over dividends. This was demonstrated earlier in Section 7.2.3, where no dividends are paid in the Miller equilibrium.[35] A large number of studies have attempted to solve the *dividend puzzle*. In recent years a number of governments have replaced the classical corporate tax with an imputation tax system that grants credits to shareholders for corporate tax collected on their dividends; it removes the double taxation of dividends and makes them subject to the same personal tax as interest income.[36] It may seem puzzling that they did not instead just abolish the corporate tax altogether. But the reason for not doing so is the same as the reason for introducing a corporate tax in the first place. In its absence firms have an incentive to pay equity income as capital gains that are subject to lower personal tax rates. Recall from an earlier discussion that there are two reasons why: first, most governments set lower statutory rates on them relative to cash income; and second, they are taxed on realization and not accrual. The more time it takes to realize capital gains, the lower the effective tax rate on them. The imputation tax system recognizes this by using the corporate tax as a withholding tax which is credited to shareholders when they receive the income as dividends. Thus, it taxes equity income on accrual inside firms and removes any incentive for then to delay paying it as capital gains (when shareholders have marginal personal (cash) tax rates less than or equal to the corporate tax rate). Governments are attracted to the imputation tax system because it removes the double taxation of dividends under the classical corporate tax system and, in so doing, is a less discriminatory tax. There are some remaining tax preferences, however, and they will be identified later in this section.

We begin the analysis with a simple proof of MM dividend policy irrelevance in the absence of taxes. Then we summarize the dividend puzzle identified earlier in the Miller equilibrium before considering a number of attempts to resolve it, including, differential transactions costs on dividends and capital gains, share repurchase constraints and agency costs. Unfortunately, none on these explanations appear to provide an adequate resolution to the puzzle, which is why many argue it is one of the most intractable problems in finance.

7.3.1 Dividend policy irrelevance

Dividend policy irrelevance can be demonstrated in a two-period certainty setting by separating equity into shares that pay dividends (D) and capital gains (G), where the optimal debt and equity choices of consumers and firms satisfy

$$\begin{aligned} \varphi(1+i_B) &= 1, \quad \text{for debt,} \\ \varphi(1+i_D) &= 1, \quad \text{for equity paying dividends,} \\ \varphi(1+i_G) &= 1, \quad \text{for equity paying capital gains,} \end{aligned} \tag{7.30}$$

leading to an equilibrium condition when the no arbitrage condition holds, of

$$i_B = i_D = i_G. \tag{7.31}$$

In the absence of taxes the three securities are perfect substitutes in a certainty setting so they must pay the same rates of return.[37] The market value of profit-maximizing firms is obtained using their payout constraint as

$$V_0 = \frac{Y_1}{1 + bi_B + gi_G + di_D}, \tag{7.32}$$

where $b = p_{aB}\, a_B/V_0$, $g = p_{aG}\, a_G/V_0$ and $d = p_{aD}\, a_D/V_0$, with $b + g + d = 1$. Clearly, when the equilibrium condition in (7.31) holds, the value of the firm is unaffected by changes in leverage or dividend policy.

7.3.2 The dividend puzzle

Miller (1988) identified the dividend puzzle by combining corporate and personal taxes in a classical finance model. Under a classical corporate tax, dividends are subject to higher tax than all other forms of corporate income for fully taxable consumers who prefer interest or capital gains. But this creates an obvious dilemma because in practice corporate firms pay a significant proportion of their income as dividends. In a sample of 156 US firms, Sarig (2004) found that on average they distributed approximately 61 per cent of their earnings, with approximately 91 per cent being paid as dividends over the period 1950–1997.[38] The dividend puzzle was isolated earlier in the Miller equilibrium using (7.28), where

$$\begin{array}{ccccc} \text{interest} & & \text{dividends} & & \text{capital gains} \\ (1-t_B^h) & > & (1-t_C)(1-t_B^h) & < & (1-t_C)(1-t_E^h) \quad \forall h. \end{array}$$[39]

The double tax on dividends makes them preferable to interest, which is subject only to personal tax, and capital gains, which are subject to lower personal tax. For that reason, no dividends are paid in the Miller equilibrium.

There have been a number of attempts to resolve the dividend puzzle. Three main explanations are considered here. The first of these is *trading costs*. Firms and shareholders incur transactions costs such as bank fees, mailing charges and stamp duty when dividends are paid. In contrast, firms that repurchase shares to pay capital gains must by law provide information about these transactions, pay broking fees and incur other transactions costs, while shareholders also incur broking fees and other transactions costs when they sell their shares. The trading costs to pay capital gains are typically much larger than the costs of paying dividends, particularly for individual shareholders. According to Barclay and Smith (1988) they are higher for capital gains, but not by enough at the margin to offset the extra tax burden imposed on dividends under a classical corporate tax system.[40]

The second explanation is *share repurchase constraints*. In some countries there are regulations that restrict share repurchases by firms. They were originally adopted to stop firms creating speculative runs to inflate their share prices above fundamentals, but in recent times they have been used explicitly to stop firms from avoiding the higher taxes on dividends. For example, in the United States penalties are imposed on firms that systematically repurchase

Box 7.16 The dividend puzzle

The dividend puzzle is illustrated in the diagram below, where the asset possibility frontier $R_C R_C$ isolates the largest amount of equity firms can supply from their aggregate net cash flows after meeting their obligations to bondholders and paying corporate tax. Since capital gains and dividends are both subject to corporate tax it does not alter the slope of the asset frontier, where both types of equity must pay the same market return for firms to supply them, with $i_D = i_G$. But personal taxes are lower on capital gains for all consumers, so their indifference schedules are steeper than the asset possibility frontier where they require $i_D(1-t_B^h) = (i_G - t_E^h)$ to trade both securities, with $i_D > i_G$. That is why firms only pay capital gains at $\hat{a}_G$. Whenever they pay dividends shareholders are driven onto lower indifference schedules due the extra tax burden imposed on them.

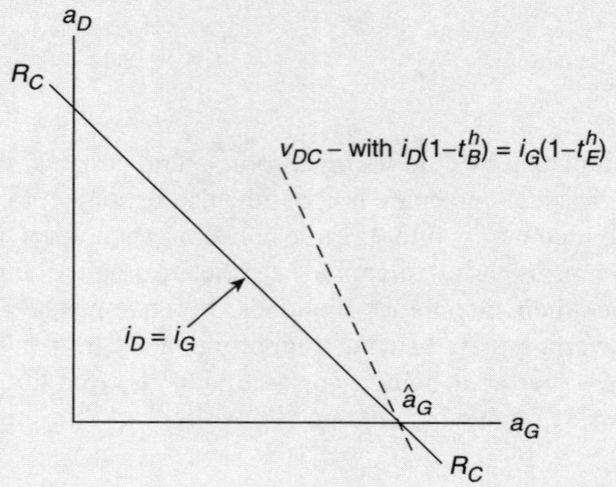

shares to avoid the higher taxes on dividends. Occasional share repurchases are permitted to allow firms to restructure their capital. Auerbach (1979), Bradford (1981) and King (1977) offered the *new or trapped view* of dividends where they argue share repurchase constraints force firms to pay dividends.

Unfortunately, though, this equilibrium outcome has an Achilles' heel because it relies on the important assumption that firms cannot trade each other's shares. Inter-corporate equity is significant in practice, and it provides a substitute for share repurchases. To see this, consider a firm A with \$100 of equity income. If it cannot repurchase \$100 of its own shares to pay capital gains it can buy \$100 of firm B's shares, and firm B then uses the proceeds to buy \$100 of firm A's shares. In the absence of transactions costs or taxes on inter-corporate equity, firm A has replaced \$100 of cash with \$100 of equity in firm B which offsets the value of its own outstanding shares. The market value of firm B is unchanged by these trades because the \$100 liability from selling its own shares is matched by the value of shares it holds in firm A, while shareholders in firm A have 100 dollars of cash that offsets the lower value of equity they now hold in firm A. Thus, the \$100 income generated by firm A has been transferred to its shareholders as capital gains.

Governments are less concerned now than they were in the past about firms trying to inflate their share valuations through share repurchase activity because institutional traders have more information about the identity of buyers and sellers and how much equity they trade. In fact, brokers frequently share this information with each other to stop traders from

Box 7.17 The dividend puzzle and trading costs

The impact of trading costs on the choice between dividends and capital gains is illustrated in the diagram below. For trading costs (T) to make dividends preferable they must be relatively higher for capital gains, where those incurred by consumers make their indifference schedules flatter (v_{DC}^T), and those by firms make the asset production frontier steeper ($R_C R_C^T$). In effect, higher trading costs raise the relative cost of capital gains for firms and reduce their relative return to consumers. In the diagram we simplify the analysis by assuming the trading costs only apply to capital gains, where this rotates the asset production frontier around the intercept $\hat{a}_D$. Dividends trade once the slope of the indifference schedules are the same or flatter than the slope of the asset production frontier. In practice, these relative trading costs do not appear large enough on their own to explain the payment of dividends under a classical corporate tax system.

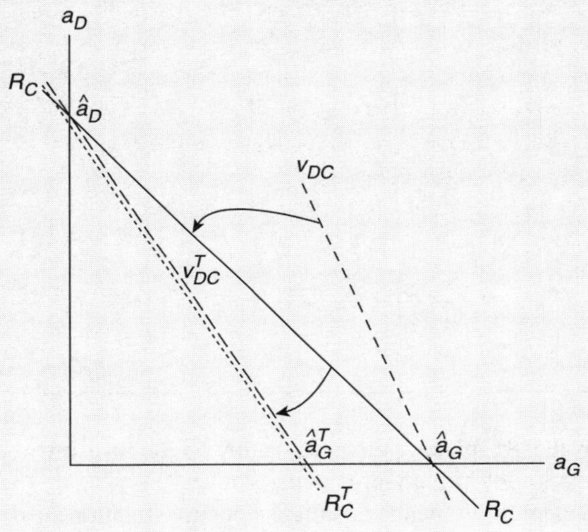

exploiting inside information, thereby making it more difficult for single traders to corner the market by spreading their trades across a number of brokers.

The third explanation is *signalling and agency costs* when there is *asymmetric information*. Bhattacharya (1979) and Miller and Rock (1985) identify circumstances where firm managers use dividend payments to signal the quality of their expected net cash flows to shareholders with incomplete information. Higher taxes on dividends are signalling costs that allow them to function as a credible signal in these circumstances. When dividend payments are optimally chosen these costs are equated at the margin to the benefits shareholders get from the information provided. Using financial data for 156 firms in the US over the period 1950–1997, Sarig (2004) finds empirical support for the *signalling benefits* of dividends, where the benefits from changes in dividends were found to be larger than the benefits from changes in share repurchases, while an increase in profitability leads initially to an increase in share repurchases and then later an increase in dividends once there is confirmation of the profitability being sustained in the long run. Rozeff (1982) and Easterbrook (1984) argue that dividends can be paid to reduce *agency costs* arising from managers consuming perquisites and from *managerial risk aversion*. Since dividend payments reduce free cash flows they limit managerial perquisites. They also force firms to go to the capital

Box 7.18 The dividend puzzle and share repurchase constraints

When there are constraints on the security trades of firms that force them to pay equity income as dividends, consumers are forced onto lower indifference schedules due to the extra tax burden. This outcome is illustrated in the diagram below where consumers are forced to locate at point $\hat{a}_D$ on the lower indifference schedule v_{DC}^D.

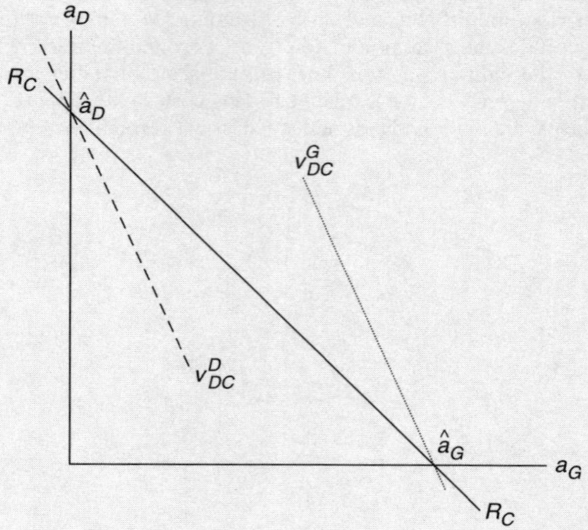

market more frequently for funds thereby placing greater scrutiny on the investment choices of risk-averse managers who underinvest in risky profitable projects.

These explanations for the payment of dividends postulate a positive relationship between dividends and the level of asymmetric information. In contrast, the *pecking order theory* of Myers and Majluf (1984) finds a negative relationship between them. When potential shareholders have less information than existing shareholders about the profitability of new projects they can discount share prices by more than the net present value of the profits. Since this makes existing shareholders worse off they reject these projects so that managers are forced to move down the pecking order and use internal funds and (risk-free) debt. Since lower dividends create a larger pool of internal funds there is a negative relationship between dividends and the level of asymmetric information. Using data for manufacturing firms that traded on the NYSE and the AMEX over the five-year period 1988–1992, Deshmukh (2005) finds empirical support for the pecking order theory over the signalling theory.

7.3.3 Dividend imputation

It is clear from the dividend puzzle examined in the previous section why a classical corporate tax distorts the financing decisions of firms. One way to eliminate the double tax on equity income is to eliminate the corporate tax altogether. But in its absence shareholders have an incentive to delay realizing this income as capital gains so they can lower their effective personal tax rates.[41] In effect, their tax liabilities are delayed at no interest cost. The corporate tax deters this activity by collecting revenue on equity income as it accrues inside firms, but the double taxation is especially problematic for dividends.

Box 7.19 The new view of dividends with inter-corporate equity

A more realistic way for firms to overcome share repurchase constraints is through inter-corporate equity trades undertaken on their behalf by financial intermediaries (F). Their role is illustrated in the diagram below. As specialist security traders their asset production frontier (R_FR_F) passes through the origin, and is linear with the same slope as the asset production frontier for corporate firms in a frictionless competitive capital market. In the presence of share repurchase constraints, firms must distribute their after-tax net cash flows as dividends at point $\hat{a}_D$. But these payouts can be converted into capital gains when financial intermediaries purchase $\hat{a}_G$ shares from corporate shareholders using funds raised by selling $\hat{a}_D$ of their own shares to corporate firms. By choosing bundle a^F the intermediaries distribute equity income of corporate firms to shareholders as capital gains, but without corporate firms buying back their own shares. Instead, corporate firms and financial intermediaries end up holding the same value of each other's shares.

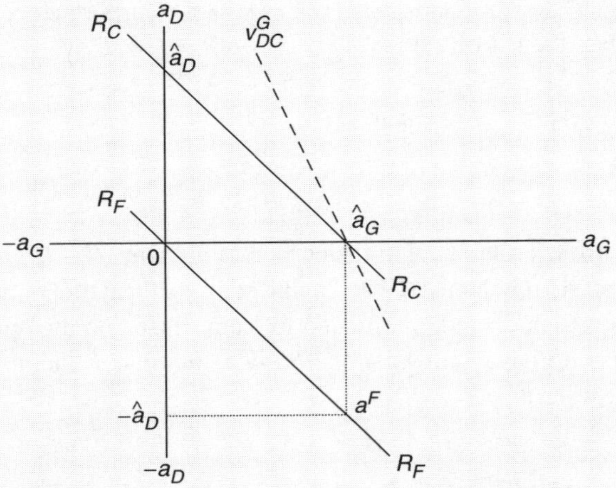

In practice, financial intermediaries incur trading costs that reduce the dividends they can convert into capital gains. These costs cause their asset frontier R_FR_F to kink downwards around the origin. However, as long as they are smaller than the extra tax on dividends paid to shareholders, and smaller than the costs incurred by corporate firms trading each other's shares, financial intermediaries will perform this role in a competitive capital market.

Governments in a number of countries have adopted an imputation tax system to remove the double tax on dividends. Any corporate tax collected on dividend income is credited to shareholders by the tax office. In effect, the corporate tax is used as withholding tax to remove the incentive for firms to delay realizing equity income as capital gains which attract no tax credits. Another important reason for keeping the corporate tax is to collect revenue on domestic income paid to foreign shareholders as personal taxes are normally levied only on the income of domestic residents.

One important aspect of dividend imputation is the distinction it makes between franked (F) and unfranked dividends (U). Franked dividends are paid from income subject to corporate tax, while unfranked dividends are paid from untaxed income. Firms have untaxed income due to differences in their economic and measured income, where economic income is the extra consumption expenditure firms generate for their shareholders. Economic and measured income were compared earlier in Chapter 2, where the main difference arises from the treatment of the changes in the values of capital assets.[42]

Under an imputation tax system optimally chosen security trades by consumers will satisfy[43]

$$\begin{aligned}
&\varphi[1+i_B(1-t_B^h)] \le 1, && \text{for debt,}\\
&\varphi\left[1+\frac{i_F}{1-t_C}(1-t_B^h)\right] \le 1, && \text{for equity paying franked dividends,}\\
&\varphi[1+i_U(1-t_B^h)] \le 1, && \text{for equity paying unfranked dividends,}\\
&\varphi[1+i_G(1-t_E^h) \le 1, && \text{for equity paying capital gains.}
\end{aligned} \tag{7.33}$$

When shareholders receive a franked dividend of $i_F p_F a_F$ they declare its pre-tax value $i_F p_F a_F/(1-t_C)$ as taxable income. They are then granted tax credits for corporate tax paid by firms, where the amount they pay the tax office is

$$\frac{i_F p_F a_F}{1-t_C}(t_B^h - t_C).$$

Shareholders with a marginal cash tax rate equal to the corporate tax rate $(t_B^h = t_C)$ make no additional tax payments, high-tax shareholders $(t_B^h > t_C)$ make additional payments, and low-tax shareholders $(t_B^h < t_C)$ get excess tax credits refunded to them. Based on the optimality conditions in (7.33), consumers will have a *demand condition* which makes them indifferent between the four securities, when

$$i_B(1-t_B^h) = \frac{i_F}{1-t_C}(1-t_B^h) = i_U(1-t_B^h) = i_G(1-t_E^h). \tag{7.34}$$

When firms choose their security trades optimally in this setting they satisfy.[44]

$$\begin{aligned}
&\varphi[1+i_B(1-t_C)] \le 1, && \text{for debt,}\\
&\varphi(1+i_F) \le 1, && \text{for equity paying franked dividends,}\\
&\varphi[1+i_U(1-t_C)] \le 1, && \text{for equity paying unfranked dividends,}\\
&\varphi(1+i_G) \le 1, && \text{for equity paying capital gains.}
\end{aligned} \tag{7.35}$$

Using these conditions we find that the *supply condition* that makes firms indifferent to the four securities is

$$i_B(1-t_C) = i_F = i_U(1-t_C) = i_G. \tag{7.36}$$

Notice how interest and unfranked dividends shield the net cash flows from corporate tax, while franked dividends and capital gains do not. By combining the demand condition in (7.34) with the supply condition in (7.36), we obtain an equilibrium condition

$$\underset{\text{interest}}{(1-t_B^h)} = \underset{\substack{\text{franked}\\ \text{dividends}}}{(1-t_B^h)} = \underset{\substack{\text{unfranked}\\ \text{dividends}}}{(1-t_B^h)} \gtreqless \underset{\substack{\text{capital}\\ \text{gains}}}{(1-t_C)(1-t_E^h)} \quad \forall h. \tag{7.37}$$

While every consumer is indifferent between cash distributions as interest and dividends, some tax preferences remain under the imputation tax system.

i All shareholders prefer to have unfranked income paid as capital gains rather than dividends because they are taxed at lower personal rates. Each dollar paid as capital gains generates consumption expenditure of $1-t_E^h$, while as dividends they generate less consumption expenditure, $1-t_B^h$. Indeed, this confirms the important role played by the corporate tax when firms cannot tax capital gains on accrual.

ii Some high-tax consumers (with $t_B^h > t_C$) can have a tax preference for equity income paid as capital gains even though it is taxed twice. They become equity specialists such as those identified earlier in the Miller equilibrium, with

$$(1-t_B^h) < (1-t_C)(1-t_E^h).$$

While dividend imputation makes debt specialists marginal investors for interest and franked dividends, it has no impact on equity specialists facing the same combination of corporate and personal taxes. Clearly, if capital gains were granted credits for corporate tax every investor would prefer them as they would be subject to lower personal tax rates than cash distributions as dividends and interest. Indeed, that is why investors prefer unfranked income to be paid as capital gains rather than dividends.

Dividend imputation is an ingenious solution to the problems we encounter when taxing capital gains because it collects tax revenue on corporate income as it accrues using the corporate tax. By crediting this revenue back to shareholders on income paid to them as dividends, it removes the double tax on dividends without making capital gains preferable for shareholders with personal tax rates less than or equal to the corporate tax rate. It also acknowledges the untaxed income of corporate firms due to differences in measured and economic income. Benge and Robinson (1986) analyse a number of other important issues not examined here. In particular, they look at transitional effects and the taxation of income paid to foreign shareholders. They also stress the importance of setting the top marginal personal tax rate at or below the corporate tax rate to reduce the incentive for tax arbitrage.

Problems

1 Consider a tax on corporate income (t_C) where the tax base is income after deducting depreciation and interest payments on debt. This is a classical corporate tax base where dividends are subject to tax but interest payments on debt are not. (Assume each firm is a price-taker in the capital market.)

i Determine how the market value of the representative corporate firm is affected by changes in its leverage. Is there an optimal debt–equity mix (i.e., choice of leverage) for the firm?

ii What is economic depreciation and why in practice do measured depreciation allowances differ from economic depreciation allowances?

2 Let $\tilde{X}$ be the random net cash flows of a firm.

i Use the CAPM to derive the firm's market value when it issues risky debt at a cost of $\tilde{i}_B$, and risky equity at a cost of $\tilde{i}_E$. Derive the firm's market value when it issues risk-free debt. Demonstrate that for both types of debt the value of the firm is independent of its financial leverage. Describe the role of the CAPM in project evaluation.

ii Explain why the firm's equity becomes more risky when it issues more risk-free debt. Why then does MM leverage irrelevance hold? Does its equity become more risky when the extra debt is risky?

3 Capel Court is a mining company in the north-west of Australia with a current market value (V) of \$6000 million. This is the summed value of its debt and equity and is computed using the CAPM when the expected net cash flow ($\bar{X}$) in 12 months is \$612m and the risk-free user cost of capital $c_F = 0.10$.

i Calculate the total risk premium Capel Court pays to the capital market when the CAPM holds. Explain how this premium is computed and calculate the covariance between the net cash flow and the return on the market portfolio (i.e., Cov($\tilde{X}$, $\tilde{i}_M$)) when the return on the risk-free asset is $i = 0.06$ and the expected return on the market portfolio is $\tilde{i}_M = 0.14$ with a standard deviation of $\sigma_M = 0.4$.

ii Use the information provided above to obtain the CAPM equation for pricing risky assets. Carefully explain why assets are priced in this way. What is the expected return on a risky asset (k) when it has a correlation coefficient with the return on the market portfolio of $\rho_{km} = 0.6$ and a standard deviation of $\sigma_k = 0.5$?

iii Compute the current market value of the total equity issued by Capel Court when its debt is risk-free and equity is expected to pay a return of $\tilde{i}_E = 0.08$ based on the CAPM equation in part (ii) above. What is Capel Court's debt–equity ratio? Explain how the share price would change with a fall in this debt-equity ratio.

4 Consider two firms with the following information about their cash flows and leverage.

	Firm K	*Firm J*
$\bar{X}$	\$840m	\$950
β_x	\$1600m	\$1000m
b	0.8	0.75

i Use the CAPM to compute the current market value of each firm when $\tilde{i}_M - i = 0.15$ and $c_F = i - \Phi_F = 0.10$. Explain your workings. Find the share of the project risk bondholders bear in each firm when both firms pay a risk premium on debt of 0.01. Calculate the risk premium paid on each dollar of equity for both firms and explain how it is measured by the CAPM. In particular, explain how risk is measured and priced.

ii Now suppose the two firms are merged into a single new firm G which takes over their debt without changing its expected return and converts their equity into its own new shares. If the mean and the variance of the aggregate net cash flows are unchanged by the merger, what share of the project risk will shareholders bear in firm G, and what will the risk premium be on each dollar of its equity? Calculate the expected user cost of capital for firm G and explain what it measures. Is it possible for the value of the firm to rise when the aggregate expected net cash flows fall after the merger? (Assume the CAPM holds.)

iii Explain why the value of these firms is unaffected by their leverage policies when the CAPM holds and then identify circumstances where leverage policy remains irrelevant even though the CAPM fails to hold. What are the important assumptions for MM leverage irrelevance?

5 MM leverage irrelevance totally ignores the fact that as you borrow more, you have to pay higher rates of interest. Do you agree with this statement?

6 Derive an expression for a corporate firm's user cost of capital when there is uncertainty and a classical corporate tax.
  i How does the tax affect the equilibrium expected returns on debt and equity? Can the expected return on equity be higher?
  ii When does the cost of capital depend on leverage in a competitive capital market?
  iii Identify government policies that directly impact the user cost of capital.
  iv In the absence of the corporate tax do bankruptcy costs result in an all-equity equilibrium in the capital market?

7 The Miller equilibrium relies on personal taxes to explain the presence of equity when firms are subject to classical corporate tax.
  i Illustrate this equilibrium in the debt–equity space for a corporate tax of 40 per cent when there are investors in each of the following three personal tax brackets:

Tax brackets	*Marginal cash tax rate (%)*	*Marginal capital gains tax rate (%)*
A	25	15
B	52	20
C	64	30

  (Assume all the tax rates are constant and endowed on consumers. To read the table note that the investor in bracket A has a tax rate on cash distributions of 25 per cent, and a tax rate on capital gains of 15 per cent.) Explain why, in this equilibrium, investors only hold their tax-preferred securities when there is uncertainty. Consider whether tax arbitrage would be possible and identify two ways it can be constrained. What would happen in the absence of such constraints?
  ii Re-do part (i) when there are no investors in the tax bracket B. Consider whether MM leverage irrelevance holds for individual firms in this setting. Identify the conditions that are crucial to this irrelevance result.
  iii Re-do part (i) when the corporate tax rate is 50 per cent. Does MM leverage irrelevance hold for individual firms under these circumstances? Illustrate your answer in the debt–equity space.

8 Taxes on income paid to shareholders and bondholders have important impacts on the user cost of capital for corporate firms.
  i Examine the way changes in financial structure affect the value of corporate firms when there is a 30 per cent classical corporate tax and marginal cash tax rates of 20 per cent for low-tax investors and 50 per cent for-high tax investors. For both groups of investors the marginal tax on capital gains is 50 per cent of their marginal cash tax rate. Compute the after-tax consumption flow to investors from a dollar of income paid as interest, dividends and capital gains, and identify their tax preferences for debt and equity. Consider how the user cost of capital and financial structure are affected when the corporate tax is raised from 30 per cent to 40 per cent. (Assume there is certainty, the capital market is competitive and there are no leverage-related costs.)
  ii How would your answer in part (i) above be changed by the introduction of an imputation tax system that provides tax credits for any corporate tax collected on dividend income?

Identify circumstances where investors will have tax preferences for capital gains over dividends under the imputation tax system.

9 In most countries corporations pay tax on shareholder income. This income is also subject to personal tax when it is realized by shareholders. (Assume there is certainty when answering the following questions.)

i Carefully explain the dividend puzzle by summarizing the after-tax income investors receive on corporate income paid as interest, dividends and capital gains when there are two groups of investors who are separated by their marginal personal tax rates. Within each group investors face the same tax rates; group 1 have a personal cash tax rate of $t_B^1 = 0.5$, while group 2 have a personal cash tax rate of $t_B^2 = 0.3$. Both groups have marginal tax rates on capital gains that are half their respective marginal cash tax rates, and the corporate tax rate is $t_C = 0.3$. Explain why governments tax equity income twice.

ii Derive an expression for the user cost of capital when corporate firms sell debt and equity to the investors in part (i). Consider whether firm leverage decisions will affect their market value in this setting. What is the market rate of return on equity when the interest rate on corporate debt is 10 per cent?

iii Explain how share repurchase constraints are used to solve the dividend puzzle. Demonstrate the way inter-corporate equity undermines this explanation.

iv Derive the after-tax income in part (i) when corporate tax is credited back to shareholders against their personal tax liabilities on dividends. How will this affect the relationship between the market rates of return to debt and equity?

10 Consider an economy where half the investors have a marginal personal tax rate on cash distributions of $t_B^L = 0.25$, while the other half have a cash tax rate of $t_B^H = 0.75$. (When answering the following questions assume there is certainty, no transactions costs and the capital market is competitive.)

i Find the personal tax rates on capital gains that would make each group of investors indifferent between debt and equity when there is a classical corporate tax rate of $t_C = 0.25$. (Assume there is certainty and no transactions costs, all investors pay income taxes and all investment is undertaken by corporate firms.) Now suppose both groups of investors have a marginal personal tax rate on capital gains of $t_G = 0.15$. Identify any investor tax preferences for the way firms distribute their income in the presence of these taxes and explain what this means for the aggregate debt–equity ratio in the economy. Consider whether changes in leverage by individual firms will affect their market valuations under these circumstances.

ii Examine the way investor tax preferences are affected by abolishing the corporate tax in part (i) above, and then explain why the Australian government adopted the imputation tax system instead. Identify circumstances where investors have tax preferences for the way corporate firms distribute income under the imputation tax system.

11 When equity income is double-taxed under a classical corporate tax system there is a tax bias against equity in favour of debt. The Australian government took steps to remove this bias by introducing dividend imputation; companies pay corporate tax on their income, and it is credited to shareholders as an offset to any personal tax they are liable to pay on dividends. When the company pays dividends (i_D), shareholders gross them up by any corporate tax paid ($i_D/(1-t_C)$) and this is used to determine their personal tax liability. The after-tax return to shareholders on a dollar of fully franked dividends is

$$\frac{i_D}{1-t_C}(1-t_P^i),$$

where t_P^i is the marginal personal tax rate which rises in steps with income. If personal tax payable under this calculation is equal to the corporate tax already paid, shareholders pay no personal tax on dividend income; it is subject just to corporate tax. (Assume initially that no capital gains are paid by firms to consumers, that is, all equity income is paid as cash dividends.)

i Compute the tax payable (or tax credit received) by shareholders on fully franked dividends.

ii Derive the demand and supply relationships between equilibrium security returns when consumers can utilize all their corporate tax credits. Are there any tax clienteles like those identified in the Miller equilibrium? (Assume there is certainty.)

iii Can you identify any tax clienteles like those identified in the Miller equilibrium when there are some shareholders who cannot utilize all their corporate tax credits (when $t_P^i < t_C$)? (Assume there is certainty.)

iv Why is there a distinction between franked and unfranked dividends? (Franked dividends are paid from income which has been taxed at the corporate tax rate, while unfranked dividends are paid from income which has not been taxed at the corporate rate.)

v Explain how the inclusion of capital gains affects your answer in (iii) above when they are subject to personal tax on realization rather than accrual.

vi Can you provide reasons why the Australian government chose dividend imputation rather than to abolish the payment of the corporate tax altogether?

12 In the Miller equilibrium under certainty, firm capital structure choice is irrelevant because there are marginal investors who are willing to hold debt and equity. All other investors form clienteles holding just one of the securities determined by their tax preferences. Explain how the Miller equilibrium obtains with uncertainty where consumers have tax and risk preferences for corporate securities. Why in practice do consumers hold bundles of debt and equity when they have a tax preference for one of them? Does this mean that MM leverage irrelevance fails?

13 i Examine the Miller equilibrium in a certainty setting, and explain why MM leverage irrelevance holds. Extend the model to uncertainty with no marginal investors to provide a critical evaluation of the statement by Edwards. Carefully explain how risk and tax preferences are satisfied in the Miller equilibrium when investors divide into strict tax clienteles.

ii Consider the effects on the Miller equilibrium of an imputation tax system where shareholders receive tax credits for corporate tax collected on income distributed as dividends. Derive the equilibrium relationship between the market rates of return on debt and equity, and illustrate this in the aggregate debt–equity space. Explain the equilibrium outcome in a series of steps by starting with no taxes, and then introduce the corporate tax followed by the personal taxes. Identify investor tax preferences for securities when there are high-tax investors and no tax credits received on income paid as capital gains.

14 The following quotation taken from Edwards' (1989, p. 162) is a summary of the finance literature on corporate leverage decisions:

> Auerbach and King (1983) show that the Miller equilibrium requires the existence of certain constraints on investors: without such constraints (on, for example,

> borrowing and short-selling) questions arise concerning the existence of an equilibrium, for with perfect capital markets realistic tax systems provide opportunities for unlimited arbitrage at government expense between investors and firms in different tax positions. Auerbach and King also show that the combined effect of taxation and risk is to produce a situation in which gearing is relevant. With individual investors facing different tax rates and wishing to hold diversified portfolios the Miller equilibrium can no longer be sustained: investors who on tax grounds alone would hold only equity may nevertheless hold some debt because an equity-only portfolio would be too risky.

Carefully evaluate this statement. In particular, assess the proposition that the Miller equilibrium cannot be sustained in the presence of risk when investors have tax preferences for debt and equity. Explain why investors will hold only their tax-preferred securities in this setting when the capital market is not double-complete. Why are short-selling constraints used in the Miller equilibrium? Examine the impact of leverage on firm values when there are no marginal investors.

8 Project evaluation and the social discount rate

In competitive economies without taxes and other market distortions, private and public sector projects are evaluated in the same way (when distributional effects are not taken into account). That is, their future net cash flows are discounted using the same marginal opportunity cost of time and risk. In reality, however, a number of market distortions and distributional effects drive wedges between social marginal valuations and costs where different rules are used to evaluate private and public projects. Taxes and subsidies are the most familiar distortions, but others include externalities, non-competitive behaviour and the private underprovision of public goods. In this chapter we evaluate public projects where the government provides a pure public good in a tax-distorted economy with aggregate uncertainty. The analysis is initially undertaken in a two-period setting with frictionless competitive markets where consumers have common information and trade in a complete capital market.

This chapter consists of two sections: the first isolates conditions for the *optimal provision of a pure public good* in each time period, while the second derives the *social discount rate* for public projects in the presence of tax distortions. To make the analysis less complicated we assume the public goods are only supplied by the government, which maximizes social welfare.[1] One can think of the public good as national defence which, by law, cannot be supplied by private traders in most countries. Initially we obtain Samuelson conditions for the optimal provision of the public goods (G_t) in each time period ($t = 0,1$) without taxes and other distortions. This familiar condition equates the current value of the summed marginal consumption benefits from a public good (MRS_{G_t}) to the current value of its marginal production cost (MRT_t). When the consumption benefits and resource costs from providing the public good in the second period are risky they are discounted using a stochastic discount factor which is the same for all consumers and firms.

In the presence of taxes on market trades the optimality conditions for public goods change whenever resources are reallocated in distorted markets. We derive the Samuelson conditions when the government raises revenue with lump-sum taxes, but in the presence of distorting trade taxes. There are additional welfare effects when the projects impact on activity in tax-distorted markets. They can raise or lower welfare, and are not taken into account by the private sector when evaluating projects. The analysis is then extended by deriving revised Samuelson conditions when the government raises revenue with the distorting trade taxes. Their marginal excess burden increases the marginal social cost of public funds and reduces the optimal supply of the public goods. In an intertemporal setting projects in one period can affect economic activity in both periods, where additional welfare effects from changes in taxed activities affect the optimal supply of the public goods.

In Section 8.2 we derive the social discount rate in the presence of a tax on capital income. This measures the extra future consumption expenditure generated by saving another dollar of capital in the first period. Since the income tax distorts intertemporal consumption choices the private discount rate deviates from the social discount rate. To make the analysis less complex, and to focus on a number of key issues, we assume the tax rate is the same for all consumers and applies to all capital income. In practice, consumers have different marginal tax rates, and taxes differ across capital assets. For example, consumers in most countries face progressive marginal personal tax rates on income, with higher tax rates on cash distributions, such as dividends and interest, than on capital gains. Moreover, equity income is double-taxed under a classical corporate tax system, once at the corporate rate and then again at the personal tax rates of shareholders. While these are important aspects of taxes in most countries, a much simpler tax system is adopted here to focus on the way income taxes in general impact on the social discount rate. This allows us to anticipate how the social discount rate will change under more realistic tax systems.

There has been considerable controversy over what discount rate to use when evaluating public projects in the presence of income taxes and risk. In a two-period certainty setting, Harberger (1969) and Sandmo and Drèze (1971) find the social discount rate is a weighted average of the borrowing and lending rates of interest in the presence of a uniform income tax. By including additional time periods, Marglin (1963a,1963b) finds it should be higher than the weighted average formula, while Bradford (1975) finds it should be approximately equal to the after-tax interest rate paid to savers. Sjaastad and Wisecarver (1977) show how these differences are explained by the treatment of capital depreciation. In a common information setting where private saving rises to replace depreciation of public capital the discount rate becomes the *weighted average formula* in a multi-period setting. Marglin assumes there is no adjustment in private saving so that depreciation allowances are consumed, while Bradford adopts a Keynesian consumption function which makes saving a constant fraction of aggregate income, thereby precluding endogenous changes in private saving to offset depreciation in public capital. Since optimizing agents make consumption choices in each time period based on their wealth, a Keynesian consumption function seems unsuitable. Private wealth depends on the expected benefits generated by publicly provided goods and services and the taxes levied to fund them. However, it seems unlikely in practice that consumers correctly compute the expected depreciation on every item of public capital, where the discount rate will exceed the weighted average formula.

Samuelson (1964), Vickery (1964) and Arrow and Lind (1970) argue the social discount rate should be lower on public sector projects because the government can raise funds at lower risk. They claim the public sector can eliminate diversifiable risk and spread aggregate uncertainty at lower cost than the private sector. Bailey and Jensen (1972) argue these claims are implicitly based on distortions in private risk markets which the public sector can overcome more effectively. They contend, however, that the reverse is much more likely in practice. That is, private markets are likely to provide the same or better opportunities for trading risk, and at lower cost, as private traders are specialists facing better incentives than the public sector.

The analysis commences in Section 8.1 using a two-period model of a tax-distorted economy with aggregate uncertainty. A conventional welfare equation is obtained for changes in the provision of the pure public goods and distorting trade taxes in each time period. The Samuelson conditions for these goods are obtained under different funding arrangements to examine the role of tax distortions and risk on optimal policy choices. The model is extended in Section 8.2 by including a tax on capital income. It is used to derive the weighted average formula for the social discount rate before using the analysis in Bailey and Jensen to reconcile the different discount rates obtained by Marglin and Bradford. Finally, we summarize the claims made by Samuelson, Vickery, and Arrow and Lind that the social discount rate should be lower when projects are risky.

8.1 Project evaluation

To illustrate the impact of time and risk on project evaluation we simplify the two-period Arrow–Debreu model examined in Chapter 3 by adopting a single private good (x) and introducing a pure public good (G).[2] In previous chapters tax revenue was returned to consumers as lump-sum transfers, but now we introduce a government budget constraint to accommodate public spending. The analysis is undertaken in a competitive equilibrium where consumers with common information maximize time-separable expected utility functions by trading in a complete capital market. In this setting the problem for each consumer is to

$$\max\left\{ EU^h(x^h,G) \left| \begin{matrix} (p_0-t_0)x_0^h \le (p_0-t_0)\bar{x}_0^h - p_0 z_0^h + L_0^h \\ (p_s+t_1)x_s^h \le (p_0+t_1)\bar{x}_s^h + p_s y_s^h + L_s^h \ \forall s\in S \end{matrix} \right. \right\},^{3} \tag{8.1}$$

with $EU^h(x^h,G) = U^h(x_0^h,G_0) + \delta\, E[U^h(x_s^h,G_s)]$ and $x_t^h := \{x_0^h, x_1^h, x_2^h, \ldots, x_S^h\}$. Scarcity in the economy is defined by endowments of the private good in each period, $\bar{x}_0^h$ and $\bar{x}_S^h\ \forall s$, where the second-period endowments are state-contingent. Output in the second period is also state-contingent, and the good trades in competitive markets in both periods at equilibrium prices p_0 and p_s for all s, respectively. All consumers are net suppliers in the first period, with $\bar{x}_0^h - x_0^h > 0$ for all h, where the market value of their saving ($p_0 z_0^h > 0$ for all h) is invested in private firms who make state-contingent payouts of $p_s y_s^h$ in the second period. There are taxes on market trades, where net supplies in the first period are subject to specific tax t_0 and net demands in the second period (with $(\bar{x}_s^h - x_s^h) > 0$ for all h) are subject to specific tax t_1.[4] Supply of the public good in both periods is exogenously determined by the government and is constant across states of nature.

Finally, the government makes lump-sum transfers to consumers in each period of L_0^h and L_s^h for all s, respectively. They are used in a conventional Harberger (1971) cost–benefit analysis to separate the welfare effects of marginal changes in each policy variable. For example, when the government increases the supply of a public good, and funds it using a distorting tax, we separate the welfare effects of each component of the project by making lump-sum transfers to balance the government budget. The welfare effects from extra output of the public good are separated from the welfare effects from marginally raising the tax to fund its production cost, where the transfers allow them each to be computed with a balanced government budget.[5] The final change in the distorting tax is determined by combining these separate components inside the project, where the tax change balances the government budget and offsets the hypothetical lump-sum transfers used to separate the welfare changes.[6]

If we write the state-contingent payouts to saving as $p_s y_s^h = (1 + i_s)p_0 z_0^h$, and use the first-order condition in the consumer problem in (8.1) for optimally chosen saving, we obtain state-contingent discount factors of

$$m_s = \delta \frac{\lambda_s^h}{\lambda_0^h} = \frac{1}{1+i_s}\ \forall s, \tag{8.2}$$

where λ_0^h and λ_s^h are Lagrange multipliers on the budget constraints in (8.1), and δ the measure of impatience, with $0 < \delta \leq 1$. In a complete capital market consumers and firms use the same discount factors, where optimally chosen investment satisfies

$$\frac{p_s}{1+i_s}\frac{\partial y_s^j}{\partial z_0^j} = p_0 \ \forall s. \tag{8.3}$$

Resource flows through the public sector are summarized by the government budget constraints in each time period, where:

$$\begin{aligned} T_0 &\equiv t_0(\bar{x}_0 - x_0) = MRT_0 G_0 + L_0, \\ T_s &\equiv t_1(x_s - \bar{x}_s) = MRT_s G_1 + L_s, \ \forall s, \end{aligned} \tag{8.4}$$

with endowments and consumption of the private good and the lump-sum transfers aggregated over consumers.[7] We assume that the marginal cost to government revenue of producing each public good is constant, with $MRT_0 = p_0$ and $MRT_s = p_s$ for all s.[8] Thus, there is risk in the cost of producing the public good in the second period.

In a competitive equilibrium the government balances its budget and producer prices adjust endogenously to equate demand and supply for the private good in each time period and in each state, where the respective market-clearing conditions are $\bar{x}_0 = x_0 + z_0 + G_0$ and $\bar{x}_s + y_s = x_s + G_1$ for all s. These equilibrium prices also equate aggregate saving and aggregate investment, with $\bar{x}_0 - x_0 - G_0 = z_0$.

8.1.1 A conventional welfare equation

In the following analysis projects are evaluated as combinations of marginal changes in the exogenous policy variables G_0, G_1, t_0 and t_1.[9] Their impact on individual consumers is obtained by totally differentiating the constrained optimization problem in (8.1) at an interior solution and using the stochastic discount factors in (8.2), where the dollar change in expected utility is[10]

$$\begin{aligned} \frac{dEU^h}{\lambda_0^h} &= (\bar{x}_0^h - x_0^h)dq_0 - z_0^h dp_0 + MRS_0^h dG_0 + dL_0^h \\ &\quad + \sum_s \pi_s m_s \{-(x_s^h - \bar{x}_s^h)dq_s + y_s^h dp_s + MRS_s^h dG_1 + dL_s^h\}, \end{aligned} \tag{8.5}$$

with $dq_0 = dp_0 - dt_0$ and $dq_s = dp_s + dt_1$ being changes in the consumer prices of the private good, and $MRS_0^h \equiv (\partial U^h/\partial G_0)/\lambda_s^h$ and $MRS_s^h \equiv (\partial U^h/\partial G_1)/\lambda_s^h$ the consumption benefits from marginal increases in the public good.

Despite its apparent complexity, the terms in (8.5) are familiar changes in private surplus. Higher consumer prices make consumers better off in the first period when they are net sellers of the private good, with $(\bar{x}_0^h - x_0^h)dq_0 > 0$, and worse off in the second period when they are net consumers, with $-(x_s^h - \bar{x}_s^h)dq_s < 0$. Endogenous changes in producer prices affect consumers by impacting on their share of profits in private firms, where higher prices make them worse off in the first period by raising the input cost, with $-z_0^h dp_0 < 0$, and better off in the second period by increasing sales revenue, with $y_s^h dp_s > 0$ for all s. Extra output of the public goods endow consumption benefits on consumers, with $MRS_0^h dG_0 > 0$ and $MRS_s^h dG_1 > 0$ for all s, while lump-sum transfers raise private surplus directly by increasing their money income, with $dL_0^h > 0$ and $dL_s^h > 0$ for all s. Most of these changes in private surplus are transfers between consumers and producers, and between the private and public sectors of the economy, where, in the absence of distributional effects, they have no impact on aggregate welfare. Thus, once we aggregate the welfare changes in (8.5) over consumers and use the government budget constraints in (8.4) to solve the revenue transfers, the final welfare changes are determined by changes in final consumption. And that makes sense because consumers ultimately derive utility from consuming goods. There are additional welfare changes when the transfers of private surplus have distributional effects.

At this point we must decide how to aggregate the welfare changes in (8.5) using a social welfare function. A large literature looks at deriving them as functions of non-comparable ordinal utility functions assigned to consumers. Since they do not contain enough information to allow interpersonal comparisons, we follow the conventional approach and use a Bergson–Samuelson *individualistic social welfare function*.[11] This is a mapping over fully comparable cardinal utility functions when consumers derive utility from their own (individual) consumption bundle, with $W(EU^1, EU^2, \ldots, EU^H)$, where the aggregate welfare change solves

$$dW = \sum_h \beta^h \frac{dEU^h}{\lambda_0^h}, \tag{8.6}$$

with $\beta^h = (\partial W / \partial EU^h)\lambda_0^h$ being the *distributional weight*; this is the change in social welfare from marginally raising the income of each consumer h.[12] In a *conventional Harberger analysis* consumers are assigned the same welfare weights on the grounds that aggregate dollar gains in expected utility can be converted into Pareto improvements through a lump-sum redistribution of income. For most policy changes there are winners and losers, but aggregate gains can be converted into Pareto improvements by transferring income from winners to compensate losers.[13] Thus, they represent potential Pareto improvements.

A *conventional welfare equation* is obtained by assigning the same distributional weights to consumers in (8.6), with $\beta^h = 1$ for all h, and using the market-clearing conditions for the private good in each time period, the dollar changes in expected utility in (8.5), and the government budget constraints in (8.4), to write the aggregate welfare change as

$$\begin{aligned} dW &= (MRS_0 - MRT_0)dG_0 - t_0 dx_0 \\ &\quad + \textstyle\sum_s \pi_s m_s \{(MRS_s - MRT_s)dG_1 + t_1 dx_s\}.^{14} \end{aligned} \tag{8.7}$$

All the policy changes examined in following sections will be solved using this welfare equation. Direct welfare changes from marginal increases in the public goods are isolated by the net benefits in the first and third terms, where consumers have consumption benefits (*MRS*) endowed on them less the reductions in private surplus when the government balances its budget to fund the production costs (*MRT*). Net benefits in the second period are discounted to cover the opportunity cost of time and risk. The remaining terms in (8.7) capture welfare effects from endogenous changes in tax-distorted activities. Whenever policy changes expand taxed activities the extra tax revenue isolates welfare gains from undoing the excess burden of taxation. For example, the welfare change from marginally raising trade tax t_0 is

$$\frac{\partial W}{\partial t_o} = -t_0 \frac{\partial x_0}{\partial t_0} + \sum_s \pi_s m_s t_1 \frac{\partial x_s}{\partial t_0}, \tag{8.8}$$

where the first term is the conventional measure of the marginal welfare cost of taxation illustrated as the cross-lined rectangle A in the left-hand panel of Figure 8.1. It isolates the increase in the familiar deadweight loss triangle when the net supply of the private good falls in the first period. If current and future consumption of the private good are gross complements then the tax change also increases future demand, where the extra tax revenue is the welfare gain illustrated as the cross-lined rectangle B in the right-hand panel of Figure 8.1.[15] It is a related market effect from the tax change, where the final welfare change is $A - B$. If the extra revenue in B exceeds the welfare loss in A, the tax change actually raises welfare.

8.1.2 Optimal provision of pure public goods

Now we are ready to find the optimality conditions for the provision of the public goods. The original Samuelson condition was derived in an economy free of any distortions where the summed marginal consumption benefits from the last unit of the public good supplied is equated to its marginal production cost, with *MRS* = *MRT*. We extend the analysis to an economy with tax distortions, and then obtain a revised Samuelson condition when the government raises its revenue using them. One obvious extension is to include time and risk in the analysis.

The Samuelson condition in an economy without distortions

The original Samuelson condition is obtained by evaluating a public project that marginally increases the supply of a public good in an economy without market distortions, where at a social optimum the net welfare change is zero. For the public goods supplied

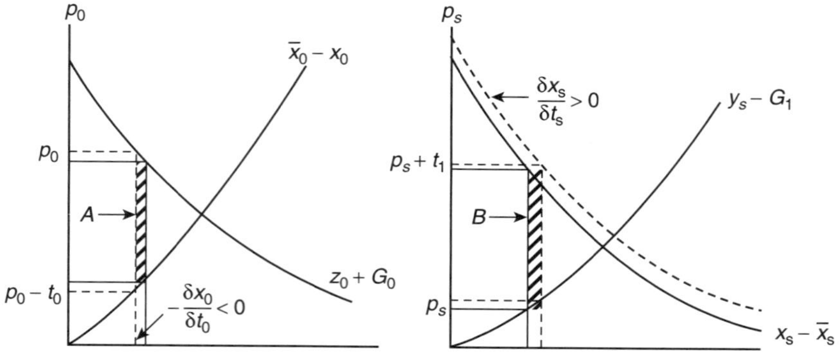

Figure 8.1 Welfare effects from marginally raising the trade tax in the first period.

in each time period we use the conventional welfare equation in (8.7), with $t_0 = t_1 = 0$, where we have

$$\frac{dW}{dG_0} = MRS_0 - MRT_0 = 0,$$
$$\frac{dW}{dG_1} = \Sigma_s\, \pi_s m_s (MRS_s - MRT_s) = 0. \tag{8.9}$$

Thus, in an economy free of any distortions and distributional effects, the Samuelson conditions, are:

$$MRS_0 = MRT_0,$$
$$\Sigma_s\, \pi_s m_s MRS_s = \Sigma_s\, \pi_s m_s MRT_s \tag{8.10}$$

The first of these is the original Samuelson condition which was obtained in a single period certainty setting, while the second one extends it to an intertemporal setting with uncertainty. In the absence of risk, the second condition also collapses to the original condition, with $m_s = \delta = 1/(1 + i)$ for all s and $MRS_1/(1 + i) = MRT_1/(1 + i)$, where i is the risk-free interest rate, so that $MRS_1 = MRT_1$. The same thing happens when consumers are risk-neutral, although the Samuelson condition is state-contingent, with $m_s = \delta = 1/(1 + i)$ for all s and $MRS_s/(1 + i) = MRT_s/(1 + i)$ for all s, where $MRS_s = MRT_s$ for all s. Risk plays no role in the analysis if the summed consumption benefits and marginal production costs are perfectly positively correlated as they are discounted using the same discount rate. When they are less than perfectly correlated the expected consumption benefits can deviate from the expected marginal production cost in each state, with $\Sigma_s\pi_s MRS_s \neq \Sigma_s\pi_s MRT_s$, due to differences in the risk premium in their different discount factors. If the consumption benefits are more risky, we must have $\Sigma_s\pi_s MRS_s > \Sigma_s\pi_s MRT_s$ to compensate consumers for the extra risk, while the reverse applies when the production costs are more risky.

In practice, many public goods are capital projects where governments incur production costs that generate consumption in later periods. Thus, each dollar of benefits has a lower current value than the costs due to the opportunity cost of time (and risk). If the production costs are incurred in the first period the optimal provision of the public good in the second period satisfies $\Sigma_s\pi_s m_s MRS_s = MRT_0$, where expected benefits must exceed expected costs (even in the absence of risk), with $\Sigma_s\pi_s MRS_s > MRT_0$, to compensate consumers for the opportunity cost of time.

The Samuelson condition in a tax-distorted economy

Welfare effects of public projects are rarely confined to markets where they have direct effects. For the public good projects being considered here there are direct consumption benefits for consumers and production costs which impact directly on the government budget. But this changes the real income of consumers and affects their demands for other goods and services. When these related markets are subject to taxes and other distortions there are additional welfare effects that can affect the optimal supplies of the public goods.

Box 8.1 An equilibrium outcome in the public good economy

Numerical solutions are derived here for equilibrium outcomes in a *public good economy* with a single aggregated consumer in a two-period certainty setting. When the consumer can trade a risk-free security in a frictionless competitive capital market the optimization problem is summarized as

$$\max\left\{U = \ln x_0 + \ln G_0 + \delta \ln x_1 + \delta \ln G_1 \left| \begin{array}{l} q_0x_0 + \delta q_1 x_1 \le q_0\bar{x}_0 + L \\ L = T - p_0G_0 - \delta p_1 G_1 - R \\ T = t_0(\bar{x}_0 - x_0) + \delta t_1 x_1 \end{array} \right.\right\},$$

where $q_0 = p_0 - t_0$ and $q_1 = p_1 + t_1$ are consumer prices of the private good in each respective time period, $\delta = 1/(1+i)$ the rate of time preference and T the present value of tax revenue collected by the government. Notice there is no endowment of the private good in the second period here, where some of the current endowment of $\bar{x}_0 = 500$ is allocated to future consumption expenditure by trading the risk-free security at market interest rate $i = 0.03$. Thus, saving in the economy is equal to $z_0 = \bar{x}_0 - x_0 - G_0 - R$. To simplify the analysis we adopt a linear production possibility frontier to hold producer prices constant at the constant marginal cost of production in each period. Since the private good can be stored and transferred to the second period at no cost, its producer price is higher by the interest rate, with $p_0 = 1$ and $p_1 = p_0(1 + i) = 1.03$. With log utility the ordinary (Marshallian) demands for the private good in each period are

$$x_0^M = \frac{I(1+i)}{(2+i)(p_0 - t_0)} \text{ and } x_1^M = \frac{I(1+i)}{(2+i)(p_1 + t_1)}$$

The general equilibrium (Bailey) demand schedules are obtained by substituting aggregate income, $I = (p_0 - t_0)\bar{x}_0 + T - p_0G_0 - \delta p_1 G_1$, into these ordinary demand schedules. Thus, even in circumstances where consumer prices are unaffected by policy changes, income effects will flow through the government budget constraint. For example, extra output of public goods funded by lump-sum taxation will impact directly on the government budget constraint through the increased production costs, and indirectly through endogenous changes in taxed activities.

First-best solution: When the government uses lump-sum taxation to fund its spending the equilibrium allocation is summarized as follows:

Trade taxes (%)		*Public goods*		*Bailey demands*	
t_0	t_1	G_0	G_1	x_0	x_1
0	0	127	123	127	123

This gives the consumer the largest possible utility of $\hat{u} = 19.0324$ from the initial endowment of the private good. Any other policy choices will lower utility. It may be possible to raise aggregate welfare in an economy with heterogenous consumers by redistributing income between them when they have different distributional weights in the social welfare function.

Once we introduce distorting trade taxes, the welfare effects for the two projects at a social optimum are obtained using the conventional welfare equation in (8.7) as

$$\begin{aligned} \frac{dW}{dG_0} &= MRS_0 - MRT_0 + \frac{dT}{dG_0} = 0, \\ \frac{dW}{dG_1} &= \sum_s \pi_s m_s (MRS_s - MRT_s) + \frac{dT}{dG_1} = 0, \end{aligned} \tag{8.11}$$

where dT/dG_0 and dT/dG_1 are the present value of endogenous changes in tax revenue.[16] These related market effects were initially identified by Diamond and Mirrlees (1971) and Stiglitz and Dasgupta (1971). Atkinson and Stern (1974) named them spending effects, which Ballard and Fullerton (1992) and Kaplow (1996) argue can reduce the marginal cost of supplying public goods thereby raising the optimal level of government spending. This is confirmed by the Samuelson conditions obtained from (8.11), where

$$MRS_0 = MRT_0 - \frac{dT}{dG_0},$$
$$\sum_s \pi_s m_s MRS_s = \sum_s \pi_s m_s MRT_s - \frac{dT}{dG_1}. \tag{8.12}$$

When each project raises additional tax revenue by expanding taxed activities, with $dT_0/dG_0 > 0$ and $dT/dG_1 > 0$, the spending effects reduce the size of the government budget deficit, where, at a social optimum, we have $MRS_0 < MRT_0$ and $\Sigma_s \pi_s m_s MRS_s < \Sigma_s \pi_s m_s MRT_s$, respectively. With diminishing marginal valuations the optimal supplies of the public goods are larger in these circumstances.[17]

The first optimality condition in (8.12) is illustrated in Figure 8.2, where it is assumed that the project expands taxed activities in both time periods and in each state, with

$$\underbrace{MRS_0}_{C} = \underbrace{MRT_0}_{D-PV(E)} - \underbrace{\frac{dT}{dG}}_{A+PV(B)}.$$ [18]

The summed marginal consumption benefits are the cross-lined area C (with $MRS_0 = C$), while the production cost is the present value ($PV(\cdot)$) of the reduction in consumption of the private good isolated by the shaded rectangles, with $MRT_0 = D - PV(E)$. In the presence of the trade taxes there is a positive spending effect isolated in the cross-lined rectangles as $dT/dG_0 = A + PV(B)$; it is the welfare gain from expanding taxed activities.

It is possible to illustrate the spending optimality condition in (8.12) using the same diagrams, but as the analysis is similar it will not be repeated here. The main difference arises from the need to discount the consumption benefits and production costs for the opportunity cost of time and risk.

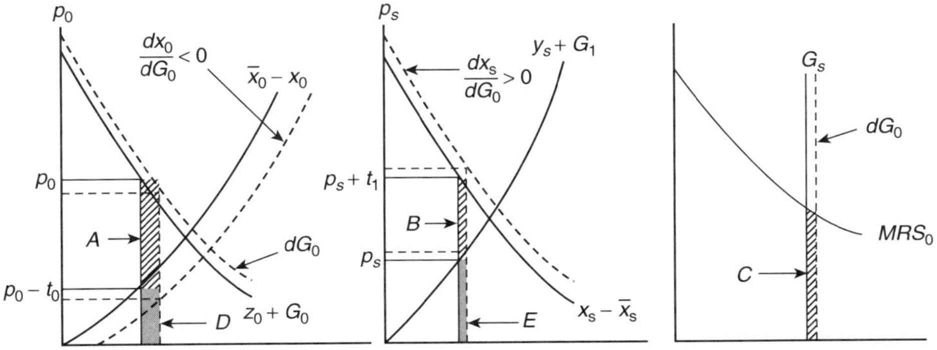

Figure 8.2 The Samuelson condition in the first period.

Box 8.2 Estimates of the shadow profits from public good production

We introduce trade taxes into the two-period certainty economy in Box 8.1 and evaluate the following equilibrium allocation that generates utility of $\hat{u} = 18.6936$.

Trade taxes (%)		*Public goods*		*Bailey demands*	
t_0	t_1	G_0	G_1	x_0*	x_1*
20	10	85	70	202	143

Aggregate utility can be raised whenever the shadow profit from marginally increasing each public good is positive. When extra output is funded using lump-sum taxation, we have

$$\pi_0 = \Sigma\, MRS_0 - p_0 + \frac{dT}{dG_0} \approx \$0.98,$$

$$\pi_1 = \delta\, \Sigma\, MRS_1 - \delta p_1 + \frac{dT}{dG_1} \approx \$1.32.$$

We obtain π_0 by first computing the dollar value of the (summed) marginal utility it generates:

$$\Sigma MRS_0 = 1/(\lambda G_0) = 1/(0.00618149 \times 85) \approx \$1.90,$$

where $1/G_0$ is the marginal utility from extra output of the good and $1/\lambda = 0.00618149 \approx \$161.77$ is the dollar value of a marginal increase in utility. Even though prices are unaffected by the project there are income effects that impact on the demands for private goods, where the endogenous change in tax revenue solves

$$\frac{dT}{dG_0} = -t_0 \frac{\partial x_0(q_0, q_1, I)}{\partial I} \frac{dI}{dG_0} + t_1 \frac{\partial x_1(q_0, q_1, I)}{\partial I} \frac{dI}{dG_0},$$

with the change in aggregate income being

$$\frac{dI}{dG_0} = \frac{dT}{dG_0} - p_0.$$

Notice how the income effect feeds through the ordinary demand functions where the consumer chooses private goods facing given prices and money income. After substituting the change in aggregate income, we have

$$\frac{dT}{dG_0} = \frac{-\theta\, p_0}{1 - \theta} \approx \$0.08,$$

with

$$\theta = -t_0 \frac{\partial x_0(\cdot)}{\partial I} + t_1 \frac{\partial x_1(\cdot)}{\partial I} \approx -0.0820645.$$

Thus, the shadow profit above is decomposed as

$$\pi_0 = \Sigma MRS_0 - p_0 + \frac{dT}{dG_0} \approx \$0.98.$$
$$(1.9) - (1) + (0.08)$$

There are similar workings for calculating the shadow profit of G_1. In total, both projects raise utility by approximately \$2.30. In a more general analysis with a non-linear aggregate production frontier, the equilibrium price changes are solved using the market-clearing conditions for each good. For an example of the calculations, see Jones (2005).

The revised Samuelson condition in a tax-distorted economy

Governments rarely, if ever, raise revenue with non-distorting taxes. Indeed, it is difficult to find taxes on activity that are non-distorting as few goods are fixed in supply, especially in the long run when resources can be moved between most activities. Poll taxes are perhaps the closest thing to non-distorting taxes but they are politically unpopular. Pigou (1947) recognized that governments raised most of their revenue using distorting taxes with excess burdens that reduce the optimal level of government spending by raising the marginal social cost of public funds. We can confirm this reasoning by using the conventional welfare equation in (8.7) to compute the welfare effects for the two public good projects when they are funded with revenue raised with distorting trade taxes, as

$$\begin{aligned} \left(\frac{dW}{dG_0}\right)_{t_0} &= MRS_0 - MCF_0\left(MRT_0 + \frac{dT}{dG_1}\right) = 0, \\ \left(\frac{dW}{dG_1}\right)_{t_1} &= \sum_s \pi_s m_s (MRS_s - MCF_1\, MRT_s) + MCF_1 \frac{dT}{dG_1} = 0, \end{aligned} \tag{8.13}$$

where the *marginal social cost of public funds* (MCF) for each tax measures the current value of the direct cost to private surplus from transferring a dollar of revenue to the government budget, with

$$\begin{aligned} MCF_0 &= (\bar{x}_0 - x_0)\Big/\frac{dT}{dt_0}, \\ MCF_1 &= \sum_s \pi_s m_s (\bar{x}_s - x_s)\Big/\frac{dT}{dt_1}. \end{aligned} \tag{8.14}$$

These are conventional Harberger (1964) measures of the MCF where the welfare effects of tax changes are separated from the welfare effects of government spending funded by the extra tax revenue.[19] We derive them by using the conventional welfare equation in (8.7) to compute the marginal excess burden of taxation (MEB) for each tax and adding them to unity, with $MCF = 1 + MEB$, where MEB is the marginal welfare loss on each dollar of tax revenue raised.[20] We demonstrate this for tax t_0 using Figure 8.3, where

$$MEB_0 = \frac{a}{b + c - a}.$$

The welfare loss from marginally raising the tax is the cross-lined rectangle in a, while the extra tax revenue is $b + c - a$. Thus, each dollar of revenue the government collects by using this tax will have an excess burden of MEB_0.

Whenever the government uses tax t_0 to fund the budget deficit it is multiplied by MCF_0 to account for the excess burden of taxation, where consumers lose a dollar of surplus on each dollar of revenue raised plus MEB_0 due to the excess of burden of taxation. Thus, in project evaluation the MCF is used as a scaling coefficient on revenue transfers made by the government to balance its budget. It is illustrated in Figure 8.3 as

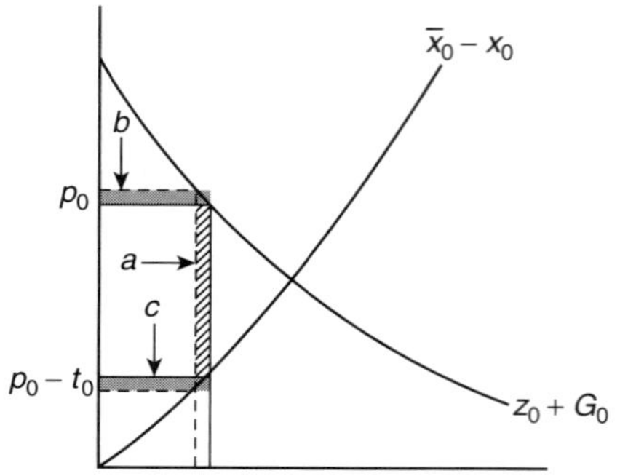

Figure 8.3 The revised Samuelson condition in the first period.

$$MCF_0 = 1 + MEB_0 = \frac{b+c}{b+c-a} > 0,$$

where private surplus falls by $b + c$ when the government collects tax revenue of $b + c - a$. If the net supply of the private good is fixed there is no welfare loss from the tax and the MCF is unity. Thus, each dollar of revenue the government raises will reduce private surplus by a dollar. Once the tax change drives down activity the fall in private surplus is larger than the revenue raised.

The revised Samuelson conditions are obtained from (8.13) as

$$MRS_0 = MCF_0\left(MRT_0 - \frac{dT}{dG_0}\right),$$
$$\sum_s \pi_s m_s MRS_s = MCF_1\left(\sum_s \pi_s m_s MRT_s - \frac{dT}{dG_1}\right). \qquad (8.15)$$

It is more costly for the government to fund budget deficits when the MCF exceeds unity, so the optimal supply of each public good will fall (relative to the optimal supplies determined by (8.12)). Since the terms inside the brackets measure the changes in the budget deficit, they are multiplied by the MCF for each trade tax. The welfare changes for the first optimality condition in (8.15) are illustrated in Figure 8.4 when the project has no net impact on trades of the private good. Thus, the reduction in net demand from the higher consumer price is undone by the net increase in demand resulting from extra output of the public good.[21]

In this special case the welfare loss from increasing the tax to balance the government budget by raising revenue $D + E$ exactly offsets the spending effect in the cross-lined area A, where the revised Samuelson condition can be summarized, as

$$MRS_0 \quad = \quad MCF_0\left(MRT_0 - \frac{dT}{dG}\right)$$
$$C \quad = \quad \frac{D+E}{D+E-A}\left(D+E-A\right) = D+E$$

Box 8.3 Estimates of the marginal social cost of public funds (MCF)

The MCF provides important information for policy-makers because it tells them how much private surplus falls when the government raises a dollar of tax revenue. This loss in private surplus exceeds tax revenue when distorting taxes are used, where the excess burden is minimized when all taxes have the same MCF. In the single (aggregated) consumer economy examined earlier in Box 8.2, the MCFs for the two trade taxes are

$$MCF_0 = \frac{\bar{x}_0 - x_0}{dT / dG_0} \approx 1.10 \text{ and } MCF_1 = \frac{\bar{x}_1 - x_1}{dT/dG_1} \approx 1.16.$$

Thus, the government could increase aggregate utility by raising more of its revenue with t_0 instead of t_1. We will summarize the workings for computing MCF_0, where the reduction in private surplus from marginally raising tax t_0 is computed, using the Bailey demand schedule, as

$$\bar{x}_0 - x_0 \approx 500 - 202.22 \approx 297.78.$$

The change in tax revenue solves

$$\frac{dT}{dt_0} = (\bar{x}_0 - x_0) - t_0 \frac{\partial x_0(\cdot)}{\partial q_0}\frac{dq_0}{dt_0} - t_0 \frac{\partial x_0(\cdot)}{\partial I}\frac{dI}{dt_0} + \delta t_1 \frac{\partial x_1(\cdot)}{\partial q_0}\frac{dq_0}{dt_0} + \delta t_1 \frac{\partial x_1(\cdot)}{\partial I}\frac{dI}{dt_0},$$

with $x_t(\cdot) \equiv x_t\,(q_0, q_1, I)$ being the ordinary (Marshallian) demands in each time period $t = 0$, 1. With fixed producer prices, we have $dq_0/dt_0 = -1$, where the change in aggregate income $(I = q_0\bar{x}_0 + T - p_0G_0 - \delta p_1G_1 - R)$ solves

$$\frac{dI}{dt_0} = -x_0 - t_0\frac{dx_0}{dt_0} + \delta t_1 \frac{dx_1}{dt_0}.$$

After substitution, and using the Slutsky decomposition, we have:

$$\frac{dT}{dt_0} = (\bar{x}_0 - x_0) + \frac{t_0(\partial \hat{x}_0(\cdot)/\partial q_0) - \delta t_1\,(\partial \hat{x}_1(\cdot)/\partial q_0)}{1-\theta} \approx 270.34,$$

where $\theta = -\,t_0\,(\partial x_0\,(\cdot)/\partial I) + t_1(\partial\, x_1\,(\cdot)/\partial I) \approx -0.0820645$ isolates the income effects. The compensated demand functions for the private goods are

$$\hat{x}_0(\cdot) = \frac{e^{u_0/2}q_1^{1/2}}{G_0^{1/2}G_1^{1/2}q_0^{1/2}} \text{ and } \hat{x}_1(\cdot) = \frac{e^{u_0/2}q_0^{1/2}}{G_0^{1/2}G_1^{1/2}q_1^{1/2}},$$

where $t_0\partial\hat{x}_0(\cdot)/\partial q_0 \approx -21.78$ and $\delta t_1 \partial \hat{x}_1(\cdot)/\partial q_0 \approx 7.92$, for $u_0 = 18.6936$, $q_0 = 0.80$, $q_1 = 1.133$, $G_0 = 85$ and $G_1 = 70$. By combining these welfare changes, we have

$$MCF_0 = \frac{\bar{x}_0 - x_0}{dT / dG_0} \approx \frac{297.78}{270.34} \approx 1.10.$$

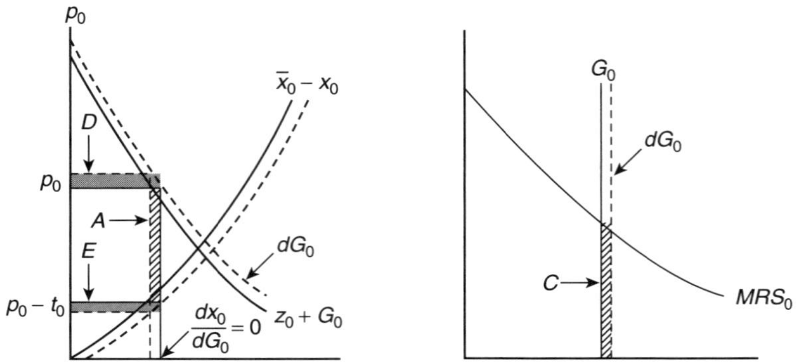

Figure 8.4 MCF for the trade tax in the first period.

There are other ways of financing the budget deficit for each project when the government can transfer resources over time by trading bonds. For example, it could sell bonds to fund extra output of the public good in the first period and then redeem them by raising the trade tax in the second period. We would then use MCF_1 instead of MCF_0 in the Samuelson condition above, which is an attractive alternative when $MCF_1 < MCF_0$ However, the MCF is independent of the tax used to balance the government budget when taxes are (Ramsey) optimal, with $MCF_1 = MCF_0$.

Box 8.4 Estimates of the revised shadow profits from public good production

In Box 8.p2 we computed the shadow profit for each public good when the extra outputs were funded using lump-sum taxation. But they were measured in the presence of distorting trade taxes, which suggests the government cannot raise all its revenue using lump-sum taxation. Indeed, if it could do so it would be preferable to eliminate the trade taxes entirely. When the extra outputs are funded using distorting trade taxes we need to compute their *revised shadow profits* by multiplying the net change in government spending by the MCF for each tax. Using the estimates of the MCF in Box 8.3, we have

$$(\pi_0)_{t_0} = \underset{(1.9)-(1.10)[(1)-(0.08)]}{\Sigma MRS_0 - MCF_0\left(p_0 - \frac{dT}{dG_0}\right)} \approx \$0.89$$

and

$$(\pi_1)_{t_1} = \underset{(2.24)-(1.16)[(1)-(0.08)]}{\delta\Sigma MRS_1 - MCF_1\left(\delta p_1 - \frac{dT}{dG_1}\right)} \approx \$1.17,$$

where the marginal excess burden of taxation reduces the shadow profit for both public goods by 11 per cent. Instead of raising utility by \$2.30, as was the case in Box 8.3 when the goods were funded using lump-sum taxation, they now raise it by \$2.06. Thus, the optimal supply of each public good is lower in these circumstances.

8.1.3 Changes in real income (efficiency effects)

Dollar changes in expected utility are unreliable welfare measures for discrete (large) policy changes when the marginal utility of income changes with real income. In particular, they are path-dependent, which means welfare measures can be manipulated by reordering a given set of policy changes. This problem is overcome by measuring compensated welfare changes. They isolate the impact of policy changes on the government budget when lump-sum transfers are made to hold constant the utility of every consumer. If a policy change generates surplus revenue (at constant utility) it can be used by the government to raise the utility of every consumer, while the reverse applies when it drives the budget into deficit. Thus, compensated welfare changes are changes in real income that get converted into utility when the government balances its budget. How these changes in real income are distributed across consumers depends, in part, on endogenous price changes and also on the tax changes the government makes to balance its budget.[22]

We measure compensated welfare changes for the projects examined in the previous section by including foreign aid payments (R measured in units of domestic currency) in the first-period government budget constraint in (8.4), with $T_0 = MRT_0G_0 - L_0 + \mathrm{R}$, where the conventional welfare equation in (8.7) becomes

$$\begin{aligned} dW &= (MRS_0 - MRT_0)dG_0 - t_0 dx_0 \\ &\quad + \Sigma_s \pi_s m_s \left\{(MRS_S - MRT_S)dG_1 + t_1 dx_s\right\} - dR. \end{aligned} \qquad (8.7')$$

Endogenous changes in R isolate surplus government revenue from the policy changes when expected utility is held constant at its initial level, with $dW = 0$, where the *compensated welfare equation* is obtained from (8.7′) as

$$\begin{aligned} d\hat{R} &= (MRS_0 - MRT_0)dG_0 - t_0 d\hat{x}_0 \\ &\quad + \sum_s \pi_s m_s \left\{(MRS_s - MRT_s)dG_1 + t_1 d\hat{x}_s\right\}.^{23} \end{aligned} \qquad (8.16)$$

Welfare gains are surplus revenue the government could pay as foreign aid ($d\hat{R} > 0$), while welfare losses are gifts of foreign aid it would need to receive ($d\hat{R} < 0$) at unchanged domestic utility.[24] Thus, they isolate the changes in real income from policy changes. The compensated welfare changes for the projects that provide public goods have the same structure as the dollar changes in utility obtained in the previous subsection, but with endogenous changes in activity determined solely by substitution effects. All the income effects for projects are removed by compensating lump-sum transfers that are referred to as the *compensation variation* (CV). Rather than rework all the cases examined in the previous subsection, we consider the project that provides an extra unit of the public good in the second period, where the change in real income is solved, using (8.16), as

$$\frac{d\hat{R}}{dG_1} = \sum_s \pi_s m_s (MRS_s - MRT_s) + \frac{d\hat{T}}{dG_1},^{25} \qquad (8.17)$$

with

$$\frac{d\hat{T}}{dG_1} = - t_0 \frac{\partial \hat{x}_0}{\partial G_1} + \sum_s \pi_s m_s t_1 \frac{\partial \hat{x}_s}{\partial G_1}$$

being the compensated spending effect.

The compensating transfers (CVs) for this project are obtained from (8.5), with $dEU^h = 0$ for all h, as

$$\begin{aligned} CV_0^h &= \frac{d\hat{L}_0^h}{dG_1} = -(\bar{x}_0^h - x_0^h)\frac{\partial \hat{q}_0}{\partial G_1} + z_0^h \frac{\partial \hat{p}_0}{\partial G_1} - MRS_0^h \\ CV_s^h &= \frac{d\hat{L}_s^h}{dG_1} = (x_s^h - \bar{x}_s^h)\frac{\partial \hat{q}_s}{\partial G_1} - y_s^h \frac{\partial \hat{p}_s}{\partial G_1} - MRS_S^h \ \forall s, \end{aligned} \tag{8.18}$$

where the current value of the aggregate *expected CV* is

$$E(CV) = \sum_h CV_0^h + \sum_h \sum_s \pi_s m_s CV_s^h. \tag{8.19}$$

Since these transfers hold the utility of every consumer constant in each time period and in each state of nature, they completely reverse any distributional effects from the project. Thus, they isolate the change in real income at the initial equilibrium outcome. Graham (1981) and Helms (1985) identify an ex ante measure of the CV that we use here to obtain a measure of the welfare effects from the changes in risk bearing. For the policy change under consideration the *ex-ante CV* is the single lump-sum transfer in the current period that would hold expected utility constant, and is solved for each consumer using (8.5), with $dEU^h = 0$, as

$$\begin{aligned} CV_{\text{ex ante}}^h = \frac{d\hat{L}_0^h}{dG_1} &= -(\bar{x}_0^h - x_0^h)\frac{\partial \hat{q}_0}{\partial G_1} + z_0^h \frac{\partial \hat{p}_0}{\partial G_1} - MRS_0^h \\ &\quad + \sum_s \pi_s m_s \left((x_s^h - \bar{x}_s^h)\frac{\partial \hat{q}_s}{\partial G_1} - y_s^h \frac{\partial \hat{p}_s}{\partial G_1} - MRS_s^h \right), \end{aligned} \tag{8.20}$$

with $d\hat{L}_s^h / dG_1 = 0$ for all s.

When summed over consumers, we have $CV_{\text{ex ante}} = \Sigma_h CV_{\text{ex ante}}^h$. Notice how this CV holds expected utility constant but allows utility to change across states of nature in the second period. Thus, it measures the change in real income from the project without undoing its impact on consumption risk. Weisbrod (1964) refers to the ex-ante CV as the option price which Graham uses to compute the option value for a project by deducting its ex-ante CV from the expected CV in (8.19):

$$OV = CV_{\text{ex ante}} - E(CV). \tag{8.21}$$

This conveniently provides a welfare measure of the project's impact on consumption risk. Since the expected CV holds utility constant in every future state of nature it completely undoes all aspects of the policy change on real income, including its mean and variance. In contrast, the ex-ante CV measures the change in real income from the project without eliminating its impact on consumption risk. Thus, a positive option value in (8.21) tells us the project reduces consumption risk, while a negative option value indicates it increases consumption risk.[26] The project with efficiency losses could be socially profitable when the risk benefits are large enough. And when that happens the expected CV must be smaller than the ex-ante CV, as the expected CV completely undoes the reduction in consumption risk. When consumers are risk-neutral, or the project has no impact on consumption risk, the option value is zero, with $CV_{\text{ex ante}} = E(CV)$, and both measures of the CV will isolate the change in expected real income.

8.1.4 The role of income effects

The analysis in the previous subsection makes it clear how income effects from policy changes play two roles when there is uncertainty. They redistribute income across consumers as well as across states of nature. In this subsection we relate compensated welfare changes to actual dollar changes in expected utility. Consider the compensated welfare change for the project evaluated in (8.17). It isolates the change in real income (that the government could pay as foreign aid at no cost to domestic utility) when the expected CV is used to hold constant the utility of every consumer in both time periods and in every state. Thus, it measures the extra real income for the true status quo. Once this surplus revenue is distributed through lump-sum transfers back to domestic consumers the income effects raise their expected utility by the welfare change (dW/dG_1) in (8.11). This relationship can be formalized as a generalized version of the Hatta (1977) decomposition by writing the social welfare function used in (8.6) over the exogenous policy variables G_0, G_1, t_0, t_1, and R, as $W(G_0, G_1, t_0, t_1, R)$ where the change in foreign aid payments that would offset the welfare effects from marginally raising output of the public good in the second period solves

$$dW(\cdot) = \frac{dW}{dG_1} d\hat{G}_1 + \frac{dW}{dR} d\hat{R} = 0. \tag{8.22}$$

We obtain the generalized Hatta decomposition for the project by rearranging these terms, as

$$\frac{dW}{dG_1} = S_R \frac{d\hat{R}}{dG_1}, \tag{8.23}$$

[27]

where $S_R = -\,dW/dR = 1 - dT/dR$ is the *shadow value of government revenue*; it measures the amount social welfare rises when a dollar of surplus revenue is endowed on the government who transfers it to domestic consumers to balance its budget. This is an important decomposition for two reasons.

First, all the income effects from marginal policy changes are isolated by S_R, including distributional effects across consumers and states of nature. By measuring the option value defined in (8.21), we can separate the welfare effects of income distribution across consumers from the income redistribution across states of nature. Two main approaches are used to account for distributional effects across consumers in project evaluation. The first is recommended by Boadway (1976) and Drèze and Stern (1990) where different distributional weights are assigned to consumers in (8.6), while the second approach by Bruce and Harris (1982) and Diewert (1983) tests for Pareto improvements. Most policy analysts are

Box 8.5 The shadow value of government revenue in the public good economy

In the two-period certainty economy summarized in Box 8.2 the shadow value of government revenue is less than unity. In other words, endowing another dollar of income on the economy will raise aggregate utility by less than a dollar. And this occurs because extra real income contracts the tax base. If a dollar of income is endowed on the economy (with $dR < 0$) the dollar change in utility is

$$S_R = 1 - \frac{dT}{dR},$$

where the change in tax revenue solves

$$-\frac{dT}{dR} = t_0 \frac{dx_0}{dR} - t_1 \frac{dx_1}{dR} = t_0 \frac{\partial x_0(\cdot)}{\partial I}\frac{dI}{dR} - t_1 \frac{\partial x_1(\cdot)}{\partial R}\frac{dI}{dR},$$

with $-dI/dR = 1 - dT/dR$. After substitution, we have

$$-\frac{dT}{dR} = \frac{\theta}{1-\theta} \approx -0.08,$$

with $\theta = -t_0(\partial x_0(\cdot)/\partial I) + t_1(\partial x_1(\cdot)/\partial I) \approx -0.0820645$. There is good economic intuition for this change in tax revenue. With the log-linear preferences summarized in Box 8.1 the demand for the private good in each time period is normal. An extra dollar of income initially raises demand for them and reduces tax revenue by θ as the tax base contracts due to the fall in supply of the good in the first period. When the government transfers this amount from the consumer to balance its budget the income effect increases tax revenue by θ^2. In the next round it falls by θ^3, and so on, until the change in tax revenue solves the infinite sequence $\theta + \theta^2 + \theta^3 + \ldots = -\theta/(1-\theta)$. Thus, the final welfare change is

$$S_R = 1 - \frac{dT}{dR} = \frac{1}{1-\theta} \approx \$0.92.$$

It is illustrated in the following diagram where the cross-lined areas are changes in tax revenue. The extra real income contracts the tax base in the first period by reducing supply and expanding the tax base in the second period by increasing demand.

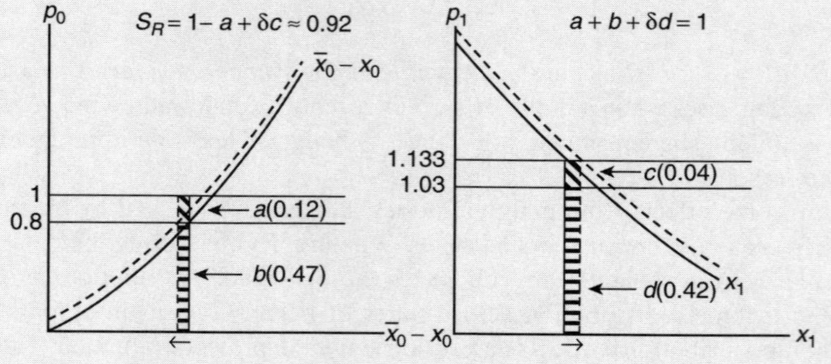

reluctant for their subjectively chosen distributional weights to have a major influence on policy outcomes, particularly in circumstances where policies with efficiency losses are promoted on distributional grounds. That is why analysts frequently report the efficiency and distributional effects separately. Other analysts, very much in the spirit of a conventional Harberger analysis, recognize the influence governments have over distributional outcomes when they make tax changes to balance their budgets. For that reason, Bruce and Harris (1982) and Diewert (1983) test to see whether patterns of transfers can be chosen to convert extra real income into Pareto improvements.[28]

Second, for a positive shadow value of government revenue, there must be efficiency gains from policy changes ($d\hat{R}/dG_1 > 0$) whenever dollar changes in expected utility are positive ($dW/dG_1 > 0$). And since S_R is an independent scaling coefficient for marginal policy changes, income effects play no role in project evaluation.[29]

8.2 The social discount rate

A major controversy in the evaluation of public sector projects is over the value of the social discount rate. Some argue it should be the same discount rate used by private operators, while others claim it should be lower. In economies with distorted markets due to taxes, externalities and non-competitive behaviour, the social discount rate will, in general, be different from the discount rate used by private investors for the same project. In particular, income taxes drive wedges between the cost of capital for investors and the after-tax returns to savers. Harberger (1969) and Sandmo and Drèze (1971) show how this makes the social discount rate a weighted average of the borrowing and lending rates of interest in a two-period certainty setting. By extending their analysis to additional time periods Marglin (1963a, 1963b) finds it is higher than the weighted average formula, while Bradford (1975) finds it is approximately equal to the after-tax interest rate. Sjaastad and Wisecarver (1977) show how these differences are explained by the treatment of depreciation in public capital. Whenever private saving adjusts to replace this depreciation the weighted average formula also applies in a multi-period setting.

Others claim the discount rate for public projects is affected by risk. Samuelson (1964), Vickery (1964) and Arrow and Lind (1970) claim it should be lower than the discount rate used by private firms undertaking the same project. Samuelson and Vickery argue this happens because the public sector undertakes many projects with uncorrelated returns that allow them to eliminate diversifiable risk. Arrow and Lind take a different approach by arguing the public sector can use the tax system to spread risk over a large number of consumers when project returns are uncorrelated with aggregate income. Essentially, both arguments rely on the government being able to eliminate diversifiable risk and trade aggregate uncertainty at lower cost than private markets. Bailey and Jensen (1972) claim this is not, in general, the case, where the risk premium in the discount rate should be the same for the public and private sector when undertaking the same projects.

In this section we derive the weighted average formula of Harberger, and of Sandmo and Drèze, before extending their analysis to accommodate uncertainty. Then we consider the social discount rates obtained by Marglin and Bradford when there are more than two time periods, and reconcile them with weighted average formula using the analysis in Sjaastad and Wisecarver. This allows us to isolate the important role of depreciation in public capital. Finally, we examine the arguments by Samuelson, Vickery, and Arrow and Lind that discount rates for public projects should be lower.

8.2.1 Weighted average formula

In the presence of distortions market prices do not, in general, provide us with true measures of the marginal valuation and marginal cost of goods and services. For example, a consumption tax drives a wedge between marginal consumption benefits and marginal production costs, where consumer prices overstate social costs and producer prices understate social benefits. With downward-sloping demand schedules and increasing marginal cost schedules the true (social) value of any good is a weighted average of its consumer and producer prices. This same logic applies to the discount rate that determines the opportunity cost of current consumption. We demonstrate this formally by introducing a tax on capital income in the two-period uncertainty model used earlier in Section 8.1. And to simplify the analysis it is set at the same rate (τ) for all consumers who face common discount factors of

$$m_s = \frac{1}{1+i_s(1-\tau)} \forall s. \tag{8.24}$$

This is confirmed by writing the state-contingent payouts to saving $(p_0 z_0^h)$ by each consumer in (8.1) as $p_s y_s^h = [1+i_s(1-\tau)]p_0 z_0^h$, where optimally chosen saving satisfies (8.24). It is the same for all consumers because they can trade in a complete competitive capital market. A further adjustment must also be made to the government budget constraints in (8.4) to include income tax revenue in the second period:

$$\begin{aligned} T_0 &\equiv t_0(\bar{x}_0 - x_0) + \tau i_s p_0 z_0 = MRT_0 G_0 - L_0, \\ T_s &\equiv t_1(x_s - \bar{x}_s) = MRT_s G_1 - L_s \forall s. \end{aligned} \tag{8.4$'$}$$

We obtain the social discount rate by measuring the welfare change from marginally increasing the first-period endowment of the private good. In effect, this is equivalent to an exogenous increase in the supply of capital to the economy, where the welfare change is referred to as the *shadow value of capital* (S_K). It is the current value of the extra consumption generated by a marginal increase in capital. By allowing this endowment to change exogenously in the presence of the income tax, we obtain an amended conventional welfare equation,

$$\begin{aligned} dW = {} & (MRS_0 - MRT_0)dG_0 - t_0 dx_0 + p_0 d\bar{x}_0 \\ & + \sum_s \pi_s m_s \{(MRS_s - MRT_s)dG_1 + t_1 dx_s + \tau i_s p_0 dz_0\}, \end{aligned} \tag{8.7$''$}$$

where $p_0 d\bar{x}_0$ measures the direct welfare gain from marginally increasing the private endowment, and $\tau i_s p_0 dz_0$ the welfare gain from a reduction in the excess burden of the income tax when private investment expands endogenously.[30] Using this equation, we obtain a shadow value of capital of

$$S_K = p_0 \Sigma_s \pi_s m_s (1+\psi_s),^{31} \tag{8.25}$$

where

$$\psi_s = i_s(1-\tau) + \tau i_s \frac{\partial z_0}{\partial \bar{x}_0} - \frac{t_0}{p_0}\frac{\partial x_0}{\partial \bar{x}_0}[1+i_s(1-\tau)] + \frac{t_1}{p_0}\frac{\partial x_s}{\partial \bar{x}_0}$$

is the social discount rate which measures the amount by which private consumption grows in each state of nature.

In the absence of taxes and other distortions the social discount rate is equal to the private discount rate, with $\psi_s = i_s$ for all s, and the shadow value of capital is its market price, with $S_k = p_0$. That is not in general the case, however, in the presence of the taxes. A marginal increase in the supply of capital is absorbed into the economy through endogenous changes in private saving and investment which have different social values in the presence of the income tax. This causes the social discount rate to deviate from the private discount rate. To identify the separate effects of taxes and risk we derive the social discount rate for a number of special cases.

Certainty without trade taxes

This replicates the analysis used by Harberger, and by Sandmo and Dréze, who obtain a weighted average formula for the social discount rate. By setting $t_0 = t_1 = 0$, and using the market-clearing condition for the private good in the first period (with $\bar{x}_0 = x_0 + z_0 + MRT_0 G_0$), the social discount rate in (8.25) becomes

$$\psi = \alpha i + (1-\alpha) i (1-\tau), \qquad (8.26)$$

[32]

where $\alpha = \partial z_0 / \partial \bar{x}_0$ is the endogenous change in private investment, and $1-\alpha = \partial x_0 / \partial \bar{x}_0$ the endogenous change in private saving. It is illustrated as the cross-lined rectangles in Figure 8.5 where a marginal increase in the supply of capital ($d\bar{x}_0$) is absorbed into the economy by a lower interest rate which expands private investment demand by α and contracts private saving by $1 - \alpha$. (The dashed lines isolate the new equilibrium outcome.)

Since ψ measures the growth in aggregate consumption from investing another dollar of capital, it is the social discount rate to use when evaluating public projects. In other words, socially profitable projects must match or better this future change in aggregate consumption. The interest rate is the marginal social value of extra private investment, while the after-tax interest rate is the marginal social value of the reduction in private saving, where, from (8.26), we have

$$i \geq \psi \geq i\,(1-\tau).$$

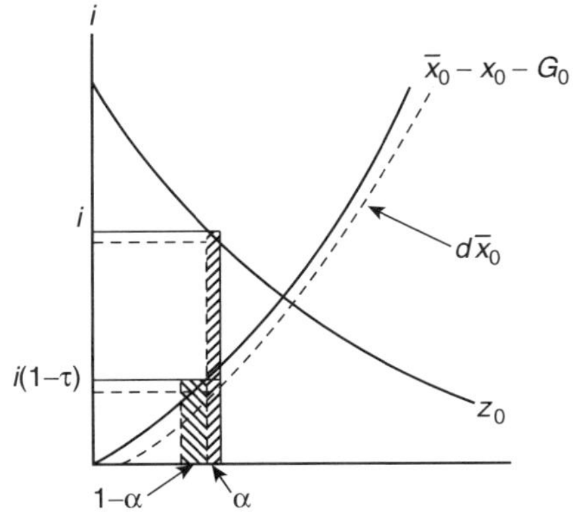

Figure 8.5 Weighted average formula.

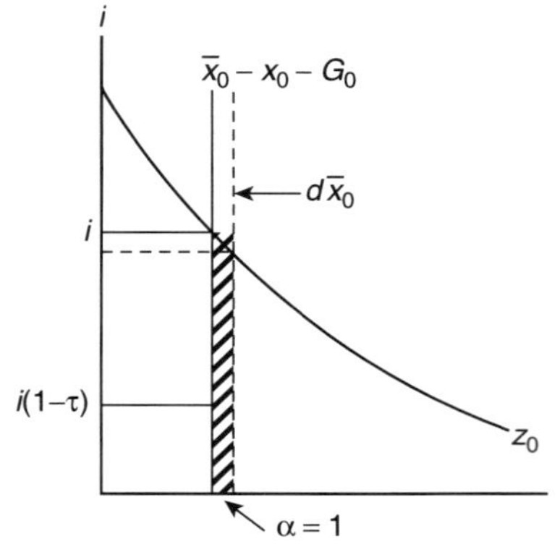

Figure 8.6 Fixed saving.

Clearly, the interest elasticities of private investment and saving determine where the social discount rate lies within these bounds. With fixed private saving additional capital must be absorbed into the economy by an equal increase in private investment, with $\alpha = 1$, where the social discount rate in (8.26) becomes $\psi = i$. It is illustrated by the cross-lined rectangle in Figure 8.6 as the present value of the net increase in consumption due to extra private investment. The same thing happens when private investment is perfectly price-elastic due to a constant net marginal product of capital.

With fixed private investment demand the additional capital is absorbed into the economy by crowding out private saving, with $\alpha = 0$, where the social discount rate in (8.26) becomes $\psi = i\,(1 - \tau)$. This welfare change is illustrated as the cross-lined rectangle in Figure 8.7. It is the value of the net benefits from consuming more of the private good in the first period when saving falls.

In general, however, these extremes are unlikely, especially in the long run when consumption and production are more responsive to changes in real income.

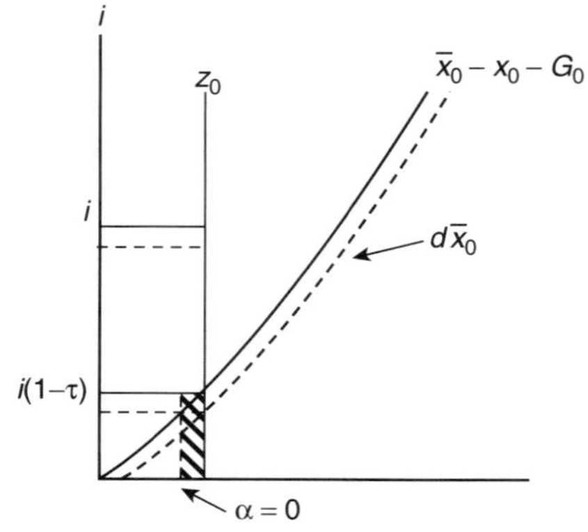

Figure 8.7 Fixed investment demand.

Box 8.6 The weighted average formula in the public good economy

Here we obtain a numerical estimate of the weighted average formula for the shadow discount rate in the two-period certainty model summarized in Box 8.1 for the initial equilibrium allocation.

Taxes (%)			*Public goods*		*Bailey demands*	
τ	t_0	t_1	G_0	G_1	x_0	x_1
40	0	0	85	70	175	170

In the presence of a 40 per cent tax on interest income and no trade taxes, the shadow price of capital solves

$$S_K = \frac{dU}{d\bar{x}_0} = p_0 + \delta\tau i p_0\left(1 - \frac{dx_0}{d\bar{x}_0}\right),$$

with

$$\delta = \frac{1}{1 + i(1-\tau)} \approx 0.98.$$

The change in private saving can be decomposed using the ordinary demand schedules as

$$1 - \frac{dx_0}{d\bar{x}_0} = 1 - \frac{\partial x_0(\cdot)}{\partial I}\frac{dI}{d\bar{x}_0},$$

where the income effect is obtained, using aggregate income of $I = q_0\bar{x}_0 + \delta\tau i\, p_0\,(x_0 - x_0 - G_0 - R) - p_0G_0 - \delta p_1G_1 - R$, as $dI/d\bar{x}_0 = S_K$. After substitution, we have

$$S_K = \frac{p_0(1+\delta\tau i)}{1-\theta} = \$1.01,$$

with $\theta = -\delta\tau i p_0 \partial x_0(\cdot)/\partial I \approx -0.006$. Since $S_K = p_0\delta(1 + \psi)$ defines the relationship between the shadow price of capital and the social discount rate, we have

$$\psi = \alpha i + (1-\alpha) i (1-\tau) \approx 0.024,$$

where $\alpha = 1 - dx_0/d\bar{x}_0$ is the change in private investment which is solved, using the ordinary demand schedules, as

$$\alpha = S_R\left(1 - p_0\frac{\partial x_0(\cdot)}{\partial I}\right) \approx 0.49,$$

with $S_R = 1/(1 - \theta) \approx 0.994$. Thus, the shadow discount rate lies between the pre- and post-tax interest rates,

$$\underset{(0.018)}{i(1-\tau)} \leq \underset{(0.024)}{\psi} \leq \underset{(0.03)}{i}$$

Private saving falls, despite an unchanged interest rate, because the income effect from increasing the endowment of the private good raises current demand.

If we include the trade taxes in Box 8.2 the shadow price of capital falls to $S_K \approx 0.93$, and the discount rate becomes negative at $\psi \approx -0.054$. This fall in welfare is due to the larger excess burden of taxation as the tax base contracts with the extra real income.

Aggregate uncertainty

An interesting, and important, extension to the analysis of Harberger and of Sandmo and Dréze introduces aggregate uncertainty. When evaluating public projects we use a social discount rate that captures the full social opportunity cost of capital, including a risk premium when the net cash flows impose costs on risk-averse consumers. We extend the analysis in the previous section by including aggregate uncertainty in the presence of the uniform income tax (and without trade taxes), where, from (8.25), the social discount rate becomes the state-contingent weighted average formula,

$$\psi_s = \alpha i_s + (1-\alpha) i_s (1-\tau) \forall s. \tag{8.27}$$

In this setting there is a risk premium in the return to capital, and it is computed in the same way for private and public sector projects when the government has no advantage over the private sector in trading risk.

We can see from the general expression for the social discount rate in (8.25) that it can deviate from the weighted average formula when there are other market distortions – in this case, trade taxes. By using the capital market clearing condition, we have

$$\psi_s = \alpha i_s + (1-\alpha) i_s (1-\tau) - \frac{t_0}{p_0}(1-\alpha)[1 + i_s(1-\tau)] + \frac{t_1}{p_0}\frac{\partial x_s}{\partial \bar{x}_0} \forall s, \tag{8.28}$$

where the last two terms are welfare effects from resource movements in distorted markets. When private saving falls, it reduces the net supply of the private good and exacerbates the excess burden of the trade tax, where the reduction in trade tax revenue in the second last term is a welfare loss. In contrast, the additional tax revenue in the last term is a welfare gain from reducing the excess burden of the trade tax in the first period. Whether these additional welfare changes move the social discount rate above or below the weighted average formula depends on the change in net demand for the private good in the second period. If it generates a welfare gain (in the last term) that is large enough to offset the welfare loss from the reduction in current trade tax revenue (in the second last term) the social discount rate rises above the weighted average formula. Once trade tax revenue declines in present value terms, the discount rate falls below the weighted average formula. Ultimately, the final outcome depends upon the size of the taxes as well as consumer preferences and production technologies.

These related market effects are often overlooked in the evaluation of small-scale project evaluation because they are too costly to measure. Typically project outputs and inputs have cross-effects in a number of distorted markets, and they can be isolated using a general equilibrium model with parameter values calibrated on data taken from the economy. Alternatively, they can be estimated directly from data using empirical analysis. But these options are often too costly to undertake, where the distortions on project outputs and inputs are the only ones taken into account. Goulder and Williams (2003) find income taxes on capital and labour inputs have the most important welfare effects. Indeed, they often dominate the welfare effects arising from taxes and other distortions on project outputs. Thus, for small-scale projects it would seem prudent to include welfare effects arising from distortions on project outputs and inputs, and to ignore welfare effects from indirect cross-effects in other distorted markets.

A more realistic measure of the social discount rate would accommodate progressive income taxes and include a corporate tax. We could also include distributional effects by assigning different distributional weights to consumers in the welfare change in (8.6). A number of these extensions are examined in Jones (2005) where social discount rates are personalized for consumers facing different taxes on income and different distributional weights. While these extensions make the social discount rate more accurate, they make the analysis more complex without adding greatly to the insights already obtained earlier. Instead, we extend the analysis in the next section by adding more time periods to examine the impact of capital depreciation on the social discount rate.

8.2.2 Multiple time periods and capital depreciation

In a two-period setting depreciation plays no role in the analysis because all capital is liquidated in the second period. With extra time periods capital can be carried beyond the second period, where (economic) depreciation measures the change in the market value of the asset in each year of its life. Unless investment rises to replace depreciated capital, future consumption will fall. Marglin (1963a, 1963b) and Bradford (1975) find the social discount rate deviates from the weighted average formula when they add time periods to the analysis of Harberger, and Sandmo and Drèze. Sjaastad and Wisecarver (1977) show that this occurs because depreciation is not matched by additional private saving. Using certainty analysis with an infinite time horizon, Marglin finds the discount rate is higher than the weighted average formula in (8.26). This is demonstrated for a public project that generates a payout of $1 + \delta$ in the second period of its life and none thereafter. It is socially profitable when

$$\frac{1+\delta}{1+i(1-\tau)} \geq (1-\alpha)+\frac{\alpha i}{i(1-\tau)} \qquad (8.29)$$

This condition makes the present value of the net consumption flow greater than or equal to its social cost. Since this project increases the demand for capital in the economy it is satisfied through a rise in private saving and/or a reduction in private investment, where Marglin identifies the social cost of forgone current consumption due to the increase in private saving as $1 - \alpha$, and the present value of forgone future consumption (αi) in perpetuity due to the increase in private investment as $\alpha i/[i(1 - \tau)]$. Rearranging (8.29), we find the project is socially profitable when

$$\delta \geq \psi + \alpha\tau i > \psi. \qquad (8.30)$$

Using a Keynesian consumption function that makes saving a constant fraction of income in each time period, Bradford finds the same project is socially profitable when

$$\frac{1+\delta}{1+i(1-\tau)} \simeq 1, \qquad (8.31)$$

which implies $\delta \simeq i(1-\tau) < \psi$.

These findings by Marglin and Bradford create a dilemma for policy analysts, as they suggest the social discount rate can range in value from $i(1 - \tau)$ to something above the weighted average formula (ψ). Clearly, some projects may only be viable at a low discount rates and others only at high rates – it depends on the timing and values of their benefits and costs.

Sjaastad and Wisecarver show how these different views are explained by the treatment of depreciation in public capital. Once consumers adjust their saving to replace this depreciation, the weighted average formula applies in a multi-period setting. They demonstrate this for the project considered by Marglin, where the payout in the second period becomes

$$1+\delta-\alpha-\alpha i,$$

with $1+\delta$ being the direct consumption benefit from the project, α the fall in current consumption when saving rises to offset the depreciation in public capital, and αi the fall in consumption due to the reduction in private investment. Now the project is socially profitable when

$$\frac{1+\delta-\alpha-\alpha i}{1+i(1-\tau)} \geq 1-\alpha,$$

where, after rearranging terms, we have $\delta \geq \psi$.

It is likely that consumers will adjust their saving, at least partially, when they observe depreciation in public capital. As wealth-maximizing agents they compute the expected consumption benefits from public capital and the higher expected taxes to replace depreciated capital. If, for what ever reason, consumers do not adjust their saving to offset depreciation in public capital the social discount rate rises above the weighted average formula.

8.2.3 Market frictions and risk

A number of studies argue the social discount rate can be lower for public projects when the government can trade risk at lower cost than trades in private markets. Samuelson (1964) and Vickery (1964) argue the government is a relatively large investor in the economy that undertakes many projects with uncorrelated risks that can be diversified inside the public sector. As a consequence, it can pool these risks at lower cost than the private sector by bundling securities in portfolios and purchasing insurance. Arrow and Lind (1970) argue the discount rates on public projects are lower because their returns are uncorrelated with aggregate income and the government can diversify risk across a large number of consumers through the tax system. Thus, the public sector offers better opportunities for trading aggregate risk and eliminating diversifiable risk.

Bailey and Jensen (1972) refute both these claims by arguing consumers can achieve the same, if not better, risk-trading opportunities in private markets. Indeed, the absence of a profit motive can make public employees less efficient operators, thereby raising the costs of trading risk. And since most taxes distort activity, the tax system is likely to be a more costly way of spreading risk across consumers.[33] Bailey and Jensen also argue public project returns are mostly correlated with aggregate income, which means they contain aggregate risk that cannot be diversified inside the public sector. It is frequently claimed the arguments by Arrow and Lind for using a lower discount rate on public projects can be justified by the moral hazard and adverse selection problems that arise when traders have asymmetric information. These problems, which were examined in Chapter 5, can raise the cost of eliminating diversifiable risk. If it can be eliminated at lower cost through the tax system, or by pooling it inside the public sector, the discount rate on public projects will be lower. However, as Dixit (1987, 1989) observes, the public sector is also subject to the same information asymmetries as private traders, and it may not be able to lower the cost of trading risk. For that reason it is important to examine the risk-spreading opportunities available to the public sector when it too is subject to moral hazard and adverse selections problems. In the final analysis, a lower discount rate for public projects must be based on some form of market friction (or failure) which the government is able to overcome at lower cost than the private sector, and these cost efficiencies need to be quantified to determine their impact on the discount rate.

Problems

1 The government collects revenue from a consumption tax on cigarettes (C) when the aggregate demand function (measured in thousands of cartons) is

$$C = 200 - 5q,$$

where $q = p + t$ is the consumer price per carton (measured in dollars), with p being the producer price and $t = 5$ the constant tax per carton.

- i Use a partial equilibrium analysis to compute the marginal social cost of public funds (MCF) for the consumption tax on cigarettes when they are produced at a constant marginal cost of \$6 per carton (with no fixed costs). Measure the welfare changes as aggregate dollar changes in private surplus. Calculate the marginal excess burden of taxation (MEB) for this tax and illustrate the MCF in a quantity–price $\{C, q\}$ space diagram.
- ii Redo part (i) when the marginal cost of production rises with $MC = 0.08C$.

2 Consider the capital market for a closed economy in a two-period certainty setting where the aggregate demand (D) for capital is determined by $D = a - bi$ and aggregate supply (S) by $S = c + di$, with i being the risk-free interest rate and a, b, c and d constant positive parameters.

- i Use a partial equilibrium analysis to compute an expression for the shadow discount rate when there is an income tax at rate τ on interest income paid to suppliers of capital (so that $S = c + di(1 - \tau)$). Illustrate your answer in a quantity–price space diagram and explain what the welfare changes represent. (Measure the welfare changes as aggregate dollar changes in private surplus.)
- ii Derive the shadow discount rate when $d = 0$ and illustrate the welfare changes in a quantity–price space diagram. Compare it to the discount rate in part (i) above.
- iii Derive the shadow discount rate when $b = 0$ and illustrate the welfare changes in a quantity–price space diagram. Compare it to the discount rates in parts (i) and (ii) above.

3 In a two-period certainty model a single consumer has an endowment of time ($\bar{x}_T$) in the first period (0) which is divided between leisure (x_T) and labour supply to firms.

Labour income is used to purchase a consumption good in the first period (x_0) while the rest is saved (s) and returned with interest (i) after tax ($s(1 + i - \tau_S)$) to fund the purchase of the consumption good in the second period (x_1). Thus, the consumer problem is to maximize $u(x_0, x_T, x_1)$ subject to

$$q_0 x_0 + \frac{q_1 x_1}{(1+i-\tau_S)} = (1-\tau_T)(\bar{x}_T - x_T) - s + \frac{\pi_0 + \pi_1 + s(1+i-\tau_S)}{(1+i-\tau_S)} + L,$$

where:

- L is a lump-sum transfer from the government;
- $q_i = (1 + \tau_C)p_i$ is the consumer price of the consumption good in each period $i = 0, 1$, with p_i being the producer price and τ_C a uniform ad valorem expenditure tax;
- τ_S is the ad valorem tax on interest income;
  $(1-\tau_T)(\bar{x}_T - x_T)$ is the after-tax income from labour supplied by the consumer, with τ_T being the ad valorem tax rate on labour income;
- $\pi_0 = p_0 y_0(y_T) + y_T$ is profit on private production of the consumption good in the first period, with $y_T < 0$ being labour input used; and
- $\pi_1 = p_1 y_1(k_p) - k_p(1 + i)$ is the profit from private production of the consumption good in the second period, with $p_1 y_1(k_p)$ being sales revenue and $k_p(1 + i)$ the cost of private investment in labour purchased in the current period, k_p.

We assume private firms have strictly concave production technologies and operate as price-takers. The *public sector budget constraint* (defined in present value terms) will be

$$L = \tau_T(\bar{x}_T - x_T) + \tau_C \left\{ p_0 x_0 + \frac{p_1 x_1}{1+i-\tau_S} \right\} + \frac{\tau_S s}{1+i-\tau_S} + \frac{p_1 g_1 - (1+i)k_g}{1+i-\tau_S}$$

where $p_1 g_1 - (1 + i)k_g$ is profit from public production of the consumption good in the second period, with $p_1 g_1$ being sales revenue and $k_g(1 + \text{i})$ the cost of public investment in labour purchased in the first period, k_g.

Finally, the market-clearing conditions are $x_0 = y_0$, $x_1 = y_1 + g_1$ and $\bar{x}_T - x_T + y_T = k_p + k_g = s$. There are five exogenous policy variables: τ_C, τ_T, τ_S, g and k_g.

i Derive a conventional welfare equation for marginal changes in the policy variables and use it to compute the shadow price of capital and the shadow discount rate when the tax on interest income is the only tax (with $\tau_T = \tau_C = 0$). Illustrate the shadow discount rate in a price–quantity diagram, and compare it with the cost of capital for private firms. (The interest rate and relative prices of the consumption goods are determined endogenously in a competitive equilibrium.)

ii Derive the welfare loss from marginally raising the expenditure tax when there are no taxes on income (with $\tau_T = \tau_S = 0$).

iii Derive the welfare loss from marginally raising an income tax (with $\tau_T = \tau_S = \tau$) when there is no expenditure tax (with $\tau_C = 0$).

iv Compare the expenditure and income tax bases in parts (ii) and (iii) above. You can use the first-order conditions for firms and the market-clearing condition in the labour market to show that the income tax base includes the expenditure tax base. Explain what the additional welfare change is in the income tax base. What determines the welfare cost of raising a given amount of revenue with each tax? Does one of the two taxes always have a lower welfare cost?

Notes

1 Introduction

1 It is difficult to isolate purely atemporal trades as most goods embody future consumption. For example, packets of washing powder and breakfast cereals have consumption flows in the future and are, strictly speaking, capital assets. Financial securities have a limited role in facilitating purely atemporal trades in a certainty setting where the quality and quantity of the goods are known to buyers and sellers. Once we introduce time and asymmetric information, financial securities can be used to specify the obligations on both parties to get or provide the necessary information about the product being exchanged.

2 Governments are monopoly suppliers of currency (notes and coins), but the money supply is more broadly defined to include cheque and other deposit account balances used for trading goods and services. Since financial institutions keep a fraction of their deposits as currency to meet the cash demands of depositors, there is a multiplier effect from changes in the supply of currency. The nominal price level equates supply and demand in the market for broadly defined money.

3 This is an important issue for the equilibrium asset pricing models examined in Chapter 4.

4 The terms 'risk' and 'uncertainty' are frequently treated as the same thing. Knight (1921) defined risk as uncertain outcomes over which individuals assign probabilities, while uncertainty relates to outcomes over which they do not, or cannot, assign such probabilities. But this distinction is less clear when consumers with different information assign subjective probabilities to uncertain outcomes.

5 Futures contracts are standardized forward contracts which trade on formal futures exchanges, whereas forward contracts also include tailor made agreements between buyers and sellers that trade over the counter.

6 We use the conventional analysis recommended by Harberger where aggregate welfare is the sum of the dollar changes in expected utility for consumers. In effect, this approach uses a Bergson–Samuelson individualistic social welfare function (Bergson 1938; Samuelson 1954) and ignores any distributional effects by assigning the same distributional weight of unity to all consumers. Distributional effects can be included in the analysis by assigning different weights to consumers.

7 Initially both schemes were adopted to reduce the variability in producer prices, but they eventually became price support schemes for domestic producers. Both schemes were eventually abandoned due to the very large costs they imposed on taxpayers.

2 Investment decisions under certainty

1 Capital goods are stocks of future consumption, while investment is the flow of resources into capital goods over a specified period of time.

2 Strictly speaking, the capital market is where all intertemporal trade takes place. It includes trades in physical commodities, such as apples, or financial securities which provide income streams in future periods. There are sub-markets in the capital market, including the financial market where financial securities trade, and the real estate market where property trades. A number of other markets are included in the financial market, such as banks, the stock market, the futures exchange, the bond market, and the markets for derivative securities (options, swaps, warrants, etc). In finance it is not uncommon for the financial market to be referred to by default as the capital market, where this reflects a focus on trades in financial securities.

3 Since there are $2N$ commodities, consumers are choosing bundles (x_0^h, x_1^h) from a $2N$-dimensional commodity space. When each consumer h has a weak preference relation $\succeq^h$ over these bundles that is complete, transitive, and continuous, they can be represented by a utility function, $u^h : \mathbb{R}^{2N} \rightarrow \mathbb{R}^+$, such that

$$\{x_0^{hA}, x_1^{hA}\} \succeq^h \{x_0^{hB}, x_1^{hB}\} \Leftrightarrow u^h(x_0^{hA}, x_1^{hA}) \geq u^h(x_0^{hB}, x_1^{hB}).$$

A proof of the existence of the utility function can be found in most graduate microeconomics textbooks; see, for example, Mas-Colell *et al.* (1995). This function is a contemporaneous measure of utility where each consumer chooses their intertemporal consumption in the first period. Thus, they measure utility from future consumption in the first period.

4 These constraints require each element in the set of consumption goods to be less than or equal to its corresponding element in the set of endowments in each time period.

5 For *standard preferences* we assume the utility function u^h is monotone (to rule out satiation), and strictly quasi-concave (to make the indifference schedules strictly convex to the origin in the commodity space). They are adopted by default in the following analysis.

6 We obtain this marginal rate of substitution by totally differentiating the utility function, with:

$$du = u_0'(n)\, dx_0(n) + u_1'(n)\, dx_1(n) = 0.$$

After rearranging terms, we have

$$\left.\frac{dx_0(n)}{dx_1(n)}\right|_{du=0} = -\frac{u_1'(n)}{u_0'(n)},$$

where $MRS_{1,0}(n) \equiv -dx_0(n)/dx_1(n)$ is the inverse of the slope of the indifference curve at the endowment point in Figure 2.1. From the first-order conditions for optimally chosen consumption, we have $u_t'(n) = \lambda_t(n)$ for $t \in \{0, 1\}$.

7 When consumers have homothetic preferences their rates of time preference for goods are independent of real income. In other words, their indifference schedules in Figure 2.1 have the same slope along a 45° line through the origin.

8 It should be noted that this also accommodates storage when it is the most efficient way of transferring consumption goods to future time periods. After all, production is a process that converts resources into more valuable goods and services, where in a certainty setting they are distinguished from each other by their physical characteristics, geographic location and location in time.

9 This derivation of the marginal rate of substitution uses the fact that $\partial z_0(n)/\partial x_0(n) = -1$.

10 Malinvaud (1972) distinguishes between discount rates for income and discount rates for future consumption goods. In this setting there is a personal discount rate for income of $\lambda_1^h / \lambda_0^h \equiv 1/(1+i^h)$, and a personal discount rate for each commodity $n \in N$ of $MRS_{1,0}^h \equiv 1/[1+\rho^h(n)]$.

11 Lengwiler (2004) derives income as the representative commodity in an asset economy where consumers can trade within each time period and between each time period in an uncertainty setting. We introduce financial securities in Section 2.2.3 and show how they allow consumers to choose their distribution of income over time (subject to the constraint that income sums to their wealth in present value terms). In fact, income can be used as a representative commodity in an economy without financial securities if consumers can trade intertemporally using forward contracts. What financial securities do is reduce the number of variables that consumers must determine in the first period, where they choose the value and composition of their consumption bundle and their holding of financial securities. While they decide the composition of future consumption in the first period, the choices are actually made in the second period. However, in exchange economies with forward contracts, consumers must determine the value and composition of their current and future consumption bundles in the first period.

12 When currency is held as a store of value governments collect revenue as seigniorage due to the non-payment of interest. This imposes a distorting tax on currency holders by driving a wedge between their private cost of holding currency, which is the nominal rate of interest, and the social marginal cost of printing currency. Revenue is transferred by this tax as seigniorage to the government because it uses real resources obtained by printing currency at no interest cost. The real wealth of traders who hold currency balances over time as a store of value will be affected by anticipated changes in the nominal money supply that impact on the nominal interest rate. This wealth effect is examined later in Section 2.3.

13 By 'full trade' we mean consumers can exchange goods within each time period and over time periods.

14 We use the notation defined in Section 2.2.1, where in each time period $t \in \{0, 1\}$, X_t and $\bar{X}_t$ are, respectively, the market values of the consumption and endowments for consumer h, with I_t being income (measured in units of the numeraire good).

15 The discount factor is obtained by noting that $R_1 = p_a(1 + i)$.

16 The *no arbitrage condition* makes the security of every firm a perfect substitute because it eliminates any profit from the returns they pay. In other words, they all pay the risk-free return. If firms are large in the capital market, which seems unlikely for the risk-free security but not when securities are segregated into different risk classes, they have market power in the capital market which they can exploit to generate profit.

17 $VMP^j = \partial Y_1^j / \partial Z_0^j$ is the value of the marginal product from investing a dollar of inputs in firm j when the input mix is chosen optimally to maximize profit.

18 This solution is obtained by using the envelope theorem to eliminate the welfare effects of the consumer choice variables in (2.11). For income in the first period we have $\partial v_0/\partial I_0 = \lambda_0$, and for income in the second period $\partial v_1/\partial I_1 = \lambda_1$.

19. In a certainty setting without taxes there is no meaningful distinction between shares and bonds as they are both risk-free securities.

20 The notation for the trading costs (τ_t) and net expenditures (D_t) at each $t \in \{0, 1\}$ was defined earlier in Section 2.2.2 for the consumer problem in (2.6), while the profit shares in firms (η_0) were defined in Section 2.2.4.

21 Both these optimality conditions are for an interior solution.

22 If consumers hold currency, so that $\lambda_1 / \lambda_0 = 1$, then they have not maximized utility because there are net benefits from moving resources from currency into the risk-free security when $\lambda_1/\lambda_0 > /(1 + i)$.

23 When the financial security reduces trading costs we use (2.15) to write the optimality condition for currency demand, as:

$$1 + D_0 \frac{\partial \tau_0}{\partial m_0} = \frac{1 - D_1 \frac{(\partial \tau_1)}{(\partial m_0)}}{(1+i) - D_1(\partial \tau_1 / \partial V_0)},$$

which equates the net cost of holding another dollar of currency in the first period to the discounted value of the net gain from using it in the second period.

24 In practice, there are changes in preferences, production technologies or other environmental variables traders face that cause relative price changes in the economy as resources flow between different activities. These price changes occur even when money demand and supply grow at the same rate.

25 This assumes the nominal net cash flows will rise with the higher expected rate of price inflation.

26 This expression is obtained by using $aR_1 = V_0(1 + i)$.

27 If the inflation rate rises by $\Delta\pi$ the nominal interest rate will rise by $\Delta\pi(1 + r)$ when the Fisher effect holds.

28 When interest payments are subject to tax at rate τ, with $1 + i(1 - \tau) = (1 + r^A)(1 + \pi)$, the tax-adjusted Fisher effect is

$$\left.\frac{di}{d\pi}\right|_{dr^A=0} = \frac{1 + r^A}{1\text{-}\tau},$$

Where r^A is the real after-tax interest rate.

29 Increases in the money supply are inflationary when they exceed the growth in money demand.

30 This short-term reduction in unemployment is captured by the Phillips (1958) curve which finds a negative relationship between the rate of inflation and the level of unemployment. Friedman (1968) argued wages would be set in anticipation of increases in the rate of inflation, where this can lead to short-term reductions in employment and output. And it is much more likely when governments persistently print money to finance their spending through higher levels of inflation.

31 In a general equilibrium analysis these real effects impact endogenously on economic activity, causing the saving and investment schedules in Figure 2.13 to shift. But for standard preferences and technologies these changes would reduce the size of the final increase in saving and investment without overturning it.

32 The properties of the Bergson–Samuelson welfare function are examined in more detail in Jones (2005).

33 After totally differentiating the social welfare function and using the first-order conditions for optimally chosen consumption, the aggregate welfare change is:

$$\frac{dW}{\beta} = dI_0 + \frac{dI_1}{1+i} = p_0(1+\tau_0)dx_0 + \frac{p_1(1+\tau_1)dx_1}{1+i}.$$

These changes in activity can be solved using the budget constraint for the economy. First, we sum the consumer budget constraints:

$$p_0(1+\tau_0)x_0 + \frac{p_1(1+\tau_1)x_1}{1+i} = p_0(1+\tau_0)(\bar{x}_0 + g_1) + \frac{p_1(1+\tau_1)(\bar{x}_1 + g_0)}{1+i} - p_a a_0 + \frac{p_a a_0(1+i)}{1+i}$$
$$- m_0 + \frac{m_0}{1+i} + \frac{p_1 y_1}{1+i} - p_0 z_0 + L,$$

where L is the sum of the lump-sum transfers from the government budget to consumers. These transfers are used in a conventional Harberger analysis to separate the welfare effects of policy changes, where the government budget constraint, is $L + p_0 g_0 + p_1 g_1/(1+i) = im_0^g/(1+i)$. After combining the private and public sector budget constraints, we obtain the budget constraint for the economy,

$$p_0(1+\tau_0)x_0 + \frac{p_1(1+\tau_1)x_1}{1+i} = p_0(1+\tau_0)\bar{x}_0 + \frac{p_1(1+\tau_1)\bar{x}_1}{1+i} + \frac{i(m_0^g - m_0)}{1+i} + \frac{p_1 y_1}{1+i} - p_0 z_0.$$

After totally differentiating this aggregate constraint for the economy and using the first-order condition for profit-maximizing firms and the goods and money market clearing conditions, we have

$$p_0(1+\tau_0)dx_0 + \frac{p_1(1+\tau_1)dx_1}{1+i} = -D_0\frac{\partial\tau_0}{\partial m_0}dm_0 - \frac{D_1\partial\tau_1}{1+i\partial m_0}dm_0.$$

Finally, we obtain the welfare change in (2.22) by using the first-order condition for optimal currency demand, where:

$$-\left(1 + D_0\frac{\partial\tau_0}{\partial m_0}\right) + \frac{1}{1+i}\left(1 - D_1\frac{\partial\tau_1}{\partial m_0}\right) = 0.$$

34 There are no other welfare effects because this is the only distorted market in the economy. Additional distortions are included in Chapter 8 when evaluating public sector projects.

35 For a detailed examination of private currency, see Dowd (1988), Hayek (1978), Selgin (1988) and White (1989).

36 In this setting commodity prices, asset prices and interest rates are time-specific, where in each period t the vectors of commodity and security prices are denoted p_t, and p_{at}, respectively, and the risk-free interest rate i_t. The endowments of goods in every time period can change over time, and it is relatively straightforward to include additional time periods in a certainty setting because all the equilibrium prices in the future are known in the first period by every agent. Consumers get utility from consumption expenditure in time periods out to infinity when they care about their heirs, but a lower bound has to be placed on their wealth to stop them from creating unbounded liabilities by continually borrowing to delay loan repayments until the infinite future where they have zero current value. While the interest rate and commodity prices can change over time in a certainty setting, they are known in advance by all consumers who use common discount factors on future net cash flows when they trade in frictionless competitive markets. That is not the case, however, when there is uncertainty unless agents have common information. Uncertainty is examined in the next chapter.

37 Using (2.12) we can write the share of profit for each consumer as $\eta_t^h = V_t^h - Z_t^h$ for all t, where the budget constraint in each time period becomes:

$$X_t^h \leq \bar{X}_t^h - Z_t^h \equiv I_t^h \forall_t.$$

38 The long-term interest rate for period T is the geometric mean of the short rates in each period $t-1$ to t, with

$$i_T = \sqrt[T]{\prod_{t=1}^{T}(1 + {}_{t-1}i_t)} - 1.$$

39 Frequently they are extracted earlier than this due to activity rules governments impose on titles granted for exploration and mining.

40 Since the annual interest rate is the *geometric mean* of a sequence of short rates over the year the 100-day rate solves:

$$i_{100} = \sqrt[100/365]{1+i} - 1.$$

41 This valuation assumes the expectations hypothesis holds.

42 When bondholders face this risk and information is costly the shareholders may favour more risky projects, where bondholders respond by discounting bond prices. Firms recognise this by inviting large creditors onto their boards to give them greater access to information and more say in their investment decisions. We examine these issues in more detail in Chapter 7.

43 Income taxes are levied on measured nominal income, while private investment decisions are based on economic real income which isolates the true change in consumption.

3 Uncertainty and risk

1 The hedonic prices can be estimated empirically by regressing apple prices on their different characteristics.

2 We follow Savage (1954) and define each state as a full description of the world that is of concern to the consumer; it represents an actual realization of the world at the end of time when all uncertainty is resolved. In prior time periods before the uncertainty is resolved there are possible events which are subsets of the set of true states of the world. In the first time period there is a single event that includes all possible states, while in the final time period there are as many events as there are states of the world. When there are more than two time periods there are fewer states in each event as time passes because some of the uncertainty is resolved. We provide a more complete description of the state space in Section 3.1. In the following analysis we use a two-period model where each event in the second period coincides with one of the states of nature. Thus, there are as many events as states of nature.

3 In effect, consumers have complete information about the demand for and supply of every commodity in every time period and in every state of the world. The analysis is much more complicated when consumers have different information and form different expectations about future equilibrium outcomes, which is the case when information is costly to acquire. Solving an equilibrium outcome for the economy in these circumstances requires that these costs be specified, as well as the technologies consumers use to acquire information. For example, they may take information from the initial market prices of contingent commodity contracts because they provide signals of what the market is expecting commodity prices to be in the future.
4 The economics of insurance is examined separately in Chapter 5.
5 Policy evaluation is examined in Chapter 8.
6 This closely follows the presentation provided in Lengwiler (2004).
7 A partition divides the full set of states into pairwise disjoint non-empty subsets. Thus, the state space is the sum of these subsets. As time passes the partitions become finer. That is, there are fewer and fewer states in each event, until in the final period there as many events as states of nature.
8 Ehrlich and Becker (1972) argue that assumption (iii) rules out self-protection by consumers to reduce the probability of bad outcomes. But we accommodate this activity by adding individual risk to the aggregate (state) uncertainty. In particular, we expand the possible outcomes in each state by including risk that is diversifiable across the population. For example, a portion of the population will suffer losses from car accidents, but they can self-protect and reduce the probability of accidents by driving more slowly and at safer times. Moral hazard arises when this effort to self-protect cannot be costlessly observed by insurers, where consumers have less incentive to self-protect if they are not directly rewarded with lower insurance premiums for their marginal effort. Individual risk expands the outcome space, but without affecting the state probabilities. The probability of each final outcome is the sum of the state probability plus the probability of incurring losses in that state. When individual risk can be costlessly eliminated through insurance, it is eliminated from the consumption expenditure of individual consumers.
9 It is implicitly assumed in the following discussion that consumers with more information have subjective probabilities that are closer to the 'true' underlying objective probabilities; these are the probabilities that would prevail with complete information. Moreover, consumers with the same information have the same beliefs, which is the Harsanyi doctrine. But this may not always apply in reality because consumers can have different technologies for converting information into beliefs, so that two consumers with the same information may form different beliefs. Indeed, they may have different computational skills and different inherent abilities to process information. When we characterize a competitive equilibrium in the following analysis consumers are assumed to have common beliefs so that they agree on the event-contingent prices for goods in future time periods. Allowing them to have different information and beliefs is problematic because we need to specify the way information is collected and processed and at what cost before we can solve the equilibrium outcome. For example, market prices may provide information to consumers that will change their beliefs, and this in turn will impact on prices through their trades.
10 When consumers hold different beliefs about the state-contingent commodity prices, due to incomplete and asymmetric information, the equilibrium outcomes are a function of their information sets. This creates problems when consumers obtain information from endogenously determined variables such as market prices when forming their beliefs. Radner (1972) considers the role of information and consumer beliefs on equilibrium outcomes under uncertainty.
11 Consumer preference rankings can be described by this generalized utility function when they are complete, continuous and transitive. In the following analysis we also assume they are monotonic, to rule out satiation, and strictly quasi-concave, to make the indifference curves strictly convex to the origin in the commodity space. These preferences do not separate the probabilities and utility derived from consumption in each state. This is examined in Section 3.2 where we derive the von Neumann–Morgenstern expected utility function.
12 We follow the practice adopted in the previous chapter and make good 1 numeraire when there is no fiat currency in the economy. One could easily refer to a unit of good 1 as a dollar and then continue to define values in dollar terms. The multiplier on the first-period budget constraint (λ_0^h) is the marginal utility of current income, while the state-contingent constraint multipliers (λ_s^h) are the marginal utility of income in the second period in each state s.

13 The indirect utility functions are mappings over state-contingent income when consumers optimally choose consumption bundles in each state to equalize their marginal utility from income spent on each good, with $[\partial u_s^h(\cdot)/\partial x_s^h(n)]/p_s(n) = \lambda_s^h$ for all n, s. We adopt the practice used in Chapter 2 of defining consumption expenditure in each period as $X_0 = \Sigma_n p_0(n)\, x_0(n)$ and $X_s = \Sigma_n p_s(n) x_s(n)$, respectively, and the market value of the endowments in each period as $\bar{X}_0 = \Sigma_n p_0(n)\, \bar{x}_0(n)$ and $\bar{X}_s = \Sigma_n p_s(n)\, \bar{x}_s(n)$.

14 For interior equilibrium solutions to the consumer problem the first-order conditions for the forward contract are $\lambda_s^h p_s(n) - \lambda_0^h p_{fs}(n) = 0$ for all n, s, while for current and state-contingent consumption, respectively, they are $\partial u^h(\cdot)/\partial x_0^h(n) = \lambda_0^h p_0(n)$ for all n and $\partial u_s^h(n)/\partial x_s^h(n) = \lambda_s^h(n)$ for all n, s. They are straightforward extensions of the optimality conditions in the certainty models examined previously in Chapter 2.

15 The first-order conditions for optimally supplied forward contracts are $\lambda_s^j p_s(n) - p_{fs}(n) = 0$ for all n, s.

16 In later chapters when we include taxes on income we will separate the capital and income in these payoffs, as $R_{ks} = p_k\,(1 + i_{ks})$ for all k, s, where i_{ks} is the rate of return to security k in each state s.

17 After substituting for η_0 we can write income in the first period as $I_0 \equiv \bar{X}_0 - Z_0$, where Z_0 is the amount saved.

18 For optimally chosen current consumption, we have $\partial u_0\,(n)/p_0\,(n) = \lambda_0$ for all n, and $\partial u_s(n)/p_s\,(n) = \lambda_s$ for all n, s. Thus, the constraint multipliers are the marginal utility of income in the first period and in each state s, respectively, where $\varphi_s = \lambda_s/\lambda_0$ is the marginal rate of substitution between income in future state s and the current period; it is the discount factor used by consumers to evaluate income in state s.

19 The payouts in each state have been normalized at unity.

20 A complete capital market is frequently referred to as a full set of insurance markets. DeAngelo and Masulis (1980a, 1980b) exploit this property of a complete capital market when they examine the effects of firm financial policy by working directly with primitive securities.

21 We examine the Miller (1977) equilibrium in Chapter 7 where consumers with progressive personal income taxes have different tax preferences for securities that allow them to increase their wealth through tax arbitrage. This activity continues until they eliminate their tax preferences or have borrowing constraints imposed on them.

22 A unique equilibrium will exist in the absence of taxes when consumers have strictly convex indifference sets and firms have strictly convex production possibility sets. The indifference sets are mappings from ordinal utility functions that are complete, transitive, reflexive, continuous and strictly quasi-concave, while the production possibility sets are mappings from strictly concave production functions with no fixed costs. A unique equilibrium will exist under more general circumstances, where a proof of the existence of equilibrium in the Arrow–Debreu economy is provided by Mas-Colell *et al.* (1995). Multiple equilibrium outcomes cannot be ruled out by adopting these standard assumptions on preferences and production technologies in economies with taxes and other price distortions. This is demonstrated by Foster and Sonnenschein (1970).

23 These possibilities are examined in Chambers and Quiggin (2000).

24 The utility functional $U(\cdot)$ is a cardinal preference mapping over consumption expenditure.

25 For a discussion of these difficulties, see Grant and Karni (2004) and Karni (1993).

26 Anscombe and Aumann (1963) make the distinction between roulette-wheel lotteries and horse-race lotteries so that they can identify the subjective probabilities consumers assign to states when they have state-independent preferences. It allows them to separate randomness in income within each state and between states.

27 If we adopt the common prior assumption, which is referred to as the *Harsanyi doctrine*, consumers with the same information have the same probability beliefs. But Kreps (1990) argues that since we allow consumers to have different preferences over the same consumption bundles we should also allow them to form different probability beliefs from the same information.

28 The expected utility function can be used to rank preferences over state-contingent outcomes if we extend the independence axiom. Savage does this by adopting the sure-thing principle so that rankings of outcomes depend only on states where they differ. There are also additional axioms to describe the way consumers form their probability beliefs. Ultimately the aim is for consumers to have subjective probabilities that they believe could be the true objective probabilities.

Mas-Colell *et al.* (1995) adopt the extended independence axiom that makes preference rankings over roulette-wheel type lotteries independent of the state of nature. This expands the randomness in consumption expenditure to the state space by mapping all the roulette-wheel type lotteries onto every state, which is not the case when the sure-thing principle is used.

29 Mehra and Prescott (1985) find the risk premium in equity is much larger than is predicted by the CCAPM when consumers are assigned a coefficient of relative risk aversion that is consistent with empirical evidence. Based on behavioural characteristics from experimental studies, Benartzi and Thaler (1995) argue that this puzzle can be explained by consumers having a degree of loss aversion where they place a larger weight on losses than they do on gains. Indeed, this may also be evidence that the CCAPM fails because consumers have state-dependent preferences. Other explanations for the puzzle are examined in Chapter 7.

30 The expectations operator $E_t(\cdot)$ uses probabilities that are based on information available at time t.

31 By taking a second-order Taylor series expansion of $EU(\tilde{I}) = U(\bar{I} - RP(\bar{I}))$ around $\bar{I}$, we have:

$$EU(\bar{I}) + EU'(\bar{I})(\tilde{I} - \bar{I}) + \tfrac{1}{2} EU''(\bar{I})(\tilde{I} - \bar{I})^2 = U(\bar{I}) - U'(\bar{I})RP(\bar{I}).$$

We obtain the expression for $RP(\bar{I})$ by noting that $EU'(\bar{I})(\tilde{I} - \bar{I}) = 0$ and $EU(\bar{I}) = U(\bar{I})$.

32 We obtain (3.15) by solving the risk premium as a function of the growth in consumption expenditure, where the variance in consumption can be decomposed as

$$\sigma_I^2 = E\left(\frac{\tilde{I} - \bar{I}}{\bar{I}}\right)^2 \bar{I}^2 = \sigma_g^2 \bar{I}^2,$$

with $g = (\tilde{I} - \bar{I}) / \bar{I}$ being the growth rate in consumption expenditure. By using this normalization we can solve the risk premium as

$$RP(\bar{I}) = \frac{1}{2} \sigma_{I'}^2 \bar{I} \cdot RRA.$$

33 Mean–variance preferences, where consumers only care about the first two moments of the distribution over the consumption outcomes, even when they are not normally distributed, are the less preferred basis for a mean–variance analysis.

34 Prior to Fama, the widely held view was that security prices followed a random walk. But the hypothesis has a number of important limitations which are discussed in LeRoy (1989).

35 When securities pay dividends they need to be reinvested in the security for prices to follow a discounted martingale.

36 In the following analysis we use conventional notation to define the statistical properties of random variables, where for each security k, we have *expected return*

$$E(\tilde{i}_k) = \bar{i}_k = \sum_{s=1}^{S} \pi_s i_{ks}, \text{with } \Sigma_s \pi_s = 1$$

variance $$\mathrm{Var}(\tilde{i}_k) = \sigma_k^2 = E\left([\tilde{i}_k - E(\tilde{i}_k)]^2\right) = \sum_{s-1}^{S} \pi_s (i_{ks} - \bar{i}_k)^2;$$

and *standard deviation*

$$\mathrm{Std}\,(\tilde{i}_k) = \sigma_k = \sqrt{\sigma_k^2}.$$

From an economic perspective, the standard deviation is a measure of dispersion that arises naturally in a mean–variance analysis. Since utility is determined by consumption, the welfare effects of uncertainty will depend on the expected value of consumption and, for risk-averse consumers, how far it deviates from that expected value. Since consumption is funded, at least in part, by returns to portfolios of securities, the risk in each security is determined by the covariance of its return with consumption expenditure. When security returns are less than perfectly positively correlated with each other it is possible to eliminate part of their variance by bundling them in portfolios. This diversification effect is determined by the *covariance* of security returns, given, for any two risk securities *k* and *d*, by

$$\text{Cov}(\tilde{i}_k, \tilde{i}_d) = \sigma_{kd} = E\left([\tilde{i}_k - E(\tilde{i}_k)][\tilde{i}_d - E(\tilde{i}_d)]\right) = \sum_{s-1}^{S} \pi_s (i_{ks} - \bar{i}_k)(i_{ds} - \bar{i}_d),$$

and by the *coefficient of correlation*

$$\text{Corr}(\tilde{i}_k, \tilde{i}_d) = \rho_{kd} = \frac{\sigma_{kd}}{\sigma_k \sigma_d}.$$

37 Cochrane (2001) shows how all the popular equilibrium pricing models in the literature, including the CAPM, intertemporal CAPM, APT and consumption-beta CAPM, are obtained as special cases of (3.17) by linearizing the pricing kernel $\tilde{m}$ over a set of state variables that isolate aggregate consumption risk. Cochrane makes the point that (3.17) also holds for individual consumers when the capital market is incomplete and they have different expectations, but their discount factors and consumption risk can be different in these circumstances. We derive the CBPM in a complete capital market and with a common expectations operator so that (3.17) is the same for all consumers.

38 This decomposition is obtained by writing the covariance term as

$$\text{Cov}(\tilde{m}, \tilde{R}_k) \equiv E\left\{(\tilde{m} - \bar{m})(\tilde{R}_k - \bar{R}_k)\right\} = E(\tilde{m}\tilde{R}_k) - E(\tilde{m})E(\tilde{R}_k).$$

39 Cochrane and Lengwiler refer to this equation as the consumption-based capital asset pricing model (CCAPM). In this book it is referred to as the CBPM, while the term CCAPM is used in Chapter 4 to refer to the consumption-beta CAPM derived by Breeden and Litzenberger (1978) and Breeden (1979) where the beta coefficient is the covariance between the expected return on any security *k* and the growth in aggregate consumption divided by the variance in aggregate consumption. It is a conditional beta coefficient in a multi-period setting when the variance in aggregate consumption changes over time.

40 Insurance markets specialize in pooling diversifiable risks. When consumers purchase insurance they create a mutual fund that makes payments to those who incur losses. A common example is car insurance, where drivers face a positive probability of having an accident that can impact on their consumption. By purchasing insurance they reduce this consumption risk and spread the cost of car accidents over all car insurers. However, problems can arise when there is asymmetric information between traders in the insurance market – in particular, when insurers cannot observe effort by consumers to change their probability or size of loss, or when they cannot distinguish between consumers with different risk. We examine these issues in Chapter 5.

41 Using the power utility functions in (3.20) to compute RRA in (3.15), we have

$$RRA = \begin{cases} \left(-\gamma\, \tilde{I}_{t+1}^{-\gamma-1} / \tilde{I}_{t+1}^{-\gamma}\right) \tilde{I}_{t+1} = \gamma, & \text{for } \gamma \neq 1 \\ \left(\tilde{I}_{t+1}^{-2} / \tilde{I}_{t+1}^{-1}\right) / \tilde{I}_{t+1} = 1 = \gamma, & \text{for } \gamma = 1. \end{cases}$$

42 From (3.21) we obtain the respective marginal utilities $U'(\tilde{I}_{t+1}) = \tilde{I}_{t+1}^{-\gamma}$ and $U'(\tilde{I}_{t+1}) = 1/\tilde{I}_{t+1}$. They are substituted into the stochastic discount factor.

43 The log utility CAPM holds unconditionally (which means it is independent of time *t*) when security returns are identical and independently distributed over time to rule out changes in the investment opportunity set. To see how the return on wealth can be used as a proxy for aggregate consumption in the stochastic discount factor, we solve the return on wealth over period *t* to *t* + 1, using (3.22) with $\gamma = 1$, as

$$1 + \tilde{i}_{W,t+1} = \frac{\tilde{W}_{t+1} + \tilde{I}_{t+1}}{\tilde{W}_t} = \frac{(\delta/(1-\delta)+1)\tilde{I}_{t+1}}{\tilde{I}_t \delta/(1-\delta)} = \frac{1}{\tilde{m}_{t+1}}$$

Consumption is a constant proportion of wealth for log utility because additional consumption expenditure ($\tilde{I}_{t+1}$) is exactly offset by the lower stochastic discount factor ($(\delta(\tilde{I}_{t+1}/I_t)^{-1})$). Thus, wealth is unaffected by changes in future consumption.

44 Breeden and Litzenberger (1978) and Breeden (1979) derive the CCAPM in discrete time by adopting the power utility in (3.20) with $\gamma \neq 1$ when security returns are jointly lognormally distributed with aggregate consumption. This model holds unconditionally (which makes it independent of time t) when the interest rate is constant and security returns are independently and identically distributed. The CCAPM is derived in Section 4.3.4.

45 Later in Chapter 4 we summarize the equity premium and low risk-free interest rate puzzles identified by Mehra and Prescott (1985). They show how consumers with power utility need a high CRRA to explain the large risk premium observed in historical data of returns to a stock market index. But this also means they view consumption in different time periods as highly complementary and require a higher equilibrium interest rate to get them to save in a growing economy. Indeed, the interest rate is higher than what is observed in the data. Epstein and Zin (1989) use a generalized expected utility function that separates the coefficient of relative risk aversion from the intertemporal rate of substitution in consumption to provide a solution to the low risk-free rate puzzle.

46 This section shows how diversifiable risk can be eliminated by trading risky securities. In Chapter 5 we show how it is costlessly eliminated by trading insurance in a common information setting.

47 We could allow aggregate uncertainty and then let consumers face loss L in each state of nature with probability π_L. Indeed, the loss and the probability of loss could also be made state–dependent. While this may be more realistic, it makes the analysis unnecessarily complex. Aggregate uncertainty is removed from the analysis in this section so that we can focus on diversifiable risk.

48 There are two reasons for consumers to trade primitive securities in this economy: one is to transfer income between the two time periods, while the other is to shift income between the two states in the second period. If consumers have identical preferences and income endowments there are no potential gains from transferring income between periods, but there are potential gains from transferring income between the states. In these circumstances we have $a_B > 0$ and $a_G < 0$ (with $a_B + a_G = 0$) to smooth consumption across the states. This generates aggregate net revenue in the first period of $H(p_{aB}\, a_B + p_{aG}\, a_G)$, and an aggregate net cost in the second period of $H(\pi_B\, a_B + \pi_G\, a_G)/(1 + i)$ measured in present value terms. The risk-free return is used in the discount factor here because, by the law of large numbers, $H(\pi_B\, a_B + \pi_G\, a_G)$ is a certain net payout to securities. In a competitive capital market the no arbitrage condition drives the security prices to $p_{as}^{p} = \pi_s/(1+i)$ for $s \in \{B, G\}$.

49 In models with multiple future time periods consumers also care about changes in relative commodity prices over time when they consume bundles of goods. Thus, they care about the real value of consumption expenditure in the future because it determines the combinations of goods they consume.

50 Since the derivative security has $\beta_{II} = 1$, we can use (3.31) to solve the risk premium for aggregate consumption risk, as $\psi = (\bar{i}_I - i)/\sigma_I^2$. After substitution we obtain (3.32).

51 Arrow (1971) made the important observation that quadratic preferences have the unattractive property of IARA.

52 Meyer (1987) makes the observation that joint normal distributions are drawn from a class of linear distribution functions that result in mean–variance preferences when consumers have NMEU functions. Ross (1978) identifies distributions that will lead to two-fund separation where consumers choose the same risky portfolios to combine with the risk-free security.

53 Cochrane (2001) provides a detailed and excellent exposition of the way state variables can be identified in the CBPM and how to make the stochastic discount factor linear in these variables.

54 These discount factors are obtained by using the NMEU function in (3.13) to obtain the CBPM in (3.17) when there are more than two time periods.

55 A risk-free bond pays the same real (nominal) interest payment at every event in each time period where interest is paid. Nominal risk-free bonds can be risky due to inflation risk.

56 Discount bonds are defined in Section 2.4.5. They are coupon bonds with zero coupon interest. Thus, they pay a specified cash flow at their maturity date, and nothing in prior periods.

4 Asset pricing models

1 The efficient mean–variance frontier identifies the highest expected returns to portfolios of risky securities at each level of risk.

2 The notation was defined in Chapter 3, where X_0 and X_s are the values of current and future consumption expenditure in each period, respectively, $\bar{X}_0$ the market value of current endowments, $V_0 = \Sigma_k P_{ak} a_k$ the market value of the portfolio of securities, and η_0 the share of profit in private production.

3 We remove the second-period endowments from the intertemporal budget constraints defined in (3.7) to remove endowment risk from future consumption.

4 Once consumers allocate their wealth to future consumption by choosing the value and composition of their portfolio, they indirectly choose their current consumption expenditure when, as is assumed here, there is non-satiation in each time period.

5 Current consumption expenditure is being optimally chosen in the background of the analysis when consumers choose their portfolios of securities.

6 The minimum variance portfolio is obtained by differentiating the portfolio variance in (4.3) with respect to a and setting the expression to zero, where $\hat{a} = (\sigma_B^2 - \sigma_{AB})/(\sigma_A^2 + \sigma_B^2 - \sigma_{AB})$.

7 A fully indexed bond which pays a constant real interest rate is a pure risk-free security. In most countries short-term government bonds are used as the risk-free security, but they are not normally indexed for unanticipated changes in inflation. Thus, even if the Fisher effect holds, the real interest rate on these bonds will change with unanticipated inflation.

8 At the margin all investors must be equally risk-averse along a linear efficient frontier as their indifference curves have the same slope. It takes a larger proportion of risky asset A in the portfolio of investor 2 to equate the slopes of their indifference curves.

9 The linear factor analysis relates the security returns to random values of the factors as

$$\tilde{i}_k = c_k + \beta_{k1}\tilde{F}_1 + \ldots + \beta_{kG}\tilde{F}_G + \tilde{\varepsilon}_k,$$

where c_k is a constant. By adding and subtracting $\Sigma_g \beta_{kg}\bar{F}_g$ to this expression, we have

$$\tilde{i}_k = c_k + \sum_g \beta_{kg}\bar{F}_g + \sum_g \beta_{kg}\tilde{f}_g + \tilde{\varepsilon}_k,$$

where $\tilde{f}_g = \tilde{F}_g - \bar{F}_g$ is the deviation in factor g from its mean. We obtain (4.22) by noting that $\bar{i}_k = c_k + \Sigma_g \beta_{kg}\bar{F}_g$.

10 Market risk is priced uniquely in the APT when the residuals are eliminated from the returns to the mimicking portfolios constructed to price factor risk. When this happens it becomes an exact factor analysis. We demonstrate this in Section 4.3.3 when deriving the APT pricing equation from the CBPM in (3.17).

11 The no arbitrage condition was defined earlier in Theorem 3.1.

12 Using vector notation we can write (4.23) as $a^A[1] = 0$, where a^A is the $(1 \times K)$ vector of security weights in the arbitrage portfolio and [1] the $(K \times 1)$ unit vector. As a risk-free portfolio we must have $a^A\beta = [0]$ and $a^A\varepsilon = [0]$, where β is the $(K \times G)$ matrix of beta coefficients, [0] the $(1 \times G)$ vector of zeros and ε the $(K \times 1)$ vector of residuals, which leads to $a^A\bar{i} = [0]$, with $\bar{i}$ the $(K \times 1)$ vector of expected security returns. Since a^A is orthogonal to the vector [1] and the columns in matrix β, which imply it is also orthogonal to the vector of security returns $\bar{i}$, there is a linear relationship between these vectors, with

$$\bar{i} = \lambda_F + \beta\lambda_\beta,$$

where λ_F and λ_β are, respectively, the $(K \times 1)$ and $(G \times 1)$ vectors of non-zero constants.

A crucial feature of this model is the zero price for residuals in the mimicking portfolio returns, and the no arbitrage condition. The residuals attract no premium when they have zero variance, while the absence of arbitrage profits maps security returns onto the premiums for market risk isolated by the factors. In practice, the R^2 for empirical estimates of the beta coefficients in (4.22) is less than unity, where this leaves a positive variance in the residuals. In other words, some of the market risk has not been identified by the common risk factors in the regression analysis. As the number of traded securities (K) increases, $R^2 \to 1$ and the variance in the residuals approaches zero. This is examined in detail by Cochrane (2001).

13 The pricing relationship in (4.28) will also hold when the capital market is incomplete, but consumers can have different discount rates across the states of nature.

14 In this setting we continue to assume consumers have conditional perfect foresight where they correctly predict equilibrium outcomes at each event in every future time period. The expectations operator $E_t(\cdot)$ is based on probability beliefs formed at current time t.

15 We can think of an infinitely lived consumer as someone who cares as much for their heirs as they do for themselves, which is why the same utility function is used by each consumer in all future time periods. But a lower bound must be placed on wealth to stop them creating unbounded liabilities by rolling their debt repayments out to infinity where they have zero present values.

16 The relationship between the short- and long-term stochastic discount factors in a multi-period setting is summarized in Section 3.4. For the long-term discount factor over period t to T, we have $\tilde{m}_T = \delta^{T-t}U'(\tilde{I}_T)/U'(I_t)$, which is the product of a full set of short-term stochastic discount factors, one for each consecutive time period, with:

$$\tilde{m}_T = {}_t\,\tilde{m}_{t+1}\,{}_{t+1}\tilde{m}_{t+2} \cdots {}_{T-1}\tilde{m}_T,$$

where the short-term discount factors are $\tilde{m}_{\tau,\tau+1} = \delta U'(\tilde{I}_{\tau+1})/U'(\tilde{I}_\tau)$.

17 The wealth portfolio is a combination of the risk-free bond and a bundle of risky securities. As noted earlier in Section 4.1, every consumer holds the same risky bundle (M) in the CAPM, which is why it is referred to as the market portfolio, but they hold different combinations of it with the risk-free bond according to their risk preferences. Investors who are relatively more risk-averse at the margin will hold more of the risky portfolio M in their wealth portfolio.

18 A risk-free bond pays the same rate of return in every event in each time period. But it can change over time when the term structure of interest rates (for risk-free government bonds with different maturity dates) rises or falls due to changes in the investment opportunity set.

A constant interest rate makes the term structure flat so that the interest rate on a risk-free bond is the same at each event and in each time period.

19 Stein's lemma states that if $\tilde{i}_W$ and $\tilde{R}_k$ are joint normally distributed, and $m(\tilde{i}_W)$ is differentiable with $m'(\tilde{i}_W) < \infty$, then

$$\text{Cov}[m(\tilde{i}_W), \tilde{R}_k] = E_0[m'(\tilde{i}_W)]\,\text{Cov}(\tilde{i}_W, \tilde{R}_k).$$

It is obtained using the decomposition $E(\tilde{m}\tilde{R}_k) = E(\tilde{m})E(\tilde{R}_k) + \text{Cov}(\tilde{m}, \tilde{R}_k)$ where $\tilde{m}$ and $\tilde{R}_k$ are time-dependent variables, with $E(\tilde{m}\tilde{R}_k) = \sum_{i=1}^{\infty} E(\tilde{m}_t)E(R_{kt})$.

20 Breeden (1979) extends Merton's analysis by allowing changes in relative commodity prices, while Long (1974) derives the ICAPM using discrete-time analysis where security returns and the factors used to isolate consumption risk are multi-variate normal. The normality assumption is not required in the continuous-time model of Merton as the two securities are normally distributed over infinitely small time intervals for the diffusion process used to describe security returns.

21 The wealth portfolio is a combination of the risk-free bond and a bundle of risky securities. In the CAPM every consumer holds the same risky bundle (M), which is why it is referred to as the market portfolio, but they hold different combinations of it and the risk-free bond due to differences in risk preferences. Investors who are relatively more risk-averse at the margin hold more of the risky portfolio M in their wealth portfolio.

22 We obtain (4.34) by expanding (4.28), using $\tilde{R}_k = (1+\tilde{i}_k)p_{ak}$, as

$$E[\tilde{m}(1+\tilde{i}_k)] = E(\tilde{m})(1+\tilde{i}_k) + \text{Cov}[\tilde{m}, (1+\tilde{i}_k)] = 1\ \forall k.$$

Since $E(\tilde{m}) = 1/(1+i)$, we have:

$$\bar{i}_k - i = -\,\mathrm{Cov}[\tilde{m},(1+\tilde{i}_k)]\ \forall k.$$

When security returns are joint-normally distributed Stein's lemma (summarized in note 19) allows us to decompose the covariance term as

$$\mathrm{Cov}[\tilde{m},(1+\tilde{i}_k)] = E\left(\frac{\partial \tilde{m}}{\partial \tilde{i}_w}\right)\mathrm{Cov}(\tilde{i}_w,\tilde{i}_k) + E\left(\frac{\partial \tilde{m}}{\partial \tilde{z}}\right)\mathrm{Cov}(\tilde{z},\tilde{i}_k),$$

where, from (4.32),

$$\frac{\partial \tilde{m}}{\partial \tilde{i}_W} = \delta\frac{V_{WW}p_a a^W}{V_W} \text{ and } \frac{\partial \tilde{m}}{\partial \tilde{z}} = \delta\frac{V_{Wz}}{V_W}.$$

23 Merton finds the market portfolio may not be mean–variance efficient in the ICAPM due to the additional state variables (factors). However, Fama (1998) shows that investor portfolios are in fact multi-factor minimum-variance efficient, where consumers combine the market portfolio with a risk-free security and mimicking portfolios to hedge against the factor risk. The return on each mimicking portfolio is perfectly correlated with a state variable and uncorrelated with the return on the market portfolio and all other state variables. Thus, the risk premium in mimicking portfolio returns are compensation paid to investors for bearing non-diversifiable risk described by their state variables.

24 Merton argues that if all traded securities by some quirk of nature are uncorrelated with the interest rate, the term structure of interest rates for a riskless long-term bond will not satisfy the expectations hypothesis. This is based on the observation that consumers will pay a premium for a man-made security such as a long-term bond that is perfectly negatively correlated with changes in the interest rate, and hence by assumption that is not correlated with any other asset. But this premium would be eliminated by arbitrage in a frictionless competitive capital market.

25 Since (4.22) is constructed as a regression equation the factor deviations, which have zero mean values ($E(\tilde{f}_g) = 0$ for all g), are uncorrelated with each other ($\mathrm{Cov}(\tilde{f}_g, \tilde{f}_j) = 0$ for all $g \neq j$) and the residuals have zero mean ($E(\tilde{\varepsilon}_k, \tilde{\varepsilon}_j) = 0$ for all k, j. Equation (4.22) describes the returns to each security k and not any arbitrary set of returns by assuming the error terms are uncorrelated across securities, with ($E(\tilde{\varepsilon}_k, \tilde{\varepsilon}_j) =$ for all k, j. As the factors are reported as rates of return the sensitivity coefficients in (4.22) are standard beta coefficients, with $\beta_{kg} = \mathrm{Cov}(\tilde{i}_k,\tilde{i}_g)/\mathrm{Var}(\tilde{i}_g)$.

26 Cochrane shows beta pricing models are equivalent to models with linear stochastic discount factors. To see this, start with the exact factor pricing model (without residuals) $\bar{i}_k = i + \beta_k\lambda$, where λ is the (G × 1) column vector of factor prices. Based on the linear factor model in (4.22), we have $\lambda_g = -(1+i)E(\tilde{m}\tilde{f}_g)$ for all g and $\beta_k = E(\tilde{i}_k\tilde{f}')/E(\tilde{f}\tilde{f}')$. Since $\tilde{f}'$ is the (1 × G) row vector of factor deviations from their expected values $E(\tilde{f}\tilde{f}')$ is a variance–covariance matrix. Using these decompositions we can write the APT pricing model as

$$1+\bar{i}_k = (1+i) - (1+i)E(\tilde{i}_k\tilde{f})\frac{E(\tilde{m}\tilde{f})}{E(\tilde{f}\tilde{f}')}.$$

Then, by defining $E(\tilde{m}) = a = 1/(1+i) \neq 0$ and $b' = E(\tilde{m}\tilde{f})/E(\tilde{f}\tilde{f}')$ with $E(\tilde{f}\tilde{f}')$ non-singular, we have $1+\bar{i}_k = 1/a - [E(\tilde{i}_k\tilde{f})b']/a$, for $\tilde{m} = a + b'\tilde{f}$.

27 When security prices follow a Markov process the expected price in the next period depends solely on the current price and not on prices in previous time periods.

28 Breeden derives the CCAPM with stochastic labour income but without leisure. When labour supply is endogenous, leisure has to be included in the measure of aggregate consumption.

29 For the power utility function in (3.20) with $\gamma \neq 1$, wealth can be solved as

$$W_t = E_t \sum_{t=1}^{\infty} \delta^t (1+\tilde{g}_{t+1})^{-\gamma} \tilde{I}_{t+1}$$

where $\tilde{g}_{t+1} = (\tilde{I}_{t-1} - I_t)/I_t$ is the growth rate in consumption.

30 The decomposition in (4.39) is obtained in two steps. First, ln (1 + ρ) is solved using (4.38) when $1+\tilde{g}$ is continuous and log normally distributed with mean $E[\ln(1+\tilde{g})]$ and variance $\mathrm{Var}[\ln(1+\tilde{g})]$, as

$$\begin{aligned}\ln(1+\rho) = & -\gamma E[\ln(1+\tilde{g})] + E[\ln(1+\tilde{i}_k)] \\ & + \tfrac{1}{2}\left\{\gamma^2 \mathrm{Var}[\ln(1+\tilde{g})] + \mathrm{Var}[\ln(1+\tilde{i}_k)] + 2\mathrm{Cov}[-\lambda \ln(1+\tilde{g}), \ln(1+\tilde{i}_k)]\right\}. \qquad \text{(a)}\end{aligned}$$

It is obtained by noting that when the product of two random variables A and B is lognormally distributed, we have:

$$\ln(\tilde{A}\tilde{B}) = E(\ln\tilde{A}) + E(\ln\tilde{B}) + \tfrac{1}{2}[\mathrm{Var}(\ln\tilde{A}) + \mathrm{Var}(\ln\tilde{B}) + 2\,\mathrm{Cov}(\ln\tilde{A}, \ln\tilde{B})].$$

Next, the price of the risk-free bond,

$$E(\tilde{m}) = \frac{1}{1+i} = \frac{1}{1+\rho} E(1+\tilde{g})^{-\gamma},$$

is used to solve ln (1 + ρ) when security returns and consumption growth are log-normally distributed, as:

$$\ln(1+\rho) = \ln(1+i) + \ln[E(1+\tilde{g})^{-\gamma}] \qquad \text{(b)}$$

with $\ln[E(1+\tilde{g})^{-\gamma}] = -\gamma E[\ln(1+\tilde{g})] + \tfrac{1}{2}\gamma^2 \mathrm{Var}[\ln(1+\tilde{g})]$. We obtain (4.39) by combining (a) and (b).

31 With lognormally distributed consumption growth, we have:

$$\ln[E(1+\tilde{i}_k)] = E[\ln(1+\tilde{i}_k)] + \tfrac{1}{2}\mathrm{Var}[\ln(1+\tilde{i}_k)].$$

32 There are a number of discrepancies in measures of aggregate consumption in the national accounts. Some capital expenditure is included at the time of purchase, but it should instead be the consumption flows generated over time. There are non-marketed consumption flows, like leisure and home-produced consumption, that are not included in reported data. Most countries make adjustments to include major items such as the rental value of housing services consumed by owner-occupiers. Empirical tests of the CCAPM use a consumer price index to obtain a real measure of consumption expenditure. We summarize the results for some of these tests later in Section 4.5.

33 While consumption in each time period is related indirectly through wealth, which is the discounted present value of future income that can be transferred between periods by trading in the capital market, the utility derived in each time period is independent of consumption expenditure in all other periods.

34 Optimally chosen future consumption expenditure can be summarized using means and variances because consumers have state-independent preferences. This means they care only about the statistical distribution of their consumption expenditure. The mean–variance analysis then follows from assumptions when security returns are completely described by their means and variances. A less satisfactory basis for using a mean–variance analysis is to assume consumers have quadratic preferences.

35 Empirical studies compute economic returns to publicly listed shares by measuring changes in their prices over time and adding dividend payments to them.

36 In the unconditional versions of the CAPM and the CCAPM the parameters in their stochastic discount factor are constant over time, while in the conditional versions of the models they are time-dependent.

37 The Hansen–Jagannathan bound can be obtained by using (4.28) to write the pricing relationship for security k as

$$E(\tilde{m}, 1+\tilde{i}_k) = E(\tilde{m})E(1+\tilde{i}_k) + \text{Cov}(\tilde{m}, 1+\tilde{i}_k) = 1$$

After rearranging these terms, and using $E(\tilde{m}) = 1/(1+i)$, we have

$$\bar{i}_k - i = (1+i)\ \text{Cov}\ (-\tilde{m}, \tilde{i}_k) = (1+i)\ \text{Corr}\ (-\tilde{m}, \tilde{i}_k)\sigma_m \sigma_k,$$

with $-1 \leq \text{Corr}(-\tilde{m}, \tilde{i}_k) \leq +1$. Since the correlation coefficient cannot exceed unity, we set Corr $(-\tilde{m}, \tilde{i}_k) = 1$ and measure the risk premium as

$$\frac{\bar{i}_k - i}{\sigma_k} \leq (1+i)\sigma_m.$$

There is a one-to-one relationship between consumption and wealth when consumers have aconstant coefficient of relative risk aversion. Thus, by using the power utility function $U(I_t) = I_t^{1-\gamma}/(1-\gamma)$, we can write the stochastic discount factor as $\tilde{m}_t = \delta(\tilde{I}_t / I_0)^{-\gamma} = \delta(1+\tilde{g})^{-\gamma}$, where its variance becomes:

$$\sigma_m^2 \approx \text{Var}[-\gamma\ \ln(1+\tilde{g}) + \ln\delta] \approx \gamma^2 \text{Var}[-\ln(1+\tilde{g})] \approx \gamma^2\sigma_g^2,$$

with $\tilde{g} = (\tilde{I} - I_0)/I_0$. From this we have $\sigma_m \approx \gamma\sigma_g$ in (4.42).

38 This expression is obtained by writing the risk-free discount factor in logarithmic form, as $\ln\delta - \gamma\ \ln E(1+\tilde{g}) = -\ln(1+i)$, where $\ln(1+\tilde{g}) \approx \tilde{g}$ if the variance in the discount factor (m) is small.

39 McGrattan and Prescott (2003) argue there are no puzzles about the average debt and equity returns over the last century when taxes on security returns, diversification costs and regulatory constraints imposed on US households are taken into account.

40 There are excellent technical summaries of these extensions to the standard CCAPM in Cochrane (2001), Kocherlakota (1990) and Lengwiler (2004).

41 Abel distinguishes between habit determined by past consumption of other consumers as 'catching up with the Joneses' and habit determined by current consumption of other consumers as 'keeping up with the Joneses'.

42 The risk-free rate puzzle cannot be solved when external habit is based solely only on the current consumption of others because saving is not raised in the same way as external habit based on past consumption.

43 Campbell and Cochrane are able to successfully predict changes in the risk premium (the Sharpe ratio) over time with external habit based on past consumption but with a high coefficient of relative risk aversion. In contrast, Constantinides can successfully explain the equity premium and the low risk-free rate puzzles with internal habit (if consumers are highly sensitive to their own consumption risk) but without predicting changes in the risk premium correctly.

44 This relationship was derived earlier in Section 3.3.1 in the previous chapter.

45 Heaton and Lucas find borrowing constraints can lower the risk-free rate considerably when a large enough proportion of consumers cannot sell debt. And they do so by reducing the demand for risk-free funds.

46 Using the CCAPM with a coefficient of relative risk aversion set at unity, which is consistent with estimates from empirical research, the risk premium on equity is less than 1 per cent for the low observed standard deviation in aggregate consumption of approximately 3 per cent.

47 Arrow and Lind argue the public sector faces a lower cost of capital because it can diversify risk by undertaking a large number of projects. Any remaining risk can then be spread across the population by using the tax system to fund these projects. Bailey and Jensen (1972) refute this claim by arguing the returns on most government projects are in fact correlated with national income, which means they contain market risk that cannot be diversified by combining them together. Moreover, the tax system is not a costless way of diversifying idiosyncratic risk. In fact, there are few, if any, non-distorting taxes that governments can use, where lump-sum (or poll) taxes are politically infeasible, while most taxes on trade affect economic activity. We look at how risk affects the social discount in Chapter 8.

48 This expression is obtained by starting with the value of the net cash flows at $t-1$, with $\tilde{V}_t = \widetilde{NCF}_t$, and

$$V_{t-1} = E_{t-1}(\widetilde{NCF}_t)\left(\frac{1}{1+E(\tilde{i}_t)}\right).$$

When expectations about the net cash flows are formed using (4.48), with

$$E_{t-1}(\widetilde{NCF}_t) = E_{t-2}(\widetilde{NCF}_t)(1+\tilde{\varepsilon}_{t-1}),$$

their random value at $t-1$ becomes

$$\tilde{V}_{t-1} = E_{t-2}(\widetilde{NCF}_t)(1+\tilde{\varepsilon}_{t-1})\left(\frac{1}{1+E(\tilde{i}_t)}\right).$$

After taking expectations at $t-2$, we have

$$E_{t-2}(\tilde{V}_{t-1}) = E_{t-2}(\widetilde{NCF}_t)\left(\frac{1}{1+E(\tilde{i}_t)}\right),$$

which allows us to write the value of the net cash flows at $t-2$ as

$$V_{t-2} = E_{t-2}(\widetilde{NCF}_t)\prod_{j=t-1}^{t}\left(\frac{1}{1+E(\tilde{i}_j)}\right)$$

We obtain (4.49) by iterating back to time 0.

49 By using (4.48) we can write the random value of the net cash flows at time $\tau < t$, as

$$\tilde{V}_\tau = E_{\tau-1}(\widetilde{NCF}_t)(1+\tilde{\varepsilon}_\tau)\prod_{j=\tau+1}^{t}\left(\frac{1}{1+E(\tilde{i}_j)}\right).$$

Since its covariance with the return on the market portfolio, is

$$\text{Cov}(\tilde{V}_\tau, \tilde{i}_{M\tau}) = E_{\tau-1}(\widetilde{NCF}_t)\,\text{Cov}(\tilde{\varepsilon}_\tau, \tilde{i}_{M\tau})\prod_{j=\tau+1}^{t}\left(\frac{1}{1+E(\tilde{i}_j)}\right),$$

and its expected value at $\tau-1$, is

$$E_{\tau-1}(\tilde{V}_\tau) = E_{\tau-1}(N\tilde{C}F_t)\prod_{j=\tau-1}^{t}\left(\frac{1}{1+E(\tilde{i}_j)}\right),$$

we have

$$\mathrm{Cov}(\tilde{V}_\tau, \tilde{i}_{M\tau}) / E_{\tau-1}(\tilde{V}_\tau) = \mathrm{Cov}(\tilde{\varepsilon}_\tau, \tilde{i}_{M\tau}).$$

5 Private insurance with asymmetric information

1 A more detailed presentation is available in Laffont (1989) and Malinvaud (1972).

2 In this setting state probabilities are outside of the control of consumers both as individuals and coalitions, but later we allow them to affect the probabilities of their individual risk through self-insurance. Their preferences can be summarized using NMEU functions with common information where they agree on the probabilities of all the possible outcomes, both for states and individual risk. But with asymmetric information subjective expected utility is more appropriate when consumers have different probabilities beliefs, which takes the analysis outside the classical finance model used to generate the consumption-based pricing model in (4.28) where consumers measure and price risk identically.

3 A state-independent utility function may not be appropriate for some applications, such as health insurance, where preference mappings depend on the consumers' well-being.

4 While we refer to these outcomes as good and bad states, they are not the states of nature defined earlier in Section 3.1.1 that are common to all consumers and outside their control. In contrast, the good and bad outcomes considered here are incurred by different individuals at the same time. Later we allow consumers to change the probability of bad state outcomes through self-protection.

5 There is a competitive equilibrium outcome for a single insurer when the market is perfectly contestable. The threat of entry forces the incumbent to set the price of insurance at the lowest possible marginal cost.

6 The analysis in this section draws from the analysis in Pauly (1974) and Shavell (1979).

7 Shavell (1979) considers ex-ante and ex-post observation with differential costs. Ex-post observation occurs when consumers make claims, while ex-ante observation occurs at the time the policies are written. Ex-ante observation is preferable if it is less costly than ex-post observation by an amount sufficient to offset the extra frequency of observation involved.

8 A considerable amount of work has been undertaken in this area looking at the adjustment processes to equilibrium and the existence properties of these equilibria. See Greenwald and Stiglitz (1986), Harris and Townsend (1985), Riley (1975), Stiglitz (1981, 1982) and Wilson (1977).

9 It is assumed throughout the analysis that insurance is *exclusive*, so that consumers buy all their insurance from one insurer. It can also be interpreted as meaning that all insurers know how much insurance every consumer buys and stops them from taking more than full insurance. In practice, insurance contracts contain clauses which require consumers to reveal all their insurance cover, with failure to do so releasing insurers from any of their obligations. Exclusivity stops high-risk types from locating to the right of L along the low-risk price line.

6 Derivative securities

1 Most retail outlets provide consumers with a two-week cooling-off period when they purchase major items. In some countries it is mandated by law, but firms still do it voluntarily when the option is valued sufficiently by consumers.

2 This bundle is created by taking long positions in the share and put option and being short in the risk-free bond. The two options have the same exercise price ($\hat{S}_T$), which is also the payout on the risk-free bond.

3 When the share price follows a random walk without drift its expected price is equal to its current price, where deviations in the future price are noise with zero mean and constant variance.

4 The stochastic variable z is a continuous random variable with increments that are statistically independent; it is normally distributed with mean zero and variance equal to the increment in time dt. Just like a random walk in discrete time, the variance scales with time.

5 Ito's lemma takes a second-order Taylor series expansion of the call option value, where:

$$dC = \frac{\partial C}{\partial t} dt + \frac{\partial C}{\partial S} dS + \frac{1}{2}\frac{\partial^2 C}{\partial t^2} dt^2 + \frac{\partial^2 C}{\partial t \partial S} dt\, dS + \frac{1}{2}\frac{\partial^2 C}{\partial S^2} dS^2,$$

and then uses (6.8) to substitute for $dS = S(\mu_S\, dt + \sigma_S dz)$ with $dz = \sqrt{dt}, dt^2 = 0$ and $dt\,dS = 0$, to obtain equation (6.9).

6 After substituting (6.7) into (6.9) and using $dH = iH\,dt$, we have

$$iH\,dt = dS - \frac{\partial S}{\partial C}\left\{\frac{\partial C}{\partial S}dS + \frac{\partial C}{\partial t}dt + \frac{1}{2}\frac{\partial^2 C}{\partial S^2}\sigma_S^2 S^2 dt\right\}.$$

The first two terms cancel because the risk in the share price is eliminated inside the hedge portfolio. By using $H = S - (\partial S/\partial C)C$ and then rearranging terms, we obtain (6.10).

7 The Australian Futures Exchange became a wholly owned subsidiary of the Australian Securities Exchange in 2006. It trades standardized futures contracts as well as over-the-counter forward contracts.

8 Sometimes this relationship is presented as ${}_0F_{NT} = (p_{N0} - {}_0NY_{NT})(1 + i_T)^T$, where ${}_0NY_{NT} = {}_0Y_{NT} - {}_0Q_{NT}$ is the present value of the net marginal convenience yield from storage.

9 The expected annual economic return from holding commodity N for T periods is

$$E(\tilde{i}_{NT}) = \left(\frac{E_0(\tilde{p}_{NT})}{p_{N0}}\right)^{1/T} - 1.$$

Thus, for 1 year, with $T = 1$, we have $E(\tilde{i}_{NT}) = [E_0(\tilde{p}_{NT}) - p_{N0}]/p_{N0}$.

10 Intermediate uncertainty was examined earlier in Section 4.6.2.

11 In the ICAPM all future consumption is funded solely from returns to portfolios of securities and there is no risk from labour or other income, where the risk in the market portfolio is the aggregate consumption risk in the first period, while the interest rate and relative commodity price risk determine how aggregate consumption risk changes over time.

7 Corporate finance

1 The consumer problem can be summarized using (2.11), without superscript h as:

$$\max\left\{v(I)\left|\begin{matrix} X_0 \le \bar{X}_0 + \eta_0 - p_{aB}a_B - p_{aE}a_E \equiv I_0 \\ X_1 \le \bar{X}_1 + a_B p_{aB}(1+i_B) + a_E p_{aE}(1+i_E) \equiv I_1 \end{matrix}\right.\right\},$$

where $I = \{I_0, I_1\}$ is the vector of consumption expenditures in each period. The first budget constraint makes current consumption expenditure (X_0) and the market value of the security portfolio no greater than the market value of the endowments ($\bar{X}_0$)plus profit from production (η_0), while the second constraint makes future consumption expenditure (X_1) no greater than the market value of the endowments ($\bar{X}_1$) plus the payouts to securities, where a_k is the number of units of security $k \in B, E$ held by the consumer.

2 This is the personalized discount factor defined in the Arrow–Debreu economy in (3.8) for a single state in the certainty setting, with $\varphi_1^h = \lambda_1^h / \lambda_0^h$, where λ_0^h and λ_1^h are the Lagrange multipliers on the budget constraints. By the envelope theorem these multipliers measure the marginal utility of income in each period at a consumer optimum when there is non-satiation, with $\partial v^h/\partial I_t = \lambda_t^h$ for $t \in \{0, 1\}$.

3 Some consumers may sell both securities to borrow against real income endowments in the second period.

4 In the two-period certainty model in Section 2.2.5 private firms purchase consumption goods in the first period as inputs to future production. We extend the analysis here by allowing them to finance this investment by selling debt and equity, where the problem for each profit-maximizing firm can be summarized using (2.12), without superscript j, as

$$\max\left\{\eta_0 = p_{aB}a_B + p_{aE}a_E - Z_0 \,\middle|\, a_B p_{aB}(1+i_B) + a_E p_{aE}(1+i_E) \le Y_1(Z_0)\right\},$$

where $Z_0 \equiv p_0 z_0$ is the market value of inputs purchased in the first period, and $Y_1 = p_1 y_1$ the market value of the net cash flows it generates in the second period. The constraint makes the payouts to debt and equity by each firm equal to the market value of their net cash flows. By defining leverage as the proportion of each dollar of capital raised by selling debt as $b = p_{aB} a_B / V$, we can write the problem for each firm as:

$$\max\left\{\eta_0 = V_0 - Z_0 \middle| V_0\left(1 + bi_B + (1-b)i_E\right) \leq Y_1(Z_0)\right\},$$

where $V_0 = p_{aB}\, a_B + p_{aE}\, a_E$ is its current market value. The expression in (7.3) is obtained from the payout constraint when it binds.

5 While it is fairly common practice in the finance literature to refer to consumers as being short in securities when they sell them and long when they buy them, the same practice is less well established when referring to the positions taken by firms. To avoid any confusion we will refer to firms as being short in a security when they purchase it and long when they sell it. This is consistent with the notion that consumers are in general net buyers and firms net sellers of securities. There are a number of reasons why firms may purchase securities. For tax reasons they repurchase their own shares and the shares of other firms to pay shareholders capital gains rather than cash dividends, and they also purchase securities to spread risk and arbitrage profits. These activities will be examined in the following subsections.

6 We omit the time subscripts and superscript j to simplify the notation.

7 This decomposition is obtained by writing the user cost of capital as $1 + \tilde{i}_E = \tilde{Y}(I)/V_U$, where

$$\beta_{E_U} = \mathrm{Cov}(\tilde{i}_{E_U}, \tilde{i}_M)/\mathrm{Var}(\tilde{i}_M) = \mathrm{Cov}(\tilde{Y}, \tilde{i}_M)/V_U[\mathrm{Var}(\tilde{i}_M)] = \sigma_{YM}/V_U\sigma_M^2.$$

8 We have $d\bar{i}_{E_l}/db = (\bar{i}_M - i)\beta_{E_l}/(1-b)$, where $(\bar{i}_M - i)\beta_{E_l} = \bar{i}_{E_l} - i$.

9 These conditions are obtained from the problem for each firm in (2.12) by replacing their payout constraint, with superscript j omitted, as

$$bV_0(1+i_B)(1-t_C) + (1-b)\,V_0(1-t_C+i_E) \leq Y_1(Z_0)\,(1-t_C).$$

By rearranging this expression when the constraint binds we find that the corporate tax base is

$$(1-b)\,i_E V_0 = (Y_1(Z_0) - bi_B V_0 - V_0)\,(1-t_c).$$

Since the repayment of capital to debt and equity and interest are tax-deductible expenses the tax falls on the return paid to equity. We follow the usual (often implicit) convention adopted in most finance models by returning tax revenue to consumers as lump-sum transfers. This avoids the need to explicitly model government spending. But even though the tax revenue is returned to consumers, their real income falls due to the excess burden of taxation.

10 In reality, however, the corporate tax is levied on measured income which is not in general the same as economic income. Recall from Chapter 2 that economic income measures the change in the wealth of consumers over a period of time. Thus, it includes capital gains (or losses) on their capital assets. In contrast, measured income applies decay factors to the purchase prices of depreciating assets as a proxy measure for the reduction in their market values, and only includes capital gains when they are realized. Whenever there are differences in economic and measured income the effective corporate tax rate on economic income diverges from the statutory tax rate. For example, when measured income is higher the effective tax rate on economic income rises above the statutory corporate tax rate. We avoid this complexity in the following analysis by assuming economic and measured income are equal.

11 This assumes investors do not take into account any future consumption benefits they might get from government spending funded from corporate tax revenue. In practice, individual investors do not directly link the tax they pay to the benefits they get from government spending. Since the tax each investor pays is small relative to total tax revenue, they do not expect their contribution in

isolation to have any noticeable impact on government spending. Moreover, wealth is redistributed through the government budget so that high-income taxpayers are less likely to receive the same value of benefits per dollar of tax revenue they pay. In the current setting tax revenue is returned to consumers as lump-sum transfers by including them in the budget constraints of consumers. This allows us to focus on equilibrium outcomes in the capital market without worrying about the welfare effects of government spending. The government budget constraint is explicitly included in the welfare analysis used in Chapter 8.

12 In practice, firms are not declared bankrupt in every defaulting state because bondholders may decide firm managers will operate more effectively in the future.

13 This is obtained by using the firm payout constraint

$$bV_0\,(1+i_B)(1-t_C)+(1-b)\,V_0\,(1-t_C+i_{sE})+h_sV_0\le Y_s(Z_0)\,(1-t_C)\ \forall_s,$$

where $h_s\,V_0$ is the default cost in each state s.

14 To properly account for asymmetric information in the Arrow–Debreu economy we need to explicitly introduce information sets for traders as well as the technologies they use to gather and process information.

15 When there are more than two periods the firm recovers depreciation rather than repaying capital to shareholders and bondholders, but measured depreciation allowances are rarely equal to economic depreciation, where the difference changes the effective tax rate on economic income and affects the value of the firm.

16 In Australia some corporations can trade their tax losses inside conglomerates. This happens in the mining and exploration sector where companies have large tax losses in some years. Similar losses are incurred by drug and information technology companies that undertake research and development. They are forced to bear potentially large costs from having to carry their tax losses forward without interest.

17 For a comprehensive summary of non-tax capital structure theories, see the survey by Harris and Raviv (1991) and the recent book by Tirole (2006). They also provide a summary of the results from empirical tests of these theories.

18 Barnea *et al.* (1981) argue managerial incentives and specialized securities such as convertible debt can be used to reduce, and in some cases, eliminate these agency problems.

19 Governments justify having lower tax rates on capital gains by arguing they promote investment and income growth. But this is frequently inconsistent with other objectives they have to minimize the excess burden of taxation. There is no doubt that part of the reason for the favourable tax treatment of capital gains is the political influence of corporate firms. They make large contributions to political parties, while the costs are diffused over consumers with much less political influence.

20 The reduction in the effective personal tax rate from delaying the realization of capital gains can be demonstrated by comparing the after-tax return to a consumer from realizing a dollar of income today and then reinvesting it for one period $(1-t_B^h)[1+i_E(1-t_B^h)]$ with the after-tax return from leaving the income inside the firm for a year $(1+i_E)(1-t_B^h)$. When the income is realized now rather than next period the consumer pays additional tax of $t_B^h i_E(1-t_B^h)$.

21 We obtain these first-order conditions from the consumer problem in section 2.2.5 by replacing the budget constraints in (2.11), with:

$$\begin{cases} X_0\le \bar{X}_0-p_{aB}a_B-p_{aD}a_D-p_{aG}a_G\equiv I_0, \\ X_1\le \bar{X}_1+p_{aB}a_B[1+i_B(1-t_B^h)]+p_{aD}a_D[1+i_D(1-t_B^h)]+p_{aG}a_G[1+i_G(1-t_E^h)]\equiv I_1, \\ a_k\ge \bar{a}_k,\ \text{for}\ k=B,D,G, \end{cases}$$

where securities D and G are shares that pay dividends and capital gains, respectively. Since the different personal taxes are endowed on consumers they have unbounded demands for their tax-preferred securities, where tax arbitrage can, in the absence of constraints, exhaust government revenue. Following Miller, we use short-selling constraints to restrict tax arbitrage and bound security demands. Other ways of bounding security demands are examined below.

22 This supply condition is obtained by replacing the payout constraint in the optimization problem for firms in (2.12) with

$$V_0\,(1-t_C) + i_B\,(1-t_C)\,p_{aB}\,a_B + i_D p_{aD} a_D + i_G p_{aG} a_G \le Y_1(1-t_C),$$

where $V_0 = p_{aB}a_B + p_{aD}a_D + p_{aG}a_G$ is the current market value of their capital. The tax base is obtained by rearranging this constraint, when it binds, as

$$i_D p_{aD}\,a_D + i_G\,p_{aG}a_G = (Y_1 - i_B p_{aB}a_B - V_0)\,(1-t_C),$$

with interest ($i_B p_{aB} a_B$) and the repayment of capital (V_0) being tax-deductible expenses. When there are borrowing constraints on consumers to restrict tax arbitrage it is important that there are no constraints on the security trades of firms for the no arbitrage condition to hold. Indeed, if consumers cannot arbitrage profits from security returns, firms must be able to perform the task in a competitive capital market. When firms choose their security trades optimally, they satisfy

$$\varphi(1+i_B)(1-t_c) \le 1, \quad \text{for debt,}$$
$$\varphi(1-t_C+i_D) \le 1, \quad \text{for equity paying dividends}$$
$$\varphi(1-t_C+i_G) \le 1, \quad \text{for equity paying capital gains.}$$

In the absence of arbitrage profits these conditions hold with equality and we obtain the supply condition in (7.27).

23 This assumes bondholders and shareholders can claim income payments made to securities they sell as a tax-deductible expense.

24 When governments respond to tax-minimization schemes there can be strategic interactions between the public and private sectors. Examples of this are examined in a dynamic setting by Fischer (1980).

25 Aivazian and Callen (1987) illustrate the Miller equilibrium using an Edgeworth box diagram where they show how constraints on tax arbitrage are required for exogenously endowed tax rates to bound security demands. They also identify the role of firm security trades in making firm leverage policy irrelevant.

26 Some of these issues are raised in Chapter 8 where we examine project evaluation in an intertemporal setting with tax distortions.

27 For examples, see Dammon (1988) and Auerbach and King (1983).

28 Miller (1988) also recognizes the important role of the security trades by financial intermediaries in a competitive capital market.

29 Using US data over the period 1970–1985, Simon (1996) finds that the relationship between the default-free tax exempt and taxable yields in the Miller equilibrium holds in the long run. Deviations in this relationship are due to transitory shocks to the leverage-related costs of debt and bank borrowing costs in the short run. The typical levels of these costs did not cause deviations from the Miller equilibrium in the sample period.

30 In practice, the returns to domestic and foreign securities are converted into a common currency before they are compared. Money has no real effects in the analysis undertaken here so we can use a common numeraire good for all countries. In other words, interest rate parity holds for each currency in this real analysis. Once money has real effects interest rate parity can break down, where a risk-free security can pay a different rate of return across countries due to expected changes in exchange rates.

31 This is obtained when the firm maximizes profit ($\eta_0 = V_0 - Z_0$) by choosing investment to make:

$$\left.\frac{dV_0}{dZ_0}\right|_{db=0} = 1.$$

32 Expected default costs per dollar of capital can be included if at the margin they are unaffected by changes in investment. In a common information setting they are confined to lost corporate tax shields as bankruptcy and agency costs require asymmetric information.

33 As a first-order condition this expression is evaluated with leverage set at its optimal level. Once MM leverage irrelevance breaks down, firm financing decisions affect their real investment choices, where shareholders may not be unanimous in wanting firms to maximize profit.

34 Lower income taxes expand aggregate output by reducing the excess burden of taxation. Any change in tax revenue is offset by changes in government spending through the government budget. In the current analysis the tax revenue is returned to consumers as lump-sum transfers because there is no government spending. It will be included in Chapter 8 when we undertake a welfare analysis of changes in taxes and government spending.

35 Miller (1977) also considers the role of investors such as religious and other non-profit organizations who are exempt from tax.

36 Australia adopted the imputation tax system in 1998 and New Zealand adopted it the following year. Canada and the United Kingdom adopted a partial imputation system. In the UK it was replaced in 1999 by a system that provided personal tax reductions on dividend income subject to corporate tax. These personal tax concessions range from 100 per cent for basic-rate taxpayers to 25 per cent for high-rate taxpayers. Singapore replaced a full imputation tax system in 2003 with a one-tier corporate tax system which exempts all dividends from personal tax when they have been subject to corporate tax.

37 The analysis here can be extended to accommodate uncertainty with common information by noting that the equilibrium condition on security returns holds in each state of nature when the capital market is complete.

38 Their dividend payout ratio changed over the sample period from around 50 per cent prior to the 1980s to over 60 per cent during the 1980s and 1990s. It peeked at about 100 per cent in 1982 and then declined to around two-thirds in the 1990s due largely to changes in the relative tax treatment of capital gains and dividends. Sarig finds empirical support for the information content of dividends.

39 The taxes on corporate income under a classical corporate tax system were summarized earlier in Table 7.2.

40 Barclay and Smith do, however, find empirical evidence that the benefits from the information content of dividends are large enough to offset their tax disadvantage.

41 The reduction in the effective tax rate on capital gains is illustrated in note 20.

42 Capital gains are included in economic income in the periods when they accrue but, for the most part, they are included in measured income at the time they are realized. Thus, in periods when capital gains are significant, firms with positive economic income can have negative measured income. Similar problems arise with capital losses because measured depreciation allowances are determined by applying standardized decay factors to the original purchase prices of assets, while economic depreciation allowances are determined by the reductions in their market valuations.

43 We obtain these conditions by replacing the budget constraints for consumers in (2.11) with

$$\begin{aligned} &X_0 \le \bar{X}_0 - p_{aB}a_B - p_{aD}a_D - p_{aG}a_G \equiv I_0,\\ &X_1 \le \bar{X}_0 + p_{aB}a_B[1+i_B(1-t_B^h)] + p_{aF}a_F\left[1+\frac{i_F}{1-t_C}(1-t_B^h)\right]\\ &\qquad + p_{aU}a_U[1+i_U(1-t_B^h)] + p_{aG}a_G[1+i_G(1-t_E^h)] \equiv I_1,\\ &a_k \ge \bar{a}_k \text{ for } k = B,F,U,G, \end{aligned}$$

where a_F is the number of units of franked dividend paying shares purchased at market price p_{aF}, and a_U the number of units of unfranked dividend paying shares purchased at market price p_{aU}. The borrowing constraints are used to rule out tax arbitrage and bound security demands when investors have different tax preferences for the four types of securities.

44 To capture the different tax treatment of franked and unfranked dividends, we replace the payout constraint in the problem for firms in (2.12) with

$$bV_0\,(1+i_B)(1-t_C)+d_FV_0[(1-t_C)+i_F]+d_UV_0(1+i_U)\,(1-t_C)+gV_0[(1-t_C)+i_G] \le Y_1(1-t_C),$$

where $b = p_{aB}a_B/V_0$, $d_F = p_{aF}a_F/V_0$, $d_U = p_{aU}\,a_U/V_0$ and $g = p_{aG}a_G/V_0$. When this constraint binds for profit-maximizing firms we can write their current market value as

$$V_0 = \frac{Y(1-t_C)}{(1-t_C)+bi_B(1-t_C)+d_Fi_F+d_Ui_U(1-t_C)+gi_G},$$

with $b + d_F + d_U + g = 1$.

8 Project evaluation and the social discount rate

1 We aggregate changes in utility over consumers using the individualistic social welfare function of Bergson (1938) and Samuelson (1954). It is a functional mapping over the utility functions of all consumers in the economy, who each obtain utility from their own consumption bundle. In other words, this rules out consumers deriving utility from the consumption bundles chosen by others. However, the social welfare function can take different forms to reflect variations in social attitudes to inequality, ranging from complete indifference (utilitarian) to complete aversion (Rawlsian). We initially use a conventional Harberger analysis that assigns the same distributional weights to consumers. This removes distributional effects from the welfare analysis and allows us to aggregate dollar changes in utility over consumers, where aggregate welfare gains represent potential Pareto improvements through an appropriate lump-sum redistribution. Distributional effects can be included by assigning different distributional weights to consumers.

2 A pure public good is defined to be perfectly non-rivalrous and non-excludable. It is difficult for private suppliers to extract a fee from consumers when the good is non-excludable, which is why public goods are underprovided in private markets. It creates a free-rider problem where individuals can consume the benefits of goods supplied by others without making a contribution to their cost. Indeed, this can lead to strategic interactions between private suppliers. To avoid these problems, which are not the focus of the current analysis, we assume the good is produced solely by the government.

3 The following analysis could be undertaken using generalized state preferences, but they do not allow us to separate the impact of risk on equilibrium outcomes. Moreover, expected utility is a requirement for using one of the consumption-based pricing models examined earlier in Chapter 4 to compute risk-adjusted discount rates on future cash flows.

4 In the following analysis we assume every consumer is a net supplier of the private good, with $\bar{x}_0^h - x_0^h > 0$, and a net consumer in the second period, with $\bar{x}_s^h - x_s^h < 0$ for all h. We could allow some individuals to be net consumers in the first period (with $\bar{x}_0^h - x_0^h < 0$) and some to be net suppliers in the second period, with $\bar{x}_s^h - x_s^h > 0$. However, the tax rates would then become subsidies, unless we allow them to change sign. But consumers would then face different relative commodity prices and use different discount factors to evaluate future consumption flows.

5 Since lump-sum transfers are non-distorting they make no contribution to the final welfare effects. This has important practical implications because it allows governments to separate policy evaluation across a number of specialist agencies. Treasury and finance departments can evaluate the marginal social cost of raising revenue with a range of different taxes without knowing how the funds will be spent, while departments responsible for health, education, social security and defence can evaluate the net benefits from their spending programmes independently of the way they are financed. The final changes to the distorting taxes are determined by the impact projects have on the government budget. If they drive it into deficit then distorting taxes must be raised to generate additional revenue, while the reverse applies for projects that drive the budget into surplus.

6 There is a detailed examination of the role of lump-sum transfers in a conventional welfare analysis in Jones (2005). Ballard and Fullerton (1992) argue that a conventional welfare analysis is not possible when lump-sum transfers are ruled out. But they are only hypothetical transfers that we use to separate the welfare effects of each policy variable, and they are eliminated inside projects by tax changes made to balance the government budget. This is demonstrated in Section 2.1.2.

7 In each period the aggregated endowments are $\bar{x}_0 = \Sigma_h \bar{x}_0^h$ and $\bar{x}_s = \Sigma_h \bar{x}_s^h$ for all s, aggregate consumption $x_0=\Sigma_h x_0^h$ and $x_s=\Sigma_h x_s^h$ for all s, and the lump-sum transfers $L_0=\Sigma_h L_0^h$ and $L_0=\Sigma_h L_s^h$ for all s. We allow the government to trade in the capital market so that it can transfer tax revenue between the two periods. On that basis, the government budget constraint can be computed in present value terms by using the stochastic discount factors in (8.2).

8 The model can be extended by adding more time periods and redefining the second-period budget constraints over events (e), which are time-specific subsets of the state space. To accommodate saving and investment at times beyond the second period, replace $^-Z_0$ and y_s for all s by the vector of net outputs y_e, with $y_e < 0$ for inputs and $y_e > 0$ for outputs.

9 Since λ_0^h is the marginal utility of current income, $1/\lambda_0^h$ converts expected utility into current income. Thus, dEU^h/γ_0^h is a dollar measure of the change in expected utility; it measures areas of surplus below consumer demand schedules. It is well known that dollar changes in utility are in general unreliable welfare measures for discrete (large) policy choices. Once the marginal utility of income changes with real income, dollar changes in private surplus do not map into utility at a constant rate and are therefore path-dependent. This is examined in detail by Auerbach (1985) and Jones (2005). These problems do not arise in a marginal welfare analysis because changes in the marginal utility of income have higher-order effects that do not impact on final welfare changes.

10 This expression is obtained by using the first-order conditions for optimally chosen consumption, with $\partial U^h/\partial x_0^h = \lambda_0^h p_0$ and $\delta \partial U^h/\partial x_s^h = \lambda_s^h p_s$ for all s and the first-order condition for optimally chosen saving in (8.2).

11 Bergson (1938) initially described the individualistic social welfare function, while Samuelson (1954) was the first to use it in formal analysis.

12 Individualistic social welfare functions rule out interdependencies between consumers where they get utility from their own consumption bundle as well as the consumption bundles of others. However, they can be given functional forms that reflect social attitudes to income inequality ranging from complete indifference (utilitarian) to complete aversion (Rawlsian). These determine the values of the distributional weights assigned to consumers in the aggregate welfare changes.

13 Distributional effects can be included in the welfare analysis by assigning different distributional weights to consumers. Typically there is an inverse relationship between these weights and income, where low-income consumers are assigned higher relative weights. But they are based on subjective assessments that can differ across policy analysts. In some circumstances policy changes with efficiency losses, which isolate reductions in real income, can be socially profitable due to distributional effects. Most analysts report the efficiency and equity effects separately so that policymakers can see the role played by subjectively determined distributional effects in the welfare analysis. We address these issues in more detail in Section 8.1.4.

14 Using (8.5), we can write the change in social welfare in (8.6) as

$$dW = (\bar{x}_0 - x_0)(dp_0 - dt_0) - z_0 dp_0 + MRS_0 dG_0 + dL_0 \\ + \sum_s \pi_s m_s \{(\bar{x}_s - x_s)(dp_s + dt_0) + y_s dp_s + MRS_s dG_1 + dL_s\}.$$

The changes in the lump-sum transfers are solved using the government budget constraints in (8.4) where, after substitution, we have

$$dW = -t_0 dx_0 + (\bar{x}_0 - x_0 - z_0 - G_0)\, dp_0 + (MRS_0 - MRT_0)\, dG_0 \\ + \sum_s \pi_s m_s \{t_1 dx_s + (\bar{x}_s - x_s + y_s - G_s)\, dp_s + (MRS_s - MRT_s)\, dG_1\}.$$

The conventional welfare equation in (8.7) is obtained by using the market-clearing conditions for the private good in each time period, with $\bar{x}_0 = x_0 + z_0 + G_0$ and $\bar{x}_s + y_s = x_s + G_1$ for all s respectively, to eliminate the endogenous price changes.

15 Since the tax on net future consumption demand raises the marginal valuation for the good above its marginal cost, the extra revenue is a net gain from expanding this taxed activity.

16 The changes in tax revenue are:

$$\frac{dT}{dG_0} = -t_0 \frac{\partial x_0}{\partial G_0} + \sum_s \pi_s m_s t_1 \frac{\partial x_s}{\partial G_0} \quad \text{and} \quad \frac{dT}{dG_1} = -t_0 \frac{\partial x_0}{\partial G_1} + \sum_s \pi_s m_s t_1 \frac{\partial x_s}{\partial G_1}.$$

17 Atkinson and Stern make the important observation that positive revenue effects do not necessarily mean that the optimal supply of the public good is larger than it would be in an economy without tax distortions. The summed benefits and costs are measured in different economies and will not in general be the same at each level of public good provision. In a tax-distorted economy the excess burden of taxation reduces aggregate real income and this impacts on the marginal valuations consumers have for the private and public goods, where the resulting impact on prices can change the cost of producing the public goods.

18 It is quite feasible that the project reduces net consumption of the private good in the second period, but it must increase net supply of the good (by reducing aggregate consumption demand) in the first period to release the resources used to produce extra output of the public good. When net demand falls in the second period the reduction in tax revenue is a welfare loss that increases the marginal cost of providing the good. It is possible for this loss to make the spending effect negative.

19 A number of studies obtain a modified measure of the MCF which combines the spending effects for projects with the conventional MCF in (8.14). Thus, the MCF is project-specific. For examples of this, see Ballard and Fullerton (1992) and Snow and Warren (1996). Jones (2005) derives the formal relationship between the conventional and modified measures of the MCF.

20 Formally, the marginal excess burden of taxation for t_0 is $MEB_0 = -(dW/dt_0)/(dT/dt_0)$, where the welfare loss is solved using the conventional welfare equation in (8.7) as

$$\frac{dW}{dt_0} = -t_0\frac{\partial x_o}{\partial t_0} + \sum_s \pi_s m_s t_1 \frac{\partial x_s}{\partial t_0} = \frac{dT}{dt_0} - (\bar{x}_0 - x_0).$$

It is important to note that this loss is isolated using (hypothetical) lump-sum transfers to balance the government budget. When the tax is marginally raised the government returns the revenue to consumers through lump-sum transfers. Thus, the welfare loss is measured in a balanced equilibrium which is on the economy's production possibility frontier. The welfare effects for each of the policy changes can be isolated in this way. Once they are combined inside projects the lump-sum transfers are eliminated by the tax changes. Thus, we have

$$MEB_0 = \left(\frac{dT}{dt_0} - (\bar{x}_0 - x_0)\right) \Big/ \frac{dT}{dt_0},$$

where MCF_0 in (8.14) is equal to $1 + MEB_0$.

21 This special case is examined by Ballard and Fullerton (1992), and it is the outcome when utility is (log-)linear in the public good.

22 For a detailed examination of the relationship between dollar changes in utility and the compensated welfare changes see Jones (2005), where the Hatta (1977) decomposition is generalized to accommodate endogenous price changes.

23 The hats (^) over variables indicate they are computed with utility held constant and are therefore based solely on substitution effects.

24 These foreign aid payments are purely notional and have no impact on the utility of foreign consumers. Normally any changes in real income stay in the hands of domestic consumers. We simply compute potential foreign aid payments as a way to isolate the changes in real income from policy changes that ultimately impact on the utility of domestic consumers.

25 The actual change in expected utility from the project is derived as the second equation in (8.11).

26 Graham looks at how to maximize the option value by redistributing income across states of nature. But in project evaluation we want to evaluate the option value for consumption risk resulting from the project, which is, in part, endogenously determined by consumers trading risk in private markets. If the government can reduce consumption risk by transferring income across states of nature the value of the ex-ante CV rises. However, that introduces a separate policy choice with additional costs. In particular, we need to consider whether the government can reduce consumption risk at lower cost than private traders, and since it cannot redistribute income across states of nature using lump-sum transfers, it uses distorting taxes which have efficiency costs that make redistribution costly. These same issues arise for income redistribution across consumers.

27 The Hatta decomposition was originally derived in a certainty setting with constant producer prices. Jones (2005) generalises it by allowing variable producer prices. It is also used by Dixit (1985) and Diewert (1983) in a certainty setting with variable producer prices.

28 It should be noted that there are an infinite number of ways for governments to distribute surplus revenue to consumers when using lump-sum transfers. But they may not be able to personalize the revenue transfers when using distorting taxes, which is why it is important to test for Pareto improvements in policy evaluation. Jones derives a revised measure of the shadow value of government revenue when consumers have different distributional weights and the government balances its budget with distorting taxes; it is the distributional weighted sum of personalized measures of the shadow value of government revenue, where strict Pareto improvements are possible when tax changes make these personalized shadow values positive for every consumer.

29 Foster and Sonnenschein (1970) find S_R can be negative in tax-distorted economies where multiple equilibrium outcomes are possible. When this happens extra real income reduces social welfare. They show how stable price adjustment mechanisms, like the Walrasian auctioneer in a competitive equilibrium, overcome this problem.

30 The derivation of this welfare equation is not provided here as it is similar to the derivation provided for the original welfare equation in (8.7).

31 The shadow value of capital is obtained using the welfare equation in (8.7″) as:

$$S_K = \frac{dW}{d\bar{x}_0} = p_0 - t_0 \frac{\partial x_0}{\partial \bar{x}_0} + \sum_s \pi_s m_s \left\{ t_1 \frac{\partial x_s}{\partial \bar{x}_0} + \tau i_s p_0 \frac{\partial z_0}{\partial \bar{x}_0} \right\}.$$

We obtain (8.25) by rearranging these terms to get

$$S_K = p_0 \sum_s \pi_s m_s \left\{ [1 + i_s(1-\tau)] \left(1 - \frac{t_0}{p_0} \frac{\partial x_0}{\partial \bar{x}_0} \right) + \frac{t_0}{p_0} \frac{\partial x_0}{\partial \bar{x}_0} + \tau i_s \frac{\partial z_0}{\partial \bar{x}_0} \right\}.$$

32 In a certainty setting the private discount factor is $m = 1/[1 + i(1 - \tau)]$ for all s, where in the absence of trade taxes the social discount rate becomes $\psi = i(1 - \tau) + \tau i \alpha$. This can be rearranged as $\psi = \alpha i + (1 - \alpha) i (1 - \tau)$, where from the market-clearing condition $1 - \alpha = 1 - \partial z_0 / \partial \bar{x}_0 = \partial x_0 / \partial \bar{x}_0$ is the change in private saving.

33 If risk can be traded at lower cost using the tax system it would seem logical to argue that more capital should be funded through the tax system. Indeed, in the extreme all investment would be funded in this way, where the cost reductions could be obtained without the projects being undertaken inside the public sector. The government could simply raise capital for private producers. Clearly, there are important cost advantages from the current risk trading opportunities in private markets which have created considerable wealth for most countries in recent years. Traders in private capital markets specialize in gathering information about projects being funded through sales of shares, debt and other financial instruments. They also specialize in creating risk-spreading opportunities by trading derivative securities such as options and futures contracts which were examined in Chapter 6.

References

Abel, A.B. (1990) Asset pricing under habit formation and catching up with the Joneses, *American Economic Review* 80(2): 38–42.

Aivazian, V.A. and Callen, J.L. (1987) Miller's irrelevance mechanism: a note, *Journal of Finance* 42(1): 169–80.

Aiyagari, S.R. and Gertler, M. (1991) Asset returns with transactions costs and uninsured individual risk, *Journal of Monetary Economics* 27(3): 311–31.

Alderson, M.J. and Betker, B.L. (1995) Liquidation costs and capital structure, *Journal of Financial Economics* 39(1): 45–69.

Allais, M. (1953) Le comportement de l'homme rationnel devant le risque: critiques des postulats et axiomes de l'Ecole Américaine, *Econometrica* 21(4): 503–46.

Altman, E.L. (1984) A further empirical investigation of the bankruptcy cost question, *Journal of Finance* 39(4): 1067–89.

Andrade, G. and Kaplan, S.N. (1998) How costly is financial (not economic) distress? Evidence from highly levered transactions that became distressed, *Journal of Finance* 53(4): 1443–93.

Anscombe, F.J. and Aumann, R.J. (1963) A definition of subjective probabilities, *Annals of Mathematical Statistics* 34(1): 199–205.

Arrow, K.J. (1953) Le rôle des valeurs boursiéres pour la repartition la meilleure des risques, *Económétrie*, 11: 41–47. Published in English (1964) as: The role of securities in the optimal allocation of risk-bearing, *Review of Economic Studies*, 31(2): 91–6.

Arrow, K.J. (1971) *Essays in the Theory of Risk Bearing*. North-Holland, Amsterdam.

Arrow, K.J. and Lind, R. (1970) Uncertainty and the evaluation of public investment decisions, *American Economic Review* 60(2): 364–78.

Atkinson, A.B. and Stern, N.H. (1974) Pigou, taxation and public goods, *Review of Economic Studies* 41(1): 117–27.

Auerbach, A.J. (1979) Share valuation and corporate equity finance, *Journal of Public Economics* 11(3): 291–305.

Auerbach, A.J. (1985) The theory of excess burden and optimal taxation, in A.J. Auerbach and M. Feldstein (eds), *Handbook of Public Economics*, Vol. 1, pp. 61–127. North-Holland, New York.

Auerbach, A.J. and King, M.A. (1983) Taxation, portfolio choice, and debt-equity ratios: a general equilibrium model, *Quarterly Journal of Economics* 98(4): 587–610.

Bailey, M.J. (1962) *National Income and the Price Level: A Study in Macroeconomic Theory*. McGraw-Hill, New York.

Bailey, M.J. and Jensen, M.C. (1972) Risk and the discount rate for public investment, in M.C. Jensen (ed.), *Studies in the Theory of Capital Markets*, pp. 269–93. Praeger, New York.

Ballard, C. L. and Fullerton, D. (1992) Distortionary taxes and the provision of public goods, *Journal of Economic Perspectives* 6(3): 117–31.

Barberis, N., Huang, M. and Santos, T. (2001) Prospect theory and asset prices, *Quarterly Journal of Economics* 116(1): 1–53.

Barclay, M. and Smith, C.W. (1988) Corporate payout policy: cash dividends versus open market share repurchases, *Journal of Financial Economics* 22(1): 61–82.

Barnea, A., Haugen, R.A. and Senbet, L.W. (1981) An equilibrium analysis of debt financing under costly tax arbitrage and agency problems, *Journal of Finance* 36(3): 569–81.

Barsky, R.B., Juster, F.T., Kimball, M.S. and Shapiro, M.D. (1997) Preference parameters and behavioral heterogeneity: an experimental approach in the health and retirement study, *Quarterly Journal of Economics* 112(2): 537–79.

Beckers, S. (1980) The constant elasticity of variance model and its implications for option pricing, *Journal of Finance* 35(3): 661–73.

Benartzi, S. and Thaler, R.H. (1995) Myopic loss aversion and the equity premium puzzle, *Quarterly Journal of Economics* 110(1): 73–92.

Benge, M. and Robinson, T. (1986) *How to Integrate Company and Shareholder Taxation: Why Full Imputation is the Best Answer*. Victoria University Press, Wellington, New Zealand, for the Institute of Policy Studies, Victoria University of Wellington.

Bergson, A. (1938) A reformulation of certain aspects of welfare economics, *Quarterly Journal of Economics* 68(2): 233–52.

Bhattacharya, M. (1983) Transaction data tests on the efficiency of the Chicago Board of Options Exchange, *Journal of Financial Economics* 12(2): 161–85.

Bhattacharya, S. (1979) Imperfect information, dividend policy, and the bird in the hand fallacy, *Bell Journal of Economics* 10(1): 259–270.

Binswanger, H. (1981) Attitudes toward risk: theoretical implications of an experiment in rural India, *Economic Journal* 91(364): 867–90.

Black, F. (1972) Capital market equilibrium with restricted borrowing, *Journal of Business* 45(3): 444–55.

Black, F. and Scholes, M.S. (1973) The valuation of options contracts and a test of market efficiency, *Journal of Political Economy* 81(3): 637–54.

Black, F., Jensen, M.C. and Scholes, M.S. (1972) The capital asset pricing model: some empirical results, in M.C. Jensen (ed.), *Studies in the Theory of Capital Markets*. Praeger: New York.

Blume, M.E. and Friend, I. (1973) A new look at the capital asset pricing model, *Journal of Finance* 28(1): 19–33.

Boadway, R.W. (1976) Integrating equity and efficiency in applied welfare economics, *Quarterly Journal of Economics* 90(4): 541–56.

Bodie, Z. and Rozansky, V.J. (1980) Rise and return in commodity futures, *Financial Analysts' Journal* 36(3): 27–31, 33–39.

Bradford, D.F. (1975) Constraints on government investment opportunities and the choice of discount rate, *American Economic Review* 65(5): 887–99.

Bradford, D.F. (1981) The incidence and allocative effects of tax on corporate distributions, *Journal of Public Economics* 15(1): 1–22.

Breeden, D.T. (1979) An intertemporal asset pricing model with stochastic consumption and investment opportunities, *Journal of Financial Economics* 7(3): 265–96.

Breeden, D.T. and Litzenberger, R.H. (1978) Prices of state-contingent claims implicit in option prices, *Journal of Business* 51(4): 621–51.

Breeden, D.T., Gibbons, M.R. and Litzenberger, R.H. (1989) Empirical test of the consumption-oriented CAPM, *Journal of Finance* 44(2): 231–62.

Brennan, M.J. (1970) Taxes, market valuation and corporate financial policy, *National Tax Journal* 23(4): 417–27.

Bruce, N. and Harris, R.G. (1982) Cost-benefit criteria and the compensation principle in evaluating small projects, *Journal of Political Economy* 90(4): 755–76.

Campbell, J.Y. (1993) Intertemporal asset pricing without consumption data, *American Economic Review* 83(3): 487–512.

Campbell, J.Y. (1996) Understanding risk and return, *Journal of Political Economy* 104(2): 298–345.

Campbell, J.Y. and Cochrane, J.H. (1999) By force of habit: a consumption-based explanation of aggregate stock market behavior, *Journal of Political Economy* 107(2): 205–51.

Campbell, J.Y. and Cochrane, J.H. (2000) Explaining poor performance of consumption-based asset pricing models, *Journal of Finance* 55(6): 2863–78.

Chambers, R.G. and Quiggin, J. (2000) *Uncertainty, Production Choice and Agency – The State-Contingent Approach*. Cambridge University Press, Cambridge.

Chen, N.-F., Roll, R. and Ross, S.A. (1986) Economic forces and the stock market, *Journal of Business* 59(3): 383–403.

Cochrane, J.H. (1996) A cross-sectional test of an investment-based asset pricing model, *Journal of Political Economy* 104(3): 572–621.

Cochrane, J.H. (2001) *Asset Pricing*. Princeton University Press, Princeton, NJ.

Constantinides, G.M. (1990) Habit formation: a resolution of the equity premium puzzle, *Journal of Political Economy* 98(3): 519–43.

Constantinides, G.M. and Duffie, D. (1996) Asset pricing with heterogeneous consumers, *Journal of Political Economy* 104(2): 219–40.

Cootner, P. (1960) Returns to speculators: Telser vs. Keynes, *Journal of Political Economy* 68(4): 396–418.

Copeland, T.E. and Weston, J.F. (1988) *Financial Theory and Corporate Policy*, 3rd edition. Addison-Wesley, New York.

Cox, J.C. and Ross, S.A. (1976) A survey of some new results in option pricing theory, *Journal of Finance* 31(2): 383–402.

Cox, J.C., Ross, S.A. and Rubinstein, M.E. (1979) Option pricing: a simplified approach, *Journal of Financial Economics* 7(3): 229–63.

Dammon, R.M. (1988) A security market and capital structure equilibrium under uncertainty with progressive personal taxes, *Research in Finance* 7: 53–74.

Dammon, R.M. and Green, R.C. (1987) Tax arbitrage and the existence of equilibrium prices for financial assets, *Journal of Finance* 42(5): 1143–66.

DeAngelo, H. and Masulis, R.W. (1980a) Optimal capital structure under corporate and personal taxation, *Journal of Financial Economics* 8(1): 3–29.

DeAngelo, H. and Masulis, R.W. (1980b) Leverage and dividend irrelevancy under corporate and personal taxation, *Journal of Finance* 35(2): 453–64.

Debreu, G. (1959) *Theory of Value: An Axiomatic Analysis of Economic Equilibrium*, Cowles Foundation Monograph 17. Yale University Press, New Haven, CT.

Deshmukh, S. (2005) The effect of asymmetric information on dividend policy, *Quarterly Journal of Business and Economics* 44(1/2): 107–27.

Diamond, P.A. and Mirrlees, J.A. (1971) Optimal taxation and public production, *American Economic Review* 61: 8–27, 261–78.

Diewert, W.E. (1983) Cost-benefit analysis and project evaluation: a comparison of alternative approaches, *Journal of Public Economics* 22(3): 265–302.

Dixit, A. (1985) Tax policy in open economies, in A.J. Auerbach and M. Feldstein (eds), *Handbook of Public Economics*, Vol. 1, pp. 313–74. North-Holland, New York.

Dixit, A. (1987) Trade and insurance with moral hazard, *Journal of International Economics* 23(3/4): 201–20.

Dixit, A. (1989) Trade and insurance with adverse selection, *Review of Economic Studies* 56(2): 235–47.

Dowd, K. (1988) *Private Money: The Path to Monetary Stability*. Institute of Economic Affairs, London.

Dréze, J.H. (1987) *Essay on Economic Decisions under Uncertainty*. Cambridge University Press, Cambridge.

Dréze, J. and Stern, N. (1990) Policy reform, shadow prices and market prices, *Journal of Public Economics* 42(1): 1–45.

Dusak, K. (1973) Futures trading and investor returns: an investigation of commodity market risk premiums, *Journal of Political Economy* 81(6): 1387–1406.

Easterbrook, F. (1984) Two-agency cost explanations of dividends, *American Economic Review* 74(4): 650–9.

Edwards, J.S.S. (1989) Gearing, in J. Eatwell, M. Milgate, and P. Newman (eds), *The New Palgrave – Finance*, pp. 159–163. Macmillan Press, London.

Ehrlich, I. and Becker, G.S. (1972) Market insurance, self-insurance and self-protection, *Journal of Political Economy* 80(4): 623–48.

Elton, E.J. and Gruber, M.J. (1995) *Modern Portfolio Theory and Investment Analysis*, 5th edition. Wiley, New York.

Epstein, L.G and Zin, S.E. (1989) Substitution, risk aversion, and the temporal behavior of consumption growth and asset returns I: A theoretical framework, *Econometrica* 57(4): 937–69.

Fama, E.F. (1965) The behavior of stock market prices, *Journal of Business* 38(1): 34–105.

Fama, E.F. (1970) Efficient capital markets: a review of theory and empirical work, *Journal of Finance* 25(2): 383–417.

Fama, E.F. (1977) Risk-adjusted discount rates and capital budgeting under uncertainty, *Journal of Financial Economics* 5(1): 3–24.

Fama, E.F. (1998) Determining the number of priced state variables in the ICAPM, *Journal of Financial and Quantitative Analysis* 33(2): 217–31.

Fama, E.F. and French, K.R. (1987) Commodity futures prices: some evidence on the forecast power, premiums, and the theory of storage, *Journal of Business* 60(1): 55–73.

Fama, E.F. and French, K.R. (1992) The cross-section of expected stock returns, *Journal of Finance* 47(2): 427–65.

Fama, E.F. and French, K.R. (1993) Common risk factors in the returns on stocks and bonds, *Journal of Financial Economics* 33(1): 3–56.

Fama, E.F. and MacBeth, J.D. (1973) Risk, return and equilibrium: empirical tests, *Journal of Political Economy* 81(3): 607–36.

Fischer, S. (1980) Dynamic inconsistency, co-operation and the benevolent dissembling government, *Journal of Economic Dynamics and Control* 2: 93–107.

Fishburn, P.C. (1974) On the foundations of decision making under uncertainty, in M.S. Balch, D.L. MacFadden and S.Y. Wu (eds), *Essays on Economic Behavior under Uncertainty*. American Elsevier, New York.

Fisher, I. (1930) *The Theory of Interest*. Macmillan, New York.

Fisher, S.J. (1994) Asset trading, transactions costs and the equity premium, *Journal of Applied Econometrics* 9(Supplement): S71–S94.

Foster, E. and Sonnenschein, H. (1970) Price distortion and economic welfare, *Econometrica* 38(2): 281–97.

Friedman, M. (1968) The role of monetary policy, *American Economic Review* 58(1): 1–17.

Friend, I. and Blume, M.E. (1975) The demand for risky assets, *American Economic Review* 65(5): 900–22.

Fullenkamp, C., Tenorio, R. and Battalio, R. (2003) Assessing individual risk-attitudes using field data from lottery games, *Review of Economics and Statistics* 85(1): 218–26.

Galai, D. (1977) Test of market efficiency of the Chicago Board of Options Exchange, *Journal of Business* 50(2): 167–97.

Gordon, M.J., Paradis, G.E. and Rorke, C.H. (1972) Experimental evidence on alternative portfolio decision rules, *American Economic Review* 62(1/2): 107–18.

Goulder, H. L. and Williams III, R.C. (2003) The substantial bias from ignoring general equilibrium effects in estimating excess burden, and a practical solution, *Journal of Political Economy* 111(4): 898–927.

Graham, D.A. (1981) Cost-benefit analysis under uncertainty, *American Economic Review* 71(4): 715–25.

Graham, J.R. (2000) How big are the tax benefits of debt? *Journal of Finance* 55(5): 1901–41.

Grant, S.H. and Karni, E. (2004) A theory of quantifiable beliefs, *Journal of Mathematical Economics* 40(5): 515–46.

Grant, S.H. and Quiggin, J. (2004) The risk premium for equity: implications for resource allocation, welfare and policy. Mimeo, Rice University and University of Queensland.

Gray, R. (1961) The search for a risk premium, *Journal of Political Economy* 69(3): 250–60.

Greenwald, B. and Stiglitz, J.E. (1986) Externalities in economies with imperfect information, *Quarterly Journal of Economics* 101(2): 229–64.

Guiso, L. and Paiella, M. (2001) Risk aversion, wealth and background risk. CEPR Discussion Paper 2728.

Hansen, L.P. and Jagannathan, R. (1991) Implications of security market data for models of dynamic economies, *Journal of Political Economy* 99(2): 225–62.

Hansen, L.P. and Singleton, K.J. (1982) Generalised instrumental variables estimation of nonlinear rational expectations models, *Econometrica* 50(5): 1269–86.

Hansen, L.P. and Singleton, K.J. (1983) Stochastic consumption, risk aversion and the temporal behavior of asset returns, *Journal of Political Economy* 91(2): 249–65.

Harberger, A.C. (1964) The measurement of waste, *American Economic Review* 54(3): 58–76.

Harberger, A.C. (1969) Professor Arrow on the social discount rate, in G.G. Somers and W.D. Wood (eds), *Cost–Benefit Analysis of Manpower Policies*, pp. 76–88. Industrial Relations Centre, Queen's University, Kingston, Ontario, Canada.

Harberger, A.C. (1971) Three basic postulates for applied welfare economics: an interpretive essay, *Journal of Economic Literature* 9(3): 785–97.

Harris, J.A. and Townsend, R. (1985) Allocation mechanisms, asymmetric information and the revelation principle, in G. Feiwel (ed.), *Issues in Contemporary Microeconomics and Welfare*, pp. 379–94. State University of New York Press, Albany.

Harris, M. and Raviv, A. (1991) The theory of capital structure, *Journal of Finance* 46(1): 297–355.

Hatta, T. (1977) A theory of piecemeal policy recommendations, *Review of Economic Studies* 44(1): 1–21.

Haugen, R.A. and Senbet, L.W. (1978) The insignificance of bankruptcy costs to the theory of optimal capital structure, *Journal of Finance* 33(2): 383–93.

Hayek, F. (1978) *Decentralisation of Money: The Argument Refined*. Institute of Economic Affairs, London.

Heaton, J. and Lucas, D.J. (1996) Evaluating the effects of incomplete markets on risk sharing and asset pricing, *Journal of Political Economy* 104(3): 443–87.

Helms, L.J. (1985) Expected consumer's surplus and the welfare effects of price stabilisation, *International Economic Review* 26(3): 603–17.

Hicks, J.R. (1939) *Value and Capital*. Clarendon Press, Oxford.

Hirshleifer, J. (1965) Investment decisions under uncertainty: choice theoretic approaches, *Quarterly Journal of Economics* 79(4): 509–36.

Hirshleifer, J. (1970) *Investment, Interest and Capital*. Prentice Hall, Englewood Cliffs, NJ.

Houthakker, H.S. (1968) Normal backwardation, in J.N. Wolfe (ed.), *Value, Capital and Growth*. Edinburgh University Press, Edinburgh.

Jensen, M.C. and Meckling, W.H. (1976) Theory of the firm: managerial behaviour, agency costs and ownership structure, *Journal of Financial Economics* 3(4): 305–60.

Jones, C.M. (2005) *Applied Welfare Economics*. Oxford University Press, Oxford.

Jones, C.M. and Milne, F. (1992) Tax arbitrage, existence of equilibrium and bounded tax rebates, *Mathematical Finance* 2(3): 189–96.

Kaldor, N. (1939) Speculation and economic stability, *Review of Economic Studies* 7(1): 1–27.

Kaplow, L. (1996) The Optimal supply of public goods and the distortionary cost of taxation, *National Tax Policy* 49: 523–33.

Karni, E. (1985) *Decision Making under Uncertainty: The Case of State-Dependent Preferences*. Harvard University Press, Cambridge, MA.

Karni, E. (1993) A definition of subjective probabilities with state-dependent preferences, *Econometrica* 61(1): 187–98.

Karni, E., Schmeidler, D. and Vind, K. (1983) On state-dependent preferences and subjective probabilities, *Econometrica* 51(4): 1021–31.

Keynes, J.M. (1923) Some aspects of commodity markets, *Manchester Guardian Commercial Reconstruction Supplement 29*, March. Reprinted (1973) in *The Collected Writings of John Maynard Keynes*, Vol. VII. Macmillan, London.

Kim, E.H. (1982) Miller's equilibrium, shareholder leverage clienteles, and optimal capital structure, *Journal of Finance* 37(2): 301–23.

Kim, E.H., Lewellen, W.G. and McConnell, J.J. (1979) Financial leverage clienteles: theory and evidence, *Journal of Financial Economics* 7(1): 83–109.

King, M.A. (1977) *Public Policy and the Corporation*. Chapman & Hall, London.

Knight, F. (1921) *Risk, Uncertainty and Profit*. Houghton Mifflin, Boston.

Kocherlakota, N.R. (1990) On the 'discount' factor in growth economies, *Journal of Monetary Economics* 25(1): 43–7.

Kreps, D.M. (1990) *A Course in Microeconomic Theory*. Princeton University Press, Princeton, NJ.

Kreps, D.M. and Porteus, E.L. (1978) Temporal resolution of uncertainty and dynamic choice theory, *Econometrica* 46(1): 185–200.

Laffont, J.-J. (1989) *The Economics of Uncertainty and Information* (translated by J.P. Bonin and H. Bonin). MIT Press, Cambridge, MA.

Leland, H. and Pyle, D. (1977) Information asymmetries, financial structure, and financial intermediation, *Journal of Finance* 32(2): 371–88.

Lengwiler, Y. (2004) *Microfoundations of Financial Economics: An Introduction to General Equilibrium Asset Pricing*. Princeton University Press, Princeton, NJ.

Lettau, M. and Ludvigson, S. (2001) Resurrecting the (C)CAPM: a cross-sectional test when risk premia are time varying, *Journal of Political Economy* 109(6): 1238–87.

LeRoy, S.F. (1989) Efficient capital markets and martingales, *Journal of Economic Literature* 27(4): 1583–1621.

Lintner, J. (1965) The valuation of risky assets and the selection of risky investment in stock portfolios and capital budgets, *Review of Economics and Statistics* 47(1): 13–37.

Long, J.B. (1974) Stock prices, inflation and the term structure of interest rates, *Journal of Financial Economics* 1(2): 131–70.

Macbeth, J.D. and Merville, L.J. (1979) An empirical examination of the Black–Scholes call option pricing model, *Journal of Finance* 34(5): 1173–86.

McGrattan, E.R. and Prescott, E.C. (2003) Average debt and equity returns: puzzling, *American Economic Review* 93(2): 392–7.

Machina, M. (1982) 'Expected utility' analysis without the independence axiom, *Econometrica* 50(2): 277–323.

Malinvaud, E. (1972) The allocation of individual risks in large markets, *Journal of Economic Theory* 4(2): 312–28.

Mankiw, N.G. and Shapiro, M.D. (1986) Risk and return: consumption versus market beta, *Review of Economics and Statistics* 68(3): 452–9.

Marglin, S.A. (1963a) The social rate of discount and the optimal rate of investment, *Quarterly Journal of Economics* 77(1): 95–111.

Marglin, S.A. (1963b) The opportunity costs of public investment, *Quarterly Journal of Economics* 77(2): 274–89.

Markowitz, H. (1959) *Portfolio Selection*. Yale University Press, New Haven, CT.

Mas-Colell, A., Whinston, M.D. and Green, J.R. (1995) *Microeconomic Theory*. Oxford University Press, Oxford and New York.

Mehra, R. and Prescott, E.C. (1985) The equity premium: a puzzle, *Journal of Monetary Economics* 15(2): 145–61.

Merton, R.C. (1973a) An inter-temporal capital asset pricing model, *Econometrica* 41(5): 867–87.

Merton, R.C. (1973b) The theory of rational option pricing, *Bell Journal of Economics and Management Science* 4(1): 141–83.

Meyer, J. (1987) Two-moment decision models and expected utility maximisation, *American Economic Review* 77(3): 421–30.

Micu, M. and Upper, C. (2006) Derivatives markets, *BIS Quarterly Review* (March): 43–50.
Miller, M.H. (1977) Debt and taxes, *Journal of Finance* 32(2): 261–275.
Miller, M.H. (1988) Modigliani-Miller propositions after thirty years, *Journal of Economic Perspectives* 2(4): 99–120.
Miller, M.H. and Rock, K. (1985) Dividend policy under asymmetric information, *Journal of Finance* 40(4): 1031–51.
Modigliani, F. and Miller, M. (1958) The cost of capital, corporate finance, and the theory of investment. *American Economic Review* 48(3): 261–97.
Modigliani, F. and Miller, M. (1961) Dividend policy, growth, and the valuation of shares, *Journal of Business* 34(4): 411–33.
Modigliani, F. and Miller, M. (1963) Corporate income taxes and the cost of capital: a correction, *American Economic Review* 53(3): 433–43.
Molina, C.A. (2005) Are firms underleveraged? An examination of the effect of leverage on default probabilities, *Journal of Finance* 60(3): 1427–59.
Myers, S.C. (1984) The capital structure puzzle, *Journal of Finance* 39(3): 575–92.
Myers, S.C. and Majluf, N.S. (1984) Corporate financing and investment decisions when firms have information that investors do not have, *Journal of Financial Economics* 13(2): 187–221.
Newbery, D.M.G. and Stiglitz, J.E. (1981) *The Theory of Commodity Price Stabilization: A Study in the Economics of Risk*. Clarendon Press, Oxford.
Pauly, M.V. (1974) Over-insurance and public provision of insurance: the roles of moral hazard and adverse selection, *Quarterly Journal of Economics* 88(1): 44–62.
Peress, J. (2004) Wealth, information acquisition and portfolio choice, *Review of Financial Studies*, 17(3): 879–914.
Phillips, A.W. (1958) The relation between unemployment and the rate of change in money wages in the United Kingdom, 1861–1957, *Economica* 25(100): 283–99.
Pigou, A.C. (1947) *A Study in Public Finance*, 3rd edition. Macmillan Press, London.
Pratt, J.W. (1964) Risk aversion in the small and in the large, *Econometrica* 32(1/2): 122–36.
Quizon, J., Binswanger, H. and Machina, M. (1984) Attitudes toward risk: further remarks, *Economic Journal* 94(373): 144–8.
Radner, R. (1972) Existence of equilibrium of plans, prices and price expectations in a sequence of markets, *Econometrica* 40(2): 289–303.
Riley, J.G. (1975) Competitive signalling, *Journal of Economic Theory* 10(2): 174–86.
Rockwell, C.S. (1967) Normal backwardation, forecasting and the return to commodity futures traders, *Food Research Institutes* 7(Supplement): 107–30.
Roll, R. (1977a) A critique of the asset pricing theory tests. Part I: On past and potential testability of the theory, *Journal of Financial Economics* 4(2): 129–76.
Roll, R. (1977b) An analytical valuation formula for unprotected American call options on stocks with known dividends, *Journal of Financial Economics* 5(2): 251–8.
Roll, R. (1984) Orange juice and weather, *American Economic Review* 74(5): 861–80.
Ross, S.A. (1976) The arbitrage theory of capital asset pricing, *Journal of Economic Theory* 13(3): 341–60.
Ross, S.A. (1977a) Return, risk and arbitrage, in I. Friend and J.L. Bicksler (eds), *Risk and Return in Finance*, Vol. 1, pp. 189–218. Ballinger, Cambridge, MA.
Ross, S.A. (1977b) The determination of financial structure: the incentive-signalling approach, *Bell Journal of Economics* 8(1): 23–40.
Ross, S.A. (1978) Mutual fund separation in financial theory – the separating distributions, *Journal of Economic Theory* 17(2): 254–86.
Ross, S.A. (2005) Capital structure and the cost of capital, *Journal of Applied Finance* 15(1): 5–23.
Rothschild, M. and Stiglitz, J. (1976) Equilibrium in competitive insurance markets, *Quarterly Journal of Economics* 90(4): 629–49.
Rozeff, M.S. (1982) Growth, beta and agency costs as determinants of dividend payout ratios, *Journal of Financial Research* 5(3): 249–59.

Rubinstein, M.E. (1985) Nonparametric tests of alternative option pricing models, *Journal of Finance* 40(3): 455–80.

Samuelson, P.A. (1954) The pure theory of public expenditure, *Review of Economic and Statistics* 36(4): 387–9.

Samuelson, P.A. (1964) Principles of efficiency: discussion, *American Economic Review* 54(3): 93–6.

Samuelson, P.A. (1965) Proof that properly anticipated prices fluctuate randomly, *Industrial Management Review* 6(2): 41–9.

Sandmo, A. and Dréze, J.H. (1971) Discount rates for public investment in closed and open economies, *Economica* 38(152): 396–412.

Sarig, O. (2004) A time-series analysis of corporate payout policies, *Review of Finance* 8(4): 515–36.

Sarig, O. and Scott, J. (1985) The puzzle of financial leverage clienteles, *Journal of Finance* 40(5): 1459–67.

Savage, L.J. (1954) *The Foundations of Statistics*. Wiley, New York.

Selden, L. (1978) A new representation of preferences over 'certain × uncertain' consumption pairs: the 'ordinal certainty equivalent' hypothesis, *Econometrica* 46(5): 1045–60.

Selgin, G. (1988) *The Theory of Free Banking*. Rowman and Littlefield, Totowa, NJ.

Sharpe, W. (1964) Capital asset prices: a theory of market equilibrium under conditions of risk, *Journal of Finance* 19(3): 425–552.

Sharpe, W. (1966) Mutual fund performance, *Journal of Business* 39(1): 119–38.

Shavell, S. (1979) On moral hazard and insurance, *Quarterly Journal of Economics* 93(4): 541–62.

Simon, D.P. (1996) An empirical reconciliation of the Miller model and the generalised capital structure models, *Journal of Banking and Finance* 20(1): 41–56.

Sjaastad, L.A. and Wisecarver, D.L. (1977) The social cost of public finance, *Journal of Political Economy* 85(3): 513–47.

Snow, A. and Warren Jr, R.S. (1996) The marginal welfare cost of public funds: theory and estimates, *Journal of Public Economics* 61(2): 289–305.

Stiglitz, J.E. (1974) On the irrelevance of corporate financial policy, *American Economic Review* 64(6): 851–66.

Stiglitz, J.E. (1981) Pareto optimality and competition, *Journal of Finance* 36(2): 235–51.

Stiglitz, J.E. (1982) Self-protection and Pareto efficient taxation, *Journal of Public Economics* 17(2): 213–40.

Stiglitz, J.E. and Dasgupta, P. (1971) Differential taxation, public goods and economic efficiency, *Review of Economic Studies* 38(2): 151–74.

Stoll, H.R. (1969) The relationship between put and call option prices, *Journal of Finance* 24(5): 802–24.

Swan, P.L. (2006) Optimal portfolio balancing under conventional preferences and transactions explains the equity premium puzzle. Paper presented at the inaugural Trevor Swan Distinguished Lecture in Economics at the Australian National University.

Taylor, B. (2007) GFD guide to total returns on stocks, bonds and bills. Global Financial Data Inc. http://www.globalfinancialdata.com/articles/total_return_guide.doc (accessed August 2007).

Tease, W. (1988) The expectations theory of the term structure of interest rates, *Economic Record* 64(185): 120–7.

Telser, L.G. (1981) Why there are organised futures markets, *Journal of Law and Economics* 24(1): 1–22.

Tirole, J. (2006) *The Theory of Corporate Finance*. Princeton University Press, Princeton, NJ.

Tobin, J. (1958) Liquidity preference as behaviour toward risk, *Review of Economic Studies* 25(2): 65–86.

Vickery, W. (1964) Principles of efficiency: discussion, *American Economic Review* 54(3): 88–92.

von Neumann, J. and Morgenstern, O. (1944) *Theory of Games and Economic Behavior*. Princeton University Press, Princeton, NJ.

Warner, J. (1977) Bankruptcy costs: some evidence, *Journal of Finance* 32(2): 337–47.

Weil, P. (1992) Equilibrium asset prices with undiversifiable labour income risk, *Journal of Economic Dynamics and Control* 16(3/4): 769–90.

Weisbrod, B.A. (1964) Collective consumption services of individual consumption goods, *Quarterly Journal of Economics* 78(3): 471–7.

Wheatley, S. (1988) Some tests of international equity integration, *Journal of Financial Economics* 21(2): 177–212.

White, L. (1989) *Competition and Currency: Essays in Free Banking and Money*. New York University Press, New York.

Wilson, C.A. (1977) A model of insurance markets with incomplete information, *Journal of Economic Theory* 16(2): 167–207.

Author index

Subject index